Women Across Cultures
A Global Perspective

Shawn Meghan Burn

California Polytechnic State University

Mayfield Publishing Company
Mountain View, California
London • Toronto

Library of Congress Cataloging-in-Publication Data
Burn, Shawn Meghan.
    Women across cultures : a global perspective / Shawn Meghan Burn.
      p.   cm.
    Includes bibliographical references and index.
    ISBN 1-55934-990-5
    1. Women—Social conditions Cross-cultural studies. 2. Women—Economic conditions Cross-cultural studies. 3. Women's rights Cross-cultural studies. 4. Sex role Cross-cultural studies. 5. Sex discrimination against women Cross-cultural studies. I. Title.
HQ1161.B87 1999
305.42—dc21   99-32736
                                                                                                          CIP

Manufactured in the United States of America

10   9   8   7   6   5   4   3   2   1

Mayfield Publishing Company
1280 Villa Street
Mountain View, CA 94041

Sponsoring editor, Franklin C. Graham; production editor, Julianna Scott Fein; manuscript editor, Jennifer Gordon; design manager and cover designer, Glenda King; cover art, *The World/Integration* © José Ortega/The Stock Illustration Source, Inc.; text designer, Leigh McClellan; art editor, Robin Mouat; photo editor, Brian Pecko; manufacturing manager, Randy Hurst. The text was set in 10/12 New Baskerville by Carlisle Communications, Inc., and printed on acid-free 45# Highland Plus by Malloy Lithographing, Inc.

Text Credits: Chapter 3, Box 3.1 (p. 56), Box 3.3 (p. 69), from *Where Women Stand* by Naomi Neft and Ann Levine. Copyright © 1997 by Naomi Neft and Ann Levine. Reprinted by permission of Random House, Inc.; Chapter 7, Box 7.3 (p. 181), from "Barbara Harris . . . The Lay of the Holy Land." First appeared in *Working Woman*, November/December 1996. Written by Gustav Niebuhr. Reprinted with permission of MacDonald Communications Corporation. Copyright © 1998 by MacDonald Communications Corporation; Chapter 8, Box 8.3, (p. 198), Box 8.4, (p. 202), Box 8.5, (p. 204), from F. D'Amico, "Women as National Leaders," in F. D'Amico and P. R. Beckman, eds., *Women in World Politics: An Introduction*, 1995, pp. 15–30. Reproduced with permission of Greenwood Publishing Group, Inc., Westport, CT.; Chapter 10, Box 10.5 (p. 264) from K. Tomasevski, *Women and Human Rights*, Zed Press, 1993. Reprinted with permission from the publisher.

Photo Credits: p. 10, © AP/Wide World Photos; p. 32, © Los Angeles Times Photo, Ann Johansson; p. 50, © Bruce Allen/Liaison Agency, Inc.; p. 78, © AP/Wide World Photos; p. 96, © Dave G. Houser/Corbis; p. 132, © Robert Holmes; p. 158, © Los Angeles Times Photo, Iris Schneider; p. 186, © Bill Gentile/Corbis; p. 220, © AP/Wide World Photos; p. 250, © AP/Wide World Photos.

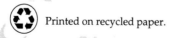 Printed on recycled paper.

Preface

*I*n the last decade, women's studies scholars made a great effort to include the voices of women from different socioeconomic classes and ethnicities within their own countries. Having sampled this diversity, we are anxious for more information about other women of the world. What we find is startling: evidence of women's low status and power, violations of their human rights due to their gender, and hope in the form of courageous women organizing for change. What we do not find, however, is a text that clearly communicates this to our students and integrates it with feminist research and thought. Given the great diversity of women as well as feminist thought, there is a need for such a work. This book chronicles women's lower status and power in the world today, provides examples of women's courageous attempts to better this situation, and attempts to explain it using feminist thought. This work addresses the diversity and similarity of women's experience and what this means for feminism.

In this book, I try to convey the scope of gender injustice and the variety of factors (e.g., economic, reproductive, political, religious) that contribute to it. I hope that readers will be struck by the scope of gender injustice but equally struck by the scope of women's resistance and the possibilities for change. Throughout the book are examples of women's actions, from the local to the global, to bring about gender justice. Furthermore, these actions demonstrate that there are many meanings of feminism based on the needs, issues, cultures, and goals of diverse women. The book's content also reflects the perspective that women's human rights and respect for cultural diversity are not mutually exclusive.

The book begins with an overview of women's status worldwide and a review of common explanations for women's lower power and status in Chapters 1 and 2. From there I move on to a discussion of reproductive choice and its relationship to women's status, power, and health in Chapter 3. Chapter 4 focuses on lesbianism and how societal reactions to lesbianism exemplify many important feminist issues. Women's unpaid and underpaid labor are discussed at length in Chapter 5 as causes and effects of women's lower power and status. Women and development is the focus of Chapter 6, with the emphasis on feminist critiques of traditional development approaches and feminist efforts to bring women into the development process. Chapter 7 presents feminist critiques of religion as well as women's efforts to reform and reconstruct religions. Although all of the chapters to some extent focus on women's empowerment, the final three look more closely at women's political efforts. Chapter 8 examines women in national politics, Chapter 9 examines women's gender equality movements, and Chapter 10 examines the international women's human rights movement. I have tried to include examples of feminist thought and action from all over the world. These examples demonstrate the point that there is great diversity in the experiences of women and in how they conceive of their struggles as women.

Statistics are used throughout the book in order to underscore points and convey diversity. Appendix A summarizes the worldwide status of women using economic, educational, and health indicators. It is alphabetized by country. The book's chapters are organized by issues rather than by country or region, whereas the appendix provides an overall sense of women's status on a country-by-country basis. Students can use this information as the basis for country or regional reports on the status of women. This information may be enhanced by use of Appendix B, a sampling of websites for women's activist and governmental organizations.

There is a lot of information in the book. As a long-time teacher, I am sympathetic to students' concerns about how to read and master textbook content. To this end, I have included a number of pedagogical elements. Subheadings are used to alert the reader to upcoming content. Important terms and concepts appear in boldface in the text and are listed at the end of each chapter. Throughout each chapter are thought-provoking quotes as well as examples of sheroes in women's history. There are also study questions listed at the conclusion of each chapter. Students may use these to make sure they understand the major points of the chapter and to structure the study of text material. Discussion questions and activities follow the study questions. These are intended to stimulate critical and creative thinking and discussion. Instructors may use these as assignments, or for class discussion.

Acknowledgments

Writing a book is a time-consuming and somewhat insane endeavor to undertake. It is also something that few of us can do without help. My students, as always, inspire me. Special thanks to Janet Decatur and Toni Duganne, students in my women's studies class in winter, 1997, and to my wonderful research interns Jennifer Adams, Christine Bailie, Ann Lescoulie, Carey Moyles, Jeff Nielsen, Kelly Seefeldt, and Amy Tewell, all of whom helped with library research. Also deserving of accolades are Sallie Harlan, research librarian at Cal Poly State University, who taught me how to surf the web, and her highly efficient colleagues from interlibrary loan. Of course the book seriously benefited from the critical eyes and minds of reviewers: Teri Ann Bengiveno, San Jose State University; Jill Borchert, Midway College; Carolyn Broadway, Empire State College; Gwyn Kirk, San Francisco State University; Letitia Ann Peplau, University of California, Los Angeles; Brenda Phillips, Texas Women's University; and Sheila Ruth, Southern Illinois University. Jayne Burn helped to prepare the summary information that appears at the end of the book. I am grateful to my colleague Patrice Engle, who inspires and encourages me. I must also thank all those who are working to bring about women's equality and all the great scholars who appear on the pages here—these are my sheroes, and I feel I have been in the presence of greatness. Last, thanks to my husband, Gene Courter; my father, Ron Burn; my son, Kane Lynch; and my stepsons, Colby and Logan Courter. Daily, they demonstrate just how wonderful men can be.

Contents

5 *Women's Work* 97

Introduction

*T*his book is about women's issues and women's equality cross-culturally. It is about feminism on a global level. Because there are many misunderstandings about what feminism is, I'll begin by defining what is meant by feminism here. Sen and Grown's (1987) understanding of feminism suits this book well. They said that, at its core, feminism entails a commitment to breaking down the structures that keep women lower in status and power. Feminism's primary goal is for women to be full and equal participants with men at all levels of societal life. However, there are diverse meanings of feminism, each responsive to the needs and issues of women in different regions, societies, and times. Feminism's issues, immediate goals, and methods are defined by different groups of women for themselves (Sen & Grown, 1987). Throughout this book, you will see that there are many cross-cultural differences in how women conceive of their struggles as women. In this way, it makes more sense to speak of feminism*s* than feminism. For instance, many Third World women connect their struggle as women to the struggles of their communities against racism, economic exploitation, and imperialism, whereas Western feminists focus on gender discrimination. Also, many of those working toward feminist goals do not identify themselves as feminists, for this label has a negative connotation in many cultures. I hope that by the time you reach the end of this book, you will more fully understand this diverse conception of feminism. Although what you read here may be alarming, my aim is that you will be cautiously optimistic about the status of women worldwide.

Status of Women Worldwide

All over the world, being female or male determines the roles that individuals occupy and the status that they enjoy. In every culture, the lives of females and males differ markedly. Unfortunately, a consideration of the evidence shows that these differences typically do not favor females. It is true that the specifics of women's lives depend upon their culture, and this is one of the topics of this book. However, it is also true that regardless of where they live, women have a lot in common: They are typically lower in status and power relative to men; they are more likely to experience sexual and domestic violence than are men; and they are able to bear and nurse children. These commonalities are also a topic of this book.

Power relations are built into social systems such that particular groups enjoy power whereas other groups do not (Lips, 1991). You will see that membership in the group male or group female is, in most parts of the world, an important determinant of status and power. Status refers to individuals' positions in a hierarchy of power relations within a social group (Lips, 1991). Power includes the ability to get others to do what you want (Cartright & Zander, 1968), as well as control over resources and core social institutions (Sherif, 1982). Power and status are closely related. High status implies a tendency to initiate ideas and activities that are taken up by the group (Sherif & Sherif, 1964). Some individuals, by virtue of their membership in a specific demographic group, are automatically conferred status relative to those in other groups. In particular, it is agreed that males are ascribed greater status than females by virtue of being male (Forsyth, 1999). This greater status is linked to the greater power of males over females.

To talk about a stratified society is to acknowledge that, although in principle people should perhaps be equal, in reality they are not. Indeed, societies are multilayered, and all groups in a society are not equally valued and equally powerful, with some groups deferring to others. The fact of the matter is that the amount of power you can accrue is highly dependent upon the class into which you are born. Furthermore, in a real sense, females, by virtue of their femaleness, are born into a lower class than are males. In other words, societies are gender stratified. For instance, in most societies, societal rules confer greater property rights and political power to men and societies sanction men's right to control the lives of women. Men's greater power and status are often cultural institutions.

Virtually all contemporary societies show some degree of men's domination over women. Sexual asymmetry is a universal fact of life, and everywhere we find that women are excluded from crucial economic and political activities by virtue of their sex (Rosaldo & Lamphere, 1974). This sexual asymmetry is also a focus of this book. Here we seek to understand why sexual asymmetry is the rule rather than the exception, where it originates, and how to achieve gender equality.

Our topic, women across the globe, is a fascinating yet difficult one. Immersed in our own cultures, we typically have little exposure to the experiences of those in other cultures. The global study of women requires that we learn about different customs, religions, and forms of government and that we imagine what it would be like to be a woman in another culture. The study of women across cultures is an exciting and wonderful way to learn about life in other places. Studying women's lives in other cultures also inspires a profound appreciation for women. The great strength that women possess and the work they accomplish despite their customary lower status and power is truly amazing. For instance, after reading *Women in the Material World* (D'Alusio & Menzel, 1996) a photojournalistic essay on women from all over the world, one of my American students wrote in her journal,

> Been thinking about the women in *Women in the Material World*. I think it's a huge chore to rinse and load the dishwasher. I detest even more having to unload it. In the book I see women who have to travel back and forth to bring water to their home to wash and cook and clean. Women that gather by the community water pump to clean their pots and pans.
>
> It's cold today. I need to open my side door, reach out, bring in a log. In the book I see pictures of women who walk for miles to gather wood for their daily fires to warm their houses and cook their meals.
>
> Good grief—it's laundry day again. I need to gather up the clothes. I might even have to reach under Josh's bed to find a dirty sock. In the book I see women that gather by a muddy stream to pound their family's laundry.
>
> The kids are hungry again! I will go to my modern kitchen and place a dish of food in the microwave oven to reheat leftovers from last night's dinner. I see women in the book that squat over the floor to cook the family's meal on the floor.
>
> Last week, I planted three packets of sunflower seeds in my garden. I see a woman who seems permanently bent as she follows her husband and the oxen to pick through the dirt clods for the weeds. And I think my life is demanding!

That women in cultures so different from our own face many of the same issues we face leads us to feel a great kinship with them. For instance, almost everywhere, women work extremely hard in both paid and unpaid labor, get married, structure their lives according to their children's needs, worry about unplanned pregnancies, and are at some risk for sexual assault. Domestic violence also cuts across international and socioeconomic lines. As another of my American students wrote,

> Domestic violence. What can I tell you about that? I did not want to rehash the years of misery I spent at the hands of a batterer. He was a charming Christian man who came from a well-known upper-middle-class family in our community. He entered my life at a time when my self-esteem was in the pits. Little did I know it would go down a lot more before my decade of terror was over. I felt like a prisoner of war. He always kept one of the children with him so I wouldn't leave. I was a hostage. I will spare you the brutal details of the bloody rape and torture I endured. Had there been a women's shelter in the early years, maybe I would have been able to escape earlier. But there was not. Financially, I was stuck. I was only able to get away later with the help of the women's shelter and welfare.

Studying Women Across Cultures

Although the task of understanding women across cultures is rich and re-warding, it is also very difficult. The world is large and diverse, and women's experiences defy simple explanation. We want to acknowledge cross-cultural similarities regarding women's experience while simultaneously acknowl-edging differences. We want to be critical of practices that are harmful to women, and at the same time we want to be culturally sensitive and avoid as-suming that our way is the right way and that the path to gender equality is the same regardless of culture. We want to talk about women's lives in dif-ferent cultures, but we must take care to acknowledge the wide range of women's experiences within any given culture—experiences often shaped by social class, ethnicity, region, and religion. We want to support interna-tional women's movements for equality while respecting the rights of women within particular countries to initiate their own movements in ways that work for them.

The saying "The truth will set you free, but first it will make you mad" applies to the subject matter of this book. At times, the study of women cross-culturally is shocking and disturbing. My students are often horrified, sur-prised, and angered at some of the gender-based abuses that continue today. However, we cannot improve the lives of women if we ignore the many of-fenses committed against them. Awareness is the first step toward change. Furthermore, although there is plenty of bad news, there is also much about which to be hopeful. In every chapter you will find examples of women com-ing together to achieve gender justice. In addition to efforts made by gov-ernments, there are literally thousands of nongovernmental organizations (NGOs) working for gender equality. These range from small, local grass-roots organizations to large international organizations. In addition to the efforts of Western women, with which you may be familiar, there is a long his-tory of struggle for women's equality in the Middle East, Latin America, Asia, and Africa. I will talk at length about efforts worldwide to increase the status of women.

As I chronicle some of the more dramatic instances of women's lower sta-tus and power, I do not want women from countries with subtler forms of gender discrimination to become complacent about sexism in their own countries. I also do not want to contribute to feelings of cultural superiority. All cultures are rich in tradition and beautiful in one way or another. Those cultural aspects that do not result in the oppression of women or others de-serve our respect and appreciation. Conversely, all cultures permit the suf-fering of identifiable groups of people. It is our responsibility to be critical of our own cultures and to bring about change in them.

Adding to the difficulty of our task is the great disagreement regard-ing the study of women cross-culturally. Some feminists suggest that it can-not be done honestly because our own cultural biases inevitably lead to dis-tortion. Others are uncomfortable with people from one culture making value judgments about the treatment of women in another culture when those judging cannot possibly understand the cultural context in which the treatment occurs. These concerns have some validity, and caution is clearly required.

In this book, I take the perspective that cultural diversity must be respected but that it must not be used to excuse the maltreatment of women. My view is that regardless of culture, it is unacceptable to deny women their equal rights. Furthermore, I do not agree that advocating for international women's rights and valuing cultural diversity are mutually exclusive. Respecting cultural diversity need not require unquestioned acceptance of all cultural practices. We are not always imposing our Western worldviews when we are critical of practices regarding women in other countries. Here I focus especially on those practices of concern to the women in their own countries—for instance, Indian women's groups striving to stop bride burnings and dowries, Islamic feminists lobbying for interpretations of the Koran that give women greater freedom, Kenyan women's groups attempting to stop female genital mutilation, Irish women's activists pursuing greater access to contraceptives and birth control information, Brazilian women's groups fighting to reduce domestic violence, and Mexican feminists battling to reduce rape. We support these movements toward equality when we share organizational strategies, call attention to abuses, lobby for international organizations to classify violations of women's rights as violations of human rights, contribute money, and compare stories of struggle.

One last thing: I cannot begin to convey the diversity of women's lives worldwide or to speak for all women everywhere. As Gross (1996, p. 51) says, "The more diversity is affirmed, the more difficult inclusivity becomes, simply because human diversity is almost infinite." Given the enormity of the task of studying women globally and the fact that information is still difficult to obtain, my job will be to give you some overall sense of the variety of issues affecting women and the variety of their responses, and how both of these are affected by culture and women's role as reproducers.

Overview of the Book

I begin the book with an overview of women's status in the world today. Chapter 1 makes the case that women are indeed disadvantaged in today's world. The chapter briefly documents women's lower status and power, both politically and economically. The fact that most societies place higher value on males than females is also explored in a discussion of son preference and the greater value assigned to male activities. I also discuss the social stigma of divorce as a factor contributing to women's social and economic dependency on men—a dependency that makes it difficult to challenge men's control over women's lives. A major theme in the chapter is violence against women,

women's sexual objectification, and how these relate to women's economic and political power.

Chapter 2 offers explanations as to why females are usually lower in status and power. Biological, psychoanalytic, and sociocultural explanations are presented. I discuss how patriarchy developed, arising out of biology but becoming culturally entrenched over time. The chapter also presents some ideas as to why female activities are less valued than male ones. In concluding Chapter 2, I consider whether societies have always been male dominated and suggest that patriarchy is not as natural as it may first appear.

The topic of Chapter 3 is reproductive choice, including women's ability to control the number and spacing of their children and their access to a range of birth control methods from which they may freely and knowledgeably choose. I discuss how women's reproductive choice is connected to women's status, power, and health and how issues of diversity must be considered in discussions of reproductive choice. One theme in the chapter is that women's reproductive choice typically lies in men's hands. In many countries, there are few contraceptive options, and women rely on abortions, often performed under life-threatening conditions. In some countries, women are coerced into using forms of contraception that are reliable but that have undesirable side effects. The global economy and international politics are also major players in women's reproductive choice. Ironically, when it comes to contraception, women's interests often come last. This means that the liberating and positive health potentials of birth control often go unrealized. There are many examples of women's activism around issues of reproductive choice.

Chapter 4 examines lesbianism. The chapter explains that the study of global lesbianism exemplifies many feminist issues. I document the incidence of lesbianism worldwide and how it varies within and across cultures. The chapter also discusses the issue of how, worldwide, lesbianism is viewed as a violation of the traditional female role and the severe consequences of that violation. I also discuss lesbian feminism as a worldwide political movement encompassing a range of lesbian struggles against patriarchy.

Chapter 5 investigates the topic of women's work. Feminists frequently point out that women's labor is typically unpaid or underpaid and that this is both a cause and an effect of women's lower power and status. Women's unpaid household labor is the first major theme of the chapter. I discuss how the burden of this work falls largely on women, even when they work full-time for pay. Despite the importance of this work to the well-being of families, communities, and nations, its importance is masked, and it is not typically calculated as work by government statistics. Women's paid labor is the second major topic of Chapter 5. This discussion includes an examination of the worldwide gender pay gap, the glass ceiling, the responsibilities of women to home and family and how they impact their paid work, government maternity and child-care policies, and sexual harassment. I also discuss the employment of women in multinational factories and women's micro- and small-scale enterprises (their work in the informal sector). Throughout the chapter, I explore the role of legislation, women's cooperatives, and labor organizing as solutions to women's labor inequality. The chapter concludes by considering the relationship between women's paid and unpaid labor and their power in the domestic and public domains.

Feminists generally believe that economic development should be an agent of women's empowerment, not their subordination. Chapter 6 takes a close look at women in economically developing countries. The chapter begins by describing traditional approaches to economic development and common feminist critiques of the traditional development process. Next I consider in some detail the ways in which development efforts frequently fail to consider women and the effects of this on women's status and development goals. The chapter also explores feminist efforts to bring gender into the development process, and it chronicles the evolution of these efforts from those that simply include women in some way to those that attempt to empower women. The important role of women in sustainable development—development that meets the needs of the present without compromising the future—is one of the last topics explored in the chapter. Finally, I clarify the role of women's nongovernmental organizations (NGOs) in bringing about change.

Chapter 7 tackles the subject of women and religion. Many feminists view religion as part of the social system that acts to keep women subordinate to men. Feminist critiques of religion and feminist theology are presented here. These include the male imagery and language used by most of the world's major religions, the divinely ordained subordination of women by many religious texts, and the exclusion of women from important religious ceremonies and positions. Despite religions' negative influence on women's status, many feminists remain convinced that religion is profoundly important to women. Feminist efforts to reform existing religions or to create new women-centered religions are another major topic in Chapter 7.

Feminists agree that women's political activity is one key to their equality, and Chapter 8 examines women in national politics. This chapter explores the causes of and solutions to women's poor representation in political parliaments, congresses, and cabinets. As well, the chapter provides an analysis of female national leaders in the twentieth century. I investigate the common assumption that female politicians lead differently than male politicians. To this end, I try to determine whether female leaders are more peaceful, whether they are more likely to promote domestic policies favorable to women and children, and whether they typically pursue feminist agendas. The chapter concludes with a discussion of women's political activity in social protest movements. When we consider this form of political activity it is evident that women are more political than they might appear at first glance.

Chapter 9 investigates women's movements worldwide. The chapter begins by noting the many forces that operate against women's activism and how, despite these, women still frequently protest gender injustice. One of the main points of the chapter is that women's movements assume a variety of forms. In most countries you will find women's rights activist groups that focus on national policy, women's research groups that attempt to document the status of women and raise public awareness, and women's grassroots organizations that help women on a local level by providing shelter for battered women, providing credit for women-owned businesses, and so on. The chapter also points out that local and national political and economic conditions affect women's movements, both positively and negatively, throughout the world. The chapter concludes with a discussion of the successes and failures of women's movements.

Women's activists have also tried to bring about change by connecting women's rights to human rights, which are protected under international law and are monitored and enforced by the United Nations. This is the focus of Chapter 10. The chapter explores the role of the United Nations in global feminism, including the four international UN women's conferences and important treaties and conventions such as the Convention on the Elimination of All Forms of Discrimination Against Women (CEDAW). The challenges facing the global women's human rights movement are an important theme in the chapter. These challenges include the development of an inclusive women's rights agenda, such that the interests of diverse women are represented, and greater implementation and enforcement of international laws protecting the rights of women. Another challenge comes from cultural relativists who argue that there are no legitimate cross-cultural human rights standards—it is up to a given culture to determine what is right and wrong. The chapter ends with discussion of the cultural relativist position that the international human rights approach is incompatible with respect for cultural diversity. I conclude that the success of the movement requires women's political activity from the local to the global level, as well as an acknowledgment of both universal human rights and cultural difference.

Throughout each chapter, you will find thought-provoking quotes from women scholars and activists, as well as examples of "sheroes" and women's history. The end of each chapter provides a list of terms and concepts that are boldfaced within the text, study questions, and discussion questions and activities. The terms and concepts and study questions are intended to help you structure your studying of the information provided in the chapters. The discussion questions and activities are provided to stimulate your critical thinking on issues raised in the chapters.

Appendix A provides a summary, alphabetized by country, of women's status worldwide. This information was compiled from UN documents, Neft and Levine's *Where Women Stand,* Seager's *The State of Women in the World Atlas,* and Morgan's *Sisterhood Is Global.* This appendix provides information on the geographic location of each country and averages on age of females at marriage, educational level, life expectancy, rates of maternal death, deaths from abortion, contraceptive use, and number of children. Statistics are also provided on percentage of women who make up the paid workforce, percentage of women in professional and technical jobs and administration and management, and percentage of women in governmental legislatures and parliaments. Figures on violence against women are also listed by country. This data reminds us of the great diversity of women's status worldwide. However, information on the status of women is often hard to come by, as many governments do not compile accurate statistics, or, if they do, they may only release them periodically. This means that these statistics should be regarded cautiously, and it means that throughout the text you will frequently find statistics that are several years old. Appendix B offers a sampling of Web sites for women's activist and governmental organizations.

The scope of gender injustice is striking, but equally striking is the scope of women's activism.

Women's Low Status and Power

Although we are divided by race, class, culture, and geography, our hope lies in our commonalities. All women's unrenumerated household work is exploited, we all have conflicts in our multiple roles, our sexuality is exploited by men, media, and economy, we struggle for survival and dignity, and, rich or poor, we are vulnerable to violence. We share our "otherness," our exclusion from decision making at all levels.

PEGGY ANTROBUS, Coordinator of Development with Women for a New Era (DAWN) and Director of Women and Development at the University of the West Indies

This chapter provides a brief overview of the current status of women all over the world (refer also to Appendix A). More specifically, it offers a variety of evidence showing that females worldwide are generally lower in status and power, relative to males. This may be called **gender stratification,** although it is sometimes referred to as gender inequality, sexism, patriarchy, and female disadvantage (Chafetz, 1990). Pay careful attention to the ways in which most modern societies are structured such that women are dependent on men economically and for social status. Women's work is generally underpaid or unpaid, and in most countries, an adult woman has little or no status if she does not marry and remain married. Women's economic and social dependencies on men, and their exclusion from political and economic decision making, symbolize and perpetuate women's lower status and power.

Status is not easy to define or to measure. Sanday (1974) suggests that **female status** is generally defined in terms of the degree to which females have authority and/or power in the domestic and/or public domains, and the degree to which females are accorded deferential treatment and are respected and revered in the domestic or public domains. These may operate independently. For instance, Latin American women are often respected and revered in the domestic domain (also called the **private sphere**) although they may not have much control (power) over family resources. They do not generally hold power in the public domain (also called the **public sphere**) as evidenced by their low numbers in political and economic power positions. Although many cultures, especially Western ones, clearly relegate women to the private sphere, in some cultures, the demarcation between public and private spheres is somewhat blurry. For instance, in many African countries women engage in both household and extra-household economic activities and play important public roles in maintaining families, villages, and communities (Mikell, 1997). Also, a woman's status within a society may vary based on her economic class, sexual orientation, and ethnic group membership.

Males' Greater Economic Power

Many feminists have worked toward achieving workplace parity because they view men's greater **economic power** and, correspondingly, women's economic dependence on men to be at the heart of women's hardship. Worldwide, women have less leisure time than men, but because their labor is more likely to be unpaid or underpaid, they have lesser economic power. I return to the topic of women's labor in later chapters. For now, let's focus on general indicators of men's greater economic power. For instance, on average, employed women earn between 50 and 95 percent of what men earn (International Labour Organization, 1995). Reports issued from the UN in 1995 indicate that

1. Poverty has a woman's face. Of the 1.3 billion people in poverty, 70 percent are women.
2. Women fare worse than men by almost all economic measures.
3. Women's economic contributions are undervalued to the tune of $11 trillion a year.
4. In virtually all countries, women work longer hours than men yet share less in the economic rewards.

Males' Greater Political Power

Politics is another arena in which women's low power and status is apparent. As a result, in many countries, women's activists concentrate on increasing women's political power. Figures from the United Nations (Summer 1995) show that only 11.3 percent of the world's lawmakers are female. The United States ranked forty-third among the 105 countries surveyed. A dozen countries had no female representatives: Bhutan, Saint Lucia, Mauritania, Papua New Guinea, the Comoro Islands, Saints Kitts-Nevis, Micronesia, Kiribati, Djibouti, the United Arab Emirates, and Kuwait. The Nordic countries have the highest percentages of female representatives (38%) and the Arab states the lowest (3.4%) (Inter-Parliamentary Union, 1999).

Political power is often built into social systems. In most countries, it is only recently that women have been permitted to participate in politics. As well, voting rights have only been awarded to women in the last thirty years. Even in the United States, it was not until 1920 that laws were changed to permit women to vote. In some countries, such as Kuwait and the United Arab Emirates, laws continue to prohibit women from occupying political posts. Other countries, such as Algeria, have given men the right to vote on behalf

Huda Shaarawi (1879–1947) was the founder of the modern Egyptian women's movement and encouraged Egyptian women to participate in politics. She organized meetings of Arab feminists from other countries and led delegations of Egyptian women to international conferences.

of their female relatives (Helie-Lucas, 1993). Despite their poor representation in formal politics (parliaments, congresses, heads of state), women are often very political. In later chapters you will see that much of women's political influence comes from their activities in grassroots organizations that place pressure on formal political institutions.

Males' Higher Status

Part of being the underclass is that your group is less valued than the upper class, despite your group's contribution to the economy or culture. Anthropologist Michelle Zimbalist Rosaldo (1974) points out that what is striking is that male activities, as opposed to female activities, are always recognized as predominantly important, and cultures bestow authority and value on the activities of men. She notes, for example, that in parts of New Guinea where women grow sweet potatoes and men grow yams, yams are the prestige food distributed at feasts. In a Philippine society she studied, men hunted in groups while women for the more part gardened individually. Although the family's diet was made up primarily of what the women gardened, meat was the most highly valued food.

Margaret Mead, the famous anthropologist and one of the first scholars to pay serious attention to the activities of women, noted, "Whatever the arrangements in regard to descent or ownership of property, and even if these formal outward arrangements are reflected in the temperamental relations between the sexes, the prestige values always attach to the activities of men" (1935, p. 302).

Job prestige is yet another example of women's lower status. According to the UN, women worldwide are almost always in less prestigious and lower-paid jobs than men. As the level, prestige, and pay of a job increase, so do the numbers of men in those job categories (Burn, 1996). This is true even in countries you might think of as progressive. For example, in the United States, the majority of prestigious and professional jobs are held by men: 70 percent of scientists, 74 percent of doctors, 57 percent of college and university professors (women are only 10 percent of tenured professors, the highest status), 83 percent of architects, and 91 percent of engineers (U.S. Department of Commerce, 1997).

Not only are male activities valued over female ones, but in most countries, there is a greater preference for male children over female children—**son preference**. All over the world, people greet the birth of boys and girls differently (Mosse, 1993). For instance, among the Turkana people of northern Kenya, great feasting accompanies the birth of a boy, but there is no feasting if the baby is a girl. Son preference is especially profound in China, Korea, India, Pakistan, and Bangladesh. In these countries, daughter neglect and selective abortion of female fetuses (practices called *femicide* or *female feticide*) significantly affect the sex ratio of the population. In Asia, the numbers of "vanished" females have reached 100 million and are put at 30 million for China (Tomasevski, 1993).

"Daughters are not for slaughter."
Indian women's movement slogan

Amniocentesis is used (by those who can afford it) to determine the sex of unborn children, and female fetuses are aborted. Approximately 78,000 female fetuses were aborted from 1978 to 1982 in India (Mosse, 1993). The Women's Centre, a leading Bombay feminist group, was instrumental in passing legislation to ban tests for the use of sex determination in 1988 (in the Indian state of Maharashtra). Although the Bombay feminists were initially criticized by feminists in other states for focusing on a problem seen as specific to the higher classes, the Women's Centre documented the growth of bargain clinics offering the service for low prices to the middle class and the poor. These clinics played on the fear of dowry with such slogans as "Better 500 rupees now than 500,000 later" (Bumiller, 1990).

The UN (1991b) reports higher mortality rates for female infants in Pakistan, Haiti, Nepal, Bangladesh, Thailand, Syria, Colombia, Costa Rica, the Dominican Republic, the Philippines, Sri Lanka, Peru, Mexico, Panama, Turkey, the Republic of Korea, and Venezuela. This is the case even though males are genetically more susceptible to most causes of infant death (United Nations, 1998). Female children aged 1 to 4 are more likely to die than male children in all countries in southcentral Asia (India, Bangladesh, and Nepal) and in nearly three-quarters of the countries in northern Africa and western Asia (U N, 1998). Child mortality among girls is at least 10 percent higher than boys in Burkina Faso, Burundi, Cameroon, Namibia, Niger, Togo, Guatemala, Haiti, China, the Philippines, Bangladesh, India, Nepal, and Pakistan (United Nations, 1998). The UN attributes these differences to the better nutrition, health care, and support that male children receive in some countries. Femicide (female infanticide) is also a contributing factor in some cases. Discrimination against girls in ways that affects their health and survival is far from universal in developing countries and exists to the greatest extent in the countries of southcentral Asia and China. However, these countries contain half of the world's population, and about 250,000 girls die each year because they experience disadvantage relative to boys (United Nations, 1998).

Why is it that male children are more desirable than female children? One reason is that daughters are seen as wasted investments. An Indian proverb says, "Raising a daughter is like watering a shady tree in someone else's courtyard." In India, daughters are expensive—they leave home to marry and take a significant portion of the family income with them as **dowry.** In contrast, when a son marries, the family accrues wealth from the new daughter-in-law's dowry. Similarly, the title used to describe the female Muslim child translates to "another's wealth." This refers to the fact that any investment made in a girl is enjoyed only by her husband's family when she moves in with them upon marriage. Because she is in a sense a wasted investment, she will receive less attention and fewer resources than her brother (Goodwin, 1994).

Dowry inflation is a problem in many countries, particularly Greece, India, and Pakistan. It costs more and more to marry off one's daughter, and the provision of dowry may command a major portion of a family's wealth (see discussion below on dowries). For this reason, daughters are often seen as liabilities. Sons are particularly valued in cultures such as India and China where it is seen as the responsibility of the son to take care of elderly parents, whereas daughters usually take care of elderly in-laws . For instance, in rural India, 90 percent of elderly men and 82 percent of elderly women live with their sons (Narayan, 1993). In China, son preference and femicide are aggravated by the one-child policy implemented in 1979, which permits only one child per family. Interestingly, in the last decade, daughters' value has grown in some parts of the world as rural daughters go to work in the city and send their money home to the family. There is some evidence of this pattern in rural China, Mexico, and Guatemala. You might expect that a scarcity of females due to femicide might also increase their value, but this has not yet occurred despite shortages of females available for marriage in some parts of the world.

Although boy preference is not as obvious in the West, there is still great value placed upon producing a male heir to carry on the family name. Girls are expected to grow up, marry, take their husband's name, and have babies. In many families, their only achievement is expected to be to have children, who, because they have their husband's name, are not credited as achievements to her family but rather to his. Conversely, a son's achievements—financial successes, property ownership, education, and so on—are credited to his family of origin.

Females as Property

When people are considered as commodities or property, they are, by definition, diminished and dehumanized. In many cultures, a woman is property—first of her father and then of her husband. In Pakistan, fathers may take their daughters to court if their daughters marry without their permission; the court may nullify their marriage and even charge them with the crime of having sex outside of marriage. Even in countries where this is no longer the case there are customs with historical vestiges of women as property. For instance, in the United States, the majority of women give up their father's last name and take their husband's last name upon marriage, and fathers "give their daughters away" at the wedding. Up until recently, it was customary for the wedding vows of the American bride to include a promise to "love, honor, and *obey*" her husband.

In some countries, women are still objects of exchange between families—used to enhance a family's social status, to gain resources, or to settle disputes. According to Amnesty International (1997), in Pakistan's North West Frontier Province and the tribal territories, a practice called *swara* persists. The practice involves handing over young girls and women to rival partners in order to settle conflicts. The idea is to end feuds between enemies by establishing a blood tie. In Ethiopia, women are a means of barter in a practice known as **exchange marriage** whereby men arrange with one another to exchange sisters (Mertus, 1995). In other places, such as the United Arab Emirates and northern Africa, women follow parental orders to marry cousins so as to keep property in the family (Goodwin, 1994; Mertus, 1995).

As mentioned previously, the paying of dowries, which is common in India and Pakistan and parts of Africa, Portugal, China, Greece, and Turkey, is also reminiscent of women as property. Hundreds of years ago, dowries were property of the bride and provided her economic protection within the marriage. However, as currently practiced, dowries consist of goods or money *given to the groom and his family* by the bride's family. For instance, in India, approximately 90 to 95 percent of marriages are arranged by the parents, and the parents of the bride must typically pay a dowry to the parents of the groom if it is requested. These dowries usually consist of material goods such as televisions and personal items such as jewelry, but sometimes they include money and land. As Anu, an Indian woman interviewed by one of my students said, "Even if the wedding is not arranged by the parents, the groom's family can ask for money or goods from the bride's family. They don't always ask for a dowry, but if they do, the bride's family is expected to pay." Although dowry was outlawed by the Indian Parliament in 1961, the practice has actually spread as a way for families of sons to increase their wealth.

Physical Violence Against Women

Throughout the book you will see how women's social, political, and economic subordination are not only issues in and of themselves but are interrelated and influential in a variety of women's issues. The remainder of this chapter, which focuses on physical and sexual violence against women, shows how these factors combine to produce a situation in which women are dishonored. You will see how the perception of women as men's property contributes to their abuse by husbands, to war rape, and to the selling of daughters into prostitution or marriage. Women's lack of political power means that legal and police protections against domestic and sexual violence are often absent or minimal. Women's lower status leads to an acceptance of violence against them by families and authorities. Women's lack of economic power leads to prostitution, to mail-order brides, and to women staying in situations of sexual and physical abuse.

Domestic Violence

"It is very little to me to have the right to vote, to own property, et cetera, if I may not keep my body and its uses, in my absolute right."
*Lucy Stone,
suffragist, 1855*

Domestic violence includes bodily harm, usually accompanied by verbal threats and harassment, emotional abuse or the destruction of property as means of coercion, control, revenge, or punishment on a person with whom the abuser is in an intimate relationship (Human Rights Watch, 1995). Domestic violence is a common concern of feminists worldwide. Precise statistics on the incidence of domestic violence are unavailable, although the United Nations (1991b) concluded that domestic violence against women is common and exists in all regions, classes, and cultures. The World Health Organization reported in 1996 that in twenty-four countries across four continents, 20 to 50 percent of adult women had been victims of domestic violence at some point in their lives (Human Rights Watch, 1998). Box 1.1 shows the incidence of domestic violence in selected countries. In the United States, battery is the leading cause of injury to adult women; in Peru 70 percent of all crimes reported to the police concern women beaten by their partners; in India 8 of 10 wives can expect to be the

BOX 1.1   *Domestic Violence in Selected Countries*

60%*	Chile	41%	Belgium
60%	Ecuador	40%	Zambia
60%	Sri Lanka	39%	Malaysia
60%	Tanzania	27–36%	Canada
59%	Japan	28%	United States
49%	Guatemala	25%	Norway
46%	Uganda	21%	Netherlands
42%	Kenya		

Source: Neft & Levine, 1998.

*The percentages are of women reporting physical abuse by a male partner in the years 1986 to 1993.

victim of domestic violence (Mosse, 1993). In a 1992 Japanese study, 77 percent of the women reported being victims of physical, emotional, or sexual domestic violence, and 44 percent said they had been subjected to all three types (Hada, 1995). Surveys from Kenya indicate that 42 percent of women had been beaten by their husbands; in Papua New Guinea, 67 percent of rural women and 56 percent of urban women report being victimized by their husbands (Human Rights Watch, 1995). A third of Egyptian women report that they are beaten at home, and the penalty for killing an adulterous wife is typically one to three years in jail (Daniszewski, 1997). In 1990, Iraq passed a law allowing men to kill their wives for adultery—and the husband does not have to prove she was guilty (Helie-Lucas, 1993). Until 1991, wife killings by husbands in Brazil were considered noncriminal honor killings (see discussion below), and in one year alone nearly 800 husbands killed their wives (Mertus, 1995). According to Human Rights Watch (1995), Brazil's lower courts continue to acquit men who killed their wives or lovers because of the women's alleged infidelity.

Domestic violence is clearly related to the idea that a woman is the property of her husband or male partner and that he has the right to control her. As the UN report Violence Against Women in the Family (1989) concluded, "In the end analysis, it is perhaps best to conclude that violence against wives is a function of the belief, fostered in all cultures, that men are superior and that the women they live with are their possessions or chattels

"Through violence men seek both to deny and destroy the power of women. Through violence men seek and confirm the devaluation and dehumanization of women."
Rhonda Copelon, professor of law and Co-Director of the International Women's Human Rights Clinic

that they can treat as they wish and as they consider appropriate." In many countries, neither government laws nor the police protect women from domestic violence, for it is viewed as a private family matter and a husband's right. Unfortunately, laws prohibiting domestic abuse are little protection when police refuse to take men into custody and judges refuse to punish them. In investigations of Brazil, Russia, and South Africa, Human Rights Watch (1995) found the domestic abuse of women to be common despite laws forbidding it. This lack of attention from authorities sends the message that domestic violence is acceptable.

The majority of nations also have no legislation considering rape in marriage a crime, because a woman is considered the property of her husband. Providing sex on demand is an unwritten part of the marital contract in many cultures. For instance, in present-day Iran, a married woman must at all times be willing to meet her husband's sexual needs or she may lose her access to shelter, food, and clothing (Mirhosseini, 1995). Between 10 and 14 percent of U.S. women report being raped by their husbands. The prevalence among battered women is at least 40 percent (Heise, 1995). The phrase "el me usa" (he uses me) that many married Mexican women use to refer to sex reflects that sexual intercourse is often an unpleasant duty rather than an act of mutual love and respect (Heise, 1995). Only a small percentage of countries in the world enforce marital rape laws—Australia, Canada, Israel, Italy, Netherlands, New Zealand, Sweden, Switzerland, United Kingdom, and the United States (Neft & Levine, 1998). A number of countries do not treat marital rape as a crime. These countries include Argentina, Brazil, Colombia, Egypt, Germany, Nigeria, the Philippines, and Thailand (Neft & Levine, 1998).

Carillo (1992) links domestic violence against women to the socially constructed dependency of women on men (Carillo, 1992). This dependency is frequently economic and results from a multilayered system of sex discrimination. First, much of women's labor is unpaid and therefore not valued. Second, even in paid jobs, women work for longer hours for lower pay with fewer benefits and less security. Women's dependency on men is more than economic, however. Carillo points out that women are trained to believe that their value is attached to the men in their lives—fathers, husbands, and sons. They are often ostracized if they disobey these men, and there are frequently social norms that equate being a good woman with being an obedient woman. Bradley (1988, in Carillo, 1992, p. 109) said, "Threats of violence control women's minds as much as do acts of violence, making women act as their own jailers. This means that a woman makes her choices not on what she wants to do or believes is best, but on what she thinks her husband will allow her to do."

Women's socioeconomic and psychological dependency on men makes it difficult for them to leave situations of violence or sexual harassment (sexual harassment is discussed in detail in Chapter 5). Adding to this problem is the fact that in many countries it is difficult for women to obtain a divorce and there is great social stigma associated with divorce. A discussion at the end of the chapter speaks to how this further reduces women's freedom to leave abusive situations. Furthermore, the majority of countries do not provide assistance for women who want to leave abusive situations, making it difficult for women to do so. For instance, although domestic abuse is prevalent in Japan, as of 1995 there were only five shelters for battered women (Hada, 1995). If women's families do not support their leaving and they have nowhere to go and no way to survive outside of marriage, they will stay.

Dowry Death

Dowry deaths occur in India and Pakistan when the bride's family is unable to provide the agreed-upon dowry, when the husband's family wants to get rid of her so that they may get another dowry from a new bride to increase their family's wealth, or when a woman does not produce a son. Her husband or his family then stages her death. In India, dowry deaths are sometimes called bride burnings because most victims are held over the cooking stove until their saris catch fire. In 1995, the Indian government reported over 7,000 of these fatalities (Neft & Levine, 1998). Forbes (1987) notes that dowry deaths are related to the historically low valuation of women and a modern consumerism (influenced by the West) that has produced a new way of exploiting women's dependency. Dowry deaths are also an example of viewing women as property. Seeing women as objects of exchange between two families is responsible for the killing of wives who do not bring enough money or material goods to the marriage (Mosse, 1993). Since the 1970s, dowry deaths have been a leading concern of Indian feminists. They have raised public awareness of the problem and in 1986 won their battle to strengthen the Dowry Prohibition Act of 1961. Unfortunately, these activists must continue to fight for enforcement (Bumiller, 1990; Forbes, 1987; Ray, 1999).

Honor Killing

Honor killing is a tradition whereby a man is obliged to kill a close female blood relative (fratricide) if she does something that is believed to sully the honor of the family. The most common transgression is for an unmarried woman to have sex. Because a woman is expected to be a virgin when she marries, honor killings are seen as a way to keep moral stability. Honor killings are rarely punished and, when they are, it is minor, for honor killing is considered "murder with special circumstance" (Curtius, 1995). Iran is one country in which honor killings are permissible; this was not true of Iran in this century until after the Islamic fundamentalist revolution of 1979. Currently, an Iranian husband, father, or brother has the right to kill his wife, daughter, or sister—and go unpunished—if he finds her committing an "immoral" or "unchaste" act (Mirhosseini, 1995). In Morocco, the law permits a husband to kill an adulterous wife (Neft & Levine, 1998). Honor crimes make up about a third of the murders reported each year in Jordan, and men who are convicted generally serve only three months to a year in prison (Golden, 1998). Honor killing is also lightly punished in Egypt (one to three years in prison), although murder normally carries the death penalty (Daniszewski, 1997). Honor killing is also found in parts of Iraq, Lebanon, Pakistan, and Turkey (Golden, 1998).

Rana Husseini, reporter for the Jordan Times, received the 1998 Reebok Human Rights Award at age 26. Despite the risk of serious physical harm, she continues to investigate and write about the practice of honor killing in Jordan.

Sexual Violence and Exploitation

Women routinely experience sexual assault in ways that have no immediate parallels for men (Chowdhury et al., 1994). Women are disproportionately sexually victimized (as in the case of rape) and sexually exploited (sexually abused for others' sexual gratification or for financial gain, as in the case of prostitution and pornography). This is further evidence of women's lower power and status, for if women and men were equal, women would not be sexually subjugated, and, if they were, there would be severe consequences. Barry (1995) summed it up well when she said that **sexual exploitation** objectifies women by reducing them to sex; this **sexual objectification** incites violence against women and reduces them to commodities for market exchange: "In the fullness of human experience, when women are reduced to their bodies, and in the case of sexual exploitation to sexed bodies, they are treated as lesser, as other, and thereby subordinated" (Barry, 1995, p. 24). When sex is treated as a thing to be taken, or to be bought, the human being is rendered into a thing, and her dignity and humanity are destroyed (Barry, 1995).

Rape

Rape is a concern of women worldwide. Rape haunts the lives of women on a daily basis: It is the stranger approaching on the street; the violent husband or partner at home (Niarchos, 1995). All over the world, you will find women's activists working to strengthen rape laws and their enforcement, educating men to see rape as wrong, and providing assistance to rape victims, largely through rape crisis centers. Rape is a concern of feminists for a number of reasons. First, it is a very real threat to women everywhere. For instance, in the United States, a woman has a 1 in 5 to 1 in 7 chance of being raped in her lifetime (Seager, 1997). Second, in many places, rape laws are weak and rarely enforced (for more information, see Appendix A, keeping in mind that rape is one of the most underreported of crimes). Likewise, in most countries, there is little support for rape victims who feel shamed and humiliated; in many countries, a woman who is raped brings shame upon her family. Third, the threat of rape limits women's freedom of movement and denies them control over their sexuality. More than any other crime, fear of rape leads women, consciously and unconsciously, to restrict their movements and their life choices or, alternatively, to prepare for battle armed with mace, tear gas, and rage (Niarchos, 1995). Fourth, many of the victims of rape are girl children and adolescents, often raped by an adult relative or acquaintance (Neft & Levine, 1998). Finally, some feminists, such as Brownmiller (1986), view the threat of rape as the basis of men's power over women. That men can and do rape women, whereas the reverse is not true, intimidates women and gives power to men. Rape is an expression of dominance, power, and contempt, a rejection of women's right to self-determination (Niarchos, 1995). The threat of rape also makes women dependent on fathers, brothers, or husbands to protect them. This places women in a subordinate position to men. Brownmiller

(1986) suggests that, historically, marriage and women's subjugation by men arose because women needed men to protect them from other men. Furthermore, says Brownmiller (1986), the price a woman paid for this protection was her male protector's exclusive ownership of her body.

That rape is frequently viewed as an offense against men rather than women is also evidence of women's lower status. Indeed, most of the world's rape laws conceive of rape as an act against the property of another man— either the father of the unmarried woman or the husband of the married woman (Mosse, 1993). Traditionally, rape is condemned as a violation of a man's honor and exclusive right to sexual possession of his woman/property, and not because it is an assault on a woman (Copelon, 1995). **War rape** is a variation on this woman-as-property theme, when rape is used by one side's soldiers as the ultimate humiliation and punishment of the men on the other side. The desecration of the female is viewed as the torture of the male (Chesler, 1996). For instance, during the war in the former Yugoslavia, women were raped to "pay" for the attitudes and behaviors of their husbands, sons, brothers, or fathers (Nikolic-Ristanovic, 1996). The rape of women during wartime is not merely a matter of being in the wrong place at the wrong time (Chinkin, 1993). Women are the male enemy's property, and they are used as an instrument to defeat or punish the enemy (Brownmiller, 1986; Nikolic-Ristanovic, 1996). Many of the rapes occur in the presence of the victim's family, the local population, or other victims, and many involve sexual torture and sadism (Niarchos, 1995).

Writings from as early as 420 C.E. document the rape of women during wartime. During World War II, Moroccan soldiers raped Italian women, Japanese soldiers raped Korean women, Nazi soldiers raped Jewish women. In the 1970s, Pakistani soldiers raped Bengali women. In the 1980s, war rapes occurred in the Central American countries of El Salvador and Guatemala. Human Rights Watch (1995) documented war rapes in the 1990s. Bosnian Serb soldiers raped between 20,000 and 50,000 Muslim women in the former Yugoslavia. In Somalia's civil war, all factions raped women to punish rival factions. In Haiti (before Aristide's return) the military raped female family members of male "subversives" and raped women's rights activists. Indian soldiers raped women in the rebellious Kashmir territory. In Peru, rapes were committed by government security forces as well as by their opposition (soldiers of the Shining Path resistance). An estimated 250,000 to 500,000 women and girls were raped in less than 100 days in Rwanda in 1994.

The rape of women during wartime is often organized in the form of forced prostitution in what amounts to "rape camps." For instance, during World War II, the Japanese enslaved between 200,000 to 400,000 Korean, Filipino, Chinese, Indonesian, and Dutch women in "comfort stations" for sexual use by Japanese soldiers (Copelon, 1995). Ninety percent of these women died in captivity (Copelon, 1995). In Uganda in the late 1980s rebels forced girls 12 years and older into sexual slavery; later these rebels received amnesty under a government program. Box 1.2 offers an account of forced prostitution in the Bosnian conflict in the 1990s. War magnifies the gendered structure of violence (Nikolic-Ristanovic, 1996). Not only are women deprived of

BOX 1.2   *The War Rape of Marijana*

I met Marijana in a hospital in Zagreb. Her doctor told me she had arrived from Bosnia several days earlier. Though our interview was difficult, 17-year-old Marijana was beyond tears: dry, tense little face, little child's body. She didn't exactly tell me what had happened; I had to coax the words out of her, one by one. One day in April, Serb irregulars came to the village, near Tesanj, in central Bosnia, where Marijana, a Muslim Croat, lived with her family. Marijana, her mother, and her 7-year-old sister were tending their vegetable garden. The soldiers raped Marijana and her mother there, then loaded Marijana on a truck, along with twenty-three other women from the village. This was the last time she saw her mother or her sister. Raping continued on the truck. The soldiers took the women to an improvised camp in the woods that operated as a military brothel. Women between the ages of 12 and 25 were kept in one room and raped daily. Marijana became pregnant in the first month. After four months, the soldiers let her and seven other visibly pregnant women go.

Source: Kuzmanovic, 1995.

The persistence and painstaking research of **Yoshiaki Yoshimi**, a Japanese history professor, was instrumental in getting the Japanese government to admit that Japanese soldiers had used girls and women from Korea and China as "comfort women." The Japanese government had covered up the situation for more than forty years.

weapons, but they are deprived of the protection that they normally have as citizens and subordinates to men. They generally have no voice in deciding to go to war, but, they must pay for men's decision to fight.

Up until 1996, the UN postwar courts had never prosecuted sexual assault as a crime of war. Although postwar courts did hear evidence of rape, it was treated as secondary to other abuses. This changed on June 27, 1996, when a United Nations tribunal indicted eight Bosnian Serb military and police officers in connection with the rapes of Muslim women during the Bosnian war. The tribunal's chief prosecutor, Richard Goldstone, noted that "rape has never been the concern of the international community. . . . We have to deal openly with these abuses" (Simons, 1996).

In 1998, the world's governments agreed to form a permanent war tribunal, to be called the International Criminal Court (ICC). The ICC is to ensure redress for and protection against human rights violations committed in the course of war. Frankson (1998) reports that women's activists and legal experts are working to have women's concerns and gender perspectives incorporated into the draft treaty establishing the ICC. They formed the Women's Caucus for Gender Justice in February 1997 and have the backing of more than 300 nongovernmental organizations from around the world. Says Director Alda Facio, a human rights lawyer from Costa Rica,

> Our main goal is to see that crimes committed against women—because they are women—will not go unpunished. Most laws and legal institutions were created without a gender perspective, which means that most atrocious human rights violations against women are made invisible or trivialized. . . . Women weren't there when the United Nations was created to make sure our concerns and perspectives were incorporated into the treaty. We're not going to be left out this time. (in Frankson, 1998)

The concerns of the caucus have already been incorporated into the draft treaty in parentheses, meaning that the subtleties of the wording have not yet been agreed upon by governments.

Prostitution

Prostitution is plainly about the sexual objectification of women, and it is clearly driven by economics. It is about women as commodities to be bought and sold and about how women's few economic options may force them into prostitution. The effect of prostitution on women is overlooked by governments such as Thailand, Korea, and the Philippines who use prostitution to boost tourism and their economies, and by militaries, such as the U.S. Army, who see "sexual recreation" as vital to the well-being and morale of their troops. Although the prostitute herself typically earns barely enough to survive, an extended network of people profit from her body and her labor—for example, the police and other government officials; pimps; bar, brothel, and hotel owners who get a cut of her wages, airlines and travel agencies, and foreign customers. It is estimated that 80 to 95 percent of prostitution is controlled by pimps who find naive and needy young women, manipulate them into prostitution, and then take the majority of their money (Barry, 1995). Barry (1995) argues that, in general, prostitution is a form of sexual slavery because women and girls are held over time for sexual use and because getting out of prostitution requires escape.

Worldwide, most prostitutes are women with no other economic choices because of multilayered systems of sex discrimination. The greatest numbers of prostitutes are found in countries where there are few jobs for women and where **sexual tourism** is a major source of cash for economic development. Sexual tourists are the hundreds of thousands of men, many of them businessmen, who travel to other countries for sex holidays. Sex tourists come primarily from Australia, Canada, France, Germany, Japan, Kuwait, New Zealand, Norway, Qatar, Saudi Arabia, Sweden, the United Kingdom, and the United States (Seager, 1997). Their main destinations are Brazil, Cambodia, Costa Rica, Cuba, the Dominican Republic, India, Indonesia, Hungary, Kenya, Morocco, the Philippines, and Thailand. Barry (1995) points out that sex industries capitalize on racial bigotry in that they satisfy the racist curiosities of customers by providing racially different bodies for sex-market exchange.

Thousands of poor women worldwide are essentially sold into sexual slavery and taken away from their home countries, and in many cases such women are an important part of sexual tourism operations. According to a 1991 UN report, "It is noted with concern that the traffic in persons and exploitation of the prostitution of others remain rife in various parts of the world. . . . These ancient scourges are being transformed into sordid international businesses." Typically, an agent uses the offer of domestic work to entice poor women to illegally immigrate to other countries. Sometimes they are lured through false marriage offers. Upon arrival, however, their agent or "fiancé" sells them to a brothel. According to Human Rights Watch, the recruiters often take advantage of families known to have financial difficulties and recruit during lean times before harvest.

"From 1970 I had been involved in initiating radical feminist action against rape, but until I learned of the traffic in women and explored pimping strategies in prostitution, I did not fully grasp how utterly without value female life is under male domination. Women as expendables. Women as throwaways. Prostitution—the cornerstone of all sexual exploitation."
Kathleen Barry

Josephine Butler (1828–1906) of Great Britain was one of the first Western women to organize against prostitution and the trafficking of women. Despite threats of violence against her, she proved that the state-licensed brothels were participants in White slave traffic and the sale of children for prostitution throughout Europe.

Women in forced prostitution can rarely escape the life (Barry, 1995; Human Rights Watch, 1995; Pyne, 1995). These uneducated, unpaid, or underpaid women in an unfamiliar land do not know how to return home. Due to their shame about the loss of their virginity and often sick with AIDS and other sexually transmitted diseases, they are discouraged from trying to escape. The conditions of their so-called employment make it that much more difficult. Almost all are controlled through debt bondage. They must first repay with interest the money given to their family at the time of recruitment. This debt mounts as they are charged for food, shelter, and clothing. Should they try to leave the brothel without paying their debt, they are likely to experience physical punishment by the brothel owner or the police. To keep them there, they are threatened with harm to their parents and with being arrested as illegal immigrants. Lack of familiarity with the local language or dialect puts them at a further disadvantage. To make things worse, they may be prosecuted for illegally leaving their own country should they attempt to return home.

Women forced into prostitution are exposed to significant health risks (Human Rights Watch, 1995; Pyne,1995). In brothels, unplanned pregnancies are often prevented by injections of the hormonal contraceptive Depo-Provera but because the same needle is used repeatedly, the likelihood of HIV transmission is increased. The women are exposed to other sexually transmitted diseases as well because they are not allowed to negotiate the terms of sex and have sex with many clients. Although condoms may be available to clients, the client has the choice of whether or not to use them. Many of the women and girls do not know about HIV and the role of condoms in preventing its transmission, and they think that using condoms is painful because of the additional friction.

Thailand is one of the most obvious offenders. Thailand specializes in sexual tourism, with men from all over the world traveling there to take advantage of the brothels. This industry generates approximately $3 billion annually. In addition, it is estimated that 75 percent of Thai men have sex with prostitutes. Younger and younger girls are sold because it is assumed that they are less likely to be infected with the AIDS virus. As of January 1994, the number of Burmese girls working in Thai brothels was estimated by Human Rights Watch to range from 20,000 to 30,000, with approximately 10,000 recruits being brought in each year. Human Rights Watch's research on such women found that most of the women and girls had to work between ten and fourteen hours a day, with only a few days off each month for menstruation. They averaged about ten clients a day, but some had twenty a day on weekends. The case of Lin Lin, a young woman from Burma (Myanmar) is described in Box 1.3. Brazil also has a thriving sex tourism business that includes an estimated 500,000 girls under the age of 14 (Neft & Levine, 1998).

The practice of luring, abducting, and tricking young women into sexual slavery also occurs in India with the trafficking of Nepalese women and girls to Indian brothels, and in Pakistan with Bangladeshi women and girls trafficked to Pakistani brothels (Human Rights Watch, 1995). Kuwait and Saudi Arabia also have sex industries. Poor women from Bangladesh, India, the Philippines, and Sri Lanka believe they are accepting jobs as maids or domestic laborers only to be tricked into working as prostitutes (Neft & Levine, 1998).

BOX 1.3   *Forced Prostitution: The Case of Lin Lin*

Lin Lin was 13 years old when she was recruited by an agent for work in Thailand. Her financially destitute father took 12,000 baht (equal to $480) from the agent with the understanding that his daughter would pay the loan back out of her earnings. The agent took Lin Lin to Bangkok, and three days later she was taken to the Ran Dee Prom brothel. Lin Lin did not know what was going on until a man came into her room and started touching her breasts and body and then forced her to have sex. For the next two years, Lin Lin worked in various parts of Thailand in four different brothels.

The owners told her she would have to keep prostituting herself until she paid off her father's debt. Her clients paid the owner 100 baht ($4) each time. If she refused a client's requests, she was slapped and threatened by the owner. On January 18, 1993, the Crime Suppression Division of the Thai police raided the brothel, and she was taken to a shelter run by a local nongovernmental organization. She was 15 years old and tested positive for HIV.

Source: Pyne, 1995.

Human Rights Watch points out that the trade in women and girls is clearly tied to women's unequal rights. Most of those who end up in this situation are very poor and are from regions where there are few educational and economic opportunities for females. The attraction of the Big City and the possibility of a better life lead girls with few options to accept alleged job or marriage offers far away. In some cases, the lure of money prompts the family to "sell" the daughter into a marriage that turns out to be a sham (yet another instance of females as property). These factors help maintain the supply of women and girls available for sexual exploitation. The growth of sex tourism and concerns about prostitutes' infection with HIV keep the demand high.

Although there are international and national laws that prohibit the **trafficking of women,** they are unevenly enforced. For instance, under the terms of a 1949 international treaty, the Convention on the Suppression of Traffic in Persons and the Exploitation of the Prostitution of Others, state parties agree to "punish any person who, to gratify the passions of another, procures, entices or leads away, for purposes of prostitution, another person." Human Rights Watch provides a number of recommendations to governments, to the United Nations, and to countries who loan money or do business with the offending countries. For instance, it is suggested that all governments bring their countries into compliance with international treaties pertaining to the trafficking of women and that they educate women regarding the dangers. The United Nations is advised to develop programs and strategies to curb such practices and ensure accountability. Donor countries are advised to use every opportunity to raise the issue of trafficking publicly and in official meetings.

The U.S. Army has played an important role in the **military sexploitation** of women in Southeast Asia. U.S. military bases in the Philippines, Korea, and in Okinawa, Japan, coordinated with government authorities and entrepreneurs to provide U.S. servicemen with sex. The U.S. military often set up clinics where women were licensed and monitored for sexually transmitted diseases and received "sexual health" identification cards. In general, however, the women were not given information about contraception or the prevention of sexually transmitted diseases (Coronel & Rosca, 1993). In the Philippines alone approximately 50,000 children have been fathered by U.S. servicemen over the past five decades (Coronel & Rosca, 1993). Such organized military prostitution is laced with racism as local women are turned into exoticized game (Enloe, 1996).

Women from Sri Lanka, the Philippines, Bangladesh and India who have traveled to other countries to be domestic workers share some unfortunate experiences with women forced by economics into prostitution. In Kuwait, the problem is especially acute. Rape, physical assaults, illegal confinement, and nonpayment of wages have led over 2,000 Asian maids annually to seek shelter in their home country's embassies (Human Rights Watch, 1995). According to Human Rights Watch (1995), they have little choice; they are not protected under Kuwaiti law, and the government denies exit visas to maids seeking to leave without their employer's permission. Escape is further discouraged by several other practices. For instance, it is customary for employers to take the women's passports upon arrival in Kuwait. Yet, if they are caught without a passport, they are subject to immediate arrest, detention, or fines. Also, law enforcement agencies refuse to investigate or prosecute maid abuses and usually return maids to their employers.

Mail-Order Brides

Another example of women being used as sexual commodities is the practice of marketing women from newly developing and economically underdeveloped countries as brides to men in advanced capitalist countries. By the 1990s, **mail-order bride** agencies marketing women from the Philippines, India, Thailand, eastern Europe, and Russia were established throughout Europe, the United States, Japan, and Australia. In Japan in 1995 alone, more than 19,500 Japanese men married women brought over from Korea, China, the Philippines, Brazil, and Peru (*Los Angeles Times,* 1997). Japanese feminists see these arranged marriages as reflecting Japanese men's desire for a subservient bride, referred to as *o-yome-san*—a role that Japanese women are increasingly reluctant to accept. Barry (1995) argues that mail-order bride selling is not only a form of trafficking in women but also a kind of prostitution whereby men buy women for sexual as well as domestic service. The industry exploits women who are so impoverished that marriage to a stranger and immigration to a foreign land are seen as their best chance for survival. According to Barry (1995), most of the men interested in purchasing mail-order brides are both sexist and racist because they seek a non-Western bride from a non-Western country who will provide them with an obedient and subservient wife.

Conclusion

This chapter has documented women's lower power and status. However, it might surprise you to hear that some social scientists question the assumption that indeed women are lower in status and power. For instance, Rogers (1985) argues that male dominance in peasant societies is a myth to which both men and women acquiesce—men because they want to give the appearance of power, and women because the myth satisfies men such that they leave the domestic realm to women, which in peasant societies is the real source of power. Bernard (1972) makes a similar point concerning North American marriages, saying that wives and husbands "conspire" to hide the wife's power because it is socially unacceptable.

Rosaldo (1974) points out that whether or not their influence is recognized, women do exert some power, although the ways in which they do it are not as obvious. Instead of telling people what to do and expecting they will do it, females rely on so-called indirect methods for their power. By the same token, however, the use of these methods is evidence of women's lower status. A lower status person does not have the power to influence by asserting authority—for example, "I have the right to tell you what to do," "I am the expert," "You must do as I say or there will be consequences." Instead, the lower status person must rely on indirect strategies such as dropping hints, pleading, and manipulation. A number of studies indicate that the use of indirect power strategies is associated with having little control over resources such as income and with greater dependency upon the relationship (Falbo & Peplau, 1980; Howard, Blumstein, & Schwartz, 1986; Johnson, 1976). This is the situation for many women worldwide. If a woman doesn't work for pay, she is typically economically dependent upon her male partner. This dependency gives him power over her. If she does work outside the home, she probably makes considerably less money than her male partner (see Chapter 5).

It is also important to recognize that legal and social views of divorced women significantly reduce women's power in the home. There is great stigma associated with divorce in most countries. In comparison to men, a woman's status is significantly reduced if she is divorced, and this increases her dependence upon the marriage and her husband's power over her. For instance, in India, women have no right to matrimonial assets upon divorce, divorce renders women social pariahs, and abused women have no alternatives to remaining in an abusive marriage (Jaising, 1995). In the United Arab Emirates and in Iran, a divorced mother is only entitled to custody of her children until they are 7. Men may take second wives and divorce their wives without their wives' knowledge (Goodwin, 1994; Mirhosseini, 1995). In Israel, women are not allowed to divorce their husband if the husband refuses to grant the divorce; a husband's abandonment, disappearance, or incompetence is also not grounds for divorce. However, husbands may be granted a divorce even if the wife refuses (Shalev, 1995). In the Sudan, the man has the right to unfettered divorce, and once he says the words "You are divorced," a divorce takes place (Abdel Halim, 1995). In contrast, a woman must go to court and prove she is entitled to a divorce. After the divorce, there is a three-month period in which the husband may change his mind and order the woman back. She is expected to comply. In Ireland—a country strongly influenced by the Roman Catholic Church, which is opposed to divorce—divorces were not granted until 1997. At that time there were an estimated 80,000 to 90,000 separated people who had been unable to divorce. Although now legal, divorce remains difficult for several reasons, aside from its stigma: Couples must be separated for at least four years, they must complete a rash of paperwork, and the court may still deny the petition for dissolution if it is deemed harmful to the family.

Cross-cultural psychologist Harry Triandis (1994) wonders if our definitions of power and status have led us to overlook the power and status that women have in the household. Triandis suggests that in some cultures women enjoy a "separate but equal" relationship. He discusses extensively the situation in today's Japan, where he says wives manage the household finances, are free to work, go to school, or "write poetry" while husbands are "slaves to the corporation." Upper middle-class women in the United States may be perceived similarly. Of course, most women in the world are not upper or even middle class and do not have time on their hands for personal growth activities. For example, in Japan, women make up half of the employed workforce but are concentrated in low-level jobs and earn less than men (Sugisaki, 1986). Women are also expected to maintain their domestic duties even when employed full-time (Lebra, 1984).

You may have a hard time seeing women as powerless because you may recall the power your mother had over you when you were a child. This is arguably a domain in which women are more likely to exert power in the same way that men customarily do (by asserting authority). Similarly, in some countries such as India, mothers-in-law have great power over daughters-in-law. Nonetheless, we can argue that women customarily have less power than men even in what you might think of as traditionally female domains. This is because the larger a person's monetary contribution to household income, the greater his or her decision-making power within it—and women's monetary contribution is typically lower (Lips, 1991). For instance, in Guatemalan families, the greater the woman's income in comparison to the total family income, the greater her role in family decision making (the only exception is food purchasing, which is her decision regardless) (Engle, 1993).

That contributing monetarily to the household increases one's power within it is interesting to consider regarding married upper-class women. The affluent woman's life is certainly not as overtly grueling and bleak as the lower income woman's, and she may have power over servants and children, as well as a higher status among other women. However, her affluence may mask the oppressive character of her life. In exchange for her sexual, economic, and political subordination, she shares the power of the men of her class to exploit men and women of the lower class (Lerner, 1986). The fact that she has some power and material things may make it difficult to see her as subordinated. However, affluent women are often still controlled by their male partners. For instance, some wealthy Muslim women in Nigeria must practice purdah (stay in seclusion from men) as a symbol of their husbands' success

(Howard, 1995), and in this way they have less freedom than their poorer counterparts who must venture into public spaces in search of their livelihoods. (Purdah is discussed in more detail in Chapter 2.)

Because their husbands are usually the sole breadwinners, affluent wives may not have the economic base of power that less affluent women have. The upper-class woman's main function is frequently that of an attractive trophy, which, once it loses its sheen, is replaced with a younger, more attractive model in the form of a new wife or a mistress. In order to keep her position, she must accept the mistress. In countries such as Pakistan where men can have more than one wife, she must accept the new wife or face divorce (whereby she becomes unmarriageable). Furthermore, the upper-class woman still faces sexual and domestic violence. Perhaps this is not surprising. Triandis (1994) notes that wife beating occurs in approximately 84 percent of societies, that adult women are most likely to be the victims, that adult men are typically the perpetrators, and that wife beating occurs most frequently in those societies where the husband has more economic and decision-making power. Also, the affluent woman, like her less affluent counterpart, may be discarded if she does not produce male heirs.

Lerner (1986) points out that class for men was and is based on their relationship to the means of production: Those who owned the means by which things are produced can dominate those who do not. However, the class position of women is generally consolidated and actualized through their sexual relationships with men. It is through men that women gain or are denied access to the means of production and to resources. Women share the "unfreedom" of being sexually and reproductively controlled by men, although there are "degrees of unfreedom"

> ranging from the slave woman whose sexual and reproductive capacity was commodified as she herself was; to the slave-concubine, whose sexual performance might elevate her own status or that of her children; then to the "free" wife, whose sexual and reproductive services to one man of the upper classes entitled her to property and legal rights. (Lerner, 1986, p. 215)

To suggest that women have limited power and status in comparison to men is not to overlook their great strength. Women are really quite remarkable—carrying on, often under conditions of great adversity, in order to keep their families going. Although their lives are frequently hard, they find pleasure in their friends and family. Also, despite barriers to their political activity, they fight for their rights, and they have brought about significant change in the last fifty years through their efforts. For instance, there are many organizations working on the issues discussed in this chapter. War Against Rape (WAR) is a Pakistani women's organization dedicated to providing legal, medical, psychological, and moral support to victims of rape; to creating awareness about violent crimes against women; and to keeping up the pressure on government and law enforcement in the prevention and handling of rape cases. WAR's activism was an important factor in the establishment of special women's police stations in Pakistan. Forum Against Oppression of Women (FAOW) is a group based in Bombay, India, which works on a variety of issues including rape, dowry, wife beating, and sexual harassment. FAOW networks with other women's groups, lobbies the government for change, raises consciousness, and helps individual women escape abusive situations. Global Alliance Against Trafficking of Women (GAATW) is an international alliance dedicated to coordinating national and international actions against the traffic in women. Haitian Women in Solidarity (SOFA) is a nationwide network of thousands of women. SOFA works for justice in cases of violence against women perpetrated by the military regime that seized power in 1991. As a result of their efforts, the Inter-American Commission on Human Rights declared the rape of women under the military regime a form of torture and a crime against humanity. SOFA also provides assistance to rape victims.

The point is that women do not have the status and power they deserve given their important contributions to their economies and to their cultures. Some theoretical explanations for this disparity are the topic of the next chapter.

Terms and Concepts

gender stratification	dowry deaths
female status	honor killing
private sphere	sexual exploitation
public sphere	sexual objectification
economic power	rape
political power	war rape
job prestige	prostitution
son preference	sexual tourism
dowry	trafficking of women
exchange marriage	military sexploitation
domestic violence	mail-order brides

Study Questions

1. What is gender stratification?
2. What evidence does the chapter offer for the idea that women are frequently viewed as the property of men? How is this an indicator of their lower status?
3. How common is domestic violence? How is domestic violence linked to women's social dependency on men, and why is it difficult for women to leave abusive situations?
4. Why are feminists so concerned about the rape of women?
5. How do the world's rape laws and war rape reflect the perception that women are the property of men?

6. What is sexual exploitation? How is the sexual exploitation of women evidence of their lower power and status? What is the role of economics in the sexual exploitation of women?

7. What evidence does the chapter provide that men have greater political and economic power than women?

8. What is son preference? What are its effects, and why does it occur?

9. How is women's power in the home influenced by how much money they earn and legal and social views of divorce?

10. What does Lerner mean when she says that women share the unfreedom of being sexually and reproductively controlled by men but that there are "degrees of unfreedom"?

Discussion Questions and Activities

1. In most cultures, it is expected that women will take their husband's name upon marriage, and most women do (in the United States about 90 percent do). Does this tendency reduce a female's value in her family of origin because she doesn't "carry on the family name"? Does this practice contribute to the perception that a woman is the property of her husband and secondary to him? What do you think of the practice of women taking their husband's name upon marriage?

2. The chapter stated that women are socialized to believe that their value is attached to the men in their lives and that this is one of the factors that contributes to women's abuse by men. Some researchers have suggested that women feel like they must have a husband or boyfriend to have any social value; therefore, women will put up with a lot rather than be without a man. Do you know women who fit this model? How is your answer influenced by your culture? How is it influenced by your generation? Would it be different if you were older or younger?

3. Some researchers have argued that paradigms used to explain lower female status may reflect a Western cultural bias with its denigration of domesticity and the devaluation of informal power. What do you think? Are women really lower in status and power, or is their status and power just different from men's? Explain your answer.

4. This chapter discussed women's status in generalities, when in fact there is great diversity not only across countries but within them based on geographic location, religion, ethnicity, and social class. Interview a woman from another culture using questions developed from the topics covered in this chapter. Make sure you ask her how long she lived in the other culture, whether where she lived was rural or urban, and what social class she is from. Share with her the information about women's status in her country of origin (see Appendix A) and ask for her thoughts.

Men's control of societies is not a given. This woman, Xia Ma, lives in the remote Lugo Lake region of China. There a matriarchal society in which women have more power than men flourishes.

Explanations for Women's Low Status and Power

2

But it will be asked at once: how did all this begin? It is easy to see that the duality of the sexes like any duality, gives rise to conflict. And doubtless the winner will assume the status of absolute. But why should man have won from the start? It seems possible that women could have won the victory; or that the outcome of the conflict might never have been decided. How is it that this world has always belonged to the men and that things have begun to change only recently?

SIMONE DE BEAUVOIR, *The Second Sex* (1953)

So far I have implied that most modern societies have a high degree of gender stratification and are patriarchal. **Patriarchies** are societies that are ruled by and for men and in which males, and male activities, are valued over females and female activities. Patriarchal societies are structured such that men have higher status and power than women. In this chapter we attempt to answer the question of why women are usually lower in status and power than men, across the globe. As discussed in the previous chapter, regardless of women's true importance, women everywhere are not as culturally valued and empowered as men. According to a United Nations 1995 report, at the current rate, it will take 500 years for women globally to gain equal standing with men in jobs and positions of economic power. The report also noted that the number of women in parliaments has dropped from 15 percent in 1988 to 11 percent in 1994. In addition, women are disproportionately the victims of domestic and sexual violence.

Many people, viewing the prevalence and persistence of patriarchy, conclude that gender stratification is appropriate. Seeing that women typically occupy the mother and wife role to the exclusion of other roles leads them to believe that this must be the way it should be. After all, they reason, why would it be so common if it were not the best way, the natural way? Furthermore, they frequently go one step farther and assume that this gender order is somehow biologically encoded. Otherwise, they argue, why do we consistently find patriarchy (social systems that favor men) in otherwise diverse cultures? **Biological explanations** for the predominance of patriarchy may be among the most commonly believed and the easiest to grasp, but as you will see, they are not the only plausible explanations for women's customary lower power and status.

Biological Explanations

Common Themes in Biological Explanations

Some people contend that all human behavior, including the dynamics of male–female relationships, is biologically based. Sometimes this perspective is called the **biosocial** or **evolutionary perspective.** Those with this orientation call themselves sociobiologists, evolutionary biologists, or evolutionary psychologists. For instance, sociobiologist Edward O. Wilson (1978) suggests that differences in female and male behavior contributed to the survival of the species and therefore became more frequent in the gene pool. Evolutionary psychologists, such as Buss and Barnes (1986) and Kenrick and colleagues (1990), propose that nature favored males with traits leading to social status and dominance and favored females with traits suited for reproduction and nurturing. In other words, they maintain that the biology of males contributes in terms of food and protection to offspring, and the biology of females contributes via gestation and nurturing.

Arguments for the biologically based dominance of males can generally be grouped into four common themes (Duley, Sinclair, & Edwards, 1986):

1. *Aggression arguments,* which maintain that males have greater aggressive tendencies, leading to dominance.
2. *Physical strength arguments,* which suggest that males' greater physical strength led to their dominance.
3. *Male bonding arguments,* which propose that males have genetically programmed bonds to other males that evolved over centuries of hunting, leading them to exclude females.
4. *Reproductive arguments,* which suggest either that the childbearing role removes females from nondomestic spheres, leading to male dominance, or that childbearing makes females vulnerable to domination by males.

Evaluating Biological Arguments

Biological arguments are difficult to evaluate. For instance, it is true that cross-culturally males are larger, and this could have something to do with males' domination of females. However, although it is true that larger people *may* dominate smaller people, they do not *have* to do so and do not always do so. Indeed, it largely depends upon whether the culture or social situation permits or encourages it. The majority of men who seek to dominate women are reared in cultures with social norms condoning male supremacy and female subordination. Likewise, although gender differences in aggression are common cross-culturally, they are not nearly as large or reliable as one might expect. In fact, gender-based differences in aggression also seem to depend strongly on cultural acceptance and social norms. Furthermore, whether gender differences are found and how great these are depend on the type of aggression and the setting. For instance, Bjorkqvist and colleagues (1994) note that middle-class social norms in European and North American cultures discourage physical aggression in adult males.

It is also hard to prove or disprove the argument that men "naturally" exclude women because of a **male bonding gene** developed over centuries of male hunting groups. However, as Lerner (1986) points out, this **man-the-hunter explanation** for male dominance has been disproved by anthropological evidence concerning hunting and gathering societies:

> In most of these societies, big-game hunting is an auxiliary pursuit, while the main food supply is provided by gathering activities and small-game hunting, which women and children do. Also . . . it is precisely in hunting and gathering societies that we find many examples of complementarity between the sexes and societies in which women have relatively high status, which is in direct contradiction to the claims of the man-the-hunter school of thought. (pp. 17–18)

Scientists are certainly not prepared to identify a male bonding gene or other genes supporting the assertion of male superiority. Indeed, Fausto-Sterling (1985) shows that much of the research used to support the theory of gender-based biological differences in social behavior provides questionable support for sociobiological explanations. Sociobiologists are often selective in their presentation of animal evidence, giving only those examples that are consistent with traditional gender relations and omitting those that are not. For instance, in approximately 40 percent of the 200 known primate species, females are dominant or equal to males (Renzetti & Curran, 1995).

Another problem with the biologically determined male domination theory is that there is some question as to whether male dominance has always been the case. Indeed, it appears that much of the anthropological and archeological evidence was collected and evaluated with a bias toward seeing patriarchy as natural. For instance, anthropological accounts of Native American cultures rarely mention the fact that male dominance was not universal, or even common, until colonization (Allen, 1992). This was also true of African countries prior to European and Muslim colonizations (Mikell, 1997). (I return to this point later in the chapter.)

More plausible, perhaps, is that in many cultures, biological differences between men and women *indirectly* led to men's domination of women. The argument goes something like this: At one time, all cultures had no means of birth control and no infant formula. This, along with men's greater size and strength, made some jobs more appropriate for males and some more appropriate for females. Women, therefore, ended

"The sexual and familial division of labor in which women mother and are more involved in interpersonal, affective relationships than men produces in daughters and sons a division of psychological capacities which leads them to reproduce this sexual and familial division of labor."
Nancy Chodorow

up doing the work that is compatible with the unavoidable female life course of bearing and nursing children (Chafetz, 1990; Lerner, 1986). Women's smaller size and their childbearing increased their dependence upon men for physical protection and economic help. This gave men power over them. Females' smaller physical size also undoubtedly contributed to their domination as well.

Women's child-rearing responsibilities also limit their public activities during crucial times in their life cycles and limit their sphere of influence to the private domain of the home (Rosaldo, 1974). Their economic and political activities are constrained by the responsibilities of child care, and their energies are directed toward children and the home. Because of this, they do not have access to sources of power in the public domain (Rosaldo, 1974).

Similarly, psychologist Bem (1993) suggests that females may have been so preoccupied with babies and children and other responsibilities that they may have had fewer opportunities to institutionalize their power. Worldwide, women continue to be overwhelmingly responsible for housework and child care, and this limits both their economic and their political power. In other words, it is not true that the hand that rocks the cradle rules the world. Indeed, to paraphrase Tavris and Wade (1984), it appears that the hand that rocks the cradle is often too tired to rule the world and is too busy with other responsibilities to institutionalize her power.

The rapid changes, historically speaking, in women's roles in the last century seem to testify to the large part that culture plays. According to Rosenthal and Rubin (1982), such changes are occurring "faster than the gene can travel" (p. 711). Besides, it is important to realize that even if there is a biological or evolutionary basis for human behavior, this does not mean that what we do has to be dictated by it. Our values are determined by us, not by evolution or natural selection (Degler, 1990). As Myers (1990) notes, evolutionary wisdom is past wisdom: It tells us what behaviors were adaptive in times past, not whether such tendencies are still adaptive and desirable today. And, as Bem (1993) argued, sociobiologists tend to pay too little attention to the ability of humans to transform themselves through cultural intervention. Simply put, there is a lot more to women's inequality than biology, and we won't get very far in understanding and changing it without considering other factors.

Psychoanalytic Explanations

Womb Envy

Most **psychoanalytic explanations** for women's lower status and power focus on the unconscious motivations for men's seeming dominance and women's seeming submissiveness. For instance, Sigmund Freud, the "father" of psychoanalysis, felt that females' lack of a penis made them feel inferior and

"To look for origins is, in the end, to think that what we are today is something other than the product of our history and our present social world, and more particularly, that our gender systems are primordial, transhistorical, and essentially unchanging in their roots."
Michelle Rosaldo

Sor Juana Inés de la Cruz (1651–1695) was a brilliant Mexican poet and intellectual. To avoid marriage and to continue her self-education, Juana entered a Catholic convent. When told by a bishop to give up her writing, she spiritedly defended the right of women to engage in intellectual pursuits, saying in a 1681 letter, "Who has forbidden women to engage in private and individual studies? Have they not as rational a mind as men do?" Ultimately, she lost her battle and was forced to give up her writing and her books.

ashamed and that females suffered from penis envy. Freud held a particularly unflattering view of women, seeing them as men's intellectual, emotional, and moral inferiors. Later, psychoanalysts such as Karen Horney (1967) rejected the idea of penis envy and suggested that male domination originates in men's envy of female reproductive powers. She maintained that men try to compensate for their inability to bear and suckle children. In short, men have womb envy!

Male Dominance as a Reaction to Maternal Power

Dinnerstein (1976) argued that males' domination of females is a reaction to the power that mothers hold over boys in childhood. This makes men ambivalent and fearful of female authority and women's bodies. They then transfer these fears into control over women. Similarly, feminist historian Lerner (1986) suggests that fear, awe, and even dread of the female must have led males to create social institutions to bolster their egos and validate their sense of worth.

Another psychoanalyst, Chodorow (1978), suggested that a division of labor in which women are the primary parents gives rise to girls embracing and internalizing motherly qualities, such as being other centered, whereas boys learn to reject the female aspects of themselves. Boys therefore grow into men with a defensive desire for autonomy based on the abstract model of the absent father. The idea is that men dominate women as part of their rejection of femininity.

Male Dominance as a Reaction to Their Otherwise Low Power

Another psychoanalytic idea is that males' domination of females may be a reaction to males' otherwise low power. We should acknowledge that, worldwide, the average man does not perceive himself to have much power, although his society probably tells him he should. He is likely dependent on those with money, resources, and land for his livelihood. Most men typically feel oppressed by their bosses, by the rich people who control the resources, and by their financial obligations to their families. The reaction of some men may be to wield power the only place they can—over women (especially because cultures so frequently encourage it). For instance, in today's Egypt, hundreds of women have been disfigured, and in some cases blinded, by frustrated men who throw sulfuric acid in their faces. In spring 1997 alone there were twenty-two reported cases in three months. Egyptian psychologist Mohammed Shaanan believes that these attacks are carried out by men who feel frustrated economically or politically. The costs of wedding ceremonies and decent apartments are beyond the reach of many young men, thus rendering them unmarriageable. Egyptian activists complain that the official reaction is indifference and complacency toward such crimes against women (Daniszewski, 1997).

"There is much to suggest that the male mind has always been haunted by the force of the idea of *dependence on a woman for life itself,* the son's constant effort to assimilate, compensate for, or deny the fact that he is 'of woman born.' "
Adrienne Rich

Perhaps it is human nature to take power where you can get it—men over women, and women over other women and over children. Social psychologists have long noted that people boost their self-esteem by derogating others and seeing themselves as superior. Furthermore, culture plays an important role in the group we choose to derogate. For instance, as you will see in this chapter, the stereotypes that most cultures have regarding the nature of females and the nature of males suggest that males are more deserving of high power and status.

Evaluating Psychoanalytic Arguments

Psychoanalytic perspectives on women's lower status are frequently criticized for being speculative and for being impossible to test scientifically. Another common criticism is that these theories are ethnocentric because they explain a particular form of gender relations common in modern Euro-American and European cultures. For instance, Chodorow's theory assumes a father who goes away to work and a stay-at-home mother. In many parts of the world, such as Africa, people still live an agrarian existence in which families work a plot of land together.

Sociocultural Explanations

Teaching Male Dominance and Female Submission

Although biological and psychoanalytic explanations are certainly intriguing, one need not refer to biology or to the unconscious motives of the individual in order to explain men's domination of women. **Sociocultural explanations** emphasize how gendered power relations are embedded in culture and passed on socially.

Our cultures communicate to us that women and men are different and should be different, and we receive social approval (or disapproval) depending upon our conformity to our gender role. Because individuals rely on their social groups for the satisfaction of their physical and social needs, they are sensitive to social information regarding what is expected of them. And we receive a lot of social information guiding us to develop and exhibit gender-appropriate behavior. Almost every culture has legends, stories, and songs attesting to the different expectations for male and female behavior. In most cultures, there is teasing, ridicule, shunning, and even physical punishment for those who deviate from their gender roles (Burn, 1996). In most cultures, chore assignment is different depending upon the child's gender (Whiting & Edwards, 1988). Many cultures have initiation ceremonies during childhood or adolescence that further emphasize the importance of gender. Social institutions, such as the law and religion, further communicate to us what our culture believes and expects regarding gender.

"At certain points we may find that the idea of equality is unpalatable to ordinary people, beyond the pale of consensus. These are the raw nerves of the social construction of sex that, when tickled, arouse ridicule; the primal roots of gender roles that, when exposed, invoke a protest of incredulity and irritation."
Carmel Shalev

Christine de Pizan (approximately 1365–1430), a Frenchwoman, was the most successful female writer of the Middle Ages. Furthermore, in her 1405 book *The City of Ladies,* she became one of the first to argue in writing against women's inferiority.

The fact that historically, in almost every culture, females and males have different jobs (Almeida Acosta & Sanchez de Almeida, 1983; United Nations, 1991b) is an important communicator of what our culture expects of us based on our gender. People are very clear on what is "women's work" and what is "men's work" and know that there is little social tolerance for deviation. Seeing the importance of appropriate gender-role behavior in our culture, we are motivated at an early age to exhibit and develop gender-conforming skills and abilities. This continues throughout our lives. Clearly, gender matters in our culture, and so it comes to matter to us as well. Therefore, it is not surprising that once children realize the importance of gender to their culture, they model accordingly. Once we identify ourselves as female or male, and note that our society expects different things of females and males, we learn and maintain appropriate gender-role behavior.

Reciprocity of Gender Roles and Gender Stereotypes

The sociocultural perspective is clearer on how patriarchy is sustained than on how it originated. One possibility is that the physical matters of women's smaller size and their bearing and nursing of children gave rise to sex-based divisions of labor. Cultures then developed **gender stereotypes** supportive of these divisions. Gender or sex stereotypes are beliefs about the psychological makeup of women and men. They are beliefs about the way females and males "are." Now, these stereotypes are used to justify traditional gender roles and men's higher status. In other words, the relationship between gender roles and gender stereotypes is reciprocal. Gender roles originally led to gender stereotypes, but now gender stereotypes lead to gender roles. That is, gender stereotypes in most societies make it seem that women are not suited for anything other than childbearing, child rearing, and supporting men in their work whereas men are best suited for power and status positions.

We have already considered the relationship between women's biological role as mothers and political power. Let's now consider how gender-based divisions of labor may have led to the development of gender stereotypes that are then used to justify keeping women in lower status positions. The beliefs we hold about the inherent qualities of a group of people create expectations regarding what members of this group should do. The qualities we believe them to have, in our mind, make them more suited to particular social roles than to others.

The most definitive work in the area of cross-cultural beliefs regarding gender stereotypes was by psychologists John Williams and Deborah Best in their book *Measuring Sex Stereotypes* (1990). Their findings suggest that men are perceived to be autocratic, independent, aggressive, dominant, active, adventurous, courageous, unemotional, rude, progressive, and wise. In contrast, women are perceived to be dependent, submissive, fearful, weak, emotional, sensitive, affectionate, dreamy, and superstitious. In general, their findings

"Clearly both men and women have the biological potential for many different kinds of behaviors. But like the external armor or shell that encases insects and other anthropods, androcratic social organization encases both halves of humanity in rigid and hierarchic roles that stunt their development."
Riane Eisler

were that masculinity is typically associated with achievement, autonomy, and striving for control (*agency*), whereas femininity is associated with interpersonal communion, communality, and the awareness and active expression of one's own feelings (*communion*).*

Gender stereotypes are used in every society to justify gender roles. The traits associated with males suggest that they are better suited to power and to control resources and others. The traits associated with females suggest that they are better suited to child rearing. Gender stereotypes that suggest that women are best suited for subordinate roles may have also arisen to justify women's exploitation. As you will see in Chapter 5 on women and work, men benefit significantly from women's unpaid labor in the home, and employers benefit significantly by underpaying women. Lower status groups typically do not deserve their lower status. Those in the upper classes typically enjoy their position because of the exploitation of those in the lower classes. That is, they were able to accrue property, wealth, and power by paying those in the lower classes minimally for their work and taking advantage of others' labor. When one group of people exploits another for economic gain, they often develop stereotypes to justify the exploitation (Myers, 1998). In this way, those with the power are able to maintain the belief that they are not bad people unjustly exploiting others for their own gain.

In summary, gender stereotypes are ancient in origin and stem from a division of labor in which women were primarily responsible for domestic labor and men for labor outside the home (Williams & Best, 1990a). This division was necessary because, once upon a time, there was no birth control, no infant formula, and few instruments that made physical strength less relevant (Bem, 1993). Because different jobs call for different qualities, and males and females held different jobs, females and males frequently exhibit different qualities. The qualities called for by the traditional female role, however, are not seen as compatible with holding and wielding power outside the home. As Lips (1991) said, in most societies being female is enough to be viewed as unfit for, and undeserving of, power.

Patriarchy as a Historic Creation

A variation on this theme can be found in Lerner (1986), who emphasizes that patriarchy is a historic creation that took over 2,500 years to develop. As

---

*The countries were Australia, Bolivia, Brazil, Canada, England, Finland, France, Germany, India, Ireland, Israel, Italy, Japan, Malaysia, the Netherlands, New Zealand, Nigeria, Norway, Pakistan, Peru, Scotland, South Africa, Trinidad, the United States, Venezuela.

she puts it, male dominance is a *historic* phenomenon in that it arose out of a biologically determined situation and became a culturally created and enforced structure over time. She too emphasizes that a sexual division of labor arose out of the necessity that women bear and nurse children. She further posits that people constructed beliefs and mores to encourage the devotion of women's adulthood to pregnancy and child care. This ensured the survival of the group through the provision of future members and laborers. She traces women's decline in status to the Neolithic period in which agriculture was developed. The economic demands of the agricultural society were such that the labor of children was needed to increase production and accumulate surpluses. Because of women's importance as reproducers, women came to be viewed as commodities—a resource to be acquired and traded. Women were exchanged or sold into marriage for the benefits of their families and conquered or enslaved because of their value as the producers of future laborers.

Greater Prestige of Male Activities

Glorifying Male Activities

It is understandable that women and men came to do different kinds of work because of their differing biologies and that gender stereotypes developed as a result. But why did those stereotypes and roles associated with males assume greater value in most cultures? And why is it that if gathering rice is women's work in one culture, it is devalued, and if it is men's work, it is valued? One explanation comes from Triandis (1994). He suggests that dangerous activities, such as hunting and fighting, were inappropriate for women and were glorified in order to get men to do them. According to him, the continued tradition of glorifying men's activities over women's are remnants of what was once a functional cultural belief.

A related explanation comes from Stockard and Johnson (1979), who argue that the problem stems from a heavily maternal system of child rearing and the identity problems it poses for boys. Lips (1991) summarizes their position as follows:

> The male child has little access to an appropriate gender role model (the father). . . . Boys growing up in almost exclusively female care are often ridiculed or punished if they act feminine. Furthermore, boys are expected, often without much positive guidance, to separate themselves clearly from dependence on their mother as they reach adolescence. Without guidance as to what being masculine means, boys in this situation may form a masculine identity based largely on an avoidance of feminine behavior and a denigration of femininity and of women. (p. 107)

"Man was not made a tyrant by nature, but had been made tyrannical by the power which had, by general consent, been conferred upon him; she merely wished that woman might be entitled to equal rights, and acknowledged as the equal of man, not his superior."
Lucretia Mott, speaking at the Women's Rights Convention at Seneca Falls, New York, 1848

Stockard and Johnson (1979) themselves put it this way:

> Societal arrangements which actually give prestige and authority to males provide the most effective and concrete support for masculine identity. The system of male dominance allows men to demonstrate concretely that they are not only different from but "better than" women. Furthermore, defining masculinity as superior, giving the highest prestige to the things males do (very much a part of male dominance), is a way of inducing men to give up "femininity" and take on a masculine identity. The greater rewards and power of masculinity then act as an inducement to men to break with femininity. (p. 209)

Exchange Value of Male Activities

Another explanation for the greater value of male activities over female ones centers around the fact that in modern times, women's work is more likely to have **private use value** than **exchange value** (Glenn, 1992). What is meant by this is that women's labor was largely for the family's use. Once societies based on money evolved, men's labor appeared to have greater value because it was done for money or the exchange of goods. Therefore, domestication of women's work and its informality have reduced its value. The important economic contributions that women make collecting fuel, taking care of animals, growing vegetables, doing laundry, preparing food, taking care of children, and so on are frequently forgotten. As already noted, it is especially true in the world today that power and status come to those who have material resources. Research, both in the United States and elsewhere, consistently finds that women's power is related to their ability to make money. However, women's ability to make money is constrained by their household responsibilities and by the designation of higher paying jobs as for men.

Rosaldo (1974) hypothesizes that women's status will be lowest in those societies that firmly differentiate between domestic and public spheres of activity and in which women are isolated from one another and placed under a single man's authority, in the home. It is interesting to think about this in relation to Muslim women. Some of the more extreme interpretations of Islam sharply delineate between the domestic and public spheres, and women live in a type of seclusion called *purdah*. For instance, in some of the more conservative regions of Pakistan, it is said that a woman should go out only three times in her life: the first when she is born, the second when she is married and taken to her husband's home, and the third when she dies and is taken to be buried. If she does go out, she must wear a burqa veil, a tentlike garment that covers her completely except for a small embroidered grill at eye level. In some Pakistani communities, the segregation of women has produced homes that are surrounded by purdah walls—8- to 10-foot walls that ensure no passing man will get a glimpse of the woman inside. Consistent with Rosaldo's claim that societies in which women are strictly relegated to the domestic sphere are those in which women suffer the most, female rape victims may be charged with the crime of having sex outside of marriage, female children may be sold into slavery or child prostitution (although most Pakistani families would not dream of doing so), and men are legally permitted to take a second wife without notifying the first.

Also consistent with Rosaldo's thesis is that economic development and the number of women working outside the home are negatively correlated with a society's gender-role ideology. Societies with more traditional gender-role ideologies believe that men are more important than women and that men have the right to dominate women. Societies with egalitarian ideologies assume that women and men are equally important and that men should not dominate women. Williams and Best (1990b) studied gender-role ideology in fourteen countries (the Netherlands, Germany, Finland, England, Italy, Venezuela, the United States, Canada, Singapore, Malaysia, Japan, India, Pakistan, Nigeria) using the SRI (Sex-Role Ideology scale) developed by Kalin and Tilby (1978). The SRI requires that respondents indicate how strongly they agree with each of thirty items, such as: "The first duty of a woman with young children is to home and family," "For the good of the family, a wife should have sexual relations with her husband whether she wants to or not," and "Women's work and men's work should not be fundamentally different in nature." Williams and Best (1990b) found significant cross-cultural variation in the extent to which respondents held traditional or modern ideologies. The order of the fourteen countries in the list above reflects their findings. The first country, the Netherlands, had the most egalitarian gender-role ideology of the fourteen countries studied and the last, Nigeria, the most traditional.

Williams and Best (1990b) then correlated the SRI scores with economic development, religion, the percentage of women employed outside the home, and the percentage of women attending universities in each country. The results from these analyses indicated that gender-role ideology shifts toward the egalitarian with economic development, that Muslim countries have more traditional ideologies than Christian countries, and that higher numbers of employed women and women in the university are associated with more egalitarian gender-role ideologies.

Matriarchal Cultures

Up until the late twentieth century, most anthropologists assumed that male-dominated societies had always been the norm. This belief arose out of a male bias in anthropology, one that viewed the world through patriarchal lenses. Slocum (1975) was one of the first to note a male bias in anthropology. According to her, historically, anthropologists assumed that most uniquely human behaviors—such as tool making, art, cooperation, and spoken language—arose out of early male hunting and that females contributed relatively little to human evolution. However, while males were out hunting and allegedly developing such skills as cooperation and inventing things such as language, tools, and weapons, females were hardly sitting around popping out babies and doing little else. Too little attention, Slocum says, has been paid to the skills required for the gathering of food (important long before hunting) and the raising of dependent young. Tools were probably developed by females to dig up roots and tubers, to open nuts, and to free the hands while carrying a baby. And, just as males had to communicate in order to hunt together, females had to communicate in order to gather food and fuel together and to train their young.

"The fact that some male-dominated religions have goddesses undercuts the thesis that there is a direct correlation between the presence of goddesses and high status for women."
Rita Gross

Today's anthropologists generally agree that in the foraging societies of early history, which covered much more time than the 120,000 years or so from the Neolithic to the present, the sexes were probably complementary and of equal importance (Ehrenberg, 1989). As Gross (1996) says, it is difficult to imagine that humanity could have survived if early humans wasted female productivity and intelligence in the way that patriarchal societies have always done. Cultures in which women and men were basically equal were also common to hunter-gatherer and horticultural societies prior to colonization (Eisler, 1987; Kehoe, 1983; Leacock, 1981; Sacks, 1982; Sanday, 1981). Even today there are some cultures with egalitarian gender relations. Examples include the !Kung people of the Kalahari Desert, the Mbuti Pygmies of Zaire, and the Vanatinai people who live on a small island southeast of Papua New Guinea (Renzetti & Curran, 1995).

Some writers argue that in ancient times **matriarchies,** or societies in which women had greater power than men, were common (cf. Bachofen, 1967; Cavin, 1985; Davis, 1971; Diner, 1975). Archeologist Marija Gimbutas (1991) extensively catalogued archeological evidence in favor of the view that matriarchies were common during the Neolithic period in Old Europe. Paleolithic foraging societies, Chatal Huyuk (a village in what is now Turkey), Old Europe, ancient megalithic cultures, and especially Crete are often discussed by advocates of this position, because there is evidence (much in the form of sculptures) that numerous, powerful goddesses were worshiped (Gross, 1996).

Many feminists are attracted to the view that matriarchies or egalitarian societies were common at one time. They would like to show that a world where women have power is possible and that, despite patriarchy's current domination of social systems, patriarchy is not as natural as it may appear. As Eisler said in her popular 1987 book *The Chalice and the Blade,* evidence from art, archeology, religion, social science, history, and many other fields show that "war and the war of the sexes are neither divinely nor biologically ordained. And it provides verification that a better future is possible—and is in fact firmly rooted in the haunting drama of what actually happened in our past" (p. xv).

BOX 2.1 *Do Matriarchies Exist Today?*

In 1995, Juanita Darling, Los Angeles Times journalist, wrote that matriarchy flourishes in the town of Juchitán, Mexico. In the tradition of the pre-Colombian Zapotec empire, women dominate public economic activities, such as buying and selling products that are mostly produced by men. They also either make or participate in all decisions regarding the household and typically control the family money because men are believed to be incompetent when it comes to family finances. Unlike in most other parts of Mexico, women are not pressured to marry or to put up with a difficult husband. When a wife feels that her husband is not doing his share, she prefers to be alone. As one woman said, "The women in other places are submissive. They are tied to a man. Well, I am not going to beg a man to give me money to buy bread. Women here work. That is the base of our economy." Art, literature, and formal politics are seen as the domains of males. Politics are one of the few areas in which men occupy leadership positions.

Lugo Lake, in a remote corner of southern China, is another place that appears to have a matriarchal society. Property and names pass from mother to daughter, and the women rarely marry. Men engage in few productive activities; for the most part, it is the women who earn and control the money and grow the food. Men have no ownership of the children they father. The women of Lugo Lake like their traditions. They point out that their self-sufficiency means that they may choose men based on love, unlike outsider women who must choose based on whether prospective husbands can provide for them. As is the case in Juchitán, the men do hold most of the formal political posts, making decisions outside of the village but not within it.

Source: Darling, 1995; Farley, 1998.

Bamberger (1974) points out that, to some, the fact that there are no *existing* matriarchal or egalitarian cultures is proof that these forms are ineffective. (Box 2.1 provides examples of matriarchal societies today.) Otherwise, the argument goes, these societies would not be extinct. Eisler (1987) responds to this by suggesting that the span of human cultural evolution is too short to make such a judgment. According to her view, patriarchy represents a 5,000-year maladaptive "detour"—maladaptive because patriarchy's emphasis on dominance and violence may lead to the ultimate destruction of the earth and humankind. She further notes that cultural progression is not in fact linear, but rather has always been characterized by periods of advancement, and then regression. To solve our mounting global problems, Eisler (1987) believes that we must reject patriarchy and its emphasis on violence. Instead, we should choose to structure our societies in ways that are "more sexually egalitarian" and that emphasize the "life-generating and nurturing powers of the universe."

Many feminist anthropologists do not think that the anthropological evidence supports the idea that matriarchies and egalitarian societies were at any time common (Duley & Edwards, 1986; Ruth, 1995). For instance, Bamberger (1974) points out that the myths that tell of female-dominated societies typically conclude with women losing their power because of in-competence, unethical conduct, or weakness. In other words, the very myths that are often used as evidence of matriarchy can, upon closer examination, be used to deny women power. Or, as Rosaldo and Lamphere (1974) say,

> Whereas some anthropologists argue that there are, or have been, truly egalitarian societies . . . , and all agree that there are societies in which women have achieved considerable social recognition and power, none has observed a society in which women have publicly recognized power and authority surpassing that of men. . . . The archeological data are more problematic. . . . Elaborate female burial rituals might, for example, indicate a world in which women were the rulers; but they could equally be the remains of wives or mistresses, concubines of male elites, or women who became heads of state in lieu of male heirs in a royal family. Female sculptures may represent goddesses, but there are historically documented and well-studied contemporary societies that manifest female fertility cults while at the same time placing political power in the hands of men. (p. 3)

To further illustrate, imagine that we are all vaporized by aliens who leave our buildings and other creations intact. They land in the United States. There they see billboards and magazines such as *Playboy,* videos, and so on plastered with images of women. They might conclude from this that women dominated the society and were worshiped. However, the truth at time of vaporization is that women in the United States held a minority of political and business power positions—for example, only 10 percent of the U.S. Congress and 4 percent of corporate executive officers are female. Although most agree that the ancient world included many powerful and impressive goddesses, some believe that those in favor of the matriarchal hypothesis infer more from the material artifacts than perhaps they should (Gross, 1996).

We may never know for sure whether matriarchies or egalitarian societies were at any time common. As Eisler herself points out, the thousands of cave drawings and sculptures depicting women could be ancient analogues for today's *Playboy* magazine, or they could be evidence of goddess worship and the veneration of women's life-giving abilities. Eisler believes the latter. Furthermore, she makes the case that, in general, archeologists and anthropologists have interpreted the evidence in ways that fit their stereotypes of prehistoric peoples and that were consistent with their own views of man as dominator and woman as secondary.

Of course, Eisler can also be accused of letting her pro-female biases tilt her reading of the archeological record. However, even if you disagree with Eisler's interpretation, remember that this does not mean that we cannot move toward greater equality. Likewise, remember that even if you agree with Eisler, this does not mean that steps toward gender equality will occur without concerted effort. As Lerner (1986) says, "the creation of compensatory myths of the distant past of women will not emancipate women in the present and future" (p. 36). In either event, activism as well as a thorough knowledge and understanding of modern cultures is required to bring about change.

Conclusion

This chapter examined a number of explanations for women's lower status and power. Note, however, that none suggest that men are by nature evil beings intent on the oppression of women. Rather, as you will see throughout the book, men's individual, intentional acts of dominance over women are reflections of cultures' overall systems of gender power relations. As Lips (1991) notes, the occurrence of many forms of routine oppression of women by men are mindless and unintentional, often unrecognized by either the perpetrators or the victims, but supported by the overall system of gender power relations. Individuals, more or less unaware of the structure of power that surrounds them, participate in, maintain, and are limited by the power structures of their societies. For instance, many cultures define masculinity in ways that encourage the denigration of women and define femininity in terms of submissiveness and subordination to men. Both males and females are socialized into cultures that emphasize men's power over women. Mothers and fathers teach their children how to participate in traditional gender systems as well. Women also participate in the social systems that oppress women. For instance, in some societies, mothers-in-law treat daughters-in-law as virtual slaves, and in others, it is adult women who perform the physically and emotionally traumatizing genital mutilations of young girls.

It is also important to realize that it is not uniquely male to create social groups in which some individuals have greater power and status than others. Groups composed solely of women are not by definition immune from these power and status dynamics. Indeed, in the face of low societal status, women often create their own female societies (within the larger culture) in which some women have greater power and status over other women. Furthermore, women of the upper classes often exploit women of the lower classes. As you will see throughout the book, it generally takes a great deal of political and social activism to override the human inclination to exploit and dominate one another.

This chapter provided some theories as to how women came to be subordinated. The following chapters pick up on the themes started here, illustrating their importance in the lives of contemporary women and their role in gender equality. For instance, Chapters 5 and 6 return to the topic of women's labor, and Chapter 7 examines women and religion. The next chapter, Chapter 3, explores how women's power and status are affected by their role as reproducer and the importance of reproductive freedom for the achievement of gender equality.

Terms and Concepts

patriarchies	sociocultural explanations
biological explanations	gender stereotypes
biosocial or evolutionary perspective	private use value
male bonding gene	exchange value
man-the-hunter explanation	matriarchies
psychoanalytic explanations	

Study Questions

1. What is the essence of biological explanations for women's lower power and status?

2. What are the four general types of biologically based arguments for the dominance of men over women, and how do critics respond to them?

3. In what way could biological differences between men and women have led *indirectly* to men's domination of women?

4. What is the essence of psychoanalytic explanations for women's lower power and status? What are the variations of this theme discussed in the chapter?

5. What are the sociocultural explanations for men's domination of women?

6. According to the sociocultural perspective, how do cultures communicate the appropriateness of male domination? In other words, how is it learned via culture?

7. How is the relationship between gender roles and gender stereotypes reciprocal?

8. What explanations are provided in the chapter for why male activities tend to be more highly valued than female ones?

9. Why are some feminists attracted to the view that matriarchies were at one time common? What types of evidence do they point to as proof that matriarchies existed? What are the problems associated with reading the archeological record that make it difficult to determine whether matriarchies were at one time common?

10. What is meant by the suggestion that the oppression of women is often routine and mindless?

Discussion Questions and Activities

1. If women were not economically dependent on men, would gender equality follow? Why or why not?

2. The society in the town of Juchitan, Mexico, described in Box 2.1, has been criticized by outsiders who see the women's strong role in public life as evidence that women there oppress men. Those who live there see their society as egalitarian and believe that Zapotec culture is more advanced and that the rest of the world is only now catching up. What is your opinion?

3. Which of the explanations for women's lower status and power most appeals to you and why? Which one least appeals to you and why?

4. Do a research project on Margaret Mead, one of the first anthropologists to pay careful attention to the activities of females and to gender roles.

Women in the U.S. demonstrate for reproductive rights. Reproductive choice is central to women's equality and health.

Reproductive Freedom

Over the past 15–20 years, women in different parts of the world have taken up issues of reproductive health. Their concern has been to empower women to control their own fertility and sexuality with maximum choice and minimum health problems by providing information and alternative services, and by campaigning for women's right to make informed choices about their fertility, for improved services and for more appropriate technologies.

Meeting of the World Health Organization and the International Women's Health Coalition, 1991

Many feminists believe that a fundamental source of women's oppression is male domination of females' bodies, both ideologically—through pornography and sexist jokes—and practically—through androcentric or male-centered marriage and property laws, denial of women's reproductive rights, and sexual violence (Peterson & Runyan, 1993). The focus of this chapter is women's reproductive rights. Women's ability to bear and nurse children profoundly affects their lives, and yet they frequently lack the freedom to control the timing and number of their children. This is both a symptom and a cause of women's unequal rights and has a significant effect on women's health. Simply stated, reproductive freedom is critical to women's equality.

This chapter notes many contradictions when it comes to women's reproductive control. Women's status is simultaneously boosted and diminished by their role as reproducers. Safe and legal abortion too often goes hand in hand with poor contraceptive availability, resulting in women being forced to use abortion as a primary form of contraception. The most effective contraceptive methods are often those that require the closest medical monitoring, yet most of the countries that offer these methods do not provide the information and monitoring necessary to ensure effectiveness and safety. Governments miss the point when they attempt to reduce overpopulation by controlling women's fertility and fail to increase women's status and the likelihood that children will live to adulthood.

At the 1968 UN International Human Rights Conference, it was acknowledged that family planning is a human right, that is, that couples should be able to freely decide how many children they want and the spacing of those children (Dixon-Mueller, 1993). The reality, however, is that the majority of women worldwide do not have these reproductive freedoms. Women

"As long as it remains possible for a woman to become pregnant without wanting to be, abortion will be a necessity and its denial a punishment of women—for having sex."
Rosalind Petchesky

often bear unwanted children, are prevented from having wanted children, and have to bear children in desperate circumstances (Morgan, 1984). This has dramatic consequences on the lives of women everywhere.

True reproductive choice involves offering women a broad range of birth control methods from which they can freely choose (Hartmann, 1995). But in most societies, reproductive choice lies not in the woman's hands but in her husband's or in the government's. The global economy and international politics are also players in women's reproductive choice—especially in terms of women's access to contraception or birth control methods (often referred to as **reproductive technologies**). As you will see in this chapter, what seems like a very personal choice (the control of one's own fertility) is in reality greatly affected by economic, political, and social institutions. This is because reproductive technologies, like other technologies, are cultural objects enmeshed in social, political, and economic systems (Ginsberg & Rapp, 1995). Furthermore, these social, political, and economic forces tend to dominate whereas women's health, power, and status take a distant backseat. As Peterson and Runyan (1993) put it, "Here the personal is political in the sense that even women's most 'private' and intimate experiences are shaped by institutions and structures that privilege male-defined pleasures and masculinist principles" (p. 118).

Reproductive Control as a Critical Feminist Issue

Reproductive control is an important feminist issue because of the intimate relationship between women's reproductive choice and their status, power, and health. The connection between women's reproductive control and issues regarding the diversity of women are another important theme.

Reproductive Control as a Symptom of Women's Low Status

According to Jacobson (1992), a woman's reproductive control can be determined by her answers to the following questions: Can she control when and with whom she will engage in sexual relations? Can she do so without fear of infection or unwanted pregnancy? Can she choose when and how to regulate her fertility, free from unpleasant or dangerous side effects of contraception? Can she go through pregnancy and childbirth safely? Can she obtain a safe abortion on request? Can she easily obtain information on the prevention and treatment of reproductive illnesses? In countries where women are socially, politically, and economically disadvantaged, the answers to these questions are likely to be no, and high rates of reproductive illness and death are usually common.

It is evident that women's health concerns are often ignored in the marketing and availability of contraception. That women are often left out of the family planning equation when their interests should be central is yet another symptom of their lower status. It is also apparent that government concerns about population control and corporate concerns about profit often endanger women's health. For instance, **hormonal contraceptive methods,** such as the Pill, Norplant, and Depo-Provera, can have significant side effects. Proper use requires medical evaluation and monitoring as well as education regarding possible risk factors and side effects. Despite this, many governments, international organizations, and corporations promote the use of hormonal contraceptives by nonmedical personnel in the Third World (Hartmann, 1995).

In many countries, women's bodies are viewed as the property of their husbands, and so it is husbands who get to make decisions regarding the number and spacing of the children. This is the case in all or parts of Bangladesh, Ethiopia, India, Korea, Nigeria, and Tunisia (Jacobson, 1992). For instance, in the Philippines, most clinics require the husband's consent for a wife's **sterilization,** a surgical procedure that prevents pregnancy (Macklin, 1996). A husband's permission is also required for a wife's sterilization in Lesotho (Kanno, 1996). It is only within the last twenty-five years that married women in the United States could easily get contraception or sterilization without their husband's permission. Many men fear that their partner's use of contraception will lead to her promiscuity, and they therefore oppose it. For instance, in Lesotho, men question their wife's loyalty if she is on the Pill or has an **IUD (intrauterine device).** They believe that if she does not fear pregnancy, she may go with another man (Kanno, 1991). Many cultures believe that if women could enjoy sexual relations and could prevent pregnancy, then sexual morality and family security would be jeopardized (Cook, 1995). Where children are a sign of male virility, men may be motivated to father many children and oppose their partners' efforts to prevent this. The family planning literature documents that women's contraceptive use is inhibited by fear of male reprisal in the form of violence, desertion, or accusations of infidelity (Heise, 1995).

Chapter 2 noted that gender stereotypes often support the subordination of women. In some societies women are believed to be too weak and irrational to be given power over their own bodies. Men are thought to have uncontrollable sexual needs that excuse sexual crimes against women and justify polygamy, extramarital affairs, and visits to prostitutes. In many countries, such as Thailand, the United Arab Emirates, Pakistan, and Kuwait, such practices have significantly contributed to the spread of AIDS. Men's higher status is also used to grant them the right to sexual favors from women, even when the women don't want it. The consequences of women's lack of power in sexual decision making are even more dire since the advent of AIDS (Heise, 1995). Most AIDS prevention programs emphasize reducing the number of sexual partners, promoting condom use, and treating other sexually transmitted diseases. However, men's greater power in sexual relationships may greatly limit women's ability to use these strategies for their own protection. For instance, in African countries where it is common for married

"Condoms are good enough, but there are men who don't want to use them. So it's men's consciousness that's lacking."
Motoko Katayama

men to engage in extramarital sexual relations, both elite and working-class women frequently express powerlessness in the face of their husband's multiple partner relationships. As the wife of a government official in Zaire said, "I can't ask him to stop, but I wish he would use condoms. Use condoms with the other women, with me, whatever. But I just don't feel I can introduce the subject. It wouldn't do any good. My husband would just get angry and tell me to mind my own business" (from Schoepf, 1997, p. 322). In many places, men's higher status and women's social and economic dependencies on men often give men condom refusal power.

The Indian state of Kerala is an interesting illustration of the relationship between women's status and reproductive control. Kerala is a state in southern coastal India. Unlike other parts of India, Kerala has fertility rates, infant mortality rates, literacy rates, and life expectancies similar to those in Europe. This is the case even though Kerala is densely populated, and its people are poor. There are a number of reasons that may account for the differences between Kerala and other Indian states, but many agree that one crucial difference is women's higher status. This higher status provides women with a source of value that is not tied to having many children and gives them greater control than most Indian women over their reproductive lives. More than 70 percent of Kerala's women are literate, three times India's national average. Kerala is the only state in India where women outnumber men (104 females to every 100 males). The average age of females to marry (22) is the highest in India. Women have greater economic independence in Kerala, for there are more jobs for women than in most other parts of the country. Kerala women have a greater say in household decisions than in other parts of India and have a history of political involvement as well.

Kerala's respect for women derives from its historically matrilineal culture. Among the dominant caste, the Nayars, a woman continued to live with her parents even once married and inherited as many shares of property as she had children (her husband lived elsewhere and visited only at night). Sons inherited only one share for themselves. Although this system was outlawed under British colonization, its impact is still felt. Also, in contrast to other Indian states, the mother goddess Bhadrakali is prominent in Kerala. Her blessings are seen as necessary for prosperity. Her centrality in Kerala culture symbolizes reverence for the female. Kerala's geographic isolation from the rest of India permitted the development of its own woman-friendly culture. Unfortunately, increasing contact with the rest of India has led to some erosion of female status in Kerala, and men are increasingly reluctant to share power with women.

Lack of Reproductive Control and Women's Low Status

As discussed previously, the fact that women must bear and nurse children plays a key role in their lower status and often perpetuates that status over time. Historically, women's inability to prevent pregnancy gave rise to a sex-based division of labor and created an economic dependence on men that gave men great power over women. For instance, women often stay in abusive relationships because of economic dependence. The huge responsibilities of caring continuously for children has also made it difficult for women to organize and participate politically. Thus, women's interests are frequently ignored in the policy process, and their power, when they have it, is specific to the domestic sphere. Because of their child-rearing responsibilities, women have reduced their earning power and, consequently, their ability to accumulate the resources of power.

Reproductive Control and Health

Reproductive control is an important feminist issue because it is a major women's health issue. The work of childbearing has major consequences for the health of millions of women. The World Health Organization estimates that over half a million women each year die from complications associated with pregnancy, childbirth, and abortion: 308,000 in Asia; 150,000 in Africa; 34,000 in Latin America; 2,000 in Oceania (Australia, New Zealand, Fiji, Papua New Guinea, Solomon Islands); and 6,000 in developed countries (Cook, 1995; Jacobson, 1992). The most frequent direct causes of maternal death are:

1. *Hemorrhage,* from botched abortions, difficult labor, uterine rupture from traditional birth practices (such as pressing on the mother's stomach during labor). This is more likely in women who have given birth frequently.

2. *Toxemia,* from high blood pressure during pregnancy. This is easily preventable with regular prenatal care.

3. *Sepsis,* a systemic infection from dirty delivery conditions, long labor, ruptured membranes, cesarean section, abortion, or retained placenta.

4. *Obstructed labor,* occurring when a child cannot be easily delivered due to a narrow pelvis (especially common with young women), many previous deliveries, twins, or a breech birth. Cesarean section is effective treatment but is unavailable to many Third World women.

5. *Complications from unsafe abortion,* hemorrhage or infection from the use of unsterilized instruments, incomplete abortion, punctures in the uterus, cervix, or other organs.

(DIXON-MUELLER, 1993; JACOBSON, 1992)

Class is clearly an issue when it comes to rates of **maternal death.** The quantity and quality of reproductive health care available to pregnant

---

BOX 3.1   *Maternal Death Rates*

The following lists a woman's lifetime chances of dying as a result of pregnancy or childbirth: 1 in

11,904 in Spain	889 in Russia
10,417 in Switzerland	526 in China
8,772 in Canada	370 in Argentina
8,333 in Norway	303 in Mexico
6,803 in Sweden	159 in Egypt
6,410 in Italy	109 in South Africa
6,173 in the United Kingdom	94 in the Philippines
5,848 in Australia	49 in India
5,102 in Israel	37 in Zimbabwe
3,968 in the United States	12 in Mali
3,922 in France	10 in Yemen
3,704 in Japan	9 in Sierra Leone
3,497 in Germany	

Source: Neft & Levine, 1998.

women—as well as women's knowledge of and ability to take advantage of the services that are available—are unequally distributed in favor of wealthier nations, urban locations, and social groups with higher incomes and education (Dixon-Mueller, 1993). Deaths and illnesses from reproductive causes are highest among poor women everywhere, as Box 3.1 shows. Indeed, over 98 percent of these deaths occur to women in developing countries. The greatest risk is to African women, who face a 1 in 21 chance of dying from pregnancy-related causes in their lifetimes compared to a 1 in 54 chance in Asia, a 1 in 73 chance in South America, a 1 in 6,366 chance in North America, and a 1 in 9,850 chance in Europe (Jacobson, 1992). In some countries such as Bangladesh, Brazil, Nigeria, and Uganda, reproductive problems now account for more than 50 percent of deaths to women in their childbearing years (Jacobson, 1992).

Demographers have estimated that about one-fourth of maternal deaths worldwide could be avoided if women's needs for family planning were met

(Winikoff & Sullivan, 1987, in Dixon-Mueller, 1993). The more pregnancies a woman has, the more frequently she is subjected to risks associated with pregnancy and childbirth; risks are also increased by having children in close succession and by having children when one is under 16 or over 35. In some parts of the world, such as Africa, many women will be pregnant and lactating for more than two-thirds of the time between the ages of 17 and 35 (Mosse, 1993). The burden of having many children in close succession means that when women have the option, they seldom choose to have as many children as biologically possible. Unfortunately, this choice is not available to many women in the world.

In some places, contraception is illegal, but in many places it is simply unavailable or there are few options. In Japan, for example, hormonal contraceptives such as Norplant and Depo-Provera are banned by the government, and only a few types of IUDs are permitted. The Pill was legalized in spring 1999 after thirty years of lobbying by women's activists. They pointed out that the government approved Viagra, a drug for male sexual dysfunction, after only a six-month review. The Japanese rely largely on condoms and **legal abortion,** which ends 1 out of every 4 pregnancies in Japan (Lazarowitz, 1997). The absence of government support for a range of reproductive choices is typically due to cost. Particularly in developing nations, medical care is largely unavailable, and the average person does not have the money for contraceptives. It is up to the government to develop distribution networks and to provide health-care workers and the contraceptive technologies. Governments often hold costs down by providing only those methods deemed cost effective and by providing minimal information and followup. For instance, governments often favor IUDs and sterilization because they are highly effective in preventing pregnancy and are irreversible without medical intervention.

Powerful religious groups may also influence the restriction of contraceptives. For instance, resistance from the Catholic Church kept contraception illegal in Massachusetts and Connecticut until 1958. Currently, contraception is legal in Chile but is largely unavailable due to resistance from the Catholic Church. Some writers suggest that the church's opposition is partly due to its desire to maintain church authority over the traditional (patriarchal) family and to its declining numbers of religious adherents (Dixon-Mueller, 1993). However, the Roman Catholic Church is not so powerful that it is always able to prevent contraceptive use, even in strongly Roman Catholic countries. For example, the great majority of Brazilian and Argentinian couples use modern contraceptive methods, 71 percent and 74 percent, respectively (Neft & Levine, 1998).

Additional threats to women's health arise from the contraceptives themselves. Women's health activists feel strongly that women should receive enough information about **contraceptive side effects** and health risks to make an informed choice. Each method has advantages and disadvantages. Box 3.2 provides an overview of the most common birth control methods. The Pill, an oral contraceptive taken daily, is highly effective

"Many of the data to measure the effect of family planning programmes focus on demographic and health objectives set by the government or by service providers, without taking into account the programmes' impact on individuals' reproductive rights."
Report of the International Conference on Population and Development, Cairo, 1994

Margaret Sanger
(1883–1966) founded the birth control movement in the United States. Despite harassment and arrest, she successfully pushed the federal courts to change laws preventing physicians from providing birth control information and devices. In 1921 she founded the organization that would later become Planned Parenthood. Although Sanger was an important figure in the history of women's reproductive choice, she was a supporter of eugenics, a movement to limit the reproduction of undesirable groups.

BOX 3.2   *Common Birth Control Methods*

Barrier Methods

Reversible, with few side effects. These methods offer some protection against sexually transmitted diseases (STDs). They are highly effective in preventing pregnancy if used properly, but because many people find them inconvenient, their effectiveness is significantly reduced.

Diaphragm—Soft rubber shallow cup that holds spermicidal jelly or cream and fits over the cervix to block and kill sperm. Proper fitting requires the help of a health-care practitioner.

Female condom—Loose-fitting polyurethane sheath that lines the vaginal wall.

Male condom—The only temporary birth control method available to men, the condom is a thin sheath, usually of latex, which covers the penis during sex.

Cervical cap—Thimble-shaped rubber cap that fits over the cervix. Like the diaphragm, it is used with a spermicide to block and kill sperm and must be fitted by a health-care practitioner.

Hormonal Methods

Reversible and highly effective but offer no protection against STDs and produce a variety of undesirable side effects.

Birth control pills (the Pill)—synthetic hormones taken daily that prevent pregnancy primarily by preventing ovulation; a prescription drug in most countries.

Norplant—Synthetic hormones released gradually from match-size capsules inserted in the arm. Prevents pregnancy for up to five years by inhibiting ovulation and thickening cervical mucus (this impedes sperm activity). Insertion and removal require a skilled health-care practitioner.

Depo-Provera—An injectable contraceptive that prevents pregnancy for up to three months by inhibiting ovulation and thickening cervical mucus.

Intrauterine Devices (IUDs)

Reversible, long-term method highly effective against pregnancy but providing no STD protection and a variety of possible negative side effects. IUDs are small devices that fit in the uterus with a small string that extends into the upper vagina. Some contain copper or hormones. No one is sure exactly how it works to prevent pregnancy, but it works until removal. Must be inserted and removed by a qualified health-care practitioner.

Permanent Methods—Sterilization

A highly effective and permanent form of birth control achieved through surgery. Generally safe with few negative side effects if performed by a skilled professional in a sterile setting. In women, the fallopian tubes are blocked or cut in a procedure called a *tubal ligation*. In men, in a procedure called a *vasectomy,* the vas deferens is cut so that sperm cannot mix with the seminal fluid. A vasectomy can be reversed surgically in some cases.

Source: Boston Women's Health Collective, 1992.

in preventing pregnancy but can cause headaches, depression, weight gain, and an increased risk for circulatory disorders. There is also some evidence that it may lead to an increased incidence of cervical cancer. Norplant, consisting of small hormonal capsules or rods implanted in the arm, is also highly effective in preventing pregnancy for up to five years. However, insertion and removal are often painful, and menstrual disorders are common. Depo-Provera, an injectable hormonal contraceptive, prevents pregnancy for three to six months. Unlike the Pill, it does not have to be taken every day, and unlike Norplant, no removal is necessary. However, menstrual disorders are common and range from heavy bleeding to no bleeding at all. Other side effects include depression, headaches, skin disorders, and loss of interest in sex. **Barrier contraceptive methods,** such as the condom and diaphragm, have the advantages of reducing sexually transmitted diseases (STDs) and causing few side effects. However, pregnancy is more likely due to inconsistent and improper use.

The point is that often, women are not informed about side effects and health risks. This is especially an issue when the government's main concern is population control. Naripokkho is a feminist activist group in Bangladesh. The group lobbies the government against the use of Norplant without the provision of appropriate medical care. Through videotaped interviews, they have proved that Norplant is widely promoted among poor women without educating them as to side effects and without adequate followup. The IUD (intrauterine device) is another example. This small plastic or copper device is highly effective in the prevention of pregnancy, and once it is inserted into the uterus, pregnancy is usually prevented until its removal. The most common side effect is heavy bleeding and cramping; this is especially a concern for women who are nutritionally deficient and for those who have difficulty obtaining clean materials for menstruation. Women with IUDs run a much greater risk of pelvic inflammatory disease (PID). PID is an infection of the upper reproductive tract that may lead to sterility. This risk is heightened if the IUD is inserted under less than sterile conditions, which is more likely in developing nations where cost considerations sometimes lead to the purchase of unsterilized IUDs, poor training of personnel, and unsanitary conditions. Despite these problems, IUD use is roughly three times greater in developing nations than in developed ones. In the United States, it took several years of activism in order to get a particular type of IUD, the Dalkon Shield, off the market in 1974. This particular device was associated with a high incidence of PID and septic abortions (miscarriage accompanied by toxic infection). Fourteen deaths and 219 septic abortions were attributed to its use from 1971 to 1974 (Hartmann, 1995).

One source of reproductive health problems for women is the practice of **female genital mutilation (FGM).** Between 80 and 114 million girls have undergone some form of FGM, and every year another 2 million girls are forced to submit to it (American Medical Association, 1995). *Sunna,* the mildest type, consists of a subtotal clitoridectomy. *Excision* consists of clitoridectomy and sometimes the removal of parts or all of the labia minor. *Infibulation* or *pharaonic circumcision* involves removal of the entire clitoris, the labia minor, and at least two-thirds of the labia major. The two sides of the vulva are then stitched together with a small opening for the passage of menstrual blood and urine. In most cases, female genital mutilations are done by a midwife or practiced village woman, although upper-class girls may be taken to a physician. Various tools may be used (knives, razors, scissors, rocks, glass), and they may or may not be sterilized. There is also variation in the use of anesthesia and antibiotics.

FGM is practiced throughout Africa and in parts of Malaysia and Indonesia. Most cases occur in eastern and western Africa in the countries of Djibouti, Mali, Sierra Leone, Somalia, Ethiopia, Egypt, and the Sudan. FGM also occurs in Europe and in the United States among immigrants from those countries where it is customary. However, Australia, Canada, France, Ghana, the Netherlands, Norway, Sweden, Switzerland, the United Kingdom, and the United States all have laws prohibiting FGM. Most Islamic countries do not practice FGM (UNIFEM, 1998).

The main purpose of FGM is to destroy a young woman's sexual sensation in order to preserve her virginity until marriage and to prevent her from succumbing to sexual temptation after marriage. There are also claims that it prevents homosexuality and "beautifies" the woman. In some societies a girl is unmarriageable unless she has undergone FGM. Upon marriage, if a woman is uncircumcized or inadequately circumsized, her husband may divorce her or insist upon proper circumcision. Even where it is illegal, it is often still practiced.

Asma El Dareer (1982), a Sudanese physician and herself circumcised at age 11, conducted research on the medical consequences of FGM. Her research along with information from the World Health Organization is reported here. Short-term medical consequences include pain, severe bleeding, and infection. There are some deaths from shock, bleeding, and infection. The long-term consequences of genital mutilation are serious, especially in the case of infibulation. Due to the small size of the remaining opening (a matchstick is often used), women who have undergone this procedure have difficulty urinating, menstruating, having sex, and giving birth. Inadequate drainage is responsible for the accumulation of deposits in the vagina, which may then cause tears (fistulae) in the tissue separating the vagina from the urinary tract and the bowel, resulting in the leakage of urine and feces, which creates many social problems. Intervention is necessary to enlarge the opening for birth, and recircumcision is common after delivery. Prolonged labor, harmful to both mother and child, is often a consequence. Decircumcision is often necessary in order to have sex. Sometimes this is done by a doctor, nurse, or midwife. Sometimes the opening is enlarged with a knife by the husband, who is too embarrassed to admit he cannot penetrate his wife. Sexual pleasure is negatively affected by all forms of female genital mutilation.

In the last decade, women have worked hard to draw attention to female genital mutilation. Activists in Gambia broadcast programs critical of FGM on state-owned radio and television stations, following a widely supported letter campaign (Brandell, 1998). The UN condemns the practice and has tried to reduce it by pointing out that it is incompatible with the Convention on All Forms of Elimination of Discrimination Against Women. CEDAW, as it is called, proceeds from the assumption that all practices that harm women, no matter how deeply they are embedded in culture, must be eradicated. The World Health Organization also condemns the practice. One hopeful sign that activism against FGM may finally pay off came at the November 1997 meeting of the Organization of African Unity (OAU). Brandell (1998) reports that the OAU secretariat pledged its commitment to working with its fifty-three member governments to eradicate FGM in Africa. The plan calls for the integration of FGM prevention and education programs into the governmental health and development ministries, as well as alternative employment programs for former practitioners. Meanwhile, women's organizations work to provide alternatives to FGM as a rite of passage. For instance, Kenyan women's organizations, along with the NGO Program for Appropriate Technology (PATH), are providing an alternative to FGM in the form of a new ceremony incorporating song, dance, and educational drama (Thomas, 1998).

Government Control of Women's Reproductive Choice

The UN treaty called the Convention on the Elimination of All Forms of Discrimination Against Women (CEDAW) requires that policymakers, governments, and service providers view fertility regulation and reproductive health services as a way to empower women, and not as a means to limit population growth, save the environment, and speed economic development (Plata, 1994, in Cook, 1995). However, it is not uncommon for governments to control women's reproduction in the name of social needs or national interests.

As it turns out, government support for family planning typically has little to do with enhancing women's control over their own bodies and has much more to do with governments' desire to control the size of their populations. Although ideally **population control programs** should provide women with greater reproductive control, the family planning services provided by many countries are coercive and deny women control over their bodies. As Waring (1988) puts it, "Powerful patriarchs of legislative, religious, and cultural bodies deny women the right to control their own fertility, and thus to control the reproduction of the labor force"(p. 188).

Pronatalism

Countries with **pronatalist** policies deny women birth control in order to increase population for a variety of reasons: to replace wartime casualties, to increase the workforce, or to increase the number of religious adherents. This is often done by outlawing contraception and abortion. For example, the Romanian government outlawed contraception in the 1970s and 1980s because it was feared that population growth was too low to keep up with projected labor needs. Another example comes from the 1980s. Following large casualties from its war with Iran, the country of Iraq banned contraceptives,

In 1998, the World Health Organization (WHO) of the United Nations appointed Dr. Gro Harlem Brundtland as its new director. She is the first woman to head the agency, just as she was the first woman to be elected Prime Minister of Norway (she served from 1981 to 1997). Brundtland is a committed feminist and an outspoken advocate of abortion and reproductive rights. She is well known for publicizing the link between poverty, health, and the environment. In 1987 she chaired the UN's World Commission on Environment and Development, producing an influential document on sustainable development now known as the "Brundtland Report."

waged a campaign stressing motherhood, and encouraged men to take second wives in order to increase the number of children.

Coercive Antinatalism

More common than pronatalist countries are societies that strongly encourage and even require that women limit their fertility. Social scientists sometimes call this coercive **antinatalism** (Dixon-Mueller, 1993). Coercive antinatalism typically occurs when concerns about reducing population growth eclipse concerns about women's health and control over their bodies. On the face of it, the superseding of individual reproductive rights in the larger interest of society may make coercive antinatalism seem justifiable. Indeed, it seems logical to the average middle-class person from a First World country that overpopulation is the source of Third World problems and that drastic measures must be taken. However, it may very well be but a myth that those in poverty create their own poverty by overbreeding. According to Hartmann (1995), overpopulation is not as great a problem as it is made out to be. Birth rates are actually falling in most areas of the Third World, and increases in agricultural yields mean that the carrying capacity of the earth is greater than once thought. Second, Hartmann emphasizes that in many parts of the world, having a large family is a rational mode of survival. In agricultural settings, children's labor contributes significantly to family production, and in urban settings children may earn income as servants or messengers or care for younger siblings while parents work. It is also children who care for parents in old age, for in many societies there are no pension plans and government aid for the elderly. It is often the sons who are expected to care for their parents, making them especially valuable. In some parts of the world where infant and child mortality rates are high, parents have many children in order to ensure that one or two sons survive and that they have enough children to contribute to the family economy.

Hartmann's point is that high birth rates are often a distress signal that people's survival is endangered. To find workable solutions, the real sources of high birth rates must be addressed. Persuading, tricking, and even coercing individuals into sterilization or contraception, as many international and government programs do, may not be a necessary evil after all. Indeed, there is good reason to believe that birth rates drop when standards of living are improved, when infant and child mortality is reduced, and when women have other ways of achieving status and value. Focusing on these goals obviously seems like a more desirable way of achieving population reductions.

Government desires to reduce population may come at the expense of reproductive health and choice. Family planning programs are frequently divorced from concerns about women's health, and women's health advocates worry that an emphasis on effectiveness has come at the expense of safety. As

"One birth in the United States is the 'ecological equivalent' of twenty-five births in India in terms of the consumption of valuable resources."
Kalini Karkal, consultant to the World Health Organization

we've already noted, governments are usually the major providers of contraceptive information and devices. Because governments' interests in family planning are largely motivated by a desire to reduce population growth, the contraceptive methods they provide are frequently the ones with the lowest failure rates, irrespective of the health risks these methods pose.

As Dixon-Mueller (1993) notes, the concept of birth control as potentially liberating for women and the poor is often submerged. Typically, women do not get the information necessary to make an informed choice about contraception; instead, they are steered toward high-tech and high-risk options such as birth control pills, Depo-Provera shots, Norplant, and IUDs. Safer methods, such as the barrier and rhythm methods, are unlikely to be promoted because of their greater failure rates, the time required for training women to use them, and the assumption that women cannot be trusted to use them correctly. All this means that state-sponsored family planning programs rarely provide them as options.

State policies surrounding reproductive control disproportionately affect women from the lower economic classes and sometimes exemplify reproductive racism. Steering women toward Norplant, Depo-Provera, and sterilization without providing them with information about risks is especially likely when the target group is lower income women or women from an ethnic group deemed undesirable by government officials. Sterilization, targeted at poor women, is often pushed by government programs. For instance, in the United States, minority women have a significantly higher rate of sterilization than do White women. Up until 1980, the United States government had a history of sterilizing poor women in federal programs without their consent, or by obtaining consent with misleading information, or by coercing consent through threats of loss of welfare or medical aid (Renzetti & Curran, 1995). In 1976, for instance, it was revealed that the U.S. government had sterilized 3,000 Native American women in a four-year period without obtaining adequate consent (Hartmann, 1995). Women from the upper classes tend to have access to private physicians who monitor their reproductive health, and they typically have access to a wider variety of contraceptives. Rich women from countries where contraceptives are illegal may get them while vacationing in countries where they are not illegal. For instance, upper-class Japanese women obtain hormonal contraceptives from abroad.

Although governments frequently argue that the risks of high-tech methods (including sterilization) are outweighed by the risks of pregnancy and childbirth, it is important to realize that

1. This penalizes poor women for their poverty—if conditions were not so poor, this would not be the case (Hartmann, 1995).
2. This comparison fails to ask why the risks of childbearing or abortion are so high in the first place (Dixon-Mueller, 1993).

3. This comparison fails to ask how the safety of contraceptives can be improved (Dixon-Mueller, 1993).

4. Even if contraception is safer than pregnancy, this does not justify denying women the right to make their own choices regarding such costs and benefits. Of course, many women will choose effectiveness and convenience over certain safety, inconvenience, and possible pregnancy, but this should be an informed choice.

Coercive antinatalism may be selective within a country. For instance, in the United States, considerable federal funds are devoted to reducing the population of Blacks, Native Americans, and Latin Americans (French, 1992). In Australia, Depo-Provera, a controversial injected contraceptive, has been given by government agencies to Aboriginal women but only rarely to women of Anglo descent (Morgan, 1996). There is a paradox here: On the one hand, women in poverty need access to contraceptives, and having smaller families is one key to their liberation; on the other hand, there are concerns within minority communities that the government's provision of such services is part of a genocidal conspiracy—that is, it is an attempt by the government to reduce what is seen as undesirable populations. Thus, many women are torn between loyalty to their ethnic group and a personal desire for a smaller family (Dixon-Mueller, 1993).

Indonesia, Thailand, Sri Lanka, Bangladesh, the Republic of Korea, Colombia, Mexico, Tunisia, and India all have antinatalist programs that incorporate persuasion, widespread family planning services, and small-scale incentive schemes (Dixon-Mueller, 1993). For instance, Bangladesh's incentive program gives each person who agrees to sterilization the equivalent of several weeks' wages as well as a sari (female clothing item) or a lungi (male clothing item). Hartmann (1995) states that government figures indicate that sterilizations in Bangladesh increase dramatically during the lean months before the harvest. Health workers in India are given targets that they must meet, or they will be docked pay or demoted. They must persuade a certain number of people to use IUDs, condoms, and birth control pills. They must also convince a certain number of people to be sterilized. In order to meet their targets and receive bonuses, they sometimes use bribery (Bumiller, 1990). Whether one considers these programs to be coercive may be a matter of opinion. However, most people would agree that China's one-child family policy is clearly coercive antinatalism.

In 1979, when one-child policy programs were initiated, China's population was approaching 1 billion. In 1980, following a successful pilot program in the Sichuan province, the Chinese congress approved the policy for the entire country. The Chinese government's goal was, and is, to bring China into the modern era. This requires high economic growth coupled with low population growth. On the face of it, this is an admirable and understandable goal. However, the coercive way in which it is pursued is disturbing. Although the government does provide incentives for couples to have only one child, it also strongly punishes those who have more than one. According to Hartmann (1995), parents who have additional children must pay the government 10 to 15 percent of their income for ten to sixteen years. Other penalties may include loss of wages and job demotion (Chow & Chen, 1994).

In some places, the one-child policy is enforced by carefully watching women to make sure they do not become pregnant. Hartmann (1987) reports that family planning workers watch for women who appear to have morning sickness or begin to restrict their activities. Elderly woman, called Granny Police, make home visits to make sure women are using contraception. The Chinese government claims that the one-child policy is strictly voluntary; however, there are many reports of forced abortions and sterilization (Hartmann, 1995).

For women, the one-child policy is paradoxical. Theoretically, it should reduce women's time spent on childbearing and rearing and thus free them to pursue activities traditionally dominated by men. Workplace participation without a series of interruptions due to multiple children should result in greater economic power for women. Lowered fertility may also mean that Chinese women will suffer less from the dual burden of work and family responsibilities (Chow & Chen, 1994). Hong (1987) suggests that an unbalanced sex ratio due to the favoring of male offspring and female infanticide should in the long run create a shortage of females, which will give them greater power.

Others have argued that China's one-child policy strengthens, rather than weakens, patriarchy. Stacey (1983) points out that historically Chinese men have controlled the fertility of Chinese women. Now that the state seeks this role, Chinese women are in a tug-of-war where the state and the patriarchal family seek control. Chen and Chow (1994) suggest that the one-child policy has actually led to a strengthening of the belief that more children are better—when you can't have something, frequently that makes you want it that much more. Furthermore, the continued preference for male offspring means that the one-child policy has placed considerable pressure on women and, in some cases, has led to wife beating and abandonment. It should also be noted that because women bear the children, they face a disproportionate amount of the blame and punishment if additional pregnancies occur, or if they have a daughter.

Chow and Chen's (1994) study comparing one-child families with multiple-child families in China did not find one-child families to be more gender egalitarian. Furthermore, they found that the great value of the only child in China and a continued emphasis on the Chinese woman as mother means that Chinese women are not spending less time with child and household responsibilities. In fact, they argue, the one-child policy has inadvertently encouraged the privatization of women in domestic labor and reproduction in the home. The preciousness of the single child prompts more housework and motherhood, not less.

The Global Economy and Women's Reproductive Choice

Making a Profit at Women's Expense

Pharmaceutical companies from industrialized countries make high-tech contraceptives and aggressively market them to government-run population control programs with the goal of monetary profit. Profit is increased by keeping research and development costs down and by emphasizing benefits and downplaying side effects and risks. Corea (1991) gives a good example of this with regard to Depo-Provera. She provides evidence that Upjohn, the developer of Depo-Provera, did questionable research and presented incomplete information from Depo-Provera drug trials in order to receive U.S. Food and Drug Administration approval so that Depo-Provera could be used in population control programs. It is alarming, she notes, that what Upjohn terms "minor side effects" are experienced as major side effects to women. In particular, she laments the downplaying of the common side effects of depression and loss of sexual arousal. "Depression is a minor side-effect that merely destroys the entire quality of a woman's life," says Corea. "It is doubtful that in a male hormonal contraceptive (should one ever see the light of day) the risks of 'loss of libido' and/or orgasm would be judged 'acceptable' or labeled 'minor' " (p. 165).

The case of the Dalkon Shield is another famous example. Recall that this IUD was taken off the United States market in 1974 as a result of increasing evidence that it led to PID and spontaneous abortion. What did AH Robbins do once it became obvious that U.S. sales would decline? They sold unsterilized Dalkon Shields at a discount, and with inadequate instructions, for distribution by population control programs in the Third World (Ehrenreich, Dowie, & Minkin, 1979).

Population Agencies and Pharmaceutical Companies

Population agencies in Third World countries are key to the profits made by pharmaceutical companies. These agencies play a major role in advertising, promoting, and distributing pharmaceutical contraceptives developed in First World capitalist countries such as the United States (Hartmann, 1995). Furthermore, the major U.S. agencies that promote international development and population control (for example, Aid for International Development) are heavily influenced by pharmaceutical companies. Owners and presidents of these companies sit on the boards of international population organizations, donate money to them, and lobby Congress for population appropriations (Hartmann, 1987). In short, the local availability of different birth control technologies may depend very much on international politics and economics of other countries.

Women's Activism

Women's groups frequently act as government watchdogs, calling attention to contraceptive abuses and the lack of appropriate reproductive health care.

Here are some examples. In Bangladesh, women's groups critique the government's focus on women as the cause of poverty. Although supportive of the general idea that birth control is a good idea for women's liberation, they question the lack of information given to women and the few choices afforded them; and they pressure the government to make changes (Jahan, 1995b). In China, women's activists explore the conflicts between the government's family planning program and women's health care, the negative effects of certain contraceptive methods, abortion abuse, and the connections between the government's program and female infanticide (Zhang & Xu, 1995). In Namibia, the women's group Namibian Women's Voice organizes campaigns against the government's use of Depo-Provera (Hubbard & Solomon, 1995). In the United States, feminists of color drew attention to discriminatory government policies, such as those pressuring Native American and Puerto Rican women into sterilization (Wolfe & Tucker, 1995).

Abortion

Unwanted pregnancies are a fact of life for women everywhere. Contraceptives fail. Contraceptives may be unavailable. Unwanted pregnancies may result from unwanted intercourse. Religions may discourage the use of contraception. All this means that women worldwide rely on abortion and have for centuries. In fact, historically, it was not until relatively recently that abortion became controversial. Indeed, abortion before "quickening" (movement of the fetus around the fifth month) was allowed under European, British, and American law until the 1800s. Even the Catholic Church was relatively tolerant of abortion for much of history. It was not until 1869 that Pope Pius IX declared all abortion to be murder (Hartmann, 1995; United Nations, 1993).

Hadley (1996) points out that discomfort with abortion is based in part on culture. For instance, British, American, Irish, and German women report more guilt feelings about having abortions than do women in Holland and Denmark. The difference is that there is greater openness in Holland and Denmark regarding women's sexuality. Third World women (and poor First World women) may see abortion as a selfless and necessary act that increases the likelihood that existing children will survive (there will be more food to go around). Indian women who opt to abort a female fetus after amniocentesis may believe that this is an act of love if it is near certain that a female child would experience a grim life as an unwanted daughter. Hadley also suggests that in those countries that are especially contemptuous of women who have abortions, abortion is viewed as a defiance of the ideology that defines women in terms of heterosexuality, marriage, and motherhood. The fetus is portrayed as a child, and the woman who gets an abortion as unwilling to make the maternal self-sacrifice that defines true womanhood. Where this ideology predominates, women may feel like abortion is a crime, even when it is legal.

"Abortion is a parody of choice, when there is no contraception."
Janet Hadley

Legality of Abortion

Sanctions against abortion historically originated on behalf of the family, tribe, state, or husband. The idea was that a woman did not have the right to deprive these agents of their "property" (Petchesky, 1984). Today's American notion that abortion should be legal because of a women's right to privacy and to have control over her own body is, globally speaking, a relatively unusual basis for legalized abortion. Laws regarding the legality or illegality of abortion are a clear example of the state regulating women's bodies, and these laws change according to the state's needs. For example, in 1966, Romanian leader Nicolae Ceauşecu banned abortion when he determined that more workers would be needed (French, 1992). Similarly, many European anti-abortion laws arose in the 1800s during times of colonial expansion when the state anticipated the need for more people to administer and populate new colonies (United Nations, 1993).

Abortion is *not* available by request (without restrictions) in the majority of countries for which the UN was able to gather information for a 1993 report, as shown in Box 3.3. However, in many of the world's countries, it is permitted under special circumstances. These circumstances vary widely. In at least twenty countries, including Argentina, Burundi, Costa Rica, Ethiopia, and Saudi Arabia, the only grounds permitted are to save the woman's life and to preserve her physical health. The preservation of mental health is an additional circumstance in seventeen countries such as Jamaica, Pakistan, Sierra Leone, Trinidad and Tobago. In some countries, abortion is only permitted in cases of rape or incest (Algeria, Bolivia, Ecuador, Zimbabwe). Australia, Belgium, Finland, France, Hungary, Italy, and Poland also allow abortion in cases of social or economic hardship (Neft & Levine, 1998).

It is important to understand that even where abortion is legal, it may not be readily available. In many countries, abortion is legal only under limited, and often vague, circumstances. Lack of legal clarity about when abortion is allowed has made many doctors reluctant to perform abortions lest they land in criminal court. In other countries, there are so many strings attached, it is difficult to get approval for an abortion. In Zambia, for instance, three doctors must approve the abortion, it must be deemed medically necessary, and it must be performed in a hospital. Most women there resort to **illegal abortions.** Abortion, even when legal, may be beyond the financial means of many women. In the United States, the average cost of an abortion is $250. A law prohibiting the use of federal health-care monies for abortion (except in cases where a woman's life is at risk) makes abortion financially untenable for many women.

In many countries, the right to a safe and legal abortion is under attack. In the United States, women seeking abortions often face anti-abortion picketers who plead with them not to "kill their babies." Many states have managed to pass laws requiring a waiting period or parental consent for those under 18. Because of budget cuts, lack of medical personnel, and effective

BOX 3.3 *Abortion Worldwide*

Least Restrictive

About 38 percent of the world's population live in countries where abortion is available by request:

Albania, Armenia, Austria, Azerbaijan, Belarus, Bosnia-Herzegovina, Bulgaria, Canada, China, Croatia, Cuba, Czech Republic, Denmark, Estonia, Georgia, Greece, Kazakhstan, Korea (North), Kyrgystan, Latvia, Lithuania, Macedonia, Moldova, the Netherlands, Norway, Puerto Rico, Romania, Russia, Singapore, Slovakia, Slovenia, South Africa, Sweden, Tajikistan, Tunisia, Turkey, Turkmenistan, Ukraine, the United States, Uzbekistan, Vietnam, Yugoslavia

With Conditions

About 46 percent live in countries where abortion is only available under certain circumstances, including threats to the mother's physical or mental health, fetal impairment, pregnancy from rape or incest:

Algeria, Angola, Argentina, Australia, Belgium, Bolivia, Brazil, Burkina Faso, Burundi, Cameroon, Congo, Costa Rica, Ecuador, Egypt, El Salvador, Eritrea, Ethiopia, Finland, France, Germany, Ghana, Guinea, Haiti, Hungary, India, Iraq, Israel, Italy, Jamaica, Japan, Jordan, Kenya, Korea (South), Kuwait, Liberia, Malawi, Malaysia, Mexico, Morocco, Nepal, New Zealand, Pakistan, Panama, Peru, Portugal, Rwanda, Saudi Arabia, Sierra Leone, Spain, Sudan, Switzerland, Taiwan, Thailand, Togo, Trinidad and Tobago, Uganda, United Kingdom, Uruguay, Poland, Zaire, Zambia, Zimbabwe

Restrictive

About 16 percent live in countries where abortion is only permitted to save the woman's life:

Afghanistan, Bangladesh, Benin, Cambodia, Central African Republic, Chad, Colombia, Dominican Republic, Guatemala, Honduras, Indonesia, Iran, Ireland, Ivory Coast, Laos, Lebanon, Libya, Madagascar, Mali, Mauritania, Mozambique, Myanmar, Nicaragua, Niger, Nigeria, Paraguay, Philippines, Senegal, Somalia, Sri Lanka, Syria, Tanzania, United Arab Emirates, Venezuela, Yemen

Forbidden

A few countries completely forbid abortion:

Andorra, Chile, Djibouti, Malta

Source: Neft & Levine, 1998.

lobbying by anti-abortion groups, many clinics have closed in a number of countries including the United States, Britain, India, Poland, Slovakia, Lithuania, and Hungary. Anti-abortion groups led by the Roman Catholic Church have been particularly influential in Poland, Slovakia, Lithuania, Italy, and Hungary. In the strongly Catholic country of Italy, many doctors and hospitals refuse to perform abortions. Although a first-trimester abortion has been legal since 1978, the law permits any health-care worker or administrator to claim conscientious objector status and to refuse to participate. In the first year, 72 percent of Italian doctors became objectors (Boston Women's Health Collective, 1992).

As is the case with contraceptive devices, women from the upper classes in most countries can get a safe abortion even when abortion is illegal. Nepal offers an example of this double standard. There, abortion is illegal, even in cases of rape and incest, and is typically punished with a jail sentence. However, the law is generally only applied to impoverished women. The elite are able to go to private clinics in Katmandu to receive hygienic abortions. These women and their doctors are not prosecuted (Goodwin, 1997). According to the Family Planning Association of Nepal (FPAN), as many as 75 percent of women in prison are there for having abortions. Furthermore, unsafe abortions are the cause of half of all maternal deaths in Nepal (Lang, 1998).

When Abortion Is Illegal

Interestingly, whether or not abortion is legal has remarkably little to do with its incidence. According to Hartmann (1995), of the 40 to 50 million abortions performed annually worldwide, 25 to 45 percent are illegal. Although many people oppose abortion on moral grounds, the fact of the matter is that women will have them when they face the possibility of having a child they cannot support. Even in strongly Catholic countries, illegal abortions are common as women perceive little choice other than to abort their pregnancies. For instance, in Colombia, the majority of women seeking abortions are married, Roman Catholic, and have at least three children (Morgan, 1984). In Greece, where family planning was outlawed until 1980 because of the influence of the Greek Orthodox Church, family size was controlled through the use of the withdrawal method and condoms, backed up by abortion (United Nations, 1993). It is estimated that in Brazil as many as 3 million abortions are performed every year (Neft & Levine, 1998). Where abortion is illegal or difficult to obtain, women customarily rely on other women for information about where to obtain an abortion or what to take to induce one. Box 3.4 describes "Jane," a women's collective that served this purpose.

There is a clear correlation between the availability of birth control devices and education and the number of abortions performed in a country (United Nations, 1993). For instance, until 1966 abortion was legal in Romania, and women depended upon it because contraceptives were difficult to obtain. In 1965, 80 percent of known pregnancies were aborted there (French, 1992). The average Soviet woman had between twelve and fourteen abortions during her lifetime because of the scarcity of contraceptives. Today, a woman in Russia has between five and seven abortions in her lifetime (Hadley, 1996). The United Nations reports shortages of contraceptives and lack of knowledge as important factors in creating high abortion rates. Contrast Holland's annual abortion rate—about 6 for every 1,000 women— with that of Britain, where it is 14; the United States, where it is 28; and Russia, where it is 111. Holland's rate is the lowest in the world, even though abortion is legal, free, and widely available. This low abortion rate is attributable to Holland's openness regarding the sexuality of young people, the easy availability of contraception, and sex education for young people (Hadley, 1996).

BOX 3.4 *Women Helping Women: "Jane"*

In 1969, abortion was illegal in the United States, and many women with unwanted pregnancies resorted to illegal and often unsafe abortions. A Chicago women's group hired doctors to perform safe abortions and referred women to them. Clients paid $375. The abortion collective was called "Jane," and everyone associated with the clinic went by the name Jane in order to protect their anonymity. After a time, it was discovered that one of the doctors was not a doctor after all, although he had performed competently.

The women who ran the collective decided that if he could do it, then they could learn too. At its peak, Jane performed 300 abortions a week for a price of $40. By 1973, when abortion was legalized in the United States, Jane had performed 11,000 abortions with a safety record comparable to legal abortions performed in medical facilities. No longer needed, Jane closed.

Source: Boston Women's Health Collective, 1992.

In European countries where abortion is illegal or difficult to obtain, women who can afford it often travel to neighboring countries where abortion is legal. Until liberalization of French abortion law in 1975, approximately 35,000 French women a year traveled to Britain for abortions. Conservative estimates indicate that at least 4,000 Irish women travel to England annually for abortions; other estimates go as high as 15,000 (Hadley, 1996). German women who have trouble getting abortions under Germany's restrictive laws travel to Holland—4,500 in 1993 alone. In the United States, prior to the Supreme Court decision legalizing abortion, abortion was legal in a few states. Women who could afford it often traveled to these states for safe and legal abortion.

Availability of Legal Abortion and Mortality Rates

Hartmann (1995) notes that, in general, legalization of abortion leads to reductions in mortality rates. In the United States, for example, prior to legalization in 1973, an average of 292 women died per year from illegal abortions. In 1973, the figure fell to 36. In countries where abortion is illegal or restricted to cases in which the mother's health is threatened, illegal abortions are a leading cause of death for young women. For instance:

- In Latin America, 30 to 50 percent of all maternal deaths are due to improperly performed illegal abortions or complications following abortion attempts.
- Every ten minutes in 1980, an Indian woman died of a septic abortion (abortions accompanied by toxic infection).

- In India, 20 percent of maternal deaths are caused by unsafe abortions; in Malawi, 17 percent; in Madagascar, 16 to 40 percent (higher figure true of rural areas); in Mauritius, 60 percent; in Nepal, 50 percent (United Nations, 1993); in Chile, 38 percent (Morgan, 1996).
- More than half of all live births in Venezuela are out of wedlock, and illegal abortion is the leading cause of death for women in Caracas, Venezuela.
- In the 1980s in Brazil, 25 percent of all hospital beds were filled by women whose illegal abortion attempts failed (Morgan, 1984).

These high rates of death and illness occur when abortion is illegal because abortions are usually performed under unsanitary and substandard conditions (United Nations, 1993). For instance, in Nigeria, contraceptives and birth control information are rare and abortion is illegal, but women use abortion in cases of premarital pregnancy and to limit or space their children. However, as many as 60 percent of abortions are performed or induced by nonphysicians, physicians with little training in the procedure, or by the women themselves (Simmons, 1998).

Women's Activism for Legalization of Abortion

All over the world women are striving to legalize abortion. This is because where there are no safe and affordable abortions, almost all women have themselves experienced or know someone who has experienced the dangers of illegal abortion. For instance, Nigerian activists push for legalization of the procedure as well as for improved sex education and contraceptive availability (Simmons, 1998). In 1988, when Brazil was rewriting its constitution, Brazilian women's activists presented a petition to the government for an amendment to legalize abortion. The petition included 30,000 signatures. Although abortion was not legalized, activists felt that their efforts were successful in that the stricter penalties advocated by the Catholic Church were not adopted (Soares et al., 1995). In Poland, following the end of communist rule, the Catholic Church moved quickly to outlaw abortion. This led to the formation of hundreds of women's organizations established to exert pressure on Parliament to refrain from criminalizing abortion (Matynia, 1995). The Polish Parliament decided that only the physician performing the abortion was to be punished, not the woman undergoing it (Matynia, 1995). Mexican feminists in the 1970s and 1980s also worked toward the legalization of abortion, but fierce resistance from the political right and from the Catholic Church (complete with physical intimidation and posters accusing women of murder) have led most feminists to focus their efforts on other issues (Lamas et al., 1995). In Nepal, the Family Planning Association of Nepal is working for the passage in the Nepalese Parliament of a bill that would legalize abortion (Lang, 1998). In the 1970s, feminists in the United States and western Europe worked for legalization by lobbying legislatures and staging demonstrations and speak-outs (Jenson, 1995; Wolfe & Tucker, 1995).

Today, many feminist organizations, such as the National Organization for Women (NOW) in the United States, fight to keep abortion legal and available. Because of feminist activism, in 1998 South Africa passed one of the world's most liberal reproductive rights laws. Women and girls are now able to have abortions during the first twelve weeks of pregnancy. Prior to the law, approximately 425 deaths occurred annually from illegal abortions.

Conclusion

A key theme of international feminism is that of diversity and, in particular, how women's issues and rights are affected by culture, ethnicity, and socioeconomic status (SES, or class). The study of reproductive choice illustrates this theme quite well. For example, reproductive choice is too often tied to socioeconomic status such that rich women are almost always guaranteed this choice whereas other women are not. Women in developing nations face greater reproductive health risks than women in more developed nations, but women in the most developed of nations still suffer from lack of reproductive choice. In some countries, the right to choose abortion and contraception is the issue; in others, the right to refuse it is the issue.

It is increasingly apparent that a broad range of reproductive health services is necessary because the best choice for a given woman is affected by many things—her health, her sexual relationships, the stage she has reached in her reproductive life, her status in society, her risk of suffering violence, her possible exposure to infected partners, and her access to education and information (Plata, 1994). For example, the likelihood of women's exposure to HIV from heterosexual contact varies significantly across cultures such that the effects of a contraceptive technology on HIV transmission may be more relevant in one culture versus another (hormonal methods do not reduce HIV transmission whereas barrier methods do).

The effectiveness and safety of different contraceptive technologies also may not generalize across cultures. As seen in the section on reproductive health, the danger of a given reproductive technology depends upon the information and medical care received. A good example is the contraceptive pill. In most Western countries, the Pill is prescribed by a physician, and a woman must have a Pap smear once a year to get her prescription renewed. This permits screening for cervical cancer and allows the dosage to be adjusted if there are side effects. The prescription requirement also provides the opportunity for screening out those women for whom the Pill is contraindicated, such as those with heart disease or diabetes and those who smoke. However, in some countries (including Brazil, Mexico, and Bangladesh), the Pill is sold without a prescription in pharmacies and stores. Depo-Provera is sold over the counter in Nigeria and even along the roadside (Pearce, 1996). Long distances to health-care facilities often preclude the monitoring that increases the safety and effectiveness of contraceptive methods. For instance, in rural India, where 80 percent of the country's population lives, there is only 1 doctor for every 15,000 people (Bumiller, 1990).

It is also the case that some side effects may be more tolerable in some societies than in others. Hartmann (1995) gives a number of such examples. For instance, the heavy bleeding that may accompany use of Depo-Provera and IUDs is especially difficult for poor women who face practical difficulties in coping with the bleeding, because they have only unsterile rags to use. Prolonged bleeding is also a problem for women in some Muslim countries where a woman's everyday activities are curtailed during menstruation for religious reasons (Jacobson, 1992). Conversely, one of the most common reasons cited for discontinuing hormonal methods of contraception is disruption of the menstrual cycle (Jacobson, 1992). To many women, such bleeding is a sign of good health and fertility, and in some cultures it is viewed as a cleansing of bad blood or spirits.

Reduced lactation caused by hormonal contraceptives containing estrogen is another side effect that affects women in some countries more than others. Hartmann (1995) suggests that it is one of the greatest dangers of the contraceptive pill in the Third World. For millions of infants, breast milk is the main source of nutrition for several years. Use of hormonal contraceptives during lactation can contribute to infant malnutrition and higher infant mortality rates. In short, greater attention needs to be paid to the variable social and biological circumstances of women's lives so that available methods can be appropriately applied (Snow, 1994).

Feminists are expanding their notions of reproductive control to be more sensitive to cultural differences. Some feminists equate women's control over their own reproduction with the use of contraceptive methods that do not require contact with the overly technical (and often male) health system. The rhythm method, the diaphragm, the cervical cap, and spermicidal sponges are examples of methods that allegedly foster greater control by women because a woman's decision to initiate or discontinue use is not in the hands of medical professionals. For instance, women in many countries may have difficulty getting doctors to remove Norplants or IUDs because their medical professionals think that the women have enough children.

Ironically, however, feminists who emphasize the negatives of high-tech contraceptives may inadvertently reduce women's reproductive choice. If too much scary information is disseminated about particular methods, women don't use them, and market forces reduce their availability. To some extent this happened in Brazil, where organized women's groups have endorsed the diaphragm and vetoed Norplant (Hardy, 1996). Once again, true reproductive control means that women can make *informed* choices about which of a *variety* of contraceptive options to use. Of course it should be noted that, in general, feminists have worked hard to expand women's reproductive options. For instance, in the United States, women's groups ushered the cervical cap through the FDA (Food and Drug Administration) approval process and lobbied for the legalization of RU486, the nonsurgical abortion pill. Groups such as the United States' Boston Women's Health Collective and Egypt's Cairo Women's Health Collective publish books to help women take charge of their reproductive health. Organizations such as the International Women's Health Coalition (IWHC) inform policymakers on women's reproductive health issues.

Another good point is made by Snow (1994), who observes that the Westernized feminist concept of user-controlled contraception ignores cultural and class differences. For instance, if women did not have to consult with a clinic in order to receive contraception, many women in Third World countries and poor women in First World countries would not receive important health information and screening (Pap smears, for instance). To this extent, a clinic visit may provide them with greater control over their health. Likewise, a three-month contraceptive injection that does not require incriminating paraphernalia in the house allows the Gambian woman whose husband is against contraception to control her fertility without his knowledge. Unfortunately, little research has been conducted on cultural variations in women's preferences for different contraceptive technologies.

Feminists generally feel strongly that women must be able to control the number and spacing of their children before they can achieve equality. However, this too must be placed in cultural context. As Dixon-Mueller (1993) points out, a reduction in fertility in the absence of other social changes can actually worsen women's status in societies where childbearing is their main source of satisfaction and claim to social consideration. Many cultures place a high value on a woman having a large number of children and on men who father large numbers of children. Mexico is one such country, as is Nepal. In many African countries, the women strive to bring to maturity at least six children and view childbearing as a primary responsibility (Mikell, 1997). In societies where women feel that they must be married in order to achieve any kind of respect, they may have children in order to bind their husbands more securely to them.

It is paradoxical that having children is simultaneously a source of fulfillment and social value for women and at the same time a factor in women's oppression. Oddly, women's ability to give life frequently inhibits rather than enhances their power. After all, there is no greater contribution than to provide a society with its future laborers and to provide a culture with children to carry on family names, traditions, and legacies. However, as you saw in this chapter, this source of power has been usurped by public and private patriarchy, social systems that deny women control over their bodies. Reproductive control is clearly both a reflection and a determinant of women's equality.

The next chapter discusses lesbianism. As you will see, most cultures find lesbianism threatening because it challenges women's role as heterosexual wife and mother. Furthermore, like reproductive control, lesbianism is also about women's control over their bodies and their right to make choices about their sexuality.

"In a sane world, it would seem, humankind would place a high value on life and those able to provide it."
Marilyn Waring

Terms and Concepts

reproductive technologies

reproductive control

hormonal contraceptive methods

sterilization

IUD (intrauterine device)

maternal death

legal abortion

contraceptive side effects

barrier contraceptive methods

female genital mutilation (FGM)

population control programs

pronatalism

antinatalism

pharmaceutical companies

illegal abortion

Study Questions

1. What is reproductive control?

2. In what way is a lack of reproductive control a symptom of women's low status and power?

3. How does women's lack of reproductive control perpetuate their lower status?

4. Why is reproductive control a major women's health issue?

5. How do race and class affect reproductive choice?

6. How do government population control programs frequently interfere with women's reproductive choice and health? What is pronatalism? What is antinatalism? What are some of the faulty assumptions underlying antinatalist programs?

7. What is female genital mutilation? Where is it practiced? What is its purpose? What health problems does it create?

8. Why should feminists expand their notions of reproductive control to be sensitive to cultural differences?

9. What role does profit making play in women's reproductive choice?

10. What are some of the factors influencing rates of abortion? Does legality affect the incidence of abortion? What is the relationship between legality and mortality rate? Why may abortion be legal but largely unavailable?

Discussion Questions and Activities

1. Does feminist advocacy of abortion rights mean that feminists must condone the use of abortion for the sex selection of sons over daughters?

2. Why is it that women end up being largely responsible for contraception? To what extent is it symbolic of their lower power? Would leaving it up to men represent a loss of control over women's bodies?

3. First World countries often make financial aid to developing nations contingent upon their reducing population growth. To this end, the First World countries often encourage the antinatalist programs of developing nations. Do First World countries have the right to do this?

4. Interview several people from another generation. Ask them about the birth control methods available when they were of childbearing age and ask what happened when unplanned pregnancies occurred. Were they able to decide how many children they wanted and the spacing of those children?

Deepa Mehta (left), the director of the film "Fire," participates in a candlelight vigil outside the Regal Theater in New Delhi, India, in December 1998. "Fire" was pulled from theaters all over India after protests against the film's subject matter (a lesbian relationship) disrupted showings. Worldwide, lesbianism is viewed as a violation of the traditional female role and is often punishable.

Lesbianism

4

In India, two young nurses hang themselves when it becomes apparent that their families will not permit them to live together.

In a courtroom in Germany, a woman loses custody of her child because the court rules that her lesbianism disqualifies her as a parent.

Two women in the Philippines are fired from their jobs at a human rights organization because they are in a relationship with each other.

A 19-year-old Brazilian woman gives her girlfriend a kiss in front of her school and is pelted by cans and insults and is expelled.

A woman in the British Navy is raped by a male soldier, and it is suggested that her problem with it is due to her being a lesbian. When she admits she is, the rape is virtually forgotten, and she is interrogated and then discharged for being a lesbian.

An Iranian's lesbian relationship is discovered by her family, who beat her so severely she is hospitalized. She is forced to marry two weeks after she is discharged. Her husband rapes her repeatedly when told of her past lesbian relationship.

Unspoken Rules: Sexual Orientation and Women's Human Rights, 1995.

Lesbianism and Our Study of Global Women

This chapter focuses on lesbianism cross-culturally. Simply put, **lesbians** are female homosexuals, women affectionally and sexually attracted to women. However, there are other definitions as well—some that focus on the politics of lesbianism and others that focus on self-identification as a lesbian. Also, the construction of lesbianism is greatly influenced by cultural context; there is no one way to be lesbian.

The inclusion of lesbianism in our topic of global women follows logically from two important points made so far. The first point is that all over the world, women's lives are heavily determined by traditional gender roles, and women do not typically have the option to stray from these. Most societies direct women toward a female role centered on heterosexual marriage and family. Women are expected to marry or pair with men, and women's social status is typically based upon their ties to men. Furthermore, in most societies, the work of adult women is unpaid or underpaid. Consequently, women are economically dependent upon marriage to men. This restricts

"Enforced heterosexuality is tied to women's lack of economic power and the restriction of female activity to the domestic sphere. Further, the embeddedness of sexuality with gender roles in Western societies proscribes homosexual activity and defines women as male sex objects."
Evelyn Blackwood

"When any woman curtails her freedom or fails to take an action or say what she believes out of fear of being labeled a lesbian, then homophobia has denied her independence and sapped her strength."
Charlotte Bunch

the freedom of heterosexual and homosexual women alike. However, this restriction may be especially great for lesbian women who must falsely live a heterosexual life. In short, the struggle for lesbians' right to control their lives is part of women's general struggle to control their own lives. A second and related point is that those who challenge traditional female roles experience serious social consequences. In no way is this more true than in the case of lesbians. Societal pressure toward heterosexual marriage makes anything else deviant and unnatural. This translates into significant discrimination and hardship for lesbians worldwide.

The point of this endeavor, the cross-cultural study of women, is to include and value a wide range of women's experiences. Although allegedly committed to women's diversity, heterosexual feminists have regularly overlooked their lesbian sisters, despite the fact that many women are not heterosexual.

Another reason to include lesbianism in this book is that **homophobia** (fear of homosexuals) and **heterosexism** (prejudice against homosexuals) is often used as a weapon against feminism. Pharr (1988) suggests that homophobia, along with economics and violence against women, acts to keep sexism in place. These weapons threaten women with pain and loss should they challenge women's subordination to men. Women often distance themselves from feminism for fear of being labeled "lesbian" and the losses that this label entails (such as, in employment, approval of friends and family, community, children, and safety). Calling feminists lesbians is a way of ostracizing and disempowering feminism. As Pharr (1988) says,

> So what does one do in an effort to keep from being called a lesbian? She steps back into line, into the role that is demanded of her, tries to behave in such a way that doesn't threaten the status of men, and if she works for women's rights, she begins modifying that work. When women's organizations begin doing significant social change work, they inevitably are lesbian-baited; that is, funders or institutions or community members tell us that they can't work with us because of our "man-hating attitudes" or the presence of lesbians. (p. 263)

"Normalizing" lesbianism is one way to diffuse this phenomenon. As Pharr (1988) puts it, "We know that as long as the word lesbian can strike fear in any woman's heart, then work on behalf of women can be stopped; the only successful work against sexism must include work against homophobia" (p. 263).

It is interesting to consider this equation of feminism with lesbianism given the real facts of the matter. Indeed, it may surprise some readers to find that despite stereotypes to the contrary, mainstream feminism is at times guilty of ignoring lesbianism. Lesbian activists from Colombia, Hong Kong, the Philippines, Malaysia, Thailand, India, Germany, the United States, the United Kingdom, and Italy have all reported barriers to advancing lesbian rights within their feminist movements (Dorf & Perez, 1995; Mak et al., 1995; Nur, 1995; Rondon, 1995). Women's movements vary significantly in the extent to which they address issues of sexual orientation (Basu, 1995). It is not that such feminists are always unsympathetic to lesbianism, but rather that they want to enhance their credibility with the larger public. Basu (1995) notes that the stronger women's movements are, and the less worried they are about survival, the more likely it is that they will raise questions concerning sexual orientation. In addition, heterosexual feminists are sometimes unaware of lesbian issues. These things lead heterosexual feminists to focus their attention on heterosexual women's issues.

Just as it is true that most feminists are not lesbians, it is also true that most lesbians are not feminists. Yes, it is true that lesbianism can be a feminist political statement, a point discussed later in the chapter. But feminism is not the usual motivator of lesbianism—except in the sense that feminism leads to greater economic independence, thus freeing lesbians from heterosexual marriage. Indeed, for most lesbians, lesbianism is a quiet, personal matter that arises out of a natural sexual attraction to women or from falling in love with a woman. In most cases, lesbianism is not intended as a political statement. Lesbians, like heterosexual women, are diverse in their feminism and vary in their awareness of women's issues and in their activism for women's equality.

One last point before continuing. Although most societies currently view homosexuality and bisexuality as sicknessness or deny their existence entirely, most psychologists and biologists believe that they are just instances of many human variations. Following significant lobbying by lesbian and gay political organizations, the American Psychiatric Association removed homosexuality from its list of mental disorders in 1974. The APA currently takes the position that it is no more abnormal to be homosexual than it is to be left-handed (which 15 percent of the population is). I will not dwell here on the causes of lesbianism, as I do not wish to add to the perception that it is an abnormality in need of explanation, prevention, or treatment. For instance, people generally do not ask why heterosexuals are heterosexual for it is viewed as normal and not in need of explanation. A more pertinent question is why romantic love between women may be met with such severe social consequences and what this tells us about women's expected roles.

> "What is important is not the gender of the two people in the relationship with each other but the content of that relationship. Does that relationship contain violence, control of one person by the other? Is the relationship a growthful place for those involved?"
> *Suzanne Pharr*

The Incidence of Lesbianism

Women in every culture and throughout history have undertaken the task of independent, nonheterosexual, women-connected existence (Rich, 1980). Examinations of ancient literature, art, and anthropology reveal that lesbianism has always existed and has not always been viewed as unacceptable and deviant. The designation *lesbian* comes from ancient Greece and the life of the lyric poet Sappho, who lived on the island of Lesbos (600 B.C.E.). Some of her poetry described her strong love for women. Cavin (1985) notes that it is ironic that lesbians are omitted from discussions of early society because, according to her, the earliest recorded history, art, and literature of Western society documents their existence: Ruth and Naomi among the Hebrews in the Bible (pre-800 B.C.E.); Lesbians in Sparta and Crete (400 B.C.E.); and among the Celts described by Aristotle. Lesbianism was also reported in Athens (450 B.C.E.) and in Rome (100 C.E.). Several ancient Chinese sexual handbooks also describe lesbian activities, and lesbian relationships are celebrated in a number of Chinese plays and stories dating from the tenth to the eighteenth centuries (Ruan & Bullough, 1992).

Anthropological accounts from the twentieth century indicate that lesbianism was acceptable in a number of cultures prior to Western colonization (Blackwood, 1986). For instance, Native American women from the Mohave, Maricopa, Cocopa, Klamath, and Kaska tribes could marry other women and make love with other women without being stigmatized (Blackwood, 1984). As Kendall (1998) says of her studies of lesbianism in Lesotho, "Love between women is as native to southern Africa as the soil itself, but . . . homophobia . . . is a Western import" (p. 224).

In many cultures, female–female romantic relationships occur prior to heterosexual marriage, and during heterosexual marriages where men are away for long periods of time. Faderman (1981) found innumerable examples of female–female romantic love relationships among European women from the seventeenth through the early twentieth centuries when she studied their letters to each other and the poetry and fiction written by women at that time. Many of these relationships took place prior to heterosexual marriage. Likewise, in Lesotho, a South African country, it is not uncommon for women to have romantic relationships with each other prior to and even during heterosexual marriage (Gay, 1986; Kendall, 1998). However, it appears that the acceptability of such relationships is due in part to their not being defined as "sexual" relationships (because no penis is involved!). For instance, Faderman's exploration suggests that it was not until after World War I, when the possibility of their sexual nature was acknowledged, that these intense romantic friendships were stigmatized. Similarly, Kendall (1998) concludes that although lesbian or lesbianlike behavior is common among Lesotho women, it is not viewed as sexual, nor as an alternative to heterosexual marriage. Both Kendall (1998) and Gay (1986) note the decline of lesbianlike relationships in Lesotho women exposed to Western ideas.

Lesbian Invisibility

In most contemporary societies, lesbianism has been rendered invisible by cultures that cannot deal with it and by lesbians who keep their lesbianism to themselves. For instance, in China, where lesbians may be jailed or forced to receive electroshock or aversion therapy, lesbianism requires great secrecy (Dorf & Perez, 1995; Ruan & Bullough, 1992). This global tendency for **lesbian invisibility,** for lesbians to live quiet, hidden lives, makes it difficult for us to get an accurate picture of lesbian experience worldwide.

Lesbianism is also underdocumented because most cultures prefer to ignore its existence. One of India's top scientists insisted that homosexuality is alien to India because "there are laws against it" (Dorf & Perez, 1995). Likewise, some country representatives at the UN's Fourth Women's World Conference balked at resolutions designed to protect lesbian rights. They claimed that there were no lesbians in their countries and that lesbianism was

BOX 4.1   *A Sampling of Lesbian and Gay Organizations Working for Lesbian Rights*

Lesbians a la Vista is an Argentinean group demonstrating for lesbian rights as human rights.

Colectivo Ciguay is a group in the Dominican Republic working against discrimination and harassment in a country that considers homosexuality an "offense against morality."

Gays and Lesbians of Zimbabwe struggles against social and political discrimination, homophobia, and laws that outlaw homosexuality.

Afro Lesbian and Gay Club in Ghana works against laws that ban homosexuality as "unnatural carnal knowledge" punishable by up to three years in jail.

Gay and Lesbian Organisation of Witwatersrand works to ensure that South Africa's new constitution provides civil rights protection to lesbians and gays.

The Asian Lesbian Network includes Asian lesbian groups from Bangladesh, India, Indonesia, Japan, Malaysia, Singapore, Thailand, the United States, the United Kingdom, the Netherlands, and Australia. These groups work together to document and combat discrimination.

RFSL is a Swedish group that has successfully assisted gay and lesbian refugees from the Middle East, Asia, and Latin America in their quest for political asylum in Sweden.

AKOE is a lesbian and gay group in Greece that provides support, protests antigay acts, and networks with other Mediterranean lesbians and gays.

Fiida is a group of Black lesbians in the Netherlands that works to combat discrimination based on race and sexual orientation.

Lambda became the first official gay and lesbian organization in Poland in 1992.

Society for the Protection of Personal Rights is an Israeli group working for legislation to protect lesbians and gay men.

International Lesbian and Gay Association (ILGA) documents human rights abuses against homosexuals worldwide and builds international bridges among homosexual groups.

_____

Source: Amnesty International, 1997.

---

a Western cultural notion. However, as a statement from Third World lesbians at the 1985 UN Women's Conference in Nairobi said, if it seems that lesbianism is confined to Western White women, it is only because Third World lesbians and lesbians of color face more obstacles to visibility (Bunch, 1995). Box 4.1 lists organizations working for lesbian human rights. A glance at this list makes it clear that lesbianism is a worldwide phenomena.

In anthropology, lesbianism has received far less study than male homosexuality (Blackwood, 1986). Cavin (1985) examined the Human Relations Area Files, the main anthropological database, for studies of lesbianism. Her search led her to conclude that Western anthropologists have hardly addressed the subject of lesbianism and that widespread societal sanctions against lesbianism have inhibited the free flow of information regarding it. Even so, in the Human Relations Area Files, she found evidence of lesbianism in thirty different societies from all over the world. Lesbianism did not appear to be more common to any one type of economy, family or household type, marriage form, stratification system, or marital residence. In other words, lesbianism reaches across a number of societies and social categories.

The social stigma associated with lesbianism also means that accurate information is difficult to attain. For instance, although survey research in the

"For the lesbian of color, the ultimate rebellion she can make against her native culture is through her sexual behavior. . . . We're afraid of being abandoned by the mother, the culture, *la Raza,* for being unacceptable, faulty, damaged. . . . To avoid rejection, some of us conform to the values of the culture, push the unacceptable parts into the shadows."

Gloria Anzaldua

United States reveals that between 8 and 17 percent of American women are sexually involved with other women (Stevens & Hall, 1991), these figures probably underrepresent the frequency of lesbianism because many women are reluctant to share this information with interviewers. Furthermore, as Rich (1980) points out, without the profound social pressures to live a heterosexual life, the occurrence of lesbianism would probably be a lot higher. We simply do not know the numbers of lesbians who have remained in heterosexual marriages for most of their lives (Rich, 1980).

Factors Contributing to Lesbian Invisibility

Although homosexuality has not always been viewed as aberrant and unacceptable, it is generally viewed as such by contemporary cultures. For example, in Western cultures, by the nineteenth century and through much of the twentieth, lesbianism was viewed as an illness in need of treatment. Confinement in mental asylums, clitoridectomy, and psychotherapy were at times considered appropriate treatments for lesbianism. The presentation of lesbianism in the medical literature further contributed to extreme and negative stereotypes of lesbians (Stevens & Hall, 1991). In some countries, such as Russia, lesbians are still subjected to "cures" such as involuntary psychiatric treatment and electroshock therapy.

Although the lesbian experience is diverse within and across cultures, one aspect is relatively consistent today; that is, lesbianism is viewed as a violation of the traditional female role, and the social consequences of such deviation are often quite severe. Simply stated, women are expected to enter and stay in heterosexual unions and to enact a specific role as adult women. Those who don't face trouble. As feminist historian Gerda Lerner says in her book *The Creation of Patriarchy* (1986), for women historically, and in most societies today, class is mediated through their sexual ties to a man. It is through men that women have access to or are denied access to the means of production and to resources. It is through their sexual behavior that they gain access to class. Breaking the sexual rules can "declass" women and consign them to the lowest status possible.

Pharr (1988) outlines a variety of losses that threaten lesbian women in heterosexual society. For the reasons described later, lesbians most frequently stay in the closet, that is, hide their lesbian identity from others and sometimes from themselves. The stigma and risk associated with acknowledging one's lesbian identity make coming out of the closet a lifelong process. Let's take a closer look at these potential losses and elaborate upon them.

Employment

According to Pharr, almost every lesbian who is not self-employed or in a business that does not require social approval fears loss of her job should her lesbianism become known. She asks us to consider whether we know any businesses that will knowingly hire and protect people who are openly gay or

"In 1994 in Lima a very violent raid was carried out in the capital where about seventy-five lesbian women were beaten up and ill-treated by the police. Prostitutes get a very rough time in jail. But the treatment of lesbians was even worse. Lesbians were beaten up because, however degrading prostitution can be, it is still regarded as normal behavior, whereas lesbianism is seen as too threatening to the status quo."
Anonymous Peruvian witness

"Being comfortable with homosexuality in societies that view your life as being not only abnormal but in fundamental opposition to patriarchal notions of the family, love, and heterosexual norms of desire is never an easy process, no matter where one lives."
Kaushalya Bannerji

lesbian. In the United States in 1987, Arizona Governor Evan Mecham publicly called for the firing of all homosexuals working in state government. Not surprisingly, lesbians there tend to lead quiet lives (Whitam & Mathy, 1991). In Peru in 1987, police raided a lesbian bar and then arranged to have the women's departure from the police station shown on the national news. Many of the women lost their jobs, some were beaten by their families, and at least two were raped on their way home from the police station (Dorf & Perez, 1995). In Brazil, the discovery of a woman's lesbianism is also likely to lead to dismissal from her job (Martinho, 1995). In a 1993 survey of 800 British lesbians, 68 percent said that they had concealed their sexuality from some or all of those with whom they work (Palmer, 1995). In general, cross-culturally lesbians keep their sexual orientation hidden in order to hold onto their jobs.

Family

The potential loss of family approval, acceptance, and love is another threat faced by lesbians worldwide. For many families, a daughter's heterosexual marriage is an expected duty, and it is a social embarrassment to have an unmarried daughter over a certain age. Families are often angry and rejecting of daughters who disgrace them by not conforming to this social program. In Brazil, for instance, Alice Dias do Amaral was murdered by her lover's brothers after they found out about their sister's lesbianism (Dorf & Perez, 1995). In many countries, lesbians are expelled from their homes, disowned, and subjected to physical and emotional abuse by their families.

In some countries families force their lesbian daughters to marry in an attempt to cure them. This is common in Thailand (Tarawan, 1995), Zimbabwe (Clark, 1995), Mexico (Perez & Jimenez, 1995), Iran (Vahme-Sabz, 1995), Turkey (Kilic & Uncu, 1995), and India (Cath, 1995). Many lesbians marry men to avoid family and social censure. For instance, most lesbians in Japan are married to men because remaining single is a major social stigma (Ishino & Wakabayashi, 1995). The majority of Brazilian lesbians invent fictitious relationships with men or marry in order to avoid the rejection of parents and relatives (Martinho, 1995). Polish lesbians are also likely to be married to men because of pressure from their families and a desire to be accepted in society (Garnier, 1995).

Children

Lesbians must often keep their lesbianism secret for fear of losing their children. Most societies continue to believe that lesbians will create homosexual children or will sexually abuse them. In the United States, a 1995 court ruling in Virginia denied a lesbian woman custody of her son based on the presumption that the child would be harmed by growing up in a home where "active lesbianism" was practiced (Reske, 1995). In Germany, lesbian mothers are often denied custody of their children on the grounds of their "immoral lifestyle" (Duda & Wuch, 1995). This argument is used in a number of countries, including Mexico (Perez & Jimenez, 1995), the United States (Minter,

1995), and Uruguay (Martinez, 1995). Allegations of lesbianism, whether true or not, can result in a woman losing custody of her children in Serbia (Todosijevic, 1995) and in Nicaragua (Gonzalez, 1995).

These decisions are based on faulty assumptions. A number of recent research studies in the United States, Britain, and the Netherlands find no relationship between a mother's sexual orientation and her child's mental health, no evidence that homosexual parents are more likely to be sexually inappropriate with their children, and no evidence that their children are more likely to become homosexual (Cooper, 1997; Patterson & Redding, 1996). Indeed, most sexual abuse of children is heterosexual adult males' abuse of female children. Despite this, lesbians are regularly denied their right to have children through artificial insemination and adoption and are refused custody of their biological children (Dorf & Perez, 1995; Patterson & Redding, 1996).

Safety

Lesbians worldwide may be subjected to physical and verbal attacks. This is yet another reason why lesbians typically keep their lesbianism hidden. Koen and Terry (1995), in a report on lesbians in South Africa, say that lesbians in South Africa are frequently targets of rape and assault. In the United States, two lesbians were murdered in 1996 in Medford, Oregon, by a man who confessed he killed them because lesbians are "sick." Furthermore, lesbians are offered little protection by police or legal systems. For instance, in 1996 in Los Angeles, a lesbian security guard was raped by a co-worker who berated her with antilesbian slurs. Police took two weeks to investigate.

Worse yet, in some countries, it is the state that subjects lesbians to violence and cruelty. In a number of countries, lesbianism is illegal, as Box 4.2 shows. For instance, in Malaysia, lesbianism is punished by whipping. In Iran, lesbians are executed after the fourth offense. In Nicaragua, the law specifies a penalty of one to three years imprisonment for lesbianism. Lesbians are also regularly denied their basic rights to freedom from torture, punitive psychiatry, and arbitrary arrest and incarceration (Dorf & Perez, 1995).

Interestingly, there are more laws against male homosexuality than female homosexuality. The International Lesbian and Gay Association (ILGA) reports that out of the 210 countries they surveyed, lesbianism is illegal in 44, male homosexuality in 84; lesbianism is not mentioned in the law in 98 countries; male homosexuality is not mentioned in only 49 countries. Dorf and Perez (1995) point out that although lesbians may benefit from this, it is not a reflection of greater tolerance for lesbianism. Rather, it is a reflection of the inherent sexism of lawmakers and their failure to understand female sexuality. In other words, Dorf and Perez contend that the underlying assumption of many sex laws is that "sex" must involve a penis. Rosenbloom (1995) also notes that most of the world's laws and their enforcement target male homosexuality. She argues that lesbians' social invisibility is one of the primary reasons that lesbians are not as subject to state persecution as are male homosexuals. In many places, she says, lesbians are not able to establish communities or participate in public life, and denial of their existence is one of the most profound harms that lesbians endure.

"Lesbians in Iran face violence and harassment not only from the state but also within their families and their communities; with no existing lesbian organizations and no attention to lesbian issues from women's groups or other organizations, lesbians who experience such violence have few places to turn."
Vahme-Sabz

BOX 4.2   *Countries Where Lesbianism Is Illegal*

Afghanistan	Libya	Saudi Arabia
Algeria	Malawi	Senegal
Bahamas	Mauritania	Seychelles
Bahrain	Morocco	Sierra Leone
Bangladesh	Mozambique	Singapore
Barbados	Namibia	Somalia
Cape Verde	Nicaragua	Swaziland
Cuba	Oman	Turkmenistan
Djibouti	Pakistan	United Arab Emirates
Ethiopia	Qatar	United States (Arkansas, Kansas, Missouri, Montana, Tennessee)
Iran	Romania	
Kuwait	St. Lucia	Uzbekistan
Kyrgystan	Samoa, Western	Yemen
Lebanon	San Marino	Zaire

Source: Amnesty International, 1997.

It should be noted that even when there are not laws specifically prohibiting lesbianism, there are often legal means by which to arrest lesbians. For instance, in Argentina, police may arrest and hold anyone while they check the person's police record, and they may arrest lesbians under an infraction known as "incitement to commit a carnal act in the public street" (Sarda, 1995).

Mental Health

In reading lesbians' accounts from around the world, one thing is evident: There is often a feeling of exile associated with being a lesbian. There are numerous sources of psychological stress for lesbians. First, lesbians experience great psychological conflict because of a conflict between their sexual orientation and the perceived ideals of society. Raised in homophobic societies, lesbians have often internalized the societal message that homosexuals are bad. Consequently, they experience lowered self-esteem and shame, as well as guilt about maintaining a false image as a heterosexual (Friedman & Downey, 1995). The greater the invisibility of lesbians in a culture, the greater the problem this presents. Young lesbians who have never met another lesbian and whose only experience with lesbianism is that it is a sickness are especially likely to suffer. This may result in self-directed homophobia and can lead to isolation, passive acceptance of persecution, exile, and even suicide (Dorf & Perez, 1995).

Even in the most liberal of countries, stress is constant because of the ongoing effort required to conceal their sexual identity to avoid rejection, discrimination, and violence. Lesbians must continually decide who is safe to tell—that is, who is safe to "come out" to. They often worry about the negative reactions that may occur should their sexual orientation become known. This actual and expected harassment creates an emotional stress that seriously impedes personal development (D'Augelli, 1992). As Pharr says, an overtly homophobic world that permits cruelty to lesbians makes it difficult for lesbians and gays to maintain a strong sense of well-being and esteem.

Community and Credibility

Lesbians lose a sense of belongingness in their communities when they are rejected and ostracized by those with homophobic attitudes. Women who openly live as lesbians may no longer be respected, listened to, honored, or believed. They often become social outcasts. For instance, in the United States in 1992, in Mississippi, local citizens attempted to force two lesbians from their land using the state's antisodomy laws (Dorf & Perez, 1995).

The Perception of Lesbianism as Dangerous

Lesbians Are "Unnatural"

"If we come out, we are more often than not exiled by the community. If we don't come out, we still feel that sense of exile because we are unable to share a very real part of ourselves with them."
Pratibha Parmar

What kinds of arguments are made against lesbianism? The most common seems to be that it is "unnatural." Given our societies' emphasis on heterosexual coupling, it is not surprising that lesbianism is viewed as abnormal. Not only do our societies tell us it is, but lesbian invisibility further contributes to this notion because we are generally unaware of the lesbians among us. Why, though, do cultures generally propagate this notion that lesbianism is deviant and unacceptable? Is it, some have suggested (Dorf & Perez, 1995), that homosexuality's power to shake up and even rupture the social structure inspires the implementation of measures intended to marginalize those who are different?

Lesbians Threaten Men's Power

A number of feminists have suggested that lesbians are perceived to be dangerous because lesbianism is a threat to men's control over women. The general argument goes like this: To protect and sustain women's traditional heterosexual roles as wives and mothers, the culture stigmatizes and pathologizes lesbianism (Stevens & Hall, 1991). Were lesbianism to become acceptable and were women to believe that they could live independently of men, men would be less able to exploit women's sexuality and to use them as a source of unpaid labor. In short, men would have less control over women and would have sexual and emotional access to women only on women's terms. For example, Trujillo (1991) says that Chicana lesbians pose a threat to the Chicano community because they threaten the cultural beliefs that women should define themselves in terms of men and should be subservient to men. The existence of Chicana lesbians, she says, is a threat to the established order of male control and oppressive attitudes toward women.*

One of the best-known feminists with this perspective is Adrienne Rich. In her classic book *Of Woman Born* (1976), she suggests that heterosexuality is "institutionalized." By this she means that most modern cultures require that a woman be legally married to a man, and anything, including lesbianism, that threatens this social order is viewed as deviant. Patriarchy, she says, could not survive without motherhood and sexuality in their institutional forms. Therefore, societies typically present wife and motherhood as "natural" and "unquestionable." This idealization of heterosexual marriage and romance can be seen in art, literature, media, advertising, and so on.

Rich (1980) views taboos against homosexuality and the enforcement of heterosexuality as a means of assuring the male right to physical, economical, and emotional access. Our economic systems enforce **compulsory heterosexuality** by providing women with few economic options outside of marriage. Men need the labor provided by women's compliance with the traditional female gender role. This is ensured by rendering the lesbian possibility pathological and by destroying historical records of its existence. Rich adds that heterosexuality is a social institution imposed, managed, organized, propagandized, and at times maintained by force. Lesbian existence has been written out of history and portrayed as a disease, and the realities of lesbian existence are hidden as a means of keeping heterosexuality compulsory.

Lesbianism as Resistance to Patriarchy

Lesbian Feminism

At the beginning of the chapter I mentioned that for some women, lesbianism is a political feminist statement. **Lesbian feminism** may be defined as a variety of beliefs and practices based on the core assumption that there is a connection between an erotic and/or emotional commitment to women and political resistance to patriarchal domination (Taylor & Rupp, 1993). For instance, Simone de Beauvoir in *The Second Sex* (1953) presented lesbianism as a deliberate refusal to submit to the coercive force of heterosexual ideology, a refusal that acts as an underground feminist resistance to patriarchy. Similarly, Rich (1980) suggests that lesbian existence involves the rejection of a compulsory way of life and is a direct or indirect attack on male right of access to women.

"Somebody that you know, probably somebody that you care about, is gay or is a lesbian. And are you willing, really, to say that that person should be treated differently because of their sexual preference? I am not willing to do that."
Anita Faye Hill, American attorney known for her testimony against Supreme Court Justice nominee Clarence Thomas

---

Chicana and *Chicano* are used by some Latin Americans instead of *Hispanic,* a term adopted by the U.S. government and rejected by some activists.

As she puts it, "Woman-identification is a source of energy, a potential spring-head of female power, violently curtailed and wasted under the institution of heterosexuality" (p. 267). Or as Ferguson (1981) said, "The possibility of a sexual relationship between women is an important challenge to patriarchy because it acts as an alternative to the patriarchal heterosexual couple, thus challenging the heterosexual ideology that women are dependent on men for romantic/sexual love and satisfaction" (p. 164).

Lesbian feminism is a political movement that combines an interest in the liberation of women with an interest in the liberation of lesbians. Keeping homosexuals in the closet is viewed as the core of lesbian oppression. Therefore, "coming out"—that is, being open about one's lesbian identity with others—constitutes a political act. The strategy is that if everyone came out of the closet, lesbians and gays could not be oppressed because "they are everywhere" (Cavin, 1985). Cavin (1985) claims that in the twentieth century lesbian feminism has emerged twice as a political movement, first in Germany and later in the United States. In Germany lesbian feminists were politically active in both the early feminist and homosexual rights movements (1924–1935). Their activities continued until the Nazi regime sent them to the concentration camps, where they were forced to wear a pink triangle (now a symbol of lesbian and gay rights). Over 200,000 homosexuals died in Hitler's camps. The second emergence of lesbian feminism as a political movement began in the United States around 1970. It was stimulated in part by the neglect of lesbians by both the feminist and gay rights movements. Political lesbians learned that they had better speak for themselves or else they would not be heard at all (Cavin, 1985). According to Cavin, lesbian feminism is a worldwide political movement of lesbians that broadly encompasses all degrees of lesbian struggle for liberation from patriarchy. The goals range from liberal lesbians' efforts to obtain lesbian civil rights within current patriarchal systems to the radical lesbian separatist goal of overthrowing world patriarchy in order to liberate all women.

Lesbian Separatism

As suggested above, some but far from all, lesbian feminists are lesbian separatists. **Lesbian separatism** began in the United States in 1971. The idea is that lesbian liberation requires females' noncooperation with the patriarchal system. This noncooperation ranges from a woman's choice not to be involved with men socially, emotionally, sexually, politically, or economically to physical separation from the institutions and jurisdiction of patriarchy (Cavin, 1985). Originally, lesbian "homelands"—free from sexism, racism, and ageism and embodying positive female values such as caring, compassion, and community—were seen as important in accomplishing these goals. In practice, though, these are rare. American lesbian separatist Jackie Anderson (1994) says that separatists begin with the assumption that injustices against women are expressions of hatred and violence and that the way to respond to this is to separate from men to the greatest extent possible. They are pessimistic that justice for women will be attained through legal remedies and appeals to moral values, such as equity. They conceive of a future for women that does not include men and in which lesbianism is the norm (Anderson, 1994).

Lesbian Diversity

At the beginning of the chapter I offered a simple definition of lesbianism as women who are affectionally and sexually attracted to other women. This definition has come under attack by lesbian feminists who seek a broader definition that reflects the political nature of lesbianism. For instance, Ferguson (1981) defines a lesbian as "a woman who has sexual and erotic-emotional ties primarily with women or who sees herself as centrally involved with a community of self-identified lesbians whose sexual and erotic-emotional ties are primarily with women; and who is herself a self-identified lesbian" (p. 166). Zita (1981) jokingly refers to the "Lesbian Olympics," where competing lesbians are ranked, categorized, accepted, and rejected based upon their conformity to the "correct" definition of lesbianism. Taylor and Rupp (1993) also note that wars are fought in the lesbian feminist community over who best deserves the label "feminist."

These definitions are interesting and draw our attention to **lesbian diversity**—to the many dimensions of lesbianism. However, they seem to ignore the reality of lesbian experience for most lesbians and are therefore of limited usefulness when talking of lesbianism cross-culturally. Living life as a lesbian according to these definitions is simply not an option for many lesbians. Most live in countries where lesbianism must be kept secret and where they live a heterosexual life to avoid persecution or to have the necessary economic support. In some countries, the lack of a lesbian community precludes a political lesbian existence. In many places it is not possible for such communities and networks to develop. Lesbian publications are shut down, police harass women going into lesbian meeting places, and political activity on the part of lesbians is simply not allowed. Wage earning, the ability to live separately from kin, and lesbian bars and gathering places all seem to be preconditions for the development of a more political lesbianism where lesbians see themselves as an oppressed minority with a right to exist.

There is great variety in the lesbian experience. Lesbian feminist movements and lesbian communities that debate about how to define lesbianism and how to best challenge compulsory heterosexuality do not characterize the lesbian experience in most of the world. Indeed, lesbian feminist communities and organizations are more common in modern capitalistic societies, and in those, are more common among urban, educated lesbians. Blackwood (1986) suggests that in societies where women do not have control over their productive activities, and may not gain status independently of men, lesbian behavior is more "informal." In short, the construction of lesbianism is greatly influenced by cultural context, and there is no single way to be lesbian. Perhaps, then, it is more helpful to examine lesbian existence in terms of the needs women have expressed and the strategies they have used to survive as lesbians, as well as the culturally specific modes of satisfaction available for lesbian interests and desires (Zita, 1980). Unfortunately, there is very little information out there that helps us answer these questions.

Overcoming Lesbian Invisibility

Coming Out to Reduce Lesbian Stereotyping

Although it is not surprising that lesbians often choose invisibility because of fears of social disapproval, discrimination, and violence, this makes it easier for stereotypes of homosexuals to be maintained. Furthermore, when lesbianism is acknowledged by the larger heterosexual culture, it is often portrayed inaccurately. For instance, Swedish lesbian Rebecka Lindau (1993) writes about how it is only in the last few years that the existence of lesbians in Sweden has been acknowledged. Unfortunately, however, the attention given to lesbianism by the Swedish mainstream media consists largely of ridicule and pornographic portrayals of lesbians as bisexual and sadomasochistic. In a report on Hong Kong, Mak and her coauthors (1995) report that lesbianism primarily appears in pornographic films for heterosexuals. These films often end with the women turning straight. In India, lesbianism is receiving increased media attention but is still portrayed as a curiosity and abnormality (Cath, 1995). Lesbians are of increasing interest to the Japanese media, but they are often portrayed pornographically or as tragic figures who try to seduce pretty women and fail (Ishino & Wakabayashi, 1995). Contemporary portrayals of lesbians in China generally depict lesbians as ugly women who no man will have or as women who were so badly treated by men as to be uncomfortable with male sexuality (Ruan & Bullough, 1992).

In the United States, lesbianism has also remained hidden and been pathologized as unseemly and bizarre (Stevens & Hall, 1991). In the 1990s a number of popular U.S. entertainers have come out in an effort to increase lesbian visibility and the accuracy of perceptions of lesbians (comedian Ellen DeGeneres, singer k.d. lang, and musician Melissa Etheridge are examples). Likewise, in Mexico, a number of artists have publicly come out as lesbians in support of lesbian rights. These include theatrical director Nancy Cardenas, musical performer Chavela Vargas, writer/director/comedian Jesusa Rodriguez, and writer and poet Rosamaria Roffiel (Perez & Jimenez, 1995).

Lesbian Communities and Organizations

Lesbians sometimes adapt to their outsider status by developing their own lesbian communities and cultures within the larger culture. Lesbian organizations exist in Argentina, Australia, Austria, Bangladesh, Belgium, Brazil, Canada, Chile, Denmark, the Dominican Republic, Estonia, France, Germany, Honduras, Hong Kong, India, Indonesia, Ireland, Italy, Japan, Mexico, the Netherlands, New Zealand, Norway, Peru, the Philippines, Russia, South Africa, Spain, Sweden, Taiwan, Turkey, the United Kingdom, the United States, and Uruguay (Seager, 1997). These groups are important for the formation of a positive lesbian identity in the face of social stigma. They provide a social arena where lesbians do not have to hide.

Some of these groups work to enhance lesbian visibility and serve a political function as well. Depending upon the country, lesbian activists (see Box 4.1) may work for laws prohibiting discrimination on the basis of sexual orientation, the right to marry (especially important because so many governmental and employment benefits are shared with spouses), legal acknowledgment of partnerships, the right to adopt, the right to custody of their children, and the repeal of laws punishing homosexuality. For instance, South Africa's constitution now includes protection from discrimination on the grounds of sexual orientation. South Africa, Canada, Denmark, Slovenia, Spain, France, Norway, New Zealand, the Netherlands, and Sweden all have national legislation banning discrimination on the basis of sexual orientation. Austria, Belgium, Canada, Denmark, Finland, Germany, the Netherlands, Norway, Sweden, and the United States all have accepted sexual orientation as grounds for political asylum. The activities of these groups are acts of bravery, for in many countries, lesbian publications are shut down, members of lesbian organizations are harassed, and meeting places are raided and closed down. For instance, Irene Petropoulou, the lesbian editor of a Greek lesbian and gay magazine, was sentenced to five months in prison and fined 50,000 drachma for publishing so-called indecent materials (Dorf & Perez, 1995).

Recovering Lesbian Herstory

Efforts are being made all over the world to reclaim homosexuals' place in history and to create archives and libraries to render the lesbian experience visible. The idea is that recovering lesbian history (herstory) will support current lesbian culture and inspire continued resistance to compulsory heterosexuality. In the United States, for instance, there are the Lesbian Herstory Archives (LHA), the West Coast Lesbian Collections, and the Women's Collection held at the Northwestern University library. Another example is the United Kingdom's South Asian gay and lesbian organization, Shakti Khabar. It is in the process of documenting the historical presence of homosexuality in South Asia.

Conclusion

In many ways, the study of lesbianism cross-culturally mirrors our more general study of women cross-culturally. Like other topics covered in the book, the study of lesbianism points to the similarity and diversity of the female experience. Penelope (1990) points out that wherever a lesbian lives, whatever social or economic class she is born into, she lives in a heteropatriarchal society where men are the ruling class and everyone is supposed to be heterosexual. These heteropatriarchal societies deny lesbian existence, suppress evidence of lesbian life and struggle, and make lesbians invisible to one another. When lesbian existence is acknowledged, she says, lesbians are caricatured as pathetic, desperate creatures too flawed to find a man or as men's swaggering imitators.

Despite this global commonality, there are a variety of lesbian experiences even within a country. First is the degree of invisibility lesbians must maintain. The repression of lesbians is more severe in some countries and subcultures than in others. In San Francisco, for example, there is a vibrant lesbian community, but in most places in the United States, lesbians remain closeted, and lesbian cultures are harder to identify. In cultures where it is acceptable for women to be unmarried or publicly close and affectionate, lesbianism is easier to carry off. For example, Estonian lesbian Lilian Kotter (1995) notes that because there is little stigma associated with being un-married in Estonia, lesbians can live their lives in a climate of relative tol-erance. Likewise, Thai lesbian Kanokwan Tarawan (1995) says that Thai cul-ture allows two women to live together for extended periods of time, hold hands, hug in public, sleep in the same bed, and even raise a child together, without assuming the relationship is sexual. This makes it possible for les-bians to live together as long as they keep the sexual aspect of their rela-tionship hidden.

There are also many different ways of being lesbian. For instance, mid-dle- and upper-class U.S. lesbians typically eschew butch/femme roles, but working-class lesbians do not. In Latin America, there is also a key distinc-tion between the *activos* who play a more macho role and the *passivos* who play a more feminine role (Ferguson, 1990). In Swaziland, lesbian couples frequently consist of a high-status wealthy woman and a low-status depend-ent woman (Ferguson, 1990). In short, other cultural and group identities such as class and ethnicity interact with lesbianism to produce a variety of les-bian identities.

Another recurring theme is that most societies are structured to favor traditional gender roles, and those women who stray from these suffer the consequences. A good example of this is that, like heterosexual women, ho-mosexual women frequently stay in heterosexual marriages in order to avoid losing their children and their social status. Another revisited theme is that of reproductive control. Compulsory heterosexuality is a denial of women's right to control their own bodies, to choose with whom they want to share their bodies. The denial of lesbianism is consistent with a societal tendency to deny women's sexuality or to define sex as being about men's and not women's pleasure. As Bunch (1995) points out, the defense of lesbian rights is integral to the defense of all women's right to determine their own sexual-ity, to work at the jobs they prefer, and to live as they choose with women, men, children, or alone.

As with other chapters, this chapter points to the role of economics in women's oppression. The ability to lead a lesbian life is very much tied to economics. Denying women the ability to earn a living wage forces them into a heterosexual existence. An atypical example exists in Swaziland, where a high divorce rate coupled with the practice of women leaving property to their daughters created a situation in which 50 percent of women live independently of men. This has permitted the development of a lesbian subculture where lesbians live together and participate in an ac-tive lesbian social life (Ferguson, 1990). The role of economic power in bringing about women's equality cannot be underestimated. This is the fo-cus of the next chapter.

Terms and Concepts

lesbians	compulsory heterosexuality
homophobia	lesbian feminism
heterosexism	lesbian separatism
lesbian invisibility	lesbian diversity

Study Questions

1. Why is the study of lesbians important to the topic of women across cultures?
2. What is the relationship between mainstream feminism and lesbianism?
3. What evidence is given for the commonality of lesbianism?
4. What are the factors contributing to lesbian invisibility?
5. Why do so many societies view lesbianism as dangerous?
6. What does Adrienne Rich mean when she says that heterosexuality is compulsory and serves to maintain men's power over women?
7. What are some of the core beliefs and practices of lesbian feminism?
8. What are some of the ways in which lesbianism differs cross-culturally?
9. How have lesbians attempted to overcome lesbian invisibility?
10. How does the study of lesbianism cross-culturally mirror our more general study of women cross-culturally?

Discussion Questions and Activities

1. What would the world be like if homosexuality was not stigmatized? How would it affect children's play? How would it influence affection between those of the same sex? How would it affect what we wear? How would it affect what jobs we choose? How would it affect marriage?
2. Cavin says the predicament of the lesbian in heterosexist society is that of "unrecorded reality" and "recorded unreality." What did you know about lesbianism prior to reading this chapter? Where did you get your information (TV, movies, family, church, personal experience)? Given lesbian invisibility and negative stereotyping, how accurate do you think your impressions are?
3. What do you think Rich meant when she said that "feminist research and theory that contributes to lesbian invisibility or marginality is actually working against the liberation and empowerment of women"?
4. Conduct an interview with a lesbian using questions developed from the chapter section on factors contributing to lesbian invisibility.

Guatemalan women participate in the informal economy. Women's labor is critical to economies worldwide, and women do more of the world's work than men do. The undervaluing of women's work is both a cause and an effect of women's lower status.

Women's Work

> All women are working women whether they are engaged in market or nonmarket activities.
>
> MARY CHINERY-HESSE, Deputy Director-General of the International Labour Organization

Women have always worked, and work is a central part of women's lives all over the world. The woman who enjoys a leisurely life paid for by her husband is a worldwide rarity. The vast majority of mothers worldwide engage in both domestic and wage-earning work to meet their children's needs (Bruce, 1995). Paid or unpaid, most women work, and they work hard. Indeed, it may surprise you to find that if women's unpaid labor contributions are included, women do more of the world's work than men do. You may also be surprised to hear that, according to the International Labour Organization (ILO), in 1994 approximately 45 percent of the world's women between the ages of 15 and 64 were economically active, Box 5.1 lists women in the paid workforce for a sample of countries. By the year 2000, women will make up at least half the paid workforce in most countries. Unfortunately, inequality of treatment marks virtually all aspects of women's working lives, beginning with wages and employment opportunities and extending to access to decision making and managerial positions, as well as to sexual harassment (ILO, 1995).

Women's Work and Our Study of Women Across Cultures

The study of women's labor is an important part of our study of women across cultures because the undervaluing of women's labor is both a cause and an effect of women's lower status and power. Recall from Chapter 1 that women's lower pay and poorer representation in economic power positions is an indicator of women's lower status and power. Regrettably, it is still the case that women are discriminated against in the world of work. Moreover, up until the latter part of the twentieth century, few people questioned men's domination of the economic sphere.

In Chapter 2, I argued that women's lower status and power are aggravated by the fact that their work tends to be unpaid or underpaid. Women often do work that is compatible with the female life course of childbearing and nursing.

BOX 5.1   *Women in the Paid Workforce Worldwide*

The following sample of countries shows the percentage of women in the paid workforce.

Algeria (8%)	Mexico (32%)
Argentina (32%)	Mozambique (78%)
Brazil (33%)	Netherlands (38%)
Burkina Faso (77%)	Oman (10%)
Canada (58%)	Saudi Arabia (10%)
Chile (33%)	Spain (26%)
China (80%)	Sweden (75%)
Egypt (10%)	Switzerland (53%)
France (57%)	Thailand (67%)
Germany (57%)	United Kingdom (60%)
Ireland (36%)	United States (60%)
Italy (37%)	Vietnam (77%)
Jordan (10%)	

Source: International Labour Organization, 1995.

> The international economic system constructs reality in a way that excludes the great bulk of women's work—reproduction (in all its forms), raising children, domestic work, and subsistence production.
> *Marilyn Waring*

In particular, this means that women's work is often conducted in the private sphere of the home. Furthermore, historically women's work more typically had *private use value* (for the family's private use) rather than *exchange value* (something that could then be exchanged for money or other goods). In short, because women's labor was typically conducted in the private sphere of the home and was largely unpaid, its social and economic importance has been masked and, consequently, has contributed to the devaluation of women.

In her book *If Women Counted,* New Zealand economist Marilyn Waring (1988) analyzes the fact that much of women's labor is left out of governments' systems of economic accounting, and she explains why this matters. Not only is much of women's labor unpaid household labor, but women's labor often takes place in the **informal labor sector,** which receives less attention from governments. Informal sector work includes small enterprises, trading and selling at markets, work done on a contract basis in the home (such as garment sewing), and "under the table" and "off the books" employment. The national accounting systems used by most governments define labor in terms of formal employment, in the **formal labor sector.** Governments, Waring points out, make resource allocations and policy decisions based on their national accounts. Because women's labor so often remains invisible in national accounting systems, and policy is so often based on national accounting figures, policymakers make fewer policies and spend less money on programs and policies addressing women's needs. As Waring says, systems cannot respond to values that remain unrecognized.

This point, that women's labor is typically overlooked by governments in making economic policies and interventions, is further illustrated in Chapter 6 on women and economic development. That chapter examines in some detail how women's labor has been largely ignored by programs designed to bring about economic development. Most development programs focus on men's labor. The result is that women's status is not usually enhanced by development programs, and women's lives are often made even harder. Furthermore, broader goals of development, such as increased quality of life, are not achieved when women's labor contributions are overlooked. This is because women are major family providers—growing and collecting food and fuel for family consumption and providing sanitation and health care to family members. Add to this the fact that when women work for pay, they devote more of their income to family subsistence than do men, who spend more on themselves (Blumberg, 1995). Despite this, most development programs have focused solely on men's wage earning.

The fact that women's work is frequently unpaid or underpaid is closely linked to women's lower power and status, for those who control the money generally have greater power and status. This is one reason why women's activists worldwide have focused on women's economic empowerment. Many Marxist feminists view women's economic dependence on men as the primary basis of patriarchy (Chafetz, 1991; Hartmann, 1984; Vogel, 1983). Economic empowerment, though, is about more than just women's economic independence from men; it's also about equal pay for equal work, women's access to traditionally male jobs, women in business power positions, and eliminating sexual harassment. Many women do work for pay—especially those who are single heads of households because of widowhood, desertion, or divorce. However, even when women work for pay, their low wages often interfere with translating this into greater power and status.

The relationship between women's status and power and paid employment is complex, but the importance of economic power cannot be denied. Blumberg (1991) suggests that for women, economic power is probably more achievable than other sources of power. Women rarely possess the *power of force* (both at the individual violence level and the organized social force level), seldom possess *political power,* and infrequently possess *ideological power* (the power that comes from social beliefs that one's group is superior). As Blumberg says, "Only with respect to *economic* power does women's position run the full range from near-zero to near-total control of the local economy" (p. 29).

Women's Unpaid Labor

The Undercounting of Women's Work

Worldwide, who does the laundry, shopping, cooking, child care, and looks after the family's medical needs? In countries where water and fuel must be gathered and families must grow much of their own food, who takes care of these tasks? Women. It is ironic that the work women do is of tremendous importance to the well-being of families, communities, and nations and yet is poorly measured in official statistics (United Nations, 1997). Government labor statistics fail entirely to reflect the amount of work women perform for no wages at all (ILO, 1995), and approximately 66 percent of the work women do is unpaid (Seager, 1997). According to the ILO (1995), if the household duties performed by women were calculated as productive activity in the various systems of national accounting, the value of the world's GDP (gross domestic product) would increase by 25 to 30 percent. The UN's International Research and Training Institute for the Advancement of Women (INSTRAW, 1995) states that the measurement of women's unpaid labor would make clear the value of household production to economies worldwide. It would also show that the burden is disproportionately carried by women, who almost match men hour for hour in paid labor and who outwork men 2 to 1 in nonmarket activities (INSTRAW, 1995).

Why is it that women's work remains uncounted and devalued? Mosse (1993) suggests that it is because so much of women's work is seen as "natural." After all, she says, only women can become mothers and suckle their children, but this biological or natural ability has often meant that all of women's work in maintaining life—nurturing children, collecting fuel and water, growing the family food and marketing the surplus, caring for those who are sick or elderly—is also seen as "natural" rather than as "work," which is what men do. Chafetz (1990) points out that in gender-stratified societies, most elite positions are filled by men, and therefore it is men who determine what work is valuable. Not surprisingly, they produce ideologies and norms that legitimate their dominance and value.

Household Labor and Employed Women

Although there are cross-cultural variations in the jobs that men and women do, in every society women continue to do most of the household labor (Chafetz, 1990; United Nations, 1985). This is true in both industrialized and developing countries. For example, in Australia, Canada, Denmark, the Netherlands, Russia, and the United Kingdom, meals are prepared by women 75 percent of the time (Seager, 1997). Japanese women spend nearly ten times as many hours as men doing household chores; Spanish, Polish, and Israeli women devote three to five times as many hours as men; and, in the United States, Norway, and Sweden, women put in one and a half times as many hours as men (Seager, 1997). In developing countries, women spend between 31 and 42 hours a week in unpaid activities, versus 5 to 15 hours for men. For instance, Kenyan women spend ten times more hours on domestic tasks than do men, and women in India spend at least 20 hours more per week on domestic work (ILO, 1996a). **Gender-based household divisions of labor** begin early, in childhood chores (Whiting & Edwards, 1988). For instance, in Mexico, El Salvador, Argentina, South Africa, Peru, the United States, and Pakistan, it is customary for girls to cook, clean, do laundry, and care for younger siblings while boys do "outside" work such as yard chores.

One major household task for which women are unpaid is child care. Worldwide, women take care of the children (Chafetz, 1990; Sanday, 1981). This is documented in such diverse countries as West Africa (Nsamenang, 1992), China (Jankowiak, 1992), Belize, Kenya, Nepal, Samoa (Munroe & Munroe, 1992), Thailand (Tulananda, Young, & Roopnarine, 1994), the United States (Leslie, Anderson, & Branson, 1991; Pleck, 1985; Russell & Radin, 1983), Japan (Ishii-Kuntz, 1993), and Puerto Rico (Roopnarine & Ahmeduzzaman, 1993). The general worldwide pattern is that fathers spend approximately one-third of the time mothers do in providing child care (Engle & Breaux, 1994), although there are a few exceptions such as the hunter-gatherer Aka pygmies of the southern Central African Republic and the northern People's Republic of the Congo (Hewlett, 1992). Lamb (1981) suggests that this sex-based division of child-care labor is aggravated by industrialization, which requires fathers to leave the home for large parts of the day in order to work at jobs where children's presence is viewed as inappropriate. Furthermore, labor market changes eliminated the way that fathers traditionally spent time with their children (such as training children in family occupations like farming) (Lamb, 1981). Other writers (Bloom-Feshbach, 1981) have noted that in societies in which labor is such that fathers are more physically present, greater paternal involvement in child rearing occurs.

By now you've probably thought of the possibility that women do more household labor because they don't work outside the home as much as men and that this is their contribution to the household. In some cases, this is a legitimate point; however, this work is still undervalued and largely uncounted by governments. Also, it is increasingly the case that women participate in the paid labor force, and, unfortunately, research indicates that employment has relatively little effect on the amount of household labor that women do (Blumberg, 1991). This is the case because household labor and child care are stereotyped as female activities, and socialization in childhood reinforces this. Women often accept the situation as "their work." Many men do a less than competent job such that women just do it themselves. Women's employed work is seen as secondary to their primary role as wife and mother, and men's higher status is such that they have refusal power (Blumberg, 1991; Burn, 1996).

All over the world, it is common for employed women to do the majority of household labor (United Nations, 1991b). For example, this is true in Bangladesh (Ilyas, 1990), Greece (Dubisch, 1993), Iran (Ghorayshi, 1996), Israel (Anson, Levenson, & Bonneh, 1990), Japan (Lebra, 1984), the former Soviet Union (Kerig, Alyoshina, & Volovich, 1993), Switzerland (Charles &

Hopflinger, 1992), and the United States (Blair & Lichter, 1991). This is an important point. It means that women's lives are often very hard as they struggle to meet both paid and unpaid work roles. You will also see that the dual burden of employment and household labor interferes with women's pay and promotion in the workplace. The relationship goes the other way as well. The smaller the income gap between an employed woman and her husband, the smaller the gender household labor gap (Blumstein & Schwartz, 1991). Of course, the fact that women rarely match or exceed their husbands in pay means that even where women do earn money, men often still have considerable power in the home.

Women's Paid Labor

The Gender Pay Gap

Women have entered the paid workforce in record numbers, but their economic power is diminished by the fact that they frequently receive less pay for their work than do men. Depending upon the country, women earn between 50 and 96 percent of men's wages (ILO,1995). Fortunately, many countries have significantly reduced their **gender pay gap** in the last fifteen years. However, as Box 5.2 shows, this change is uneven, and in some countries, the pay gap has grown.

Why is it so common for women to be paid less than men? Seager (1997) gives three reasons: (1) Women are segregated and concentrated in lower-paying female-dominated jobs, (2) outright wage discrimination, and (3) the high percentage of women working part-time.

Gender Job Segregation   Historically, females and males have had different jobs in almost every culture (Almeida Acosta & Sanchez de Almeida, 1983; Davidson & Thomson, 1980; Munroe & Munroe, 1975). According to the United Nations (1991b), everywhere in the world the workplace is segregated by sex, and **gender job segregation** is one reason why women earn less than men (ILO, 1995). Job segregation means that women work in different jobs and occupations than men, almost always with lower status and pay and with little security and little possibility for savings, credit, or investment (United Nations, 1997).

Women generally work in such sectors as secretarial work, sales, and domestic services whereas men generally work in industry and transportation; women engage in teaching, care services, and subsistence agriculture whereas men are found in management, administration, and policy (ILO, 1995). For instance, French women work predominantly in low-status clerical and service jobs. In India the great majority work in agriculture and the rest primarily in service industries. Most of Japan's employed women work in services, retail businesses, restaurants, and manufacturing. Nigerian women work primarily as agriculturists in addition to doing sales, clerical, and factory

BOX 5.2   *The Gender Pay Gap Worldwide*

Across the world, the gender pay gap has changed dramatically in the last decade or so. The countries listed below demonstrate women's earnings as a percentage of men's in nonagricultural industries for some representative countries.

Country	1984	1995
Australia	86%	90%
Belgium	75	75
Costa Rica	72	90
Czech Republic	68	71
Denmark	84	83
France	81	81
Germany	72	74
Hong Kong	79	63
Iceland (unskilled workers)	94	90
Japan	52	51
Kenya	84	85
Luxembourg	65	66
Netherlands	74	78
New Zealand	78	81
Paraguay	85	75
Sri Lanka	70	96
Switzerland	67	66
Turkey	97	93
United Kingdom	69	71

Source: International Labour Organization, 1995.

work. In Sweden women make up the majority of those in low-paying clerical and service jobs (Neft & Levine, 1998). In the industrialized countries, 75 percent of women are employed in historically low-paying service-sector jobs, 15 to 20 percent in manufacturing, and some 5 percent in agriculture (ILO, 1995). For instance, in Canada women make up only 20 percent of the workers in the ten highest paid occupations and 73 percent of those in the lowest paid jobs (Neft & Levine 1998). One-third of employed Canadian women work in clerical jobs (ILO, 1997). Women still tend to be crowded into low-skilled, low-status, low-paid, and atypical jobs, which by definition are more precarious and prone to exploitation (Chinery-Hesse, 1995).

In most countries women find it hard to be hired into the better-paying jobs customarily held by men. Research indicates that women are less likely than equally qualified men to be hired for nontraditionally female jobs (Olson & Frieze, 1987). This is called **access discrimination** (Martinho & Gardner, 1983). For instance, Glick and colleagues (1988) found that in the United States, negative access discrimination is likely to occur when either females or males apply for a job traditionally held by the other gender. They hypothesize that employers hire based on beliefs regarding the traits desirable for an occupation as well as beliefs about whether males or females are more likely to have those traits. Kawashima's (1995) report surveying Japanese firms exemplifies this. Of the firms surveyed, 48 percent answered that they hired and assigned women to jobs that "fit their special attributes." In many countries, such as Japan and Hong Kong, many job advertisements still specify a particular sex (Kawashima, 1995; WIN, 1993). In Hong Kong, employers refuse to employ women when the job being advertised is high in pay and is managerial or technical (WIN, 1993). A study in Argentina found that professional women required more than sixteen years of seniority over male job candidates in order to be considered qualified for the same job (Neft & Levine, 1997). In short, in most countries, jobs are earmarked as male or female jobs, and typically women can only get traditionally female jobs—jobs that pay less than male jobs and for which pay is not negotiable.

The Compensating Differentials Explanation   Why is it that traditionally female jobs pay less? According to the **compensating differentials** approach, women's jobs pay less because these jobs offer pleasant work conditions, good social relations, the opportunity to serve others, flexible hours, or easy work (Filer, 1985, 1989). It is true that women are not typically found in jobs customarily held by men and that the salaries in female jobs are lower. But is there evidence that women choose these jobs over higher-paying men's jobs because they are more pleasant or conducive to mothering? No, not for the most part. For example, according to research in the United States, female jobs do not offer more flexible hours, lower levels of exertion, and other characteristics that would facilitate parenting (Glass & Camarigg, 1992). In fact, Glass and Camarigg (1992) found that the opposite is true: Greater concentrations of females in professional and blue-collar jobs is related to less flexibility, greater supervision, and less control over the timing and pacing of tasks. An analysis of 1,600 U.S. jobs by Jacobs and Steinberg (1990) suggests that female-dominated jobs involve somewhat different, but not necessarily fewer, undesirable working conditions than male jobs. Women's jobs are more likely to involve working with difficult clients, cleaning others' dirt, mindless repetition, and low autonomy (lack of control over one's work). Furthermore, they found that undesirable working conditions typically have a *negative* effect on wages for both men's and women's jobs because unpleasant jobs tend to be held by those who are low in power and cannot command the higher wages needed to offset the unpleasant work conditions. Later in this chapter, after reading about women in the global factory, you'll be convinced that women aren't getting paid less because their jobs are easy, lightweight, and conducive to mothering.

The Human Capital Explanation   Do women get paid less because they are less skilled, less educated, or less experienced than men and, therefore, less valuable? Do they get paid less because they take too much time out of the labor market in order to bear and raise children such that they have less work experience? Do they do less work for the organization because they are focused on their families? Is the wage gap due to the fact that women are more likely to work part-time? These are the types of explanations offered by the **human capital approach** (Blau & Ferber, 1987). According to research, the factors identified by the human capital approach explain part of the male–female earnings differential, but differences remain even when these factors are not operational. For instance, even when women enter traditionally male sectors of the labor market, they still earn less than men (ILO, 1995). A study in Brazil compared women and men working the same jobs. The study found that women were hired at lower salaries, and a pay gap remained ten years later. After ten years on the job, women earned seven times the minimum wage whereas men earned eleven times the minimum wage (Neft & Levine, 1998).

The United States is another example of how even when women work the same jobs as men, their wages lag behind men's. U.S. Department of Labor statistics from 1991 indicate that female computer programmers make 83 percent of what their male counterparts make, female financial managers make 67 percent of what male financial managers make, female salespeople make 58 percent of what males make, female elementary teachers make 89 percent of what male teachers make, and so on. The pay gap seems especially marked for working mothers. Waldfogel (1997), in a study using a national sample of U.S. women, found that work experience, part-time employment, and taking time out to have children did not fully explain why mothers tend to make less money than women without children. She suggests that one possibility is the assumption on the part of employers that working mothers are less committed to their work and are therefore worth less to the organization.

Part-Time Workers   The gender pay gap is partially due to women's large presence in part-time work. In industrial countries, between 65 and 90 percent of part-time workers are women (ILO, 1996a). Overall, about 1 in 4 employed women are part-time workers, and women constitute about two-thirds of all part-time workers (Thurman & Trah, 1990). The ILO (1995) suggests that the main reasons for women's high rates of part-time employment are that they cannot find full-time jobs, or they must work part-time in order to simultaneously satisfy family demands such as child care and household labor. Indeed, in most countries, married women have a higher incidence of part-time work than do other groups (Blau & Kahn, 1996). Employers have discovered the benefits of part-time workers. Part-time workers are generally paid substantially less than full-time workers, they can be easily laid off during slow periods, and, in many countries, they are not paid nonwage labor costs such as Social Security contributions (Thurman & Trah, 1990).

Gender Wage Discrimination Another explanation for the gender pay gap is simple **gender wage discrimination.** In general, women have been undervalued and so has their work—if women do it, it's worth less than if it's done by men. In some cultures, it is assumed that a woman can be paid less because her income is merely a supplement to her husband's and that her paid job is secondary to her unpaid job as wife and mother. For instance, Kawashima (1995) says that in Japan, employers view women as secondary or supplementary workers and as secondary breadwinners in the household. She also cites a survey of Japanese women suggesting that many accept low wages because of a belief that their wages are supplementary to the household income. Some might argue that paying women less has been a way to keep women in the wife/mother role (with few economic options women must depend on men). However, paying women less probably has more to do with employers' simply wanting to make more money. When employers can get away with paying women less, they often do—because saving on women's wages increases employers' profits.

Legal Remedies to the Gender Pay Gap

Many countries have laws prohibiting gender pay discrimination. The Equal Pay Act of the United States, passed in 1963, says that women's pay should be equal to men's when their positions are equal. Unfortunately, such laws are far from guarantees that discrimination will not occur because governments infrequently enforce them. Another problem is that it is difficult to prove that discrimination has occurred, and the burden of proof falls upon the individual claiming discrimination. It is also difficult to get a gender pay discrimination case to court. In the United States, for example, complaints first go through federal, state, or local agencies, which are horrendously backlogged. As reported by Crampton, Hodge, and Mishra (1997), in 1995 alone about 450 U.S. complaints were filed daily, and 193,859 were still pending resolution. Despite the fact that the Equal Pay Act has been on the books for over thirty years, significant gendered earnings differences still occur in the United States. Other countries with equal pay laws include Brazil, Britain, Canada, China, France, India, Israel, Italy, Japan, Mexico, New Zealand, and Sweden.

Equal pay legislation is one of many examples in this book of how laws, by themselves, do not bring about gender equality. In many countries, there are no penalties for violation of equal pay laws, and in others there is no enforcement of such penalties. Another problem is that most of the countries that have equal pay laws make it illegal to pay women working the *same* job as men less money, but the truth of the matter is that occupational segregation means that in most countries, women are not found in the same jobs as men. Take Japan as an example. Japan's Equal Employment Opportunity Law officially prevents companies from discriminating against women in hiring. However, many companies get around the law by using a two-track hiring system (Kawashima, 1995; Lazarowitz, 1997). The *sogoshoku* track leads to managerial positions but requires the possibility of working overtime and accepting geographic job transfers. Men are automatically placed on this track. The *ippanshoku* track is a secondary track where the work is routinized, promotions are limited, but transfers and overtime are not required. About 98 percent of Japanese women are placed on this track (Lazarowitz, 1997). According to Kawashima (1995), women are given the option of choosing either track but are expected to choose the *ippanshoku* track. Kawashima suggests that this is partly because *sogoshoku* women are expected to fit into a male workplace that does not welcome women. Furthermore, their heavy share of responsibility at home remains unchanged, which makes success in the *sogoshoku* track difficult.

Responding to concerns that gender segregation in work undermined equal employment laws, the 1994 United Nations' Commission on the Status of Women agreed to promote the idea of **comparable worth.** This approach permits the comparison of different jobs on skill, effort, responsibility, and working conditions (United Nations, 1994). The ILO is also a proponent of comparable worth and views it as potentially reducing the gender wage gap because it can deal with wage differences due to occupational segregation (Gunderson, 1995). Of course, it is one thing to endorse such an idea and quite another for it to become practice. Regrettably, widespread voluntary adoption of comparable worth programs is unlikely. Not only would their adoption result in significantly increased labor costs, but the assessment of jobs according to skill, effort, and working conditions is a large and challenging task. In addition, there is little pressure for their adoption.

> Equality of opportunity and treatment for women in employment has yet to be achieved anywhere in the world.
> *Michel Hanseene, Director-General of the UN's International Labour Organization*

Cross-Cultural Variation in the Gender Pay Gap

What accounts for cross-cultural variations in the gender pay gap? It appears that government commitment to equal pay for the genders is one important factor. In a study of the gender pay gap in eleven industrialized countries, Blau and Kahn (1996) found that countries with strong centralized unions and government participation in wage setting tended to have the smallest pay gaps. For instance, relative to most other industrialized nations, the United States has a large gender pay difference, low unionization rates, and a minimal governmental role in wage setting. Another example may be seen in Russia. In 1991, Russian women earned 75 percent of men's wages, but this proportion fell to 40 percent with the move from centralized communism to a decentralized market economy (Neft & Levine, 1998). Unionization especially reduces the pay gap for women working in traditionally male jobs because the union negotiates fixed wages for particular jobs rather than the employer deciding on a case-by-case basis. Pay raises are also more likely to be granted after a certain period of time has passed as long as one has done a serviceable job. This means that the employer does not have the discretion to reward men more adequately than women performing the same job.

Another important factor explaining cross-cultural variation in the gender pay gap is the extent to which traditional stereotypes of the genders still prevail. When traditional gender stereotypes are culturally pervasive, a gender-segregated workforce and lower pay for women is more acceptable. It is also the case that under these cultural conditions, child-care options for employed women are fewer, and the work men do in the home is less. This makes it harder for women to dedicate themselves to the work organization in the same way that men can. Consequently, women may be less likely to apply for jobs that make it difficult to satisfy their domestic role.

The Glass Ceiling

Further evidence of gender discrimination in paid employment comes in the form of a **glass ceiling.** This term is used to refer to the various barriers that prevent qualified women from advancing upward in their organizations into management power positions. According to the ILO (1998), worldwide, women hold less than 5 percent of top jobs in corporations, and women's overall share of management jobs rarely exceeds 20 percent. At the current rate of progress, it is estimated that it will take a couple of centuries for men and women to achieve equal representation at higher levels in organizations (ILO, 1995).

Admittedly, the picture is quite variable. For instance, in Australia, Finland, Italy, Norway, Portugal, Sweden, and the United Kingdom, women hold between 26 and 40 percent of administrative and managerial jobs. However, they hold 10 percent or less in Algeria, France, India, Indonesia, Iran, Nigeria, Pakistan, Singapore, Sudan, and Turkey (Seager, 1997). Box 5.3 gives a worldwide sampling of the percentage of women in administrative and managerial jobs. Keep in mind, however, that combining administrative and managerial positions, as governments so often do, paints a somewhat rosier picture than that seen without the inclusion of administrative positions. The gap also becomes more pronounced the higher you look in organizations. For example, a study of the 70,000 largest German companies found that only 1 to 3 percent of top executives and board members are women; in Brazil, only 3 percent; and in the United States, women hold just over 2 percent of the corporate positions in the 500 largest companies (ILO, 1998). Consider also that in many countries some women face the dual burden of racism and sexism in organizations (Nkomo & Cox, 1989). For instance, in the United States, Black, Latina, Asian American, and Native American women represent approximately 4 percent of women in management, leading some theorists to call the ceiling they face a **concrete ceiling.**

BOX 5.3 *Women in Administrative and Managerial Positions Worldwide*

The following list shows the percentage of women in administrative and managerial jobs and their share in the total employment for 1994 to 1995.

Countries	Administrative and Managerial Jobs (%)	Total Employment (%)
Australia	43	42
Austria	22	43
Chile	20	32
Costa Rica	23	30
Ecuador	28	38
Egypt	12	20
Finland	25	47
Israel	19	42
Japan	9	41
Malaysia	19	34
Mexico	20	32
Norway	32	46
Paraguay	23	41
Philippines	33	37
Sri Lanka	17	48
Switzerland	28	40
Turkey	10	30
United Kingdom	33	45
United States	43	46
Uruguay	28	41
Venezuela	23	33

Source: ILO, 1997.

Research on the glass ceiling does not support the idea that the reason there are few women in higher status positions is because women have personality traits or behavior patterns that make them ill-suited for managerial positions (Burn, 1996). Instead, the main culprits appear to be traditional hiring patterns, stereotypes that suggest that women are inappropriate for leadership positions, and organizational barriers such as a lack of mentoring and training of women for leadership positions. This is another important point. As Geis (1993) notes, if we are under the impression that there is equal opportunity for women and men, then we may falsely conclude that women's lower pay and power are reflections of women's inadequacies. Likewise, the ILO (1998) states "The assertion that an insufficient number of qualified women exist to fill more top jobs is rapidly becoming outmoded. While gender differences still exist in professional study choices, women worldwide are demonstrating their intellectual ability and are approaching the levels of men in educational attainment"(p. 2).

Gender Stereotypes

When you think of a leader, what types of qualities do you imagine? In your culture, are these qualities typically associated with males or females? Gender stereotypes are one contributor to the perception that women are inappropriate for leadership and managerial positions. Morrison and Von Glinow (1990) cite several studies (Freedman & Phillips, 1988; Heilman & Martell, 1986; Ilgen & Youtz, 1986) indicating that gender stereotypes suggesting that women are inappropriate for leadership positions are so strong that contrary data are often ignored in managerial selection and other managerial decisions affecting women. If it is believed that a woman's place is in the home or that women are ineffective as leaders and decision-makers, then women will be denied leadership positions (Stevens, 1984). Because our dominant images of women are in traditionally female roles that often call for different behaviors than those demanded by a managerial role, we may have a hard time envisioning women as leadership material.

Common stereotypes of women suggest that women cannot lead. For instance, many people hold stereotypes of women as emotional and indecisive—qualities that are clearly undesirable for a leader. A number of studies find that successful managers are believed to have personality traits that are more consistent with male rather than female stereotypes (Brenner, Tomkiewicz, & Schein, 1989; Heilman et al., 1989; King, Miles, & Kniska, 1991; Massengill & DiMarco, 1979; Powell & Butterfield, 1984; Schein, 1973, 1975; Schein, Mueller, & Jacobson, 1989). Schein and Mueller (1992) found males in the United States, Great Britain, and Germany to believe this. Females in Germany sex-typed the managerial positions almost as much as males in Germany. British females also sex-typed it but not as much as the German females. However, American women see women and men as equally likely to possess the traits needed for effective management.

U.S. researcher Glick (1991) found that jobs are generally seen as "masculine" or "feminine" and that job applicants are seen as more or less suitable for different jobs depending upon the applicant's sex. Likewise, in a study of job applicants and job interviewers in the Netherlands, Dutch researchers (Van Vianen & Willemsen, 1992) found that gender stereotyping influenced hiring decisions. Worldwide, if you asked people to imagine a leader or manager, most of them would imagine a man. This prototypical leader image may interfere with the hiring of women. Several research studies suggest that gender-based stereotypes associate power with men and not women (Ragins & Sundstrom, 1989). This, in combination with the fact that there are relatively few women in positions of power, may make it hard for some people to imagine a woman in such a position. Research also suggests that we rely more on stereotypes when the person under consideration is a member of a minority group (Dion & Schuller, 1990). Because women tend to be a numerical minority in the corporation, their gender is quite noticeable to perceivers. Therefore, they are likely to be judged and evaluated on the basis of gender stereotypes.

Organizational Practices

Gender stereotypes are but one cause of the glass ceiling. Another is that common organizational practices generally dictate the hiring and promotion of males, rather than females, into management positions. If social and organizational norms do not explicitly advocate hiring women into high-level positions, then those doing the hiring are likely to follow standard operating procedures and hire a man (Burn, 1996). In some cases social norms clearly communicate that women are not appropriate for high-level positions. Individuals within the organization may then comply with these norms regardless of their personal feelings regarding the appropriateness of women in leadership positions (Larwood, Szwajkowski, & Rose, 1988). Similarly, a qualified woman may not be promoted if upper management feels that employees' or clients' stereotypes might interfere with her effectiveness—for instance, they won't be comfortable taking orders from a woman or won't find her a credible authority.

Another problem is that within the organization, women may not receive the experiences needed to advance in the organization. Most organizations have entry-level jobs that lead up the organizational ladder. According to economist Bergmann (1989), these jobs are typically earmarked for men. Kanter (1976) argued that women are usually placed in jobs with less power and limited mobility, and in this way, they are "structurally disadvantaged" in the organization. In the United States, Baron and co-workers (1986) analyzed job ladders (jobs that provide promotion opportunities as opposed to so-called dead-end jobs) in 100 organizations. Jobs in these organizations were pervasively segregated by sex (only 73 of the 1,071 jobs studied had both female and male incumbents), and 71 percent of the promotion ladders in the sample were occupied exclusively by men, 6 percent exclusively by women, and 22 percent by both men and women. Women in prestigious male-typed organizations are usually segregated into female-typed specialties that offer fewer resources for power or are hired into departments with little power (Ragins & Sundstrom, 1989). This has also been noted by the ILO (1998):

> At lower management levels women are typically placed in non-strategic sectors, and in personnel and administrative positions, rather than in professional and line management jobs leading to the top. . . . It is notable that in large companies and organizations where women have achieved high-level managerial positions, these are usually restricted to those areas considered less vital and strategic to the organization such as human resources and administration. (p. 2)

Women's progress may also be limited by their relative lack of access to the political network and lack of mentoring. Mentoring occurs when a senior organizational member helps guide the career of a junior member by sharing knowledge about how to succeed in the organization. Because of their gender and concerns about intimacy and sexual attraction, women are often excluded from the informal social relationships shared by their male counterparts in which power transactions and mentoring often occur (Bhatnagar, 1988; Nelson et al., 1990; Noe, 1988; Powell & Mainiero, 1992). In many countries, it is socially inappropriate for women to interact closely with men who are not husbands or family members. In others, the seclusion of women is accepted practice among some ethnic and religious groups. This is the case in parts of Afghanistan, Bangladesh, Cameroon, Eritrea, India, Iran, Morocco, Niger, Nigeria, Oman, Pakistan, Saudi Arabia, Tunisia, the United Arab Emirates, and Yemen (Seager, 1997).

Responsibilities to Home and Family

Finally, women's responsibilities to home and family may prevent upward mobility in the organization. This can happen in two ways. First, when a woman is married and/or has children, employers often assume that her family responsibilities will interfere with her work commitment, and, consequently, they will not promote her into positions of responsibility. Second, for some women, home and family demands do mean that they are unable to put in the extra hours or travel time necessary for advancement in the organization.

Childbearing and women's primary responsibility for child rearing also affect women's pay and promotion in the workplace because many women take leaves of absence from their jobs in the formal sector while their children are small. For instance, in Japan, advancement in the organization is highly dependent upon uninterrupted service to the organization and seniority. Japanese mothers with small children generally do not participate in the paid sector because of difficulty reconciling the wife/mother role with the demands of paid employment (Tanaka, 1995). Women who interrupt their careers because of pregnancy or who leave the workforce while their children are young are disadvantaged upon their return (Kawashima, 1995).

Indeed, in Japan, unwritten policies have generally prevented the hiring of women older than 30 or 40 (Lazarowitz, 1997). As Tanaka (1995) points out, marriage is more costly to a woman's career because only women are called upon to reconcile the competing demands of work and family responsibilities. Men are able to rely on wives to take care of the household responsibilities, and this frees them to concentrate on work responsibilities. Research in the United States also indicates that women are significantly more likely to interrupt their careers for family-related reasons than men and that such interruptions affect later job advancement and career decisions, especially for women (Powell & Mainiero, 1992).

Because high work involvement is incongruent with the traditional female gender role, women who work often experience anxiety and guilt (Burke & McKeen, 1988), and this may affect their career choices. Few men see marriage or family as a constraint on the emphasis they place on their careers, whereas multiple and conflicting role demands related to parenthood frequently affect women's career choices (Powell & Mainiero, 1992). They may choose not to pursue the career track that takes them away from their families. Many choose part-time work that, although compatible with family responsibilities, is largely incompatible with pay increases and climbing the promotion ladder.

State Maternity Leave and Child-Care Policies

Women get pregnant and have babies. Women have primary responsibility for their children. These facts mean that employed women must sometimes take time out for childbirth and recovery. It also means that to work for pay, they must often find care for their children. As an ILO report said in 1995, women workers still have to juggle numerous roles with considerable difficulty and stress, and few countries provide adequate support—child-care facilities, parental leave, family-friendly workplaces—for workers with family responsibilities. There are some notable exceptions. The Scandinavian countries of Sweden, Finland, and Denmark have the most comprehensive family policies. In Sweden, parents have their jobs guaranteed by law for several years if they wish to stay home with their children, and they may receive 80 to 90 percent salary compensation for fifteen months (Haavio-Mannila, 1993). In Argentina, federal law entitles women to a ninety-day maternity leave. They cannot be fired during this time and receive Social Security payments equivalent to their full salary (Neft & Levine, 1998). Likewise, Indian and Bangladeshi women are entitled to paid maternity leave for twelve weeks; Italian women may take a five-month paid maternity leave, and Mexican women receive twelve weeks of paid maternity leave (Neft & Levine, 1998). Relative to most other industrialized countries, the United States has few family-supportive policies although a 1993 federal law permits parents who work in firms of fifty employees or more to take twelve weeks of unpaid leave to recover from childbirth or to care for a new child.

BOX 5.4 *Maternity and Child-Care Policies Worldwide*

Across the world, there is considerable variation in the maternity and child-care policies of employers and governments. The following is a sampling of some representative countries' policies.

Country	Maternity Leave	Child Care
Argentina	Full pay for 90 days, paid for by the government.	Businesses with more than 50 employees are to provide day care; not enforced.
Australia	Most women entitled to a year of unpaid leave; federal and some state employees entitled to paid leave (varies by state).	Government provides money for child-care assistance to low- and middle-income families, but a shortage of centers remains problematic.
Bangladesh	Full pay for 90 days, paid for by employer. Women often fired for getting pregnant.	Government provides some day care. Factories of 50 or more employees required to supply care, but law is not enforced.
Brazil	Full pay for 120 days, paid for by the government. Law that employers may not force women to prove they are not pregnant was passed in 1995.	Free day care up to the age of 6.
Egypt	Salary at 70 percent for 50 days, paid for by the government.	The government has established some day-care centers, and in some cases requires employers to do so. However, there are too few, and they are of poor quality.

Affordable child care also remains a significant problem for working parents. Again, Sweden is one of the best countries for working parents. A Swedish law passed in 1985 guarantees a place in a day-care center for every child between the ages of 1 and 6, and a place in a "leisure time" center for every child between 7 and 12 (Neft & Levine, 1998). France also provides government sponsored child care for children over 3 (Morgan, 1996). Box 5.4 shows some representative maternity and child-care policies across the world. In truth, however, many family and work laws are not enforced and do not apply to women working in the service and informal sectors; as well, some of these benefits work against women because employers may choose to hire men or make women prove that they are not pregnant before hiring them (Morgan, 1996; Neft & Levine, 1998). Once again, laws may be a step in the right direction, but laws alone are insufficient.

Country	Maternity Leave	Child Care
Germany	Full pay for 14 weeks, paid for by the government. The government also provides a child-raising allowance, called *Kindergeld,* for two years.	Poor availability of child care combined with half-day schedule of public schools makes careers difficult for mothers.
Mexico	Full pay for 12 weeks, paid for by the government.	Government runs some day-care centers, but there are too few, and they are too costly for many women.
Nigeria	Full pay for 12 weeks.	No government child-care policy and a shortage of public facilities.
Pakistan	Full pay for 12 weeks.	Law requires that child care be provided at factories with 50 or more employees, but it is not enforced.
Philippines	Full pay for 14 weeks, paid for by the government.	Child-care shortages are a problem. A 1991 law requiring that every village have a day-care center has not been implemented for cost reasons.

Sources: Morgan, 1996; Neft & Levine, 1998.

Sexual Harassment

Sexual harassment is yet another problem facing employed women. Sexual harassment includes requiring sex as a condition of employment or job rewards (called **quid pro quo sexual harassment**), as well as repeated and unwanted sexually suggestive words, acts, and gestures and sexually discriminating remarks (called **gender harassment**). For example, widespread sexual harassment was apparently common at the U.S. Mitsubishi automobile plant in Normal, Illinois. Women there were subjected to repeated and unwelcome physical and verbal abuse. Among the host of harassing behaviors were obscene graffiti demeaning to women, men exposing themselves to women and grabbing women's breasts, and men taunting women with crude names and pressuring them to have sex (Braun, 1998; Cray, 1997). Gruber and colleagues (1996) reviewed existing research on cultural differences in types of sexual harassment.

Their findings provide evidence of cross-cultural similarity in sexual harassment experiences. In studies with American, French, Spanish, Canadian, and Russian women, the most frequent form of harassment was verbal abuse and suggestive comments; this was followed by "sexual posturing" (including sexually suggestive looks or gestures, touching, following, and leering). Next were repeated requests for dates, sex, or a relationship; and last was outright sexual assault and coercion.

It is only within the last twenty years that industrialized countries have identified sexual harassment as a workplace problem and most systematic research on the dynamics of harassment has been conducted by U.S. researchers. In areas where women have only recently entered the formal workforce, there is still denial of the problem and reluctance to report incidents (Bullock, 1994). This explains why statistics on the occurrence of sexual harassment worldwide are hard to obtain, although available statistics suggest that sexual harassment is prevalent. The ILO (1995) reports that between 15 and 30 percent of employed women surveyed in industrialized countries say they have experienced frequent, serious sexual harassment such as unwanted touching, pinching, offensive remarks, and requests for sexual favors. A 1993 report in the *Women's International Network News* cited survey data indicating that as many as 85 percent of women in Hong Kong and 73 percent of women in Britain experienced sexual harassment in the workplace. Evidence from the United States suggests that between 40 and 60 percent have experienced some form of sexual harassment at work (Murray, 1998). Sexual harassment often results in emotional and physical stress and stress-related illnesses (Gutek & Koss, 1993; ILO, 1995; Schneider, Swann, & Fitzgerald, 1997). It is also potentially costly to organizations. Research in the United States indicates that harassment can lead to increased absenteeism, job turnover, requests for transfers, and decreases in work motivation and productivity (Knapp & Kustis, 1996).

Sexual Harassment and Power

Many sexual harassment experts agree that sexual harassment is about power. Indian researchers Shobha Menon and Suresh Kanekar (1992) suggest that sexual harassment—like wife beating, dowry, sati (when widows throw themselves on their husband's funeral pyre), feticide, and rape—is a manifestation of the power differential between men and women and its misuse by men. From a feminist perspective, sexual harassment, like other forms of gendered violence, arises from and reinforces the subordinate position of women in society (Cleveland & McNamara, 1996; Fitzgerald, 1993; Pagelow, 1992). Also like wife battering, rape, and incest, sexual harassment is considered to be a consequence of gender-role socialization processes that promote male dominance, the sexual objectification of women, and the cultural approval of violence against women (Cleveland & McNamara, 1996).

Most cases of sexual harassment occur between male superiors and female subordinates. Women's vulnerability to unemployment allows men with decision-making power to take sexual advantage of women (WIN, 1992).

For instance, at Mitsubishi, many of those who experienced sexual harassment did not complain because it was their supervisors who were doing the harassing (Braun, 1998; Cray, 1997). Ironically, according to the company's sexual harassment policy, sexual harassment complaints were supposed to be made through these very supervisors (Cray, 1997). Livingston (1982) points out that the relative social and economic power of harassers and victims influences the occurrence and severity of harassment as well as victims' responses.

Women Especially Vulnerable to Harassment

Certain groups of women are especially vulnerable to sexual harassment (Bullock, 1994). These include live-in domestic workers and women in non-traditional, male-dominated occupations. Note that in both of these cases women are often numerical or ethnic minorities. Research suggests that women who are numerical minorities are at greater risk for sexual harassment than women in jobs in which women predominate or are members of the dominant ethnic group (Gutek, Cohen, & Konrad, 1990). Furthermore, women who are ethnic minorities in the workplace may be targeted because minority group status denotes marginality and lack of power within the workplace (Murrell, 1996). Additionally, such women may be susceptible because racism toward female ethnic minorities may be expressed as sexual aggression and harassment (Collins, 1990).

It is interesting to note, for instance, that sexual harassment of women is reportedly widespread in factories owned by transnational corporations. This appears to be especially true when the supervisory staff is male and from a different country than the female subordinates. Murrell (1996) adds that the sexual harassment of ethnic minority women should be viewed as a form of racial discrimination because the sexual harassment of such women is often fueled by race-based stereotypes of women. Ethnic minority women are also likely to see their harassment as arising from their minority status (Collins, 1990; Murrell, 1996). This dual experience of racism and sexism, or sexual racism, may exacerbate the negative experience of sexual harassment (Murrell, 1996).

Sexual Harassment and Organizational Climate

It is clear, however, that women need not be ethnic or numerical minorities in order to experience sexual harassment in the workplace. Indeed, organizational climate plays a strong role in sexual harassment. More specifically, the degree to which an organization is perceived by employees to be insensitive or tolerant of sexual harassment affects its frequency and severity (Hulin, Fitzgerald, & Drasgow, 1996). Pryor and colleagues (1995) further argue that men predisposed to harass women do it when such behavior is tolerated, modeled, and encouraged in the organization. Women in such organizations are not only more likely to experience harassment but are likely to have less institutional recourse and fewer effective remedies when they do (Hulin et al., 1996). According to sexual harassment researcher Louise Fitzgerald, research indicates that 95 percent of those who experience sexual harassment do not report it because they fear losing their jobs and sabotaging their careers (Murray, 1998).

Research suggests additional reasons for low rates of reporting as well. These include victims' fears of retaliation, fears they won't be believed, and fears they will be blamed for it (Cleveland & McNamara, 1996; Gutek & Koss, 1993). These fears have basis in reality. For example, at Mitsubishi in Normal, Illinois, women who lodged complaints were subjected to hostile phone calls, the threat of rape, and stalking (Cray, 1997). *The Asian Women's Newsletter* reports that in Asia women do not dare speak out for fear of being labeled as "loose women," because people still believe that decent women do not get harassed (WIN, 1992). Likewise, studies of **maquiladoras,** assembly plants in Mexico owned by multinational corporations, reveal that sexual harassment, including rape, is common and is used to control female employees. Few women report it because they fear reprisals and feel shamed and humiliated (Nauman & Hutchison, 1997).

Sexual Harassment Interventions

Organizational Interventions   Interventions at the organizational level may make a difference in reducing sexual harassment. In particular, sexual harassment is reduced when there are clear procedures to support victims and punish harassers and when there is a clear and consistent statement from management that sexual harassment will not be tolerated. One U.S. study found that the presence and effectiveness of sexual harassment policies and procedures reduced the incidence of harassment (Hesson-McInnis & Fitzgerald, 1995, reported in Hulin et al., 1996). Sexual harassment training, designed to prevent harassment from occurring, may also be effective *if* it is accompanied by strong managerial support. Unfortunately, sexual harassment training is often offered without procedures for ensuring that complaints will be taken seriously. Once again, the Mitsubishi plant in Normal, Illinois, serves as an example. The company's standard disciplinary measure was to require the harasser to watch a thirty-minute sexual harassment video and to place a memo in the person's file (Cray, 1997). Watching the film reportedly became a companywide joke.

Legal Interventions   The majority of organizations in the world have no policies against sexual harassment or procedures for handling it. Likewise, the majority of countries in the world have no laws against sexual harassment in the workplace. Some of the few countries with laws against sexual harassment include Australia, Canada, Cuba, Denmark, France, Greece, India, Portugal, South Korea, Sri Lanka, and the United States. Laws in other countries, such as Britain, Ecuador, Finland, Japan, Norway, Pakistan, and Sweden, can be interpreted to include sexual harassment. Of course, as I have frequently noted, laws are of limited impact when they are vague or unenforced, and this is definitely the case when it comes to sexual harassment law. In the countries that have laws, violations rarely make it to court. This is partly because sexual harassment laws are often more progressive than the societies in which they are enacted. Despite laws, sexual harassment is not taken seriously by male-dominated legal systems or viewed as a crime by societies. Thus, there is relatively little motivation for prosecution. Sexual harassment law is also new and confusing, and legal systems are not yet prepared to handle sexual harassment complaints. This means that not only are there few attorneys familiar with it, but that it is often unclear what legal evidence is necessary to prove harassment. Women often have difficulty finding legal counsel willing to take these cases. Some countries require that complaints first be registered through underfunded and backlogged government agencies. For instance, in Canada, the Human Rights Commission handles complaints, and there is typically a backlog of two and a half years (Morgan, 1996).

Given this state of affairs, women frequently see little point in pursuing legal avenues of redress, especially given the high personal and financial costs of doing so. However, countries with laws against sexual harassment are to be commended, and in time, these laws may become more helpful to women. For example, in June 1998 the automaker Mitsubishi was ordered by the U.S. courts to pay $34 million to hundreds of female workers at its Illinois plant. This is the largest such settlement on record in a corporate case. Perhaps this settlement sends a message to employers that sexual harassment is unacceptable and potentially expensive and signals a new era in the United States in which sexual harassment is vigorously prosecuted.

Women in the Global Factory

Women's relatively cheap labor is the basis of export-oriented industrialization and international competition for many developing countries (ILO, 1996a). Women's manual dexterity and docility (conditioned by culture), their desperation for work, and their seemingly limitless supply have made them the choice factory workers of multinational corporations worldwide. With few options for paid work, many must work for low pay in **sweatshops**— businesses that violate wage, child labor, and safety laws. Sweatshop workers are unlikely to complain because they need the work despite the conditions. These jobs are desirable because in developing countries there are few modern wage jobs for women and because most of the jobs are concentrated in farming, domestic service, and the informal sector (Lim, 1990). The odds are good that the majority of your clothes, shoes, toys, and electronics were created with women's sweatshop labor in countries such as Bangladesh, Burma, China, the Dominican Republic, Haiti, Honduras, Indonesia, Guatemala, Malaysia, Mexico, Nicaragua, the Philippines, and Vietnam. Your good deal may be at the expense of these women. Recently, transnational corporations have begun employing women in service jobs such as telemarketing, banking, and airline reservations, particularly in the Caribbean. For instance, at one Barbados location, 100 women sit at a row of computer terminals and daily enter 300,000 ticket reservations for a U.S. airline (Bullock, 1994).

Poor Working Conditions and Pitiful Pay

The *maquiladoras* of Mexico's border towns are but one example of women in the global factory. There, over 2,000 multinational corporations have drawn over a half million workers, two-thirds of them women, who get paid between $3.75 and $4.50 a day (Nauman & Hutchison, 1997). In El Salvador, women employees of the Taiwanese *maquilador* Mandarin are forced to work shifts of 12 to 21 hours during which they are seldom allowed bathroom breaks; they are paid about 18 cents per shirt, which is later sold for $20 each (Jeffrey, 1996). Mandarin makes clothes for the Gap, J. Crew, and Eddie Bauer (Herbert, 1995). In Haiti, women sewing clothing at Disney's contract plants are paid 6 cents for every $19.99 *101 Dalmatians* outfit they sew; they make 33 cents an hour (Kernaghan, 1997). Meanwhile, Disney makes record profits and could easily pay workers a living wage for less than one half of 1 percent of the sales price of one outfit (Kernaghan, 1997). In Vietnam, 90 percent of Nike's workers are females between the ages of 15 and 28. Nike's labor for a pair of basketball shoes (which retail for $149.50) costs Nike $1.50, 1 percent of the retail price.

"Just don't buy it."
Slogan of the Global Exchange's Boycott Nike Program

Contrary to the beliefs of many Westerners who purchase sweatshop products, these wages are insufficient to escape poverty. For example, sweatshop workers in Nicaragua average from $55 to $75 a month when the average family needs $165 a month to make ends meet (Stark, 1996). In Indonesia, the government estimates that the minimum wage there is equal to just 67 percent of what is required to meet minimum physical needs, and many companies do not pay even that much (Wallace, 1992). Wages at Mexican *maquiladoras* are sufficient to provide for only one-fourth of the needs for a typical worker's family (Nauman & Hutchison, 1997). In Vietnam, a living wage is estimated to be $3 a day, but Nike workers make only $1.60 a day (Herbert, 1997). Nike's chief executive officer, Philip Knight, is one of the richest men in the world.

Health problems are reportedly common because of harsh working conditions such as inadequate ventilation, chemical exposures, and repetitive motion. However, most governments have generally failed to collect information or to carry out studies to document their severity. At the Dynamics factory in Bangkok, Thailand, where Mattel's Barbies are made, over 75 percent of the 4,500 female workers suffer severe breathing problems from the inhalation of dust (Foek, 1997). In the Lamphun province in northern Thailand, female factory workers at electronic production factories use lead and other solvents to clean electronic components. The accumulation of toxic metals in the workers' bodies is contributing to high levels of chronic illness and deaths. The government is reluctant to attribute the high rate of illness and death to occupational causes out of fear that foreign investors will go elsewhere if the costs of doing business in Thailand should rise (Rajesh, 1997). In Mexico, several studies found acute health effects due to chemical exposures as well as reproductive effects such as babies with lower birth weights (Nauman & Hutchison, 1997). In short, health and safety hazards are common, and government protections are few.

The Risks of Rebellion

Women workers in the global factory typically have little choice other than to accept these questionable work conditions. The women are often from rural areas and are unaware of their rights and are afraid of losing their jobs should they assert themselves (Nauman & Hutchison, 1997). Many are underage and work with forged birth certificates (LaBotz, 1993). There are few other jobs available for women, making the situation a desperate one (Bullock, 1994). The women at the Dynamics factory, for example, come from northeastern Thailand where the poverty is so bad that parents sometimes sell their daughters into sex slavery or cheap labor (Foek, 1997). In Guatemala, war and conflict in the countryside have led to migration to the cities, and people must take any work they can find. In the United States, illegal immigrants desperate for employment have little choice but to take what work they can. Many work in garment industry sweatshops or perform home-based sewing and assembly of garments.

Despite the risk, strikes and efforts to organize for better work conditions and pay are increasingly common, but swiftly and harshly punished. At a Nike subcontractor in Indonesia where more than 9,000 women work, workers who organized a protest of pay and working conditions were fired (Herbert, 1996). Likewise, eighteen Sony workers at a Mexican *maquiladora* were fired for union organizing. When workers protested these firings by stopping work and blocking the road to the factory, Sony brought in riot police who beat the workers (Bacon, 1997). After South Korean women successfully unionized at Nike plants in the 1980s, Nike and its subcontractors began shutting down their South Korean factories, moving them to Indonesia and Vietnam (Enloe, 1995a). Governments generally participate in the suppression of labor organizing. Competition with other economically struggling countries for foreign investment is stiff. In order to attract and keep foreign operations in their country, they must guarantee that there will be no labor conflict and little regulation.

Corporations choose to locate in countries where the unemployment is high and the people are desperate for work. As the chairman of the only union in Indonesia noted, the union is weak because there is an oversupply of labor—every year there are approximately 2.5 million new workers looking for jobs. Governments are hesitant to intervene, needing the jobs and foreign currency to pay off loans and knowing that multinational corporations will move their operations to other countries that do not enforce labor regulations. They feel that the multinationals give them no choice. The companies argue that they are doing nothing wrong because the people are better off than they would be if they had no jobs.

> It is unacceptable that any zone or enterprise should be outside the labour laws of the country where it is situated and similarly, that it should flout international labour standards.
> *Susan Bullock*

Recent free trade agreements such as GATT (General Agreement on Tariffs and Trade) and NAFTA (North American Free Trade Agreement) have aggravated poor labor conditions by making it easier for corporations to ask for and receive exemptions from laws that ostensibly interfere with free trade. These treaties have encouraged the development of free trade zones, where companies are exempted from labor, health and safety, and environmental laws and pay few, if any, taxes. As Enloe (1995a) noted, free trade as practiced today is hardly free for the workers who must accept outrageous work conditions as the price of keeping their jobs.

Dolores Huerta (1930–) is the co-founder of the United Farm Workers Union in the United States. The mother of eleven has worked tirelessly for thirty years to gain a living wage and safe working conditions for farmworkers. Her recent focus is on the right of female farmworkers to work without sexual harassment and assault. She also works to get Latina women into leadership positions in unions and in politics.

Some labor unions have begun to actively support their exploited counterparts in multinational industries. For instance, in 1993, Honeywell workers in Canada, Mexico, and the United States protested the firing of Mexican employees in Chihuahua (Nauman & Hutchison, 1997). Labor unions and NGOs in both northern and southern countries (see Chapter 6) are urging the inclusion of "social clauses" in trade agreements to protect the rights of workers (Bullock, 1996). Nongovernmental organizations, such as the U.S.'s Multinational Monitor, the London-based Women Working Worldwide, and the Dutch group SOMO, have launched awareness campaigns, organized consumer protests, and monitored working conditions in transnational factories.

Consumer protest can make some difference. The Gap, one of the United States' largest clothing chains, responded to consumer protest by stating that it will not do business with its subcontractor Mandarin unless it obeys international labor laws and rehires workers blacklisted for union activity (Jeffrey, 1996). Levi-Strauss now requires that Asian garment companies agree to provide the legal minimum wage and prohibit all worker exploitation.

Self-Employed Women

Outside the formal, organized, and visible economic sector is the informal sector. **Self-employed women** working in the informal sector far outnumber women working in multinational factories. The Cuban woman who runs a beauty shop on the roof of her apartment building, the Peruvian woman who sells vegetables from her garden by the roadside, the South African woman who brews and sells her own beer, the Filipino woman who does others' laundry for pay, the American woman who watches her neighbor's children, and the Mexican woman who sews sweatshirts in her home for the subcontractor of a transnational corporation are all working in the informal sector. Informal sector work includes petty trade, food processing, and domestic work. Informal sector work is paid, but unstructured and unregulated (Seager, 1997). Women in self-employment rely on the skills and experience they already have, and so food processing and trading, sewing, and domestic and personal services are all common (Bullock, 1994). Home-based work done for subcontractors is also part of the economic strategy of women (Beneria & Roldan, 1987; Tinker, 1995). In most cases, women are paid by the assembled piece ("piece rate"). In such cases, work at home is part of the chain of production in the formal sector, demonstrating the blurry line between formal and informal sectors.

Women generally make up at least half and sometimes more, of the informal sector (Dignard & Havet, 1995). There are more women in the informal sector in some countries than in others. Some countries with high rates of women in the informal sector are Zambia (72%), Gambia (62%), the Republic of Korea (41%), and Indonesia (65%) (ILO, 1996a). Women dominate informal sector work for several reasons. One is that it is often the only work they can find because formal manufacturing enterprises and state (government) bureaucracies have failed to create enough jobs (Dignard & Havet, 1995; ILO, 1996a). Another reason is that it permits the combining of paid work with family and household responsibilities and poses less of a challenge to the "male breadwinner ethos" (Bullock, 1994; Tinker, 1995). Remember, in many cultures a woman's primary role is to care for her home and family, and a man's role is to be the cash provider. Informal sector work, particularly home assembly work, allows women to work for pay without defaming the family or threatening men's masculinity.

Bullock (1994) notes that the concept of the informal sector has been challenged on the grounds that the word *informal* belies the importance of these economic activities and women's role in paid economic life. She reports that the Self-Employed Women's Association (SEWA), which works to protect and organize women in the informal sector in India, recommends use of the term *self-employment* out of respect for this type of work. As Bhatt (1995), one of the founders of SEWA said, "It is contradictory to describe such a vast, active work force in terms that relegate it to a peripheral position, while in reality it is central to the economy. In my view, in order to properly characterize this work force, it should be called the 'self-employed sector' or 'the self-employed'" (p. 87). Another designation gaining acceptance is **women's micro- and small-scale enterprises** (WMSEs) (Dignard & Havet, 1995).

The way that women are able to scrape together an income on the basis of almost no inputs but their own labor and ingenuity inspires admiration and respect (Bullock, 1994). Despite this, economists see these activities as "economically marginal" because women microentrepreneurs do not always use their profits for business growth (Tinker, 1995). Instead, women often return their profits to the family in the form of better food and living conditions, to what is called the "human economy" (Tinker, 1995). As noted earlier, women's work in the informal sector is also literally devalued by its exclusion from national accounting systems, although some efforts are being made to remedy this.

One problem facing self-employed women is that they do not usually have the advantage of being represented by **unions.** This means that collective action to redress labor wrongs is less available to them. Another problem is that the invisibility of women's work in the informal sector, along with it not fitting standard definitions for economically successful business, mean that women entrepreneurs have had difficulty getting credit (loans) from banks, governments, and development agencies. Berger (1995) summarizes some of the constraints on credit access for women microentrepeneurs. One of these is lack of collateral. This is a key problem as women often do not have clear title to land or property. This is compounded by the widespread practice of registering property in the man's name and by inheritance systems that favor men. Bank practices, such as those that require a male cosigner, also discourage women. In addition, many poor women, especially those with little education, have difficulty completing the complicated application forms required by lending agencies. Consequently, for credit purposes women microentrepeneurs frequently rely on moneylenders (who charge high interest rates), family, and friends (Berger, 1995).

Self-employed women are increasingly finding ways around these problems. For instance, there are a number of self-employed women's unions such as the South African Domestic Workers' Union (SADWU) and the Union of Domestic Workers of Brazil. Perhaps the best known self-employed women's union is SEWA of India, begun in 1972. One of SEWA's principal activities is the organization of cooperatives through which labor problems are addressed. Bhatt (1995) gives a number of examples. For instance, SEWA helped the "pushcart vegetables cooperative" to fight for women's right to receive vending licenses, the "paper pickers cooperative" to set up their own collection network so that they could sell directly to the paper factories and avoid middlemen, and the "cane and bamboo" cooperative to upgrade their skills and receive a greater share of their state government's harvested bamboo at a reasonable price. In addition, the SEWA Bank provides capital for women's small-scale businesses. Before the SEWA Bank, self-employed women had to obtain capital at high interest rates from moneylenders. As of 1992, SEWA had 44 different cooperatives, 46,000 members, 22,000 savings accounts, over a million U.S. dollars in working capital, and over 860,000 U.S. dollars in loans with a repayment rate of 96 percent (Bhatt, 1995).

In industrialized nations, the number of **women entrepreneurs** is also rising, although their businesses tend to be part of the formal sector and directed toward growth. For instance, in Canada, women comprise almost a third of all self-employed workers and have been starting their own businesses at three times the rate of men (Neft & Levine, 1998). Likewise, by 1996 U.S. women owned slightly more than one-third of the businesses in the country, employing 18.5 million people and generating $2.3 billion in sales (Cannon, 1997). According to the ILO (1996b), in developing countries women start their own microenterprises as a matter of survival, whereas in industrialized countries women do so in order to be masters of their own fate. In other words, in contrast to the small-scale enterprises run by women in developing nations to provide for their families' basic needs, women in industrialized nations start their own businesses to be their own bosses and to escape the glass ceiling. However, it should be noted that poor women in the United States also start small businesses in order to provide for their families' basic needs. One thing experienced by women entrepreneurs all over the world is limited access to credit. Another commonality is the role of alternative economic organizations such as women's banks, networks, and cooperatives in women's entrepreneurship all over the world.

BOX 5.5 *International Labour Organization Conventions Relevant to Women*

The Equal Renumeration Convention, 1951, provides for the equal renumeration (pay) for men and women for work of equal value.

The Discrimination (Employment and Occupation) Convention, 1958, promotes equality of rights between men and women in the workplace.

The Workers with Family Responsibilities Convention, 1981, aims to create effective equality of opportunity and treatment for men and women workers with family responsibilities.

The Part-Time Work Convention, 1994, aims to ensure protection for part-time workers in areas such as access to employment, working conditions, and Social Security.

The Home Work Convention, 1996, aims at improving the situation of home workers who are largely unrecognized in labor statistics and unprotected by legislation.

Source: www.ilo.org/public/english/140femme/feons.htm.

Conclusion

The chapter started with the suggestion that there is a relationship between women's paid work and women's status but then went on to document the low pay, glass ceilings, and poor work conditions so often experienced by employed women. The conclusion to this chapter explores two questions. First, What can be done to improve women's work conditions? Second, Do women benefit from paid work despite the negative work conditions they so often experience?

With regard to the first question about how to improve women's work conditions, one recurring theme in this book is that governments often respond to gender inequality by passing legislation. However, this observation is inevitably followed by the lament that because governments frequently fail to enforce such laws and conventions, legislation often has little impact. For example, Box 5.5 summarizes ILO conventions that specifically concern women's labor. If these conventions were indeed implemented, many of the problems facing employed women would certainly be eliminated. Bullock (1994) points out that one of the problems is lack of **legal literacy.** As she puts it, a law that no one knows about does not really exist. People need to know their rights according to the law and should have the means to defend and enforce them. Bullock (1994) suggests that the transformation of the situation of working women rests on three pillars: laws that establish equality principles, women's active participation in workers' organizations, and women's understanding of their rights. Workers' organizations along with other NGOs are important in pressing for the ratification of international labor standards and their implementation, as well as promoting women's legal literacy (Bullock, 1994).

Mary "Mother" Jones
(1830–1930 Irish
American) was a labor
organizer for fifty-nine
years. Her passionate
speeches along with
the dramatic marches
and confrontations she
organized brought
attention to the plight
of child laborers and
coal and railroad
workers.

That said, let's look at trade unions and their role in promoting women's work equality. As already noted, one customary way to advocate for workers' labor rights is through the organization of labor unions that collectively bargain for workers. The International Confederation of Free Trade Unions (ICFTU) reports that 34 percent of its membership worldwide is female (Bullock, 1994). Historically, unions have paid relatively little attention to labor rights specific to women, such as violence against women, sexual harassment, child-care facilities, and gender job segregation. According to the ILO (1997), male dominance, along with the way unions are typically structured, hinder the promotion of women's labor rights. For instance, unions frequently hold meetings at night, and women's family responsibilities make it difficult for them to attend. Also, strong male networks tend to dominate, making it difficult for women to participate. Furthermore, because women tend to hold lower status jobs, they are unlikely to be elected to important committees and bargaining teams. The ILO views labor unions as essential ingredients in women's workplace equality and in recent years has attempted to educate and encourage unions to do a better job of including women. Their recommendations to unions include such things as removing sexist language in union material; sensitizing men to the role women play in daily life; setting up a women's commission to keep attention focused on women's needs; reserving a certain number of seats for women in decision-making bodies (ideally providing extra seats so that men don't feel threatened); setting goals such that, within a certain period of time, a specific number of women occupy decision-making posts; and having meetings at times when women can attend.

The ILO's efforts, along with women's growing union membership and the work of activists and women's leaders, has resulted in some progress. For instance, Bullock (1994) reports that over 90 percent of ICFTU affiliates reported having a special structure and/or officer responsible for women's and equality issues. In cases in which mainstream trade unions have not responded to women's needs, women have often formed their own associations. India's SEWA, discussed earlier in the chapter, is one example. The Working Women's Co-operative Society (WWCS) and its offshoot, the National Union of Working Women, are other Indian examples. Also, there are the Grassroots Women Workers' Centre in Taiwan, the Korean Women Workers' Association, the South African Domestic Workers' Union, and the Union of Women Domestic Employees in Brazil.

The chapter began by suggesting that feminists view women's **economic empowerment** as the key to women's equality, but there is some debate on this point. Currently, the effects of paid work on women are somewhat paradoxical. On the one hand, earning money buys some freedom and some power in the home. On the other hand, this is often offset by the difficulties of balancing work and family, low wages, glass ceilings, and poor work conditions, including sexual harassment. The prevailing opinion is that employment is a necessary but not sufficient condition of high female status (Tinker, 1990). Indeed, Tinker notes that in some societies, women's social status is enhanced when they are economically dependent on husbands and don't have to work, and many poor, hard-working women would welcome such a situation. Furthermore, the extent to which women get to keep or control the income they generate varies greatly worldwide (Blumberg, 1991). Mere work in economic activities or even ownership of economic resources does not translate into benefits if the person has no control over them (Blumberg, 1991, 1995). The more a society's political, economic, legal, and ideological systems disadvantage women, the less a woman gets her "hypothetical dollar's worth of economic power for every dollar she brings to the household" (Blumberg, 1995, p. 213).

Overall, though, the evidence appears to support the idea that women gain significantly from paid employment. This is true in both industrialized and less developed countries. According to Lim (1990), women in developing countries often cite such benefits as the ability to earn independent income and spend it on desired consumer purchases; the ability to save for marriage or education; the ability to help support their families and "repay" their debt to parents; the opportunity to delay marriage and childbearing and to exercise personal choice of a marriage partner; and the opportunity to enjoy some personal freedom, the companionship of other women, and to experience more of what life has to offer, such as a "widening of horizons."

Research in the United States suggests that although balancing multiple social roles is indeed stressful, this stress is mitigated to some extent by the fact that multiple roles provide us with alternate sources of self-esteem, control, and social support (Rodin & Ickovics, 1990). For instance, research (Baruch & Barnett, 1986, 1987) finds that working women report higher levels of rewards than costs for their multiple roles and indicates that paid employment enhances women's satisfaction with domestic life (Crosby, 1991). Crosby (1991) found that although employed mothers were stressed by their multiple roles and longed for more time to get everything done, on balance they felt the advantages of multiple roles outweighed the disadvantages. Multiple roles give life variety and buffer the impact of negative events (Crosby, 1991).

According to Blumberg (1995), data from Third World women indicates that a woman's absolute and relative income is tied to increases in self-esteem and confidence, greater leverage in fertility decisions, and greater leverage in other household economic and domestic decisions. Other studies (Blumstein & Schwartz, 1991; Lips, 1991; Stroh, Brett, & Reilly, 1992) also suggest a link between women's paid employment and her power in the home. In particular, the greater a woman's control of income, the greater her say in other household economic and domestic decisions and the greater her "voice and vote" in the marital relationship (Blumberg, 1991, 1995). Engle (1993), for example, found that in Guatemalan families, the greater the women's income in comparison to the total family income, the greater her role in family decision making (the only exception was food purchasing, which was her decision regardless). Likewise, some researchers have noted that girl children receive more intrahousehold resource allocations when they have money-making potential.

Indeed, several studies suggest that in developing countries such as India, rural females' survival chances are increased by their participation in the paid labor force (Papanek, 1990). The suggestion is that the female's economic value to the family is higher in cases in which she may bring in money, and consequently, the family invests more resources in her survival.

It should be apparent after reading this chapter that women's disproportionate responsibility for household labor and child care features prominently in their continued subordination. Chafetz (1991) summarizes the thinking on this point by showing the interrelationships between women's paid and unpaid labor and their power in both the domestic and public domains (which she respectively calls "micro" and "macro" levels of power). The argument goes like this: Societies designate household labor (including child care) as women's work. This, combined with men's greater power in the home (**micro power**), means that men are able to avoid household labor, regardless of the other work women might do. In addition, the double work-day experienced by wage-earning women reduces women's ability to compete for better-paying jobs, and this reinforces men's micro power advantages. Men's micro power can also be used to prevent women from entering the paid labor force or may restrict them to part-time jobs (for example, husbands may forbid their wives from working for pay at all or from working full-time). This further reinforces males' micro power advantage because they continue to be the major providers of money. Chafetz points out that even when women do earn wages, their husbands' micro power is not totally eliminated because women can rarely match or exceed their husbands in the provision of economic resources. The fact that men generally enjoy greater **macro power** (public sphere power) plays into this as well. This power permits men—as employers, lawmakers, and so on—to segregate women into low-paying jobs, to restrict their opportunities to acquire skills and credentials needed for better jobs, or to even prevent them from paid employment altogether. Men's macro power is then reinforced as women tend to lack the resources to challenge it. For example, in Afghanistan the ruling Taliban government does not permit women to work unless they are widows with no other source of income. Girls are not allowed to work or go to school.

Chafetz's model suggests that changing societal conceptions of household labor as "women's work" would remove one barrier to women's achievement of higher paying work roles. This would then positively impact both their micro and macro power levels. Many feminists believe that gender roles are unlikely to change until the division of labor in the home changes. Current gender-based divisions of labor in the household are viewed as symptomatic of continuing gender inequality and gender-role socialization (Blair & Lichter, 1991). As Braverman (1991) points out, "The allocation of housework and childcare reflects in microcosm the power inequities between men and women in society at large" (p. 26). Traditional divisions of household labor may also perpetuate the lower status of females. It is apparent to the child that the person who works all day and who must then come home and cook and clean is of lower status than the one who works all day and does not have these duties when he returns home. Children may then infer that females must really be inferior, or they wouldn't have this lower status.

Traditional divisions of household labor lead children to develop gender stereotypes and to learn different skills based on their gender. When children see males and females in different roles, they assume that males and females have different qualities that make them better suited for these differing roles (Burn, 1996). These gender stereotypes then act as social norms, or prescriptions, for behavior. In other words, children come to believe that men and women should occupy different roles and have different psychological qualities.

Another implication of Chafetz's model is that women's achievement of higher paying work roles should increase women's micro power. This is why activism toward the goal of gender pay and promotion equity is so important. The model also suggests that male macro power results in gender ideologies, norms, and stereotypes that support a gendered division of labor and reinforce male power and privilege. This is one of the reasons that feminists work to increase the number of women in governmental and business power positions. Chapter 8 addresses how women come to occupy powerful political positions. In general, though, women are a minority in formal political positions.

Despite women's low power and few material resources, they do organize, mobilize, challenge, and change macro power institutions. This chapter presented evidence of this in the form of changed laws and union activity. Chapter 9 examines in more detail the dynamics of gender equality movements. Chapter 6 discusses economic development programs and women and provides additional examples of change brought about by women's activism.

Terms and Concepts

informal labor sector

formal labor sector

gender-based household
   divisions of labor

gender pay gap

gender job segregation

access discrimination

compensating differentials

human capital approach

gender wage discrimination

equal pay legislation

comparable worth

glass ceiling

concrete ceiling

quid pro quo sexual harassment

gender harassment

maquiladoras

sweatshops

self-employed women

women's micro- and small-scale
   enterprises (WMSEs)

unions

women entrepreneurs

legal literacy

economic empowerment

micro power

macro power

Study Questions

1. Why is the study of women's labor important to a study of women across cultures?

2. What evidence is there that women's labor is undercounted and undervalued? Why is this the case?

3. How is the fact that women are largely responsible for child care and household labor related to the gender pay gap, the glass ceiling, and women's micro and macro power?

4. What is the gender pay gap? How common is it? What are three explanations for it? What accounts for cross-cultural variation in the gender pay gap?

5. What is the glass ceiling? How common is it? What are the barriers to women's promotion?

6. How has legislation been used to remedy workplace gender inequalities such as the gender pay gap, the glass ceiling, sexual harassment, and inequalities arising from pregnancy and child-care responsibilities? Why has such legislation been less than effective?

7. What are the two types of sexual harassment, and how common are they? What groups of women are especially vulnerable to sexual harassment? What do sexual harassment researchers and activists mean when they say that sexual harassment is about power? What organizational factors play a role in the occurrence of sexual harassment?

8. What are sweatshops, and why do women work in them? How well paid are the women who work in them? What are the working conditions like? How can corporations get away with the way they treat these workers? What can be done?

9. Why do women make up such a large percentage of the self-employed? In what way is women's informal sector work devalued by economists? What are some of the difficulties facing self-employed women, and what have they done about them? How are self-employed women in industrialized nations somewhat different from those in less industrialized ones?

10. What does it mean to say that the effects of paid work on women are somewhat paradoxical? In what ways does working for pay benefit women?

Discussion Questions and Activities

1. Choose two jobs. One should be a "man's" job and one a "woman's" job. For each, make a separate list of the hazards, skills, and work involved, how heavy or light the work is, whether the work requires few or many decisions, whether the skills required are high or low, and whether the responsibility is high or low. Use your lists to decide the value of each job. Which is higher status? Which is paid more? What might you conclude about fairness? (adapted from Bullock, 1994)

2. Discuss with others whether they have experienced sexual harassment in the workplace. Ask them to describe the type of harassment (that is, verbal comments, sexual advances, sexual touching or posturing, sexual materials in the workplace), how it affected their productivity, and its emotional and physical effects. How did they handle it and why? How did the answers of females and males differ? Summarize your findings.

3. Where were your clothes made? Choose an article of your clothing. Write a short story about the life of the woman who made it. To make it realistic, use the information in the text on women in the global factory and information in Appendix A on the status of women in that country.

4. Discuss how the fact that women get pregnant, have children, and retain primary responsibility for children interferes with equal employment opportunities. This is a case in which women's differences from men mean that they need to be treated differently from men. Is this consistent with feminists' desire for women to be treated equally to men?

Women in Zimbabwe collect water from the village well in the Eastern Highlands for their families. Women play an important, though often neglected, role in world development.

Women and Development

6

> Development was to be a liberating project—a project for removal of poverty and leveling of socio-economic inequalities, based on class, ethnicity, and gender. While the dominant image of "development" persists as a class and gender neutral model of progress for all, the experience of "development" has been the opposite, polarizing the dichotomizing society, creating new forms of affluence for the powerful, and new forms of deprivation and dispossession for the weak.
>
> VANDANA SHIVA

*T*he study of women and development is an important part of internationally oriented women's studies (Staudt, 1995). Previous chapters have touched on the subject of women in developing countries. For instance, in Chapter 3, it was noted that family planning efforts, which are often a part of development programs, frequently fail to consider women. In the previous chapter on women and work, you learned about women in the global factory and women's work in the informal sector. This chapter takes a closer look at women in developing countries and how they are affected by economic development efforts in their countries. As you will see, gender equality has largely been ignored in development efforts. The result is that women's inequality is often untouched, and is sometimes aggravated, by development projects.

Background

Development Terminology

An introduction to development jargon is necessary first. The terms **Third World** and **developing nation** are usually used to describe the less or non-industrialized nations of the world. The United Nations identifies approximately 128 nations in Africa, Latin America, and Asia as "developing." The forty-eight identified as "least developed" are listed in Box 6.1. The **First World** countries are those such as the United States that are industrialized and market based. In recent years, the terms **northern** and **southern countries** have gained acceptance based on the relative geographic location of the industrialized nations in the north and developing nations in the south (Mermel & Simons, 1991; United Nations, 1997a).

BOX 6.1   Countries Identified as "Least Developed" by the UN

Afghanistan	Gambia	Niger
Angola	Guinea	Rwanda
Bangladesh	Guinea-Bissau	Samoa (Western)
Benin	Haiti	Sao Tome and Principe
Bhutan	Kiribati	Sierra Leone
Burkina Faso	Laos	Solomon Islands
Burundi	Lesotho	Somalia
Cambodia	Liberia	Sudan
Cape Verde	Madagascar	Tanzania
Central African Republic	Malawi	Togo
Chad	Maldives	Tuvalu
Comoros	Mali	Uganda
Djibouti	Mauritania	Vanuatu
Equatorial Guinea	Mozambique	Yemen
Eritrea	Myanmar	Zaire
Ethiopia	Nepal	Zambia

Source: United Nations, 1997a.

In a nation, development is the process of growth that may include the following: emphasis on large-scale economic growth; focus on small-scale community development projects aimed at increasing individuals' self-reliance; creation or improvement of national infrastructures such as roads; provision of credit, training, or services that enable people to participate more fully in the economic, political, and social lives of their communities; improvement in access to health care; mechanisms for increasing agricultural yield; increased access to education for women and children; and expanded opportunities for political development (Mermel & Simons, 1991). Development programs are often funded through foreign aid, either country to country (called bilateral aid) or through multilateral programs such as the World Bank, the IMF (International Monetary Fund), and other UN agencies.

Colonial History

Many of the countries in the south spent years as **colonies** of northern countries, some well into this century. For instance, the developing nation of Sri Lanka (formerly Ceylon) is an island country off the coast of India. It was dominated by Europeans for more than 400 years, first by the Portuguese in the sixteenth century, then by the Dutch, and later by the British, who controlled it until 1948. Only two countries in Africa were never colonies (Liberia and Ethiopia). The rest were controlled by Belgium, Britain, France, Portugal, Holland, Germany, and Spain until a lengthy decolonization period following World War II. As colonies, these countries were exploited as sources of cheap labor and resources. Typically, profits were not shared with the natives. These colonial experiences permanently altered cultural features such as language and economics and, some would argue, negatively impacted women's status and power. These colonial experiences also affect how developing nations interpret Western attempts to "help" them. This fact is relevant to our study here. Colonizers often defended their behavior on the grounds that they were doing native cultures a favor by remaking them in the Western image. The result, of course, was the loss of many native traditions and suspicion of Western intervention. Consequently, efforts to influence gender equality are often resisted with the charge of Western cultural imperialism.

Conditions in Developing Nations

Developing nations suffer not just from income poverty but from human poverty—a denial of choices and opportunities for living a tolerable life (United Nations, 1997a). According to the UN's 1997 *Human Development Report,* an estimated 1.3 billion people in the world live on less than $1 a day. Nearly half a billion people are illiterate, two-thirds of them women. Well over a billion people lack access to safe water, and 60 percent do not have access to adequate sanitation. Nearly a third of the people in the least developed countries are not expected to live past age 40. Nearly two-thirds of those infected with the AIDS virus live in developing countries. Box 6.2 gives a brief description of life in a developing country.

As in other parts of the world, women in developing nations are typically lower in status and power than are men, although there is some debate as to whether prior to colonialization this was as true as it is today. Many feminists argue that colonialization replaced egalitarian gender arrangements by removing women from the political decision-making spheres, limiting their access to and control over resources, and interfering with their legal rights and privileges (Boserup, 1970; Duley & Diduk, 1986; Sen & Grown, 1987). For instance, Western patrilineal notions of land ownership contributed to a situation in which women own hardly any of the world's land. Industrialization, which necessitated the movement of families into cities, increased women's dependence upon men for their livelihoods because offices and factories hire far fewer women than men, and urban work is often incompatible with the traditional female roles.

BOX 6.2   *Life in a Developing Country*

Heilbroner (1963) suggests that to understand economic development, we must have a picture of the problem with which it contends. Here is a condensed version of his attempt to take us there. Strip your house of its furniture and linens, except for a few blankets, the kitchen table, and a wooden chair. Empty your closet of clothes except for your oldest dress or pants and shirt. Empty your kitchen of appliances and food save for a box of matches, a few onions, and a dish of dried beans. Cut off the running water and the electricity. Now take away the house or apartment and move to a toolshed. You have no newspapers, books, or television (you can't read anyway). There are no government services, no hospital nearby. There is a clinic, but it is ten miles away and you have no transportation. This is what you have although you work 12 to 14 hours every day.

The **feminization of poverty** is especially marked in developing countries. Of the 1.3 billion people in poverty, 70 percent are women. In the southern countries, 60 percent of the illiterate are women, and female wages are only three-fourths of male wages. A third of married women in developing countries are battered by their husbands. More than half of the pregnant women in southern countries suffer from anemia, which leads to low birth weights and maternal illness. Over 98 percent of women's deaths and illnesses from reproductive causes occur to women in developing countries. Life expectancy, educational attainment, and income are especially low for women relative to men in the southern countries of Sierra Leone, Niger, Burkina Faso, Mali, and Ethiopia (United Nations, 1997a). As the poorest of the poor, women in developing countries work extremely hard for the basic survival of their families. In some ways women may be perceived as a last colony or as a "Fourth World." Women, and colonies, are often low-wage or nonwage producers who are structurally subordinate and dependent and overwhelmingly poor (Acosta-Belen & Bose, 1995).

Economic Development and Gender Equality

Historically, most **development programs** have focused on economic growth and a conversion to market economies. The assumption was that other forms of development (that is, political and social development) would follow. This idea is commonly associated with **modernization theory.** In reality, economic growth can lead to increased income inequalities and can leave social and political inequalities untouched. Women are among the many social groups that frequently suffer severe economic and social dislocation as a result of development plans and projects (Howard, 1995). For example, according to the Food and Agriculture Organization of the United Nations (FAO), the introduction of high-yielding varieties of rice in Asia have displaced women's wage-earning opportunities through mechanization. Development projects focusing on irrigation systems for cash crops (crops grown for cash rather than local food production) are another good example of how development projects often negatively impact women. Such projects often divert water away from home gardens and other domestic uses, making it more difficult for women to provide for their families' food and water needs.

Another good example of how development strategies often negatively impact women involves what is called structural readjustment. In the 1980s, Third World commodity prices dropped, interest rates rose, and many developing nations could not make payments on their development loans. Debtor countries were forced to turn to the International Monetary Fund (IMF), the UN's international banking agency. The IMF imposed a series of reforms as a condition of loaning additional money, for they were convinced that without reforms, debt would continue to grow. These conditions, part of what are called **structural adjustment programs (SAPs),** were imposed by governments to save and raise money. Unfortunately, many of these SAP impositions affect women more than men. For instance, cuts in wages and social services and rises in the costs of basic goods and services have a greater impact on women because it is generally women who are responsible for providing food, water, and health care for family members (Blumberg, 1995; Lorentzen & Turpin, 1996; Mosse, 1993; World Resources Institute, 1994–95). For instance, when medical services are cut, it is women's workload that increases because they are responsible for taking care of ill family members. If water service is unreliable, it is women and children who have to walk longer distances or stand longer in line. When food is in short supply, men and boys generally suffer less than women and girls, who are expected to limit their consumption so that the males can eat (Mosse, 1993).

The fact that some southern countries outperform richer industrialized countries in gender equality in political, economic, and professional activities also demonstrates that economic development does not necessarily lead to increased gender equality. For instance, Barbados is ahead of Belgium, Italy, and Greece on indicators of gender equality; Trinidad and Tobago outrank Portugal; the Bahamas does better than the United Kingdom; France is behind Suriname, Colombia, and Botswana; Japan is behind China, Guatemala, and Mexico (United Nations, 1997a). This shows that gender equality can be achieved at different stages of development and that economic development is no guarantee of women's equality.

"Experience shows that investing in women is one of the most cost-effective ways of promoting development. As mothers, as producers or suppliers of food, fuel, and water, as traders and manufacturers, as political and community leaders, women are at the center of the process of change."
Gro Harlem Brundtland

Feminist Concerns with the Development Process

The United Nations' 1986 *Declaration on the Right to Development* defines development as the right of "every human person and all peoples . . . to participate in, contribute to and enjoy economic, social, cultural and political development, in which all human rights and fundamental freedoms can be fully realized." Given such a definition you might expect that development efforts would include the promotion of gender equality. The reality is generally otherwise. Development in practice is usually defined narrowly—as activities that generate income—such that the promotion of women's equality is seen as separate from development. Success is typically measured in terms of increases in gross national product, per capita income, literacy rates, life expectancy, and decreased fertility rates (Acosta-Belen & Bose, 1995). Development programs have largely continued women's segregation in labor that generates the lowest wages and prestige (Acosta-Belen & Bose, 1995). The invisibility of women in development efforts was especially true until the 1970s, when feminists began voicing their concerns (Anand, 1993).

Failures and False Assumptions

A 1970 book by Ester Boserup, *Women's Role in Economic Development,* was perhaps the first major text in the women and development literature (Mosse, 1993). As Boserup says in the opening sentences of the book, "In the vast and ever growing literature on economic development, reflections on the particular problems of women are few and far between" (p. 5). Boserup's research fostered an understanding of the dual aspects of colonial and contemporary development policies, which ideologically denigrated women's economic contributions while relying on and exploiting their labor (Acosta-Belen & Bose, 1995). She also showed that economic development has a differential impact on men and women and that the impact on women was often negative (Beneria & Roldan, 1987).

"It is not possible to address society's needs at any level while ignoring the perspectives, priorities, and knowledge of more than half of the world's population."
Rosina Wilshire

Boserup's book stimulated a number of feminist critiques of development programs. One common criticism is that the programs fail to acknowledge that women's work both inside and outside the home is vital to development. The absence of women in the public sphere, along with an emphasis on their role as homemakers and child-rearers, has led to a devaluing of their productive labor in the development process (Anand, 1993). Because work is viewed in terms of participation in the paid labor force, all the productive labor women perform in and around their households is not considered work and therefore is not targeted for development assistance (Mosse, 1993).

A related criticism is that traditional development programs tend to focus on men's labor under the assumption that what benefits men trickles down to benefit women. Traditional development programs often assume a gender-role arrangement in which men are breadwinners and women are homemakers. Consequently, the programs focus on fostering wage earning by male heads of household and on adult women in domestic homemaking roles. For instance, through much of the 1970s, development efforts targeted at women viewed women primarily as mothers by focusing on mother–child health programs, feeding schemes, family planning, food aid, and so on. Many such programs continue today. Moser (1989) calls this the **welfare**

approach. As Mosse (1993) points out, these programs do not do much to create independence and self-reliance among women, but they are politically safe in that they do not challenge women's traditional roles.

The assumption that males should be heads of households and that all households have a male to do so has led to the channeling of development resources through men (Youseff, 1995). This has led to a situation in which women without husbands are doubly disadvantaged because they often lack even indirect access to development resources (Bryceson, 1995). Development programs have typically increased males' but not females' access to important sources of development such as land, credit, cattle, and technical know-how. All these things maintain women's dependence on men. It also means that divorced, widowed, or abandoned women are particularly vulnerable to poverty. Female-headed households are on the rise all over the world, and female-headed households are the poorest group in every country. Women already head more than a fifth of households in Africa and the Caribbean, and 15 percent of those in Latin America, the Middle East, and North Africa (Dankelman & Davidson, 1991).

Development programs often provide resources on the basis of land ownership. Land can be used as collateral for loans, and it is assumed that those who own the land also have the power to implement development suggestions. In short, secure access to land often goes hand in hand with access to development credit and training, and because laws and local practices typically disfavor women's property ownership, women are often denied development resources. In Asia, this is largely due to laws that favor male inheritance. Similarly, in many Latin American countries (such as Chile, the Dominican Republic, Ecuador, Guatemala, Mexico, and Paraguay), according to law it is the husband who is the administrator of the conjugal property. In Africa, land was traditionally "owned" collectively in the sense that it was shared by a community. As the notion of private ownership of land has developed, it has largely excluded ownership of land by women under the assumption that women will be provided for by male kin. Having little access to land for purposes of collateral, women are often unable to obtain cheap credit. This makes it difficult for them to develop economically. Likewise, lack of access to cattle ownership significantly reduces the economic power of rural women in developing nations, and development programs generally do not provide draft animals to those who are not landowners. Draft animals, which pull plows through fields, are particularly important in terms of increasing agricultural yields. Profits go down when there is no access to draft power or when it must be borrowed, exchanged, or hired.

According to the Food and Agriculture Organization (FAO) of the United Nations, extension workers also bypass women because women often do not own or control the land they farm and are therefore unable to obtain the credit to put extension education into action (FAOb). Extension programs, in which out-of-school educational services are offered to rural producers, have largely ignored the needs and priorities of women. A 1989 FAO global survey on extension services found that women only received between

2 and 10 percent of all extension contacts and a mere 5 percent of extension resources worldwide. In Africa, this may be seen in development projects in which male extension workers deliver technical information to a male clientele and in which the focus is on the production of cash crops. Because women's farming is often for cultivation of food for the family rather than for sale, their farming does not generally receive rural development moneys and attention. For instance, although women manage almost 80 percent of Africa's agriculture, they are not considered to be the farmers (Anand, 1993). In Asia, women provide 40 to 50 percent of the labor for rice production, and in Latin America, women do 30 to 40 percent of the agricultural work. Despite women's key role in agriculture, gender bias and gender blindness persist: Farmers are still generally perceived as male by policymakers, development planners, and agricultural service deliverers (FAOd).

According to the FAO, cultural and religions customs further reduce women's access to extension workers. The majority of extension workers are men, and women are not permitted to interact with men in some parts of the world. Some efforts have been made to solve this problem through the hiring and training of more female extension workers, but male extension workers still outnumber female ones. Another problem is that women's workloads are such that they cannot get to the demonstrations or take part in the training courses (FAOa).

Consequences to Women of Development's Failings

One serious consequence of the failure to consider women's work in the development process is that, in most cases, development projects have not positively influenced women's considerable workload. Women's work as the primary household food producers and preparers, and as water and fuel gatherers, goes largely unappreciated and unaided even as this workload grows because of resource depletion and pollution. For instance, in rural Africa, women have to travel longer and longer distances to collect clean water, and they must spend more and more time coaxing crops from depleted soils (Bryceson, 1995). Box 6.3 gives you an idea of the average work day for a woman in the developing nation of Nepal. You can probably readily think of tools or technologies that would significantly reduce her work burden.

Yet another problem is that by encouraging or assuming a Western version of gender-role arrangements, development programs have contributed to erosions in women's status. The development projects of the 1960s and 1970s were predicated on the notion that a male breadwinner and female housewife was a desired goal. This mentality pervaded national and international agents of development, and that, combined with local patriarchal beliefs, contributed to women's continued lower status and power relative to men. Rogers (1980), in a highly influential book called *The Domestication of Women,* argues that development efforts up to this time were designed to encourage women's conforming to Western middle-class notions of the housewife role. By failing to provide incentives for women as producers,

---

BOX 6.3   *A Typical Day's Work for a Nepalese Woman*

Get up at 4:00 A.M.

Pack up the bedding.

Prepare morning tea.

Sweep the house and the courtyard clean.

Prepare breakfast.

Process milk into yogurt, buttermilk, and ghee.

Winnow grain; prepare rice, dahls; grind spices.

Fetch fuel and water.

Clean dishes.

Feed, clothe, and wash children.

Wash and mend clothes.

Spread out bedding at night.

Mend the house.

Care for cows, chickens, and donkeys.

These things are largely done without labor-saving devices. For instance, rice is hulled with a stick, clothes are washed in the river, cow dung is used to mend the house, water is hauled from far away, and there is no plumbing.

Source: Mosse, 1993.

---

development projects eroded what had been a source of power and status for women. For instance, in many developing nations it is women who traditionally engage in improving and innovating plant and animal varieties. This important source of status and control for women is lost when development projects give men, but not women, access to improved seed varieties and other farming technologies, as is typically the case (FAOe).

As Mosse (1993) notes, many development projects resulted in women changing from being independent producers and providers to being housewives economically dependent upon men as controllers of cash income. Furthermore, with cash, men gain access to banks and other modern institutions, leaving women further behind (Mosse, 1993). The idea that progress involves the promotion of the male breadwinner/female homemaker roles also interferes with the extension of loan moneys to women entrepreneurs, although their high rates of repayment are well documented.

Women in Development Approach

These criticisms did have some impact. For instance, in 1973 the U.S. Congress enacted the Percy Amendment to the Foreign Assistance Act. It required that bilateral programs "give particular attention to those . . . activities that tend to integrate women into the national economies of foreign countries, thus improving their status and assisting the total development effort" (World Resources Institute, 1994–95). By the 1980s many development programs made at least token efforts to include women. As the negative effects on women of technocratic, growth-oriented development projects became apparent, an approach arose that is often called the **women in development (WID)** approach (Howard, 1995). WID demanded increased attention to women's development needs and emphasized women's productive labor. WID projects may be classified into three general types: (1) income-generating projects, (2) projects that provide labor-saving technologies, and (3) projects that improve women's local resource access.

Income-Generating Projects

In the 1980s, development efforts directed at women turned away from a home economics approach and began focusing on fostering women's economic participation in the public sphere. The thought is that women enhance family well-being and their own power within the household and society when they earn money, thereby increasing their status (Acevedo, 1995; Bryceson, 1995). **Income-generating projects** remain one of the most common types of women's projects.

Buvinic (1995) summarizes the effects of development projects in enhancing women's income-earning opportunities as "negligible at best, and perverse at worst" (p. 220). The typical income-generating project for women focuses on traditional female skills such as sewing, embroidery, and handicrafts—all low in marketability and profit in comparison to the skills taught to men (Bryceson, 1995; Youseff, 1995). The projects are often unsuccessful because they are launched before it has been determined that there is a market for the goods produced and because they fail to take into account the work women must also do in the household. As Bryceson (1995) put it, women's overbooked working day is a major stumbling block to their involvement in commodity production for pay, or in its improving their quality of life. Or as Buvinic (1995) says,

> The perverse effects from such poorly conceived income-generation projects for women are magnified when not only are the women unable to generate income as a result of the training, but the training itself has imposed additional demands on their time, thus negatively affecting the welfare of both the women and their children. (p. 220)

It is increasingly evident that the process of development benefits women only if and when it addresses the double burdens of production and reproduction carried by women (Afshar, 1991).

Another problem is that this type of income-generating program frequently fails to include women in the project design process. Women are typically presented with the program instead of being asked to generate their own ideas. Involving women directly in the development process would increase the likelihood that there would be a market for the item produced

"There is a need to reconceptualize a development paradigm that can promote equity, social justice, sustainability, and self-determination."
Filomina Steady

and that the choice of item could be produced within the constraints of women's workload. It would also give women organizational skills and a sense of empowerment that would last long after the donor has left the area. Under these conditions, income-generating projects can positively contribute to women's status and power. Mosse (1993) tells of such a project in Bangladesh. Each member of a women's group saved a handful of rice a week, which they pooled and sold for cash. After a year, the women had enough cash as a group to take over the lease of a piece of land. The women grew rice on the land and generated more money. This experience gave the women even more confidence to effect changes around them. They successfully lobbied to have the road to their village repaired and to reduce the amount of dowries.

Although development programs sometimes still include small-scale income-generating development projects for women, particularly in rural areas, the trend since the mid-1980s is toward the employment of women by transnational corporations. As noted in Chapter 5, these corporations have significantly increased profits by having much of their product assemblywork done by low-waged women workers in developing nations. Indeed, women's work for transnationals constitutes a growing proportion of women's work in currently developing countries, especially in Asia, Latin America, and the Caribbean (Ward & Pyle, 1995). This situation is encouraged by international development and financial institutions such as the World Bank and the IMF as a way to generate income to pay off development loans.

As you read in Chapter 5, this situation demonstrates that wage earning per se is no guarantee of a better life for women. The women working for transnationals frequently face harsh and unsafe working conditions, sexual harassment, and discrimination. In some places, such as Colombia and Indonesia, women are paid less than a subsistence wage because it is assumed they live with their family or a husband (Ward & Pyle, 1995). This situation keeps them from economic independence. Furthermore, efforts to organize for better conditions or wages often result in corporations' relocation to other low-wage countries. "Homework," assemblywork done in the home, has increased throughout the world and is often chosen by women who seek to combine wage earning with domestic responsibilities. Homeworkers are typically paid far less than factory workers. In short, women in low-level, dead-end jobs with low wages and high household workloads relative to men do not necessarily benefit from wage earning. However, traditional measures of development success, such as increased GNP and per capita income, may lead to the perception that development based on providing low-cost labor to transnationals is an effective development strategy.

Labor-Saving Technologies

Women's quality of life in developing countries is significantly affected by the lack of technologies, including relatively simple tools. Therefore, it is certainly logical that labor-saving technologies are an important aspect of development projects targeted toward women. A number of development projects have reduced women's labor loads by providing such things as grinding mills, pumps, or cooking stoves. The main criticism of these projects is that they have disseminated only a narrow range of devices that only begin to address the reality of women's multitask responsibilities (Bryceson, 1995). Also, because development agencies frequently fail to consult the women whom they wish to reach, the tools are often unsuccessful. For instance, in Ethiopia, where women are the primary water collectors, women were not consulted in the design of a water development program. Because of this, a pump that required two hands to operate was installed. Due to the traditional round-bottomed water jar used for collection, this meant that two people were required to collect the water (Mosse, 1993).

Women's Access to Development Resources

The UN's Convention on the Elimination of Discrimination Against Women (CEDAW) specifically addresses the rights of women in development. Article 14(9) of the convention promises women the right to "have access to agricultural credit and loans, marketing facilities, appropriate technology and equal treatment in land and agrarian reform as well as land resettlement schemes." As already noted, women's access to credit and loans is inhibited by the fact that they are unlikely to own land to use as collateral. But the problem is apparently more than collateral. As structural adjustment programs shifted the brunt of economic problems to the poor, they survived by creating their own livelihoods in the urban informal economic sector. For instance, women microentrepreneurs do such things as run beauty parlors out of their homes and make tortillas or clothing and sell them in the marketplace. In the 1980s and 1990s, aiding microentrepreneurs in the form of small loans became a popular form of development aid; however, male entrepreneurs are more likely to receive aid than females (Blumberg, 1995). This is partly due to the faulty assumptions that women are not serious entrepreneurs, that they would default on their loans, and that their businesses have no growth potential.

"The evidence indicates that . . . women microentrepreneurs . . . tend to do their utmost to succeed. They benefit (although they may increase their workday and self-exploitation), their children benefit, the credit project benefits, and the planet's equity account becomes a little less tilted toward power, privilege, and patriarchy."
Rae Lesser Blumberg

Loan practices also make it more difficult for women to obtain loans. For instance, many programs prohibit loaning money for certain types of activities or require a male cosigner for women (but permit men to be sole signers). Forrester (1995) points out that the reluctance to lend to women is ironic given that women have a repayment rate of 90 percent, even when interest rates are over 20 percent. Evidence from Bangladesh, the Dominican Republic, Guatemala, and Indonesia indicates that women microentrepreneurs have a payback record at least as good or better than men's (Blumberg, 1995). Furthermore, Blumberg's (1995) research in the Dominican Republic, Ecuador, and Guatemala found that women's microenterprises often produce as many or more jobs than men's and often grow faster than men's.

Although women are excluded from most conventional lending schemes, there are some programs that do extend loans to women for small-scale economic enterprises. The best-known is probably Bangladesh's Grameen Bank, which grants small loans to help women set up microenterprises. The bank now has 3 million members in 37,000 villages. Nearly half of the women who have received their grants are no longer living in poverty, according to the United States Agency for International Development (Wright, 1995a). At least five other nongovernmental agencies in Bangladesh have adopted the collateral-free loan system of the Grameen Bank (Amin & Li, 1997). At this point, there are literally thousands of nongovernmental organizations throughout Asia, Africa, and Latin America that use revolving credit funds and lend disproportionately to women (Fisher, 1996). For instance, BancoSol in Bolivia makes small loans of about 100 to 200 U.S. dollars for microenterprises, has a zero default rate, and has approximately 45,000 female clients (Buvinic, 1995). Women's credit programs benefit women in many ways. Studies indicate that women's credit programs positively impact on their contraceptive use and nutritional status via the mechanisms of increased empowerment and autonomy (Amin & Li, 1997).

Gender and Development Approach

Almost thirty years have passed since Boserup (1970) offered her critique of traditional development programs. Have development programs significantly improved in their attendance to women's needs during this time period? The answer is yes and no. It is true that many development programs make an effort to include women, but it is also true that these efforts are often token ones. Mosse (1993) notes that too many development projects still take the form of a main project for men, plus ten sewing machines tagged on to show that the project has considered gender. It is also the case that many projects still fail to consider women. A 1995 internal review of the World Bank, arguably the largest and most influential source of development aid and advice, found that only 615 of the 4,955 development projects from 1967 to 1993 included at least minimal measures to explicitly address the needs of women (Buvinic, Gwin, & Bates, 1996).

There are different ways of including women in the development process, some of which go further to address women's lower status and power than do others. Indeed, despite increased attention to women in development, development programs have for the most part failed to increase women's status. Rogers (1982), in a study of Tanzania, wrote that the failure of development programs to increase women's status is traceable to ignoring the basic structure of gender relations. Likewise, Howard (1995) argues that WID masks the need for specific women's rights activism, making it seem as though women are not being left out of the development process. She contends, though, that the inclusion of women in traditional development projects does not usually further women's rights. These projects are ineffective in promoting women's equality because they aim at increasing economic growth and not at changing the traditional cultural beliefs that underlie women's subordination. Changes in the political and ideological spheres, as well as the economic, are needed. Howard recommends the specific allocation of development moneys for women's development in the areas of education and politics. In this way, women would have the tools to advocate for their equality. She notes that although this type of development activity would not directly increase economic growth, it would likely ensure that women's rights are furthered.

These concerns are consistent with what has become known as the **empowerment approach,** or the **gender and development approach (GAD).** The GAD approach tries to take into account women's lives and labor, both inside and outside of the home. In addition, it emphasizes a "bottom-up" approach in which women are not as much integrated into development as they are the architects of their own development. Projects based on a GAD approach involve encouraging women to bring about positive change through women's organizations and activism. Mosse (1993) suggests that GAD differs from other approaches to women and development in that it sees the goals of development for women in terms of self-reliance and strength. GAD puts less emphasis on legislating for gender equality (a top-down approach) and more emphasis on empowering women themselves to work to change and transform the structures that contributed to their subordination (a bottom-up approach). Moser (1989) terms this approach the empowerment approach because of its emphasis on the full equality of women.

Feminists from the south, in particular those in the organization DAWN (Development with Women for a New Era), have been important players in the formulation of a new concept of development according to feminist ideals (Braniotti, Charkiewicz, Hausler, & Wieringa, 1994; Sen & Grown, 1987). DAWN, launched as a Third World initiative in 1984, includes representatives from Asia, Africa, Latin America, the Pacific, and the Caribbean. Many influential Third World feminists are members. DAWN's main purpose is to mobilize opinion and to create a global support network for equitable development (Dankelman & Davidson, 1988). Brandiotti and colleagues (1994) summarize the DAWN position as follows:

1. Rejecting the separation of the private and public domains.

2. Promoting women's empowerment through larger international and societal changes.

3. Advocating equitable development based on the values of cooperation, resistance to hierarchies, sharing, accountability, and commitment to peace.

4. Acknowledging that women's empowerment can only come about by examining the interrelationships between gender, race, class, and nationality.

5. Emphasizing political mobilization, consciousness raising, and popular education as crucial to women's empowerment.

This quote from Peggy Antrobus of Barbados, DAWN's current coordinator, characterizes the DAWN philosophy:

> We must clarify the links between environmental degradation and the structures of social, economic and political power . . . the links between decisions made in boardrooms, parliaments and military command centers and the conditions under which we live . . . the links between the structure of our own subordination as women and the processes by which this subordination serves to perpetuate all other systems of oppression. (Seager, 1993, pp.280–281)

It remains to be seen just how much of an influence the GAD approach will have on development programs. As Chen (1995) points out, it is increasingly evident that women's problems are not just economic but are also structural and political, and it is difficult to translate this knowledge into specific programs and policies. Development agencies are talking some good talk, but it is too soon to tell how much will translate into action. Most of the leading development agencies have added GAD-sounding rhetoric to their mission or goal statements and have at least begun to acknowledge the need to consider women in development. As the UN's 1997 *Human Development Report* points out, if development is not "engendered it is endangered," and if development strategies "fail to empower women, they will fail to empower society." Or, consider these three very GAD-sounding strategic objectives of the UN's Food and Agriculture Organization Plan of Action for Women in Development (1996–2001):

1. To promote gender-based equity in the access to, and control of, productive resources.
2. To enhance women's participation in decision and policy-making processes at all levels.
3. To promote actions to reduce rural women's workload and enhance their opportunities for remunerated employment and income.

The FAO now has a department, Women in Development Service (SDWW) devoted to the implementation of the FAO plan of action for women in development. As well, there is a committee comprised of representatives from all FAO departments charged with advising the director-general on policies and strategies for the integration of women into FAO programs.

OXFAM, a nongovernmental development aid organization based in the United Kingdom, has also made changes consistent with a gender and development approach. In 1985 the gender and development unit was created to ensure that OXFAM's development and relief programs will improve the quality of women's lives. OXFAM's gender policy states a commitment to the following: promoting the empowerment of women, confronting social and ideological barriers to the improvement of women's status, promoting women's independent access to development resources, helping women exercise their rights over their bodies and protect themselves from violence, and promoting initiatives with a gender focus.

OXFAM has put these ideas into practice in a number of different ways. For instance, in India and Serbia they provided funding to local programs devoted to making gender violence against women visible and unacceptable and that provided women with options in cases of violence against them. Another OXFAM example is that of a program designed to help families displaced by civil conflict in rural Andean Peru. Initially, OXFAM supplied seed, llamas for breeding stock, and agricultural training to male heads of households although 40 percent of the families were headed by females. Also, the initial program did not support the labor contributions that women make to their families. OXFAM brought in a team of gender advisors who noted that women were being disempowered by the way aid was being provided. The program was altered to include support for communal vegetable gardens (so that women could feed their families); funds for small livestock production (to be consumed by the family or sold and traded); training in agricultural production, nutrition, and project management; and the strengthening of women's organizations.

"Women are community managers, farmers, water collectors, entrepreneurs, caretakers of fragile ecologies, and as mothers they daily create and maintain life. Only when their expertise and value are realized will development initiatives have half a chance of succeeding."
Julia Mosse

Although these efforts represent notable progress, as Brandiotti and colleagues (1994) point out, "adding women on" in this way hasn't stimulated the more radical societal changes necessary for gender equality. The GAD view of development represents a radical departure from the way development is commonly practiced. Therefore, although popular among development practitioners working within a feminist framework, it is viewed with suspicion by many aid agencies and Third World governments (Mosse, 1993). Part of this has to do with developing nations' past history with colonialism. Western donor agencies currently espouse a neutrality toward local customs and mores to avoid charges of cultural imperialism. Of course, patriarchy being the rule rather than the exception, this would mean that development projects aimed at increased gender equality would not be in keeping with cultural neutrality. Consequently, donor agencies often play it safe by funding more traditional women in development projects.

Women, the Environment, and Sustainable Development

Vandana Shiva is an Indian physicist, spokesperson, and activist in the Indian movement for sustainable development.

In the mid-1980s, the United Nations, environmentalists, and policymakers concerned with the environment called attention to the environmental consequences of traditional development. Their main charge was that development, in both the north and the south, was not sustainable. There are a number of ways to define sustainability, but the general idea is that **sustainable development** "meets the needs of the present without compromising the ability of future generations to meet their own needs" (World Commission on Environment and Development, 1987). Another good definition comes from

Rosina Wilshire, manager of the Gender in Development Program of the United Nations Development Program. She defines sustainable development as "development that promotes human well-being and human dignity while regenerating and protecting the natural resource base so that the issues of empowerment and equity are central to development, which cannot be equated with economic growth per se" (1995, pp. 127–128.) (You will appreciate Wilshire's definition as you read further.) This section explores women's role in promoting sustainable development, but first, some sustainability basics are in order.

Sustainability Basics

Environmental indicators suggest that much of the development in both northern and southern nations is not sustainable. It is a fact that economic development has environmental consequences, many of which may significantly impact human health and survival. The environment is called an eco*system* for a reason: Like other systems, change in one part affects the others. Take the case of deforestation, a problem faced on almost every continent but especially in developing nations. Trees hold soil in place, and, consequently, deforestation contributes to soil erosion. Agricultural yields are significantly decreased when valuable topsoil washes away. But the animal waste often used for fertilizer may be burned for fuel when there are no trees left. This means that petrochemical fertilizers must be used to increase agricultural yields. However, over time these build up and increase the salinity of the soil. This results in desertification, which means that nothing will grow. Runoff of agricultural fertilizers pollutes waterways, thus reducing the amount of drinkable water and killing fish. Deforestation also contributes to global warming as trees are major consumers of deadly carbon dioxide gases. These are but some of the many effects of deforestation. The bottom line is that shortages of the basics of life, such as food, water, and clean air, may occur when development is not sustainable.

Upon reflection, it may seem obvious that development should be conducted with regard to the future. However, the situation becomes muddier when considering the role of the north in southern development. Development in the southern countries is often guided and in many cases controlled by the northern countries who supply the capital for development. These northern countries, such as the United States, gain many of the benefits and bear few of the costs of development in the south. The northern countries benefit from higher profits from lower labor and materials costs, weaker environmental laws, and lower priced goods, thus permitting the continuation of high-consumption lifestyles. The environmental costs are borne largely by the citizens of the southern countries, especially the poor, who are disproportionately women and children.

You may not understand why the southern countries accept this type of development, but this too is complex. First, you must remember that some of the fault lies at the doorstep of the economic development strategies encouraged by traditional development programs. These programs encourage the replacement of small, localized economies with market-based economies that produce goods for export to generate cash. International development programs arrange large loans (sometimes in the millions and billions of dollars) but in return often dictate what type of development is to occur. Funding is done on the basis of a project's potential to make money, with environmental sustainability rarely considered. Remember also that economic progress is typically measured in terms of short-run economic goals, such as increases in per capita income and gross national product. Developing nations must demonstrate this type of progress in order to receive more aid.

To make matters worse, what has often happened is that the cash generated goes to pay the interest on the loans. This results in a high debt burden, aggravated when international markets fluctuate and prices fall. To come up with the money simply to pay the interest on their loans, governments are often forced to sell goods at bottom prices and to exploit fragile natural resources. Multinational corporations are increasingly part of this equation. Their primary interest in their own profit and growth strategies frequently means that they are largely unconcerned with the effects of their practices on local environments and people. The people lose: They remain poor because they often cannot eat or use the commodity produced for export, and their health suffers as governments cut down on food subsidies and government health services to repay development loans. Furthermore, the environmental resources on which the people depend are often degraded in the process.

I said earlier that there are serious questions about the sustainability of development in both the north and the south, but you should note some important differences. The north's contribution to environmental degradation arises out of a consumer lifestyle. For instance, consider this evidence of consumption: Northern families spend an average of $9 billion a year on video games for their children and $7.5 billion to care for their lawns (World Resources Institute, 1994–95). The conspicuous consumption of the north, which includes a heavy diet of fossil fuels and nonrenewable resources (once they're gone, they're gone) contributes to *global* environmental problems such as ozone depletion and global warming. These are problems that degrade the global commons—the environmental resources we all share. In contrast, in the developing nations of the south, the major damage is to local renewable resources such as water and land. Furthermore, unlike in the northern countries, the damage is done in the quest to meet basic needs, not to sustain a consumer lifestyle. Currently, about half of the world's poorest people earn their livelihoods in ecologically fragile areas. Such people often have little choice for survival other than to contribute to resource depletion and pollution.

Women and Sustainability

Also, unlike in the north, the consequences of insustainable development in the south fall largely on the shoulders of the poor of those nations, especially the women. This is because women are the primary cultivators and gatherers of food, water, and fuel for family consumption in southern nations, and environmental degradation significantly increases the amount of time that must be spent on these tasks. Because poor women rely heavily on natural resources, they are among the first to notice and feel the effects of environmental stress (Steady, 1995). Environmental degradation often increases women's workloads. Women are working harder and harder to coax crops from tired soils. They are traveling farther and farther to collect fuel, fodder, and water. For example, in the foothills of the Himalayas, the gathering of firewood and fodder took no more than two hours a generation ago; now it takes a full day of walking through mountainous terrain (World Resources Institute, 1994–95). Similar cases are found in India, Peru, and in other parts of Africa (Dankelman & Davidson, 1988). Some 30 percent of women in Egypt walk over an hour a day to meet water needs, and in some parts of Africa, women and children spend eight hours a day collecting water (FAOf). In El Salvador, where 80 percent of the natural vegetation has been destroyed and 77 percent of the soil has been lost or degraded, it is increasingly difficult for peasant women to find firewood and food (Lorentzen & Turpin, 1996). Women's health is also affected by environmental degradation (Steady, 1995). For example, poor women must often cook with wood, crop residue, and animal dung, and they suffer respiratory disease, anemia, and cancer as a result (World Resources Institute, 1994–95). Carrying heavy loads of wood, often on their head, for long distances damages the spine and causes problems with childbearing (Dankelman & Davidson, 1988). As the primary water carriers and managers, they have the most contact with polluted water and are therefore most vulnerable to water-related diseases (INSTRAW, 1991). The longer hours women work because of environmental degradation also cause health problems. For example, a study of Sri Lankan women concluded that they suffered from persistent sleep deprivation because of their multiple roles (Lorentzen & Turpin, 1996).

Women of the south play a critical role in sustainable development for two main reasons. First, in many cases they are the main managers of local natural resources. According to the World Resources Institute, for centuries women have managed forests and used forest products. In developing nations, they are the ones who collect fuel, fodder, and food from trees and other plants. In the south, women are also largely responsible for collecting, supplying, and managing water. Also, in most of the developing world, women are significant agriculturists. Unfortunately, acknowledging of the role that women play in resource use has sometimes led to blaming them for environmental degradation. However, it is important to realize that Third World women often have no choice but to exploit natural resources in order to survive, even though they may have the knowledge to promote sustainability (Dankelman & Davidson, 1988). Furthermore, there is evidence that significantly more ecological damage results from development practices such as commercial logging and high-tech agricultural practices. For instance, the main contributor to deforestation is commercial harvesting and the clearing of land for large-scale agriculture, not women collecting fuelwood (Brandiotti et al., 1994; Elliot, 1996). Indeed, as Shiva (1996) suggests, development projects have impaired the productivity and

"In the Third World, because women have remained in intimate contact with nature, they often give the early warning signals that something is wrong with the environment."
Vandana Shiva

renewability of nature by removing land, water, and forests from women's management and control.

A second reason why women are important to sustainable development is that they often possess important knowledge about sustainability in their environments. For instance, they often know which varieties of seed will yield drought- and pest-resistant plants and which seeds do not require petro-chemical fertilizers. They often know which trees are easiest to grow and have the most practical value in their culture as sources of food, fuel, and medicine. Their knowledge of water sources and water quantity and quality during wet and dry seasons makes them important sources of information when water resources are being developed. Ecofeminists see this knowledge as evidence of women's interconnectedness with nature. They draw a parallel between the desire of industrialization to conquer nature and the desire of men to dominate women (Tinker, 1994). Box 6.4 briefly discusses **ecofeminism** and Vandana Shiva, an ecofeminist leader in India.

Filomina Chioma Steady from Sierra Leone was appointed special advisor on women and the environment and development to the Secretary General of the United Nations Conference on Economic Development (otherwise known as the Rio Earth Summit). According to Steady (1995), there are four main obstacles to increasing women's involvement in the promotion of sustainable development. One of these is the debt problem facing developing nations that has led to the promotion of export-led growth at the expense of the environment. A second problem arises from development programs and policies dominated by men who are not always aware of the gender implications of program planning and implementation. For instance, the fact that women are marginalized into the private sphere means that their close connection to ecosystem health is overlooked and undervalued (Elliot, 1996). The low level of participation by women in decision-making positions is a third obstacle Steady identifies. Women are not only underrepresented in the formal institutions of states, but in development agencies and nongovernmental development organizations as well. A fourth obstacle is the dominant ideology that development should be propelled by the domination of nature. Current patterns of development and the use and management of natural resources are in line with male values that see the relationship with nature as one of control (Elliot, 1996). Steady (1995) suggests that these barriers mean that women's environmental organizations and movements hold the key to sustainable development in many countries.

Although it is easy to view women as victims of ecological crisis, a look at the mobilization of women to prevent ecological destruction shows the extraordinary abilities of women to organize and combat ecological destruction (Sontheimer, 1991). As Shiva (1988) says, "I know for certain, no matter where you go, that if there is a scarcity of water, women have protested; if there has been an overfelling of trees, women have resisted it." Women's mobilization for the environment demonstrates the courage women have shown in the battle against the growing ecological degradation that surrounds them and against the traditional power structures that subordinate their needs (Sontheimer, 1991). As Elliot (1996) notes, women must not just

"Women give life. We have the capacity to give life and light. We can take up our brooms and sweep the earth."
Isabelle Letelier

BOX 6.4 *Ecofeminism*

Simply put, ecofeminism suggests that the domination of women and the domination of nature are intricately connected and that women are particularly suited to lead ecological movements to save the planet (Sachs, 1997). That being said, in truth ecofeminism means different things to different people (Merchant, 1992; Sachs, 1997; Sturgeon, 1997). For example, *cultural ecofeminists* suggest that menstruation, pregnancy, and childbirth bring women closer to nature and are a source of women's power and environmental activism. In contrast, *social ecofeminists* emphasize how capitalism and patriarchy are used to dominate both women and nature. The idea is that economic development generally entails the devaluing and conquering of nature and that women's association with nature dooms them to conquering as well.

Because of some of the more radical and theoretically problematic versions, most feminist scholars and activists currently distance themselves from ecofeminism (see Sturgeon, 1997, for discussion). For instance, Biehl (1991) criticizes ecofeminism for rejecting rationalism and for worshiping goddesses. Critics of ecofeminism also charge it with "essentialism," that is, with saying that there are essential differences between women and men. Such essentialism rubs many feminists the wrong way for essentialism has historically justified discrimina-

tion against women. However, the essentialism charge is more relevant to some ecofeminisms than others.

Vandana Shiva, trained as a theoretical physicist, is a well-known Indian ecofeminist. She works closely with the Chipko movement as well as other rural environmental movements in India. Her 1989 book *Staying Alive: Women, Ecology and Development* is already a classic for Third World ecofeminism. The book, along with later writings, argues that Western science and Western economic development have created both environmental destruction and the marginalization of women through the "death of the feminine principle." This feminine principle arises from direct experience with nature and is holistic, caring, cooperative, intuitive, nonhierarchical, welcoming, and supportive of diversity (Sachs, 1997). This feminine principle is "not exclusively embodied in women but is the principle of activity and creativity in nature, women, and men" (Shiva, 1989, p. 52). Shiva also suggests that Third World women are uniquely suited to environmental activism: "Because of their location on the fringes, and their role in producing sustenance, women in Third World societies are often able to offer ecological insights that are deeper and richer than the technocratic recipes of international experts or the responses of men in their own societies" (Shiva, 1994, p. 1).

be seen as victims of environmental degradation but as agents who must participate equally in the solution to these problems.

Women and Environmental Activism

Much of women's activism for the environment is the result of women's non-governmental organizations (NGOs). Indeed, according to Fisher (1996), NGOs now serve as principal institutional resources for sustainable development in the Third World, both because of their own activities and because of their impact on governments. Fisher suggests that NGOs take two general forms: the **grassroots organizations (GROs),** locally based groups that work to develop and improve the community, and **grassroots support organizations (GRSOs),** nationally or regionally based development assistance organizations,

"Come arise, my
brothers and sisters,

Save this mountain . . .

Come plant new trees,
new forests,

Decorate the earth."
*Song of the Chipko
movement*

usually staffed by professionals, that channel funds to grassroots organizations and help communities other than their own to develop.

The **Chipko movement** in the forests of Uttar Pradesh, India, is a famous example of a GRO. In 1974 conflict escalated between logging companies supported by the state and the natives who depended upon the forest for food and fuel. The villagers were also aware that previous logging by commercial interests had resulted in erosion and flooding from which they had suffered dearly. The village men were away on the day the contractors arrived to cut 2,500 trees, but the village women took action. They wrapped themselves around the trees (*chipko* means "hug") and refused to move until the contractors left. The contractors did leave, and Indira Gandhi issued a fifteen-year ban on commercial logging in the forests of Uttar Pradesh (Dankelman & Davidson, 1988). The Chipko movement has spread throughout the Himalayas in India, Nepal, and Bhutan (Jain, 1991). The Chipko message is spread through sustainable development camps that meet twice a year (Fisher, 1996). This shows how GROs sometimes become GRSOs, which then support grassroots organizations elsewhere. In addition, chipko-based resistance is now used throughout India to protest environmentally irresponsible road building, mining, and dam projects (Seager, 1993).

The **Greenbelt movement** in Kenya is a well-known example of the role of GRSOs in sustainable development involving women. The movement was begun in 1977 by Wangari Maathai, an ardent feminist, environmentalist, and scholar in microbiology, in conjunction with the National Council of Women of Kenya. By the 1970s, severe deforestation and soil erosion had created a shortage of fuelwood and food. The movement organized women to plant and manage trees for fuelwood and to guard against erosion. Maathai explains her focus on women by noting that it is women who use wood fuel for cooking and who also till the land (Katumba & Akute, 1993). According to the World Resources Institute, the movement now includes some 1,000 tree nurseries with more than 50,000 women participants. The women learn important leadership skills and gain economic power by the income generated by the sale of seedlings. In the last ten years, more than 7 million trees have been planted. The project also promotes organic farming and organizes workshops and seminars on sustainable development. The movement has been replicated in twelve other African countries.

Other GRSOs with a sustainability focus include the Secretariat for an Ecologically Sound Philippines, which addresses environmental problems affecting women, farmers, youth, and minorities, and KENGO, a Kenyan organization that hosted the Kenya Assembly of Women and the Environment in May 1993. International GRSOs with a sustainability focus exist as well. Some examples include the Women's Environment and Development Organization, which organized the World Women's Congress for a Healthy Planet in 1991 in preparation for the Rio Earth Summit; the International Women and Environment Network, which formed in 1989 in Managua, Philippines; and the Earth Council, formed after the Rio Earth Summit.

Wangari Maathai,
Kenyan microbiologist, feminist, and environmentalist, is considered the founder of the Greenbelt movement. In 1999, Maathai was injured by government forces when she organized women to plant trees in a forest scheduled for demolition.

Environmental degradation is now recognized as a critical development problem, and women are increasingly acknowledged as important contributors to sustainable development. This is reflected in a number of official reports and declarations, but it is important to remember that this is largely the result of women's activism. For instance, after the 1992 UN Conference on Economic Development (UNCED), Agenda 21 called for specific agreements by governments to strengthen the role of women in creating and implementing sustainable development strategies (Steady, 1995). Women and sustainability are also mentioned in the Rio Declaration from the conference, which states "Women have a vital role in environmental management and development. Their full participation is essential to achieving sustainable development." Keep in mind that NGOs worked hard for these things. The truth is that gender issues were given very little attention in the preparatory committees for UNCED and were only taken up after intense lobbying by women's NGOs (Brandiotti et al., 1994; Elliot, 1996). Indeed, the Rio Declaration clearly incorporates many ideas developed at the 1991 World Women's Congress for a Healthy Planet.

Conclusion

Feminists generally favor the gender and development approach to development because it integrates development, gender equality, and women's empowerment. It also specifically emphasizes that the agenda for women's development should be set by women themselves. Contrary to the belief that women in southern countries are content with their position, when given opportunity and support, women seek out ways of challenging and changing their situations (Mosse, 1993). Numerous cases show that local women are capable of being the agents of their own development (Moser, 1995). Although the gender and development approach has been difficult for development agencies to translate into action, because of entrenched interests that vigorously resist the emancipation of women and their release from subordination, local women have exerted pressure from the bottom up with some success (Moser, 1993). Ironically, the marginalization of women by state and international development entities has spurred the rise of women's grassroots organizations that emphasize and stimulate women's empowerment. For instance, in many countries women are entitled to own land, but local customs prevent them from assuming ownership. This, as previously noted, prevents them from obtaining development loan moneys because they have no property for collateral, and it keeps them from receiving extension training. Women's NGOs in Thailand, China, Nicaragua, Malaysia, and Cuba have fought for women's land rights. According to Fisher (1996), over 200,000 grassroots organizations exist in Asia, Africa, and Latin America, over half of them organized by women. Additionally, her research indicates that there are 30,000 to 35,000 grassroots support organizations active in the Third World.

There is growing recognition that women are not a special interest group but rather are an integral part of every development strategy (Moser, 1995). The failure to consider women in the development process not only causes harm to women but to development efforts in general. Women's work, under-compensated and undervalued as it is, is vital to the survival and ongoing reproduction of human beings in all societies (Sen & Grown, 1987). Therefore, successful development must take into account women's roles as the principal providers of basic needs (fuel, water, health care, sanitation, and so on). For instance, although rural women in most of the developing world are the main food producers for their families, agricultural research and education programs generally target cash crops grown by men. However, this focus often does not reduce periods of famine or food shortages because these cash crops do not produce food for family consumption. As the FAO put it, "Neglecting women as agricultural producers and resource managers inhibits the attainment of food security goals" (FAOb). Many water resource development and agricultural irrigation projects have also failed due to the exclusion of women's important role in water management (FAOf). Likewise, child malnutrition may increase when women prepare fewer or less nutritious meals due to time constraints.

Similarly, the relationship between women's status and important development goals such as the reduction of child malnutrition is also increasingly obvious. As Ramalingaswami, Jonsson, and Rohde (1996) note, it is all but impossible for a woman to provide high-quality child care if she herself is poor and oppressed, illiterate and uninformed, anemic and unhealthy, lives in a slum or shanty, has neither clean water nor safe sanitation, and lacks necessary support either from health services, her society, or the father of her children. Mothers also devote more of their income than do fathers to family subsistence, holding back less for personal consumption (Blumberg, 1995). As Amin and Li (1997) note, because women are more likely to look to the interests of their children, any measure that puts resources directly into the hands of women or strengthens their autonomy is likely to improve children's health and well-being. Their research shows that the children of NGO credit members in Bangladesh had higher immunization rates and lower infant and child mortality rates.

Although there is some evidence that important changes in development programs are underway, activism is still called for. As Jahan (1995a) suggests, up to now, development agencies and organizations have only tinkered with the constraints on women's equality. They have yet, she says, to come forward with bold policies, adequate budgetary allocations, and the institutional mechanisms necessary to overcome these obstacles. Despite the apparent rationality of expanding women's role in development, it probably will not occur without pressure from a variety of women's organizations. Networking and political pressure, which build on what happens at the local level, can scale out the impact of women's NGOs at the grassroots level and scale up their impact on policy (Fisher, 1996).

Terms and Concepts

Third World

developing nation

First World

northern and southern
   countries

colonies

feminization of poverty

development programs

modernization theory

   structural adjustment
   programs (SAPs)

welfare approach

women in development (WID)

income-generating projects

empowerment approach

gender and development (GAD)

sustainable development

ecofeminism

grassroots organizations (GROs)

grassroots support organizations
   (GRSOs)

Chipko movement

Greenbelt movement

Study Questions

1. How did colonization affect women's status? In what way might we conceive of women as a fourth colony?

2. How do common development strategies negatively impact women?

3. What are some common feminist criticisms of traditional development programs?

Discussion Questions and Activities

1. How do women from developing nations contribute to your community? How do their lifestyles here differ from their country of origin? (adapted from Mermel & Simons, 1991)

2. If southern women followed the footsteps of U.S. women, would they gain or lose? What cultural biases or values underlie your answers? (adapted from Duley & Diduk, 1986)

3. Do international development agencies have the right to intervene in the gender arrangements of a country? Is it morally wrong for them not to?

4. Consider this quote from DAWN's Peggy Antrobus: "We must never lose sight of the fact that the women's movement and the environmental movement are primarily *revolutionary* movements. If we give up that political challenge to the dominant paradigm, there is no hope for change." What do you think she means and do you agree?

A Jewish girl holds a tambourine at a feminist seder in the United States. Women called to serve God often reconstruct their religious traditions so that the traditions no longer support the subordination of women.

Women and Religion

Now what about Islam? And what of the other great religions? When we think about religions in general, it seems to me that, more or less, they are the same. They all have a general human call for the equality of people—regardless of color, race, or sex. One finds this conception of equality in all of the religions, as well as in Marxism or existentialism. But when we come to the specifics, when we come to the daily lives of men and women, rich and poor, one race and another, this general sense of equality does not seem to be in evidence. Here we find oppression, including the oppression of women. So we must not have illusions about religion, because religion is used, and it is used often by those in power.

NAWAL EL SAADAWI, 1987

This chapter considers the role of religion in women's lower status as well as the ways in which women have claimed and reclaimed religion. It is also a chapter on **feminist theology** (theology is the study of religious doctrines). As King (1994) said, feminist theology seeks to accomplish both a negative and positive task. The negative task is the critique of and struggle against the oppression of women whereas the positive task is one of reform and reconstruction. King (1994) suggests that feminist theology is always dynamic and pluralistic—including and expressing the voices, experiences, and approaches of many different women in very different situations and societies.

When considering the various forces that contribute to women's lower power and status, it is important to consider religion. Religion is frequently a central part of a culture and often communicates a great deal about the relative roles of women and men. Indeed, theologian Rosemary Reuther (1974) suggests that religion is the most important shaper and enforcer of the image and role of women in culture and society. Doyle (1974) also emphasizes its importance:

Feminist analysis of culture and society stops prematurely if it does not dare to tackle religion. When feminists take on religion they oppose the most deeply held motivations, beliefs and life orientations. It is this dimension of religion that makes the debate the most radical of all feminist encounters with cultural and individual thought and feeling. We should not be surprised if the dispute thus results in radical resistance within the churches and individual men and women, as well as in the possibility of radical cultural, psychological, and religious transformations for others. (p. 16)

BOX 7.1   *Some Contemporary Woman-Centered Religions*

Afro-Brazilian Religions (Brazil)

These combine elements of African tribal religions, Amerindian religions, Catholicism, and Kardecism (French Spiritism). The main features are curing and public rituals in which female mediums are possessed by spirits. They coexist with Catholicism.

Black Carib Religion (Central America)

This is a religion centered around numerous rituals to honor and appease ancestral spirits and to protect the living against evil spirits and sorcery. Old women are the spiritual leaders. Most Black Caribs are also Roman Catholic.

Burmese Nat Religion (Upper Burma)

The religion centers around the appeasement of spirits called *nats*. These *nats* are also called upon to prevent and cure illness and to bring good luck. Most rituals are performed by women, and almost all shamans are women as well. The religion exists alongside Buddhist practices.

Christian Science (United States)

This religion was founded by Mary Baker Eddy in the nineteenth century. Christian Scientists believe that healing comes about through study and prayer.

Our focus in this chapter is on the world's major religious traditions (Christianity, Hinduism, Islam, Judaism, and Buddhism), but please realize that it is difficult to generalize about entire religious traditions. Within a given religion, there are many variants, some of which are more supportive of women's equality than are others. Also, bear in mind that smaller indigenous religions often give women a greater role than do the world's major religions. For instance, in many indigenous traditions there are strong female mythological figures and female rituals and no doctrine of male superiority and dominance (Gross, 1996). Mbon (1987) illustrates this in a discussion of African religion. In many traditional African religions, women play active roles as *diviners* (who foretell the future) and as *healers* of physical and psychological illnesses. In some parts of Africa, women also occupy a central place in the practice of witchcraft, and this is a source of power for them. There are also many rituals and ceremonies that cannot be performed without women. In addition, in most traditional African religions, God is neither exclusively male nor exclusively female; God is both. It is also the case that in so-called marginal or nonmainstream religions, women often have more power and autonomy (Gross, 1996; Sered, 1994; Weissinger, 1993). These religions, however, are rare. Sered (1994) examines twelve contemporary woman-dominated religions in depth (Box 7.1 gives a sampling of her research). These are interesting in that they often exist alongside of mainstream religions and frequently emphasize the appeasement of spirits for purposes of healing and bringing good tidings.

Feminist Spirituality Movement
This is discussed at the end of this chapter.

Korean Household Religion
Korean women make offerings to gods for the well-being of their households and consult female shamans for guidance. This coexists with Buddhism.

Sande Secret Society (West Africa)
Adolescent girls are initiated into the societies at lengthy all-female retreats. At this time, they are taught about childbirth and other skills women are expected to know. Sande societies also control the supernatural and sacred realm. This coexists with male secret societies called *Poro.*

Zar (parts of Africa and the Middle East)
Zar are spirits that attack and possess women. Women then join zar cults in which they participate in rituals to appease the possessing spirit and turn it into an ally. Women's zar activities often serve as a counterpart to men's involvement in official Islamic practices.

Source: Sered, 1994.

Religion as an Ingredient of Patriarchy

Religion is an ingredient of patriarchy when it is part of the social systems that act to keep women lower in power and status. This may occur in several different ways. For instance, you have already read how in many cultures, marriage, divorce, contraception, abortion, and traditional gender power relations are regulated by religious laws and customs. Religions also communicate to us information regarding females' and males' relative status. This is done directly when a religious text states that women are to be subservient to men, as do the majority of the world's religious texts. This is done indirectly when females are not allowed to participate in the religion's major rituals and are not permitted to occupy power positions in the religion. What our religion says about gender is especially influential because we are typically encouraged to accept it unquestionably as the word of an all-knowing and all-powerful God or Allah.

Religion then, is one of the cultural agents that shapes our conceptions of female and male and prescribes different roles to them. Our conceptions of male and female come from our culture. We are not born believing that females and males should differ in specific ways. We learn this from our culture, and one important cultural messenger for most people is their religion. Religions provide a worldview, a way of looking at the world in order to make more sense out of it. A culture's values and norms are commonly communicated via religion, and participation in religious practices is generally part of the socialization process. In other words, what our society values and expects is often learned from religious stories and practices.

Although the Greek goddess **Pandora** is known as the unleasher of the world's evils, in earlier history she was known by the name Gaea and worshiped as the embodiment of earth and the giver of all.

Feminist critiques of religion suggest that the majority of the world's religions currently communicate to their adherents that men's greater power and status relative to women is appropriate and acceptable. In other words, patriarchal religion has made it more difficult to see through the injustices of the patriarchal system by legitimating and reinforcing it (Daly, 1974). This is done by the common presentation of God as male, by traditions of male leadership, by the exclusion of women from major religious rituals, and by religious texts that leave out the female experience and legitimate men's authority over women. You will see that this does not necessarily mean that feminists are ready to abandon religion (although some certainly have). Indeed, much of the work in this area has been done by religious women who wanted to serve God but were limited in their efforts because they were female. For instance, women who felt called to be rabbis, priests, and ministers found themselves barred from these vocations: Orthodox Jewish women who wanted to participate fully in worship were excluded from the praying community and were made to sit behind a screen; Catholic and Protestant women who wanted to serve communion were asked instead to serve church suppers (Christ & Plaskow, 1979). Many of these women have sought to reform and transform existing religion. Others have resurrected ancient female-centered religions or have created new ones.

Feminist Critiques of Religion

God, the Father

> "If we do not mean that God is male when we use masculine pronouns and imagery, then why should there be any objections to using female imagery and pronouns as well?"
> *Rita Gross*

Feminist critiques of religion often cite the male imagery used by so many of the world's religions and regard it as both a source and a reflection of patriarchy. For instance, God or Allah is typically presented using male imagery and language. Theologians are often quick to point out that God is not to be considered in sexual terms at all, despite such terminology. However, the actual language they use daily in worship and prayer conveys a different message and gives the impression that God is thought of in exclusively masculine terms (Pagels, 1976). That it is frequently considered daring, degrading, or alienating to speak of God using female pronouns and imagery perhaps indicates something about the way women and the feminine are valued (Gross, 1979). In other words, **masculine God language** is not as innocuous as it may appear, for linguistic conventions do indeed shape our perceptions of reality.

Feminists argue that referring to God using terms like "Our Heavenly Father" and "He" suggest that on earth men can be the only true gods. After all, God is the ultimate male and in this way deifies male power. God as male is also a stern, commanding ruler, an image that represents only one aspect of humanity: maleness (Ruth, 1995). The thought is that as long as God is only the God of our fathers and not our mothers, men will be perceived as having both a closer relationship with God and a higher religious status (Umansky, in Cantor, 1995). In addition, God's main messengers on earth are typically male. For instance, Jesus (Christianity), Muhammad (Islam), and the Buddha

(Buddhism) are all male. This too is viewed by many feminist theologians as contributing to the common cultural view that men are above women.

The effects of this on women are also an issue to feminists. Ruth (1995) suggests that the sexist and masculine focus of religion makes being a religious woman analogous with maintaining a stoic attitude about one's lower status. For instance, a friend of mine in an abusive marriage was advised by her church leaders to let her husband make all the family decisions and not to challenge him even when he was obviously wrong. She was told that this was the way for women to serve God and that God would reward her by taking care of her and her marriage. Or as Daly (1973) puts it, the males' judgment having been metamorphosed into God's judgment, it becomes the religious duty of women to accept the burden of guilt, to see the self with male chauvinist eyes, to accept male dominance.

Religious Texts and Women's Oppression

Another focus of feminist criticism of religion is **sexism in religious texts.** One key issue for feminists regarding the scriptures is the relative absence of females and female experience. Put simply, most of the stories are about men and male experience, and when women appear it is usually as characters in stories told by and about men or as objects of male concern such as the control of female sexuality. As Reuther (1985) suggests, although women's experience may be found between the lines of religious texts, for the most part the norm presented for women is one of absence and silence. When women are portrayed, it is as objects praised for obedience or admonished for disobedience to men. As Plaskow (1991) says in regard to Judaism,

> Half of Jews have been women, but men have been defined as normative Jews, while women's voices and experiences are largely invisible in the record of Jewish belief and experience that has come down to us. Women have lived Jewish history and carried its burdens, but women's perceptions and questions have not given form to the scripture, shaped the direction of Jewish law, or found expression in liturgy. (p. 1)

A second key issue for feminists with regard to the scriptures is the concern that most of these texts sacralize patriarchy (present it as sacred). As Gross (1996) puts it, the study of religious scriptures is important because scriptures are so often used to support traditional notions of women's roles. Feminist theologian Mary Daly (1985) notes that the endorsement of traditional gender roles in religious texts acts to convince women to accept their lower status. As she puts it, "ecclesiastical propaganda" seems to put woman on a pedestal by emphasizing her value as a wife and mother, but, in reality, it prevents her from genuine fulfillment and full participation in society. Religion, she notes, makes women feel guilty or unnatural if they rebel against the role prescribed to them, and this condemns women to a restricted existence in the name of religion.

"Consider the impact on your self-image of being 'in the likeness of God,' like Jesus, the Pope, and the 'Brothers of the Church' and contrast it with never finding yourself reflected in the sacred pronoun. Utter: God, He . . . ; God, Him. Now say: God, She. . . . Imagine the experience of seeing oneself reflected in the sacred images of power."
Sheila Ruth

Religious stories and texts often contain four common messages that perpetuate women's lower status and power. These are: (1) Female sexuality is dangerous and must be suppressed; (2) female religious figures are subordinate to male religious figures (they are typically portrayed in relationship to males); (3) females should be subservient wives, mothers, and homemakers; and (4) women's lower status is punishment for their sinful nature. It is hard to say with certainty why these themes are consistently found in the world's religions. However, Prusak (1974) suggests that the men who created these stories were puzzled by the power of the sexual drive and birth. Through the creation of stories that connected women with evil, they could explain why women bled every month and why they experience the pain and inconvenience of pregnancy and childbirth. By connecting women with evil, they also had a theological explanation and justification for male dominance and female subservience. As an added bonus, they were able to explain evil by identifying women as its source.

Next let's look at a sampling of the religious texts that some feminists claim argue for male supremacy and female subordination. As you read this section it is important to bear in mind that most of these texts have some passages that may be interpreted in ways favorable to women's equality, and some (such as the Sikh religious texts of India) explicitly call for the equal treatment of women. In practice, though, this seems to have little effect on the treatment of women. This is probably because, as Holm (1994) notes, historically in all major religions, it is men who have composed, transmitted, and interpreted the sacred writings. Over time these writings and their interpretations increasingly reflected men's activities, achievements, and power as well as societal views of male superiority.

Hinduism   Hinduism, the only major polytheistic religion in the world, is also the only one that worships female deities as well as male ones (Gross, 1996). Indian religion has existed for almost 6,000 years yet has no central God concept, no founder or single prophet, and no single authoritative scripture (Carmody, 1974). In these ways, Hinduism is unique. However, it is not unique in that it developed in the context of a patriarchal society and reflects this. For instance, although there are female as well as male gods in Hinduism, female gods are often portrayed as dangerously passionate, capable of giving and taking life, and needing the control of male gods so that they do not produce chaos (Carmody, 1989). Furthermore, although Hinduism is rich in female deities, most Hindus and Hindu scholars describe Hindu religious mythology as revolving around the male deities (Gross, 1996).

In Hinduism, a number of the epic heroines and scriptural texts enjoin women to worship their husbands as gods and to identify totally with the identities and interests of their families (Robinson, 1985). For example, Savitri, a prominent female figure in Hindu mythology, is so devoted to her husband that she sacrifices her life for his. Similarly, another major female figure, Sati, wife of the god Siva, commits suicide by walking into a fire to avenge her husband's honor. Fire and the preservation of the husband's honor also figure in the story of Sita. Sita is kidnapped from her husband, Rama, by the demon Ravana. She is twice victimized—first, by the terror of abduction and captivity, and again, when she is rescued by Rama and must prove to him that she remained pure and faithful to him. She steps into a sacrificial fire but emerges unscathed because she was virtuous. Sita risked death to protect the honor of her husband (Robinson, 1985).

Key concepts of Hinduism are reincarnation and karma, the idea that one's present life is the result of actions taken in previous lives. Women's lower status is to be accepted as just, for it is due to choices they made in past lives. It is also notable that in classical Hinduism it is believed that no woman can gain salvation except in a future life when she has been reborn as a man. The way to do this is by being a good wife and worshiping her husband. Men gain good karma, and therefore a higher level of rebirth, through the study of the Vedas (the earliest and most authoritative Hindu scriptures) and through meditation (Carmody, 1989).

Buddhism Although Buddha himself clearly suggested that females and males had equal potential for enlightenment, later interpreters and Buddhist writers suggested otherwise. For instance, in many Buddhist writings you can find themes quite similar to those of the Adam and Eve story in the Bible. The general idea is that women tempt men away from the divine and good and interfere with a man's attainment of holiness (Paul, 1979). Many Buddhist scriptures describe women as filled with evil desires and as harmful obstacles to men's attainment of enlightenment (Uchino, 1985). In the Buddhist tradition, women are regarded as impure, as having a more sinful karma than men, and as being unable to attain Buddhahood (the highest level of enlightenment) (Uchino, 1985). Buddhist literature is also similar to Hindu literature in that it suggests that the good wife is totally submissive and honors all her husband's wishes and commands (Carmody, 1989). There are, however, also images in Buddhist literature of women as fully enlightened beings (Barnes, 1987). Barnes (1987) argues that most of the main schools of Buddhism thriving today are egalitarian in doctrine and that the problems faced by women in Buddhist countries have more to do with social values that were not originated by Buddhist theorists.

It should also be noted that there are several forms of Buddhism and that these differ in terms of their male-centeredness. The literature of Theravada (Hinayana) Buddhism is the one most likely to view women as obstacles to spiritual progress and to suggest that women are inferior spiritual beings. In contrast is Mahayana Buddhism, which stresses that all human experience, male or female, is the source of enlightenment and that all things share one life because nothing can stand on its own. This is known as the Supreme Wisdom, Prajnaparamita, or the feminine principle (Bancroft, 1987). Tantric Buddhism—another, though less popular, form—is even more female-centered and includes the presence of strong, sexually active female sacred beings (Gross, 1996).

Islam The Koran (also spelled Qur'an) is the religious text of Islam and consists of the writings and revelations of its founder, Muhammad. The Koran has a number of passages that illustrate three of the four common religious messages regarding women (women's lower status as due to punishment for past sins is not found in the Koran). For instance, the following passage clearly conveys these sexist themes:

> Men shall protect and maintain women because God has made some of them excel others, and because they support them from their means. Therefore the righteous women are obedient, guarding the intimacy which God would have them guard. As for those women whose rebellion you justly fear, admonish them first; then leave their beds; then beat them. Then if they obey you, seek no harm against them for God is most High, Exalted, Great.

Other verses are less clear-cut but are interpreted according to common Islamic social views. For instance, Islamic societies generally view women as in need of watching and protecting because of women's seductive nature, and this has influenced the interpretation of the Koran. Consequently, the Koran verse that reads "Tell the believing women to lower their gaze and be modest, and to display of their adornment only that which is apparent, and to draw their veils over their bosoms" is used by some Muslims to justify the seclusion and veiling of women.

Judaism The Hebrew Bible (the Old Testament) is an important Jewish text and focuses primarily on the stories of men, portraying women largely in terms of their service to men. Much of Judaism is also based on various other texts, stories, and prayers not found in the Bible. One Orthodox Jewish prayer is the male's daily morning prayer: "Blessed art thou, O Lord our God, King of the Universe, who has not made me a woman." The corresponding prayer for women is: "Blessed art thou, O Lord our God, King of the Universe, who has made me according to his will" (Schulman, 1974). Such a prayer reminds women and men of their places and of God's desire for this order.

A legend from *Genesis Rabbah* in the Midrash (a record of rabbis' biblical exegeses from 200–600 C.E.) explains that menstruation is one of women's punishments for Eve's sins (Schulman, 1974):

> Why does a man go out bareheaded while a woman goes out with her head covered? She is like one who has done wrong and is ashamed of people; therefore she goes out with her head covered. Why do they [the women] walk in front of the corpse at a funeral? Because they brought death into the world, they therefore walk in front of the corpse. And why was the precept of menstruation given to her? Because she shed the blood of Adam by causing death, therefore was the precept of menstruation given to her. And why was the precept of "dough" given to her? Because she corrupted Adam, who was the dough of the world, therefore was the precept of dough given to her. And why was the precept of Sabbath lights given to her? Because she extinguished the soul of Adam, therefore was the precept of Sabbath lights given to her.

"What is it after all that Jewish women seek? They do not ask to be excused or exempt. They do not wish to turn their backs on the tradition, to wash their hands of it and walk away. Rather, they desire to enter it more fully. They long to share a greater part of the tradition, to partake of its wealth of knowledge, to delight in the richness of ritual. For these reasons, their efforts should be welcomed, not scorned."
Blu Greenberg

The Hebrew Bible, with its biblical stories, describes what it means to be Jewish. The keeping of the Torah's commandments is the pride of Jewish life, yet very few of the 613 religious injunctions in the Torah apply to women (Carmody, 1994). The Talmud, a sixty-three volume compendium that centers on the meaning of the Torah, conveys such messages as, "Wherewith do women acquire merit? By sending their children to learn Torah in the synagogue and their husbands to study in the schools of the rabbis." A woman is a "golem, a shapeless lump" until her husband transforms her into a "finished vessel" (Carmody, 1974).

Christianity The main text of Christianity, the Bible, rarely includes women as the major actors, and the stories themselves never deal with the lives of women among women (Frymer-Kensky, 1994). Due to the use of masculine God language and the portrayal of women in traditional subservient relationships to men (when they are portrayed at all), many feminists view the Bible as a patriarchal document of a patriarchal society (although this does not necessarily mean that they recommend its complete abandonment). The story of Adam and Eve (Gen. 1:3) is frequently cited by feminist theologians as one of the most influential biblical stories affecting women's status. In this story, Eve is punished for her curiosity for eating from the tree of knowledge of good and evil. She is banished from paradise, is condemned to give birth to her children in pain, and must submit to the authority of Adam (Gen. 3:16–19). Later in the Bible, it appears that Eve is held responsible for the downfall of all humankind, who must now pay for her foolishness (1 Tim. 2:13–14). The story has been interpreted by some feminists as communicating that women do not deserve their independence for they will abuse it. Furthermore, in Genesis (2:24), Eve is created as a companion to Adam from his rib. This part of the story is often used to legitimate a husband's power over his wife in the most persuasive of ways—it is presented as divinely ordained: "For man was not made from woman, but woman from man. Neither was man created for woman, but woman for man" (1 Cor. 11:8–9).

In some versions of Christianity, most notably Latin American Roman Catholicism, Jesus' mother, Mary, is an important religious figure and model of womanhood. She obediently accepts the message from the angel Gabriel that she is the mother of the baby Jesus: "Behold, I am the handmaid of the Lord; let it be to me according to your word' (Luke 1:38). Mary is also presented as the perfect mother and a spotless virgin, difficult ideals for human women to live up to (Cisernos, 1996; Drury, 1994).

Sex-Segregated Religious Practices

Most of the world's major religions distinguish between the religious activities of females and males. A number of the world's religions have different religious rituals and forms of worship based on gender. Many Hindu women, for instance, perform rituals of self-denial, such as fasting, in order to create positive energy and power for their husbands. The self-sacrifice of a woman for her

> "If God had not intended that Women shou'd use their Reason, He wou'd not have given them any, for He does nothing in vain. If they are to use their Reason, certainly it ought to be employ'd about the noblest Objects, and in business of the greatest Consequences, therefore in Religion."
> *Mary Astell, 1705*

husband is understood to be a religious offering. Men do not perform such rituals for their wives. There are also domestic rituals performed by females for fertility that are not found in Hindu texts but are passed down orally from woman to woman (Young, 1987).

The roles that women and men may hold within a religion are often based on gender. Thus, female ministers, bishops, priests, rabbis, gurus, or sadhus (holy people) remain rare or nonexistent in most religious traditions, even today. Eck and Jain (1987) note that although there have been women saints and gurus and countless local female leaders, for the most part, religious authority has been the domain of men. As Gross (1996) suggests, the ordination of women is not the only important indication of whether or not women have genuine membership in their religion, but it is a way to quickly assess the status of women in a given religion.

Denying women the right to hold positions of religious authority is justified in several ways. First, religious texts are often used as justification for why women should not hold religious leadership positions. For instance, this passage from the Bible has historically been used as a proof text for why women shouldn't hold priestly and liturgical roles: "Women should keep silence in churches. For they are not permitted to speak, but should be subordinate, as even the law says" (I Cor. 14:34–35) (Parvey, 1974, p. 128). Second, many religions keep women theologically illiterate, and thus they are unqualified to hold high positions within the religion. For instance, women may not be permitted to study religious texts, attend important religious ceremonies, or have access to theological education. Likewise, higher rates of illiteracy among females, and the lack of schooling in the languages of the texts, are in some cases obstacles. Third, in most of the world's major religions (for instance, Christianity, Islam, and Buddhism), God's messengers on earth are male, and it is often said that only males may represent them. Fourth, some religions maintain that women are spiritually inferior to men and that they are therefore unsuitable for religious leadership.

Hinduism   In India, temple rituals and rites of passage are still performed by male priests, and most Hindu teachers (gurus) remain male (Young, 1987). For a long time, one barrier was that the study of Sanskrit, the language of the religious texts, was available only to males. However, today university study of Sanskrit is mostly undertaken by women as men pursue more lucrative professions. In recent years, a number of major Indian gurus have passed their spiritual mantle to women, and even orthodox Hindu leaders have initiated a few women as ascetics and spiritual teachers (Young, 1994).

Buddhism   In Buddhism, traditionally, the main religious leaders are the male monks, or *bhikkhu*. The female counterpart is the *bhikkhuni*, sometimes translated as "nun" although it is really the female form of the word *bhikkhu*. However, in some Buddhist countries—such as Burma, Cambodia, Laos, Tibet, Thailand, Sri Lanka, Nepal, Bhutan, and Burma—there are no orders of fully ordained *bhikkhuni* (although the Dalai Lama of Tibet is supportive of their ordination). Most of these countries practice the more gender-conservative Buddhist school of Theravada, which does not ordain nuns or does so under limited conditions (Bancroft, 1987; Barnes, 1994). In these countries, there are women who shave their heads as nuns and live as Buddhist devotees (Barnes, 1994). For instance, in Thailand, women may become *bhikkhuni* that are not fully ordained, called *jis,* but they receive no public or governmental support and have low social status. All religious rituals and instruction are administered by male monks. Thai Buddhist monastic rules forbid close association with women, and the Buddhist tradition is taken to be the sphere of men (Kabilsingh, 1987). These practices have the effect of removing women from their religious heritage and rights (Kabilsingh, 1987).

In contrast to Theravada Buddhism, the Mahayana (Zen) school gives women greater freedom as religious teachers. In Taiwan, Buddhist nuns, or ascetics, have their own monasteries and enjoy social and financial support from the public. In Japan, nuns are ordained and may even perform some priestly duties in some sects. Uchino (1987) discusses how this came about in an article tracing the status elevation process of Soto sect nuns in modern Japan. Changes began in the early 1900s when Buddhist schools for nuns were established. Nuns who studied at these schools later became leaders in the nun equality movement. Beginning in 1925, the nuns held conferences and issued demands for increased equality in the world of Buddhism. Changes toward nun's equality occurred gradually over the next fifty years due to continued political pressure on the part of the nuns' organization.

In general, though, monks remain higher status than nuns. Barnes (1994) describes some of the restrictions placed on nuns relative to monks. The ordination process is more difficult for nuns, and nuns' lives are more closely regulated than monks' lives. Nuns must also adhere to eight regulations spelling out their lower status relative to male monks. These regulations are alleged to have come from the Buddha himself and require that nuns treat all monks as their superiors; nuns are required to seek out monks for instruction but not to instruct or admonish them (Bancroft, 1987; Willis, 1985).

Finally, it should be noted that despite the overwhelming dominance of male leadership, Buddhism has undergone a number of changes in this century that have created new possibilities for women in Buddhism. In particular, the old distinction between cleric (monks) and laypeople is rejected by many, and this has increased the number of Buddhist female leaders and teachers. Among the most influential of these are Ayu Khandro and Ani Lochen (Tibet), Achan Naeb (Thailand), Daw Panna (Burma), Ruth Denison and Maureen Stuart (United States), Jiyu Kennett Roshi (United Kingdom, now in the United States), and Ayya Khema (Sri Lanka, originally from the West). The recently developed American version of Buddhism, and a number of the lay versions developed in Japan and Korea, frequently have women leaders believed to possess spiritual powers (Bancroft, 1987; Barnes, 1994). Furthermore, laywomen in some Theravada countries and in Europe and America have assumed new roles as the teachers of meditation as a means to nirvana (Barnes, 1994).

Judaism Orthodox Judaism strongly delineates between the religious activities of women and men. Orthodox Judaism is a time-consuming religion

"When men know that spiritually we are the same as they are, they will have to judge us on our merits and our ability and not on what someone said thousands of years ago."
Reverend Master Jiyu Kennett Roshi ("Roshi" means Zenmaster), one of the few female heads of a Buddhist monastery in the United States

"The fact that, in traditional Judaism, women are not counted in a *minyan* (quorum required for public prayeer) or called to the Torah amounts to our exclusion from the public religious realm."
Judith Plaskow

requiring much studying and praying. However, these activities can interfere with the running of the household. Therefore, women are excluded from the majority of religious activities that take place outside of the home. The spiritual domain belongs to men; women's participation is through keeping the laws of family purity such as the ritual bath seven days after menstruation and the preparation of kosher food. In Orthodox Judaism, women do not count as members of the *minyan*, the quorum of ten males required for public religious services. Women are also segregated from men in orthodox synagogues. Women can't lead services in part because they are not allowed to read from the Torah. Indeed, the Talmud (the sixty-three volume explanation of the Torah) says: "Let the words of Torah rather be destroyed by fire than imparted to women." The reading of the Torah is a major part of worship, and that women are discouraged from studying the Torah means that they are excluded from full participation in their religion.

In the United States, the reform, reconstructionist, and conservative Jewish traditions now permit women to be ordained as rabbis. Orthodox women are still prohibited. In Israel, however, these branches of Judaism have no standing, and they are considered to be deviant groups by the orthodox (Carmody, 1994).

Islam   In Islam, leadership roles are also dominated by males. Although there are no clergy in Islam, there is a male hierarchy of mullahs who control understanding of the Koran's meaning. Historically, however, some women were viewed as authorities on the Koran. In particular, Aisha (613–678), one of Muhammad's wives, was a powerful political and religious leader in addition to being one of the originators of Sunni Islam following her husband's death.

"If women's rights are a problem for some modern Muslim men, it is neither because of the Koran nor the Prophet, nor the Islamic tradition, but simply because those rights conflict with the interests of a male elite."
Fatima Mernissi

Many current Islamic religious practices also discriminate by gender. During the month of Ramadan, for instance, Muslims are to fast from sunrise to sunset in order to receive grace. A menstruating women is regarded as ritually unclean and may not fast or pray in the mosque. Furthermore, she must pay back the missed days but receives less "grace from God" (pahala) for made-up days (Hartmann, 1987). The practice of purdah also prevents many Islamic women from going to the mosque or from receiving religious instruction, therefore further isolating them from the power sources of their culture. In general, women are more likely to pray in the home rather than in the mosque and do not necessarily follow the regular pattern of praying five times a day (Smith, 1987). Also, although women participate in the fast, it is they who prepare the fast-breaking meal (Smith, 1987).

Christianity   In the late 1960s and early 1970s, feminists pointed out how males monopolized all visible roles in Christianity beyond singing in the choir, baking, and teaching young children (Gross, 1996). Activism from this time on has led to the ordination of women and to the occupation by women of other church positions traditionally held by males, such as deacon. In the 1990s, women made up more than one-third of the student body at theological seminaries (Gross, 1996). However, change has been uneven (Eck

& Jain, 1987). For instance, the Lutheran Church of America, the United Church of Christ, the United Methodist Church, and the Episcopal Church all ordain women. However, there are Christian churches that do not. For instance, the Anglican Church and the Catholic Church do not ordain women. All women in the Catholic Church are laity, including nuns, because ordination to the clerical state is denied to women. Pope John Paul II defended this on the grounds that Jesus had no women among his twelve apostles and that because Jesus is male, only another male may represent him.

It should be noted that there were a handful of nineteenth-century Christian movements in the United States that challenged conventional notions of the family and of men and women's roles. These include the Oneida community, the Shakers, Christian Science, and the Theosophy movement. Some scholars suggest that these movements and the large numbers of women who joined them arose in part out of a rebellion against women's lower status in Protestant churches and American culture (Gross, 1996). Several of these, such as the Christian Science movement and the Theosophy movement, were founded by women.

Reformist Efforts in Feminist Theology

Although modern religion is often an agent of women's oppression, religion is profoundly important to many feminists. As feminist theologians Christ and Plaskow (1979) say, for many women, the discovery that religions teach the inferiority of women is experienced as a betrayal of deeply felt spiritual and ritual experience. To paraphrase Ruth (1995), religions that worship male gods and ideals in male language demean women's full humanity and interfere with women's development of their full potentials. Therefore, religion must be reformed or reconstructed to support the full dignity of women. This next section shows that there is great diversity in how feminists go about this. However, as Gross (1996) points out, despite these differences, feminist theologies agree on two basic things: First, human experience is the source of and authority for authentic religious expression; second, religious expressions, expressions worthy of surviving for centuries and millennia, must promote the full humanity of women as well as men.

Efforts to reform the world's major religions are typically based on the belief that deep down these religions are supportive of women's equality. Reformists assume that although it is generally the case that religion has contributed to the oppression of women, this does not have to be so. Women's personal religious experiences often lead them to believe that their religions are not fundamentally sexist. Reformists examine religious texts and religious history for evidence promoting women's equality. They work to unearth women's religious stories. They fight for the right to be ordained as rabbis and ministers, to have access to holy texts, and to worship alongside men. Plaskow (1991) says that feminism is not about attaining equal rights for women in religious or social structures that remain unchanged; rather, it is about the thoroughgoing transformation of religion and society. The goal is the creation of a society that does not promote superiority and subordination and in which all people have the opportunity to name and shape the structures of meaning that give substance to their lives.

Changing Religious Language and Reinterpreting Texts

"The first step in the elevation of woman to her true position, as an equal factor in human progress, is the cultivation of the religious sentiment in regard to her dignity and equality, the recognition by the rising generation of an ideal Heavenly Mother, to whom their prayers should be addressed, as well as to a Father."
Elizabeth Cady Stanton,
The Women's Bible,
1895

Elizabeth Cady Stanton (1815–1902), one of the founders of the American women's movement, wrote and lectured on a variety of women's issues, including religion. Her *Women's Bible,* published in 1895, was the major nineteenth-century feminist interpretation of the Bible.

One of the more common reformist efforts centers around the changing of God and prayer language to be more female inclusive. For instance, Jewish feminists have tried to add "God of our mothers" to "God of our Fathers" and the names of the foremothers Sarah, Rebecca, Leah, and Rachel to those of the forefathers Abraham, Isaac, and Jacob in Jewish prayer books (Cantor, 1995; Gross, 1996). Both Jewish and Christian feminists have tried, with some success, to address God as "She" or at least to leave out masculine references such as "He" or "our Father." The idea is that without de-emphasizing the masculine face of God, women cannot be fully equal in the religious community.

Another major reformist effort centers around the reinterpretation of traditional religious texts and stories. Such reformists argue that it is not the religions texts that have caused the problems but rather their interpretation and their editing. In other words, the suggestion is that religion has been co-opted for use in the oppression of women. As el Saadawi (1987) says, religion is flexible sometimes to the point of being manipulated by those in power. Too often, religion changes with power, and those who have the power change religion according to their own interests, not according to the interests of the people.

Currently, feminists are reexamining religious texts and history in order to use religion to promote women's equality. These feminists distinguish between those aspects of the tradition that support women's empowerment and those that do not (Gross, 1996). As Carmody (1979) says in her book on women and world religions, the task "is to winnow the wheat of authentic religion . . . from the religion's sexist chaff" (p. 14). Thus biblical scholars show how the story of Adam and Eve can be reread in a way that is not hostile to women (Trible, 1973); use biblical stories such as the one about Mary and Martha to show that Jesus accepted women as equals (Gross, 1996); translate and interpret ancient documents that provide less sexist versions of biblical stories (Arthur, 1987); show that the gospel of Luke indicates that women are significant to a full grasp of the theological meaning of Jesus' life and ministry (Via, 1987); demonstrate that in the prophetic literature and the psalms, God is represented through feminine images (Gardini, 1987); and present evidence that women were important leaders in the early Christian mission and were among Jesus' apostles (Fiorenza, 1979).

They also reinterpret biblical literature. For instance, Asian Christian and Latin American Christian "Mariologists" reclaim and redefine Mary, the mother of Jesus Christ, as a model of liberation, suffering, and struggle (Gebara & Bingemer, 1994; Singapore Asian Christian Women's Conference, 1994). Buddhists review Buddha's history and conclude that it was not his intention to restrict women's participation in Buddhism (Kabilsingh, 1987) and show that essential Buddhist teachings state that women and men have equal potential for enlightenment (Gross, 1993); Buddhist reformers work to

BOX 7.2   *Writings of Female Disciples of Buddha*

Sakyadhita, the International Association of Buddhist Women, maintains that the predominant role of males in the history of Buddhist societies has no Buddhist doctrinal support. The organization researches and promotes knowledge of Buddhist women and fosters communication on issues of relevance to Buddhist women. Here are some Poems of Enlightenment from the society that are attributed to female disciples of Buddha.

> While the breeze blows
> cool and sweet-smelling,
> I shall split ignorance asunder,
> as I sit on the mountaintop.
> *Therigatha 544*

Awareness of impermanence
practiced and developed,
exhausts all desire,
exhausts all ignorance
and removes all conceit.
Therigatha 717

I am friend to all,
companion to all,
sympathetic to all beings,
and I develop a heart full of love,
delighting in non-harming.
Therigatha 648

discredit the orthodox Theravada view of women's inferiority by showing that the scriptures were not written down until 400 years after the Buddha's death (Bancroft, 1987). Box 7.2 offers some of the Poems of Enlightenment that are attributed to female disciples of Buddha. Muslims investigate the religious heritage of Islam and conclude that Muhammad intended equality and dignity for women as well as men (Hassan, 1991; Mernissi, 1987). Hindu feminists look to the epic figure Draupadi, who does not allow men to dictate to her, and to the goddess Kali, who inspires terror and awe and is a model of female power (Gupta, 1991; Sugirtharajah, 1994).

Unfortunately the task of "winnowing the wheat from the sexist chaff" is complicated by the ambiguity of religious texts that permit varying interpretations. As Kusha (1995) notes, every religion is made up of two things: the revelations, which are "expressions of divine will and eternal truths," and interpretations of these revelations. These interpretations are part of a historic process governed by the specifics of the society in which the process unfolds. For instance, verse 31 of the Koran reads "And tell the believing women to lower their gaze and be modest, and to display of their adornment only that which is apparent, and to draw their veils over their bosoms, and not to reveal their adornment save to their husbands or fathers, or their sons." Modern Islamic fundamentalists interpret this as calling for the complete veiling of women and for the segregation of the sexes from each other. However, Islamic feminists point out that this is a recent interpretation. Because the verse before says "Say to the believing *men* that they should lower their gaze and guard their modesty," they argue that there is nothing in the Koran that requires the enshrouding of women.

Hermeneutics is the study of the principles of interpretation for religious texts. Whether one interprets a text literally (as the word of God), allegorically (as stories from which moral lessons are to be learned), or historically (as reflections of the times in which they are written) has important implications for women. For instance, given the wealth of textual passages supportive of women's subordination to men, those who believe in literal rather than historical interpretations are more likely to arrive at the conclusion that God means for women to serve God by serving their husbands. Furthermore, believing that God must certainly know what he is doing and that humans do not have access to his plan, they will accept women's subordination despite any inequity. It is interesting, however, that even so-called literal interpretations are selective, for no religion takes all of the passages found in its scriptures literally. For instance, those who argue that male dominance is required according to the scriptures do not generally argue that slavery is also required, although the scriptures of the three main monotheistic religions (Christianity, Islam, and Judaism) all allow and condone it (Gross, 1996).

Islam is a particularly interesting example as it has been interpreted in such a way as to become one of the most oppressive religions to women. However, Muhammad, the founder of Islam (610–632), abolished practices such as female infanticide, slavery, and levirate (the requirement that a widow marry her husband's brother). He also guaranteed women the right to inherit and bequeath property. He exhorted being kind to women and said, "Treat your women well, and be kind to them." Regarding polygamy, he said, "Marry of the women who seem good to you, two or three or four. And if ye fear that ye cannot do justice to so many, then marry only one." Although he said, "Men are the maintainers of women because Allah has made some of them to excel others . . . and therefore good women are obedient," he also said, "Men and women are equal as two teeth on a comb." Khadija, his first wife, was a successful international trader, fifteen years his senior, and is known to have played an important role in the development of Islam. His second wife was also quite powerful and known as an expert interpreter of the Prophet's writings (Goodwin, 1994; Kusha, 1995). Historically, it appears that women's status improved under early Islam, during the Prophet's life, but by the second and third centuries of Islam, the seclusion and degradation of women had progressed beyond anything known in the first decades of Islam (Goodwin, 1994).

In short, the Koran can be interpreted in a way favorable to women. As Nilofar Ahmad, the director of Daughters of Islam, a women's organization in Pakistan, said, "If I have any message for Muslim women it is that they must study their religion for themselves, learn what it really says, not accept someone else's idea. Only then will they be able to fight for their rights with the very weapon currently used against them—the Koran" (in Goodwin, 1994, p. 75). However, gender equality under Islam is not as simple as pointing to the textual evidence in favor of it. This is because of the ambiguities of the text. The fundamentalists can also find some confirmation for their beliefs regarding women. Furthermore, currently, the male mullahs (who decide how to interpret the text for the masses, and enforce laws accordingly) have chosen an interpretation unsympathetic to gender equality.

Contradictions in Textual Interpretations

The Bible is contradictory with regard to women, and one can find support for traditional gender roles or for gender equality. For instance, women were major figures in the founding and spread of Christianity in its early years (French, 1992; Stark, 1995), and in the Book of Revelation, Jesus is portrayed as freely talking to women, assigning them roles in his parables, and thinking of them as good friends and followers. And, the apostle Paul said, "There is neither Jew nor Greek, there is neither slave nor free, there is neither male nor female; for you are all one in Christ Jesus" (Gal. 3:28). However, in Corinthians (11:4) he says,

> Any man who prays or prophesies with his head covered dishonors his head, but any woman who prays or prophesies with her head unveiled dishonors her head—it is the same as if her head was shaven. For if a woman will not veil herself, then she should cut off her hair; but if it is disgraceful for a woman to be shorn or shaven, let her wear a veil. For a man ought not to cover his head since he is the image and glory of God; but woman is the glory of man. (For man was not made from woman, but woman from man. Neither was man created for woman, but woman for man).

By the later Epistles, the restriction of women is outright. Prayers must only be said by men; women are to dress modestly and are instructed to be quiet and fill all their hours with good deeds (1 Tim. 2:15) (Parvey, 1974).

Buddhism is another religion in which early teachings relevant to women were more sympathetic to gender equality than later ones. For instance, early teachings of Buddha suggested that in marriage the spouses were equal and had equal access to enlightenment (Bancroft, 1987). However, over time, this view was replaced with the one that women were dangerous temptations to men's virtue, especially if uncontrolled by a husband. This change probably arose out of the emphasis on celibacy as part of the road to enlightenment. In one story, Buddha is said to encounter the three daughters of Mara, the god of desire and worldliness. Mara was trying to prevent Buddha from reaching enlightenment. It was only by withstanding the seduction of the daughters—named Desire, Pleasure, and Passion—that Buddha was able to achieve nirvana. Thus, eventually Buddhist literature began to emphasize that the good woman is a submissive woman who honors all her husband's wishes and obeys all of his commands. This neutralizes her wickedness (Carmody, 1974).

Reformists in the Buddhist tradition point out that the fundamental concepts of Buddhism (the Four Noble Truths, Practice, and the attainment of nirvana) are applicable to both sexes. Buddhist reformists direct attention to those stories and texts supportive of women's equality and work toward equal participation within their religion, particularly greater respect and support for nuns. Several recent Buddhist sects give women an equal place with men and have women in top administrative positions. Won Buddhism (begun in Korea and found in Taiwan and in the United States) is one example (Holm, 1994).

It is interesting to note that it appears that women had greater status in these three religions (Islam, Christianity, and Buddhism) in the religions'

Clare of Assisi (1193–1254) was a disciple of St. Francis of Assisi and led the first female Franciscan order.

formative years. This is a pattern found in other religions as well. For instance, it is true of Sikhism (Kaur-Singh, 1994). This Indian religion was founded by Guru Nanak in 1699 C.E. He clearly asserted that women should be equal with men as evidenced in this writing and others opposing dowries, purdah, and female infanticide:

> In a woman, man is conceived,
> From a woman he is born
> With a woman he is betrothed and married.
> With a woman he contracts friendship.
> If one dies another one is sought for,
> Man's destiny is linked to woman.
> Why denounce her, the one from whom even great people are born?
> From a woman, a woman is born,
> None may exist without a woman.

Despite this, like other religions with gender-equal roots, Sikhism in practice became patriarchal. In all of these religions it appears that once the original leaders died, new writings and interpretations emerged that justified the continuation of existing patriarchal traditions. Once again, as el Saadawi (1987) says, those who have power change religion according to their own interests, not according to the interests of the people. It is then up to the people to redirect attention back to the founder's intent. For instance, Sikhism is beginning to turn back to its gender-equal roots. Although it is still the case that no woman has ever been named one of the five Sikh head priests, in 1999, a woman, Jagir Kaur, was appointed as Sikhism's top religious official (Watanabe, 1999).

The analysis of religious texts is a complex scholarly enterprise requiring archeological, historical, and linguistic study (Gross, 1996). Not only are religious scriptures often self-contradictory, but they have usually undergone numerous interpretations and translations over time. The Bible, for instance, was originally written in an ancient language that is no longer used. Furthermore, as Gross (1996) points out, most adherents of religious traditions do not read their scriptures in this scholarly way.

Revolutionary Feminist Theology and the Remaking of Religion

"Jesus Christ cannot symbolize the liberation of women. A culture that maintains a masculine image for its highest divinity cannot allow its women to express themselves as the equals of men."
Naomi Goldenberg

Some feminists question that equality for women can be found through revision of the world's major religions. They believe that the essential core of the world's major religions is so fundamentally sexist that reform efforts are all but hopeless. For instance, Hampson (1987) concludes that real equality for women cannot come from the Christian Church because it is based on religious texts from the past that are, for the most part, supportive of leaving gender relations the way they are. The medium, she says, is the message, and the Bible is not read as just any book but rather as one that conveys what is normative for humans and how we should think about God. She notes that it is clear that the biblical language for God is male (he is Father, King, Lord, Judge) and that women are, in the biblical world, subordinate to men. As Daly (1971) says, if God in *his* heaven is a *father* ruling *his* people, then it is in the nature of things and according to divine plan and the order of the universe that society be male dominated.

Seeking to reconcile their beliefs in God with their beliefs in women's equality, these feminists choose to look at God differently. For instance, Daly (1971) calls for a recasting of the God concept away from the "divine patriarch" and toward something that is transcendent and immanent yet not reducible or able to be represented by such expressions as *person, father, supreme being*. A God that is not objectified in this way cannot be easily used to legitimate oppression, she argues. Or as Hampson (1987) says, women are at a very creative point and have the possibility of creating something new. Many women are beginning to conceive God as spirit who moves among us, between us, and within us (Hampson, 1987).

Some feminists who believe that the world's major religions are fundamentally sexist are working to create new traditions. For example, a number of feminist theologians have made efforts to develop a new textual base for religion that makes women's experience visible and central. Reuther's efforts are particularly well known in Christian feminist theology. In her 1985 book *Womanguides: A Reader Toward a Feminist Theology,* she looks to the past for sources of a **revolutionary feminist theology** and begins the process of developing new texts. She notes that although there is no canon of an alternative feminist religion of ancient times, we are not left without sources for our own experience in the past. Women, she says, can read between the lines of patriarchal texts and find fragments of their own experience that were not completely erased. They can also find, outside of canonized texts, remains of alternative communities that reflect either the greater awe and fear of female power denied in later patriarchy or questionings of male domination in groups in which women did enter into critical dialogue (Reuther, 1985).

Some revolutionary feminist theologians favor an entirely new canon, one not based on existing religions but based on women's experience. Theologians such as Daly (1974) feel that the reformation of patriarchal religion is not enough and is doomed to fail given that these religions are the products of men and are designed to serve the needs of sexist societies. In general, revolutionary feminist theologians favor grounding a new theology in women's experience. Feminist experience, traditional women's experience, women's experience past and present are all potential starting points for a new feminist theology. Recurrent themes are women and nature, the significance of community with other women, women-centered stories and rituals, and the use of female imagery and symbolism (Christ & Plaskow, 1979).

Revolutionary feminist theologians share the belief that we must look to women's experiences as the basis of a new women's religion. However, they differ as to whether they look for this female experience in the present or in the past. Daly (1974) is an example of looking to the present. For example, she emphasizes that the bonding phenomenon among women has deeply spiritual dimensions and is an important source of a new women's religion. For her, the unfolding of women's consciousness is an intimation of the endless

"The Christian tradition is by no means bereft of elements which foster genuine experiences and intimations of transcendence. The problem is that their liberating potential is choked off in the surrounding atmosphere of the images, ideas, values, and structures of patriarchy."
Mary Daly

unfolding of God. Revolutionary feminists of this sort propose that this unfolding occur in a community of women who use dreams, stories, and women's literature to recover and discover women's experience.

Other revolutionary feminist theologians locate women's experiences in favor of spirituality inspired by paganism, an umbrella term for a wide variety of pre- and nonbiblical religions that include female images of the divine (Gross, 1996). These ancient religions are rich sources of positive female imagery and have the advantage of being rooted in tradition (Christ & Plaskow, 1979). According to Gross (1976), collectively, these groups are known as the **feminist spirituality movement.** Many of these focus on **goddess worship,** although as noted by King (1987), there is a lot of variation in how these groups envision the goddess. Writers such as Starhawk (1979) and Eisler (1987) and edited works such as that by Olsen (1983) point to archeological artifacts and myths showing the important role of the goddess in early religion and civilization. For instance, feminine sacred beings (goddesses) were popular in the Greco-Roman traditions that co-existed with early Christianity and remain common in many indigenous African and Native American traditions as well as in Hinduism (Gross, 1996). This quote from Starhawk (1979) gives us a feel for the important role of the goddess in women-centered religion:

> The importance of the Goddess symbol for women cannot be overstressed. The image of the Goddess inspires women to see ourselves as divine, our bodies as sacred, the changing phases of our lives as holy, our aggression as healthy, our anger as purifying, and our power to nurture and create, but also to limit and destroy when necessary, as the very force that sustains all life. Through the Goddess, we can discover our strength, enlighten our minds, own our bodies, and celebrate our emotions. We can move beyond narrow, constricting roles and become whole. (p. 9)

Feminist Wicca is a form of feminist spirituality based on ancient wiccan (witchcraft) traditions (note: this type of witchcraft is not to be associated with Satanism and devil worship). There are numerous versions of Wicca, some of which involve goddess-centered worship and some that do not. Starhawk is one of the best-known feminist spirtualists and has written several feminist Wiccan guides. Starhawk (1979) emphasizes female- and earth-centered, nature-oriented worship that venerates the goddess and that flourished before the advent of Christianity. Like many forms of feminist spirituality, this religion is rich in group and meditative rituals that emphasize women's connectedness with the earth and nature.

Those in the Wiccan movement often emphasize that in the years 1560–1760, ancient witchcraft traditions were eradicated by the Christian Church through a campaign of persecution that constituted an attack on women's power. Historian Anne Barstow (1994) says that approximately 100,000 women were killed in European witch hunts during this time period and 200,000 were accused. Old single women, seen as burdens, were especially likely to be accused, as were outspoken women and those who stepped out of the traditional female role. Accusations of witchcraft are still used today against women who displease others and are too powerful. For instance, Amoah (1987) writes about how witchcraft accusation is used in contemporary Ghana to deal with women's power. Women who are educated and successful in business are especially likely to be accused. In the United States, politician Pat Robertson declared that supporting the Equal Rights Amendment was a "socialist, anti-family, political movement that encourages women to leave their husbands, kill their children, *practice witchcraft,* destroy capitalism and become lesbians" (Barstow, 1994[italics added])!

Barstow suggests that the European and American witch hunts had a number of effects on women's power. One is that fear of being accused of witchcraft kept women quiet and obedient. Another is that the campaign took away a source of power for women. Previously, witches had a lot of power as the village healers who delivered babies, performed abortions, set bones, and prescribed and administered herbal medicines. The attack on witchcraft had the effect of taking the practice of medicine away from women. The European and American witch hunts also essentially destroyed the religion of witchcraft. Indeed, remnants of that smear campaign remain today in common perceptions of witches as casting evil spells and worshiping Satan, although these were not part of the religion of witchcraft. For this reason, women from this tradition often call their religion the **womanspirit movement** rather than witchcraft.

Conclusion

My students invariably ask if women are oppressed if they do not see themselves as so. This chapter suggested that the world's religions play a role in women's oppression, yet your experiences with religious women may suggest that these women do not seem to feel oppressed. This could be due to theological illiteracy in the sense that women may not have the tools to critique traditional theologies. It could be because they accept their religion's portrayal of the gender order. Or, as Carmody (1989) suggests, it may be because, in practice, women do not always accept the designations of their nature and roles as laid out in their religions' orthodox teachings. For instance, she says that Hindu women may believe that it is not necessary to be reborn as a man to gain salvation, despite what they are taught. Christian women denied the right to be ministers could take pride in the other work they did for the church and know that the church was losing out on some great leadership. Women also adapt by developing their own rituals conducted by and for women. For instance, an important part of the lives of many Muslim women is the practice of healing and semi-magical practices (Smith, 1987).

The Jewish theologian Judith Plaskow (1987) also points out that traditional religious women do not necessarily experience themselves as oppressed. Religious women often have a sense of importance in their religions from the knowledge that without them, those parts of religious traditions that take place in the home would not occur. Sered (1994) also maintains that even in many highly

Sonia Johnson (1936–) was excommunicated from the Mormon Church for supporting the Equal Rights Amendment in 1979. Despite this, she founded Mormons for ERA and in 1981 wrote about her experiences in the book *From Housewife to Heretic.*

patriarchal cultures women sacralize their domestic lives through holiday food preparation. In many cultures, food is one of the few resources controlled by women, and it plays a central role in women's religious lives (Sered, 1994).

Many religious women maintain that just because women's role in religion is largely a private one, it is not a lesser one. Indeed, it is interesting that in virtually every culture the heart of the religious tradition, at the local level and in the home, is performed, maintained, and transmitted by women (Eck & Jain, 1987). For instance, in most American Christian homes, it is the mother who gets the children ready for church and who prepares all religious holiday meals. In Orthodox Judaism, the spiritual domain belongs to men, but women participate by keeping the laws of family purity such as the ritual bath seven days after menstruation, preparing kosher food, and running a smooth household such that the men may study the Torah. One Orthodox Jewish woman said that at first the most difficult thing for her to accept in her religion was that the men were separated from the women in the synagogue. However, she now feels that "there is so much going on in the home, with rituals, teaching our children, keeping kosher, that I don't feel left out at the synagogue. At times I feel like a priestess, paying attention to the details of life in a holy way" (Rourke, 1997).

Plaskow (1987) suggests that one benefit of the sex-segregated nature of religion is that it provides women with a common life, or **womanspaces,** where power and integrity come from their shared experiences and visions as women. For instance, in India it is not uncommon for a married woman to live with her in-laws, and a household may consist of a number of sisters-in-law as well. Together these women run the household, and this domestic space is frequently a source of feminine support and friendship. Indeed, most of us can remember our mothers spending many hours working together with other women preparing for religious celebrations. Many of us have done this ourselves and can recall the special times spent with other women as we shared intimacies while we worked to prepare for elaborate meals and rituals (and then cleaned up afterward).

Looked at this way, women's differing role in religion does not seem quite so bad. After all, the practice of religion would grind to a halt without the work of women, and women do have some special times with other women as a result of the sex-segregated nature of most religions. However, as Plaskow cautions, perhaps these womanspaces are simply preserving an unjust system by rendering it bearable and providing shared self-validation. Also, as Eck and Jain (1987) note, here again we confront an old and pervasive disjunction: the indomitable presence and influence of women at the domestic level and the virtual absence of women at the public level. (See Box 7.3 for a look at the numbers of women in power positions in U.S. religions.) The problem with this is twofold. First is that the appearance of this arrangement in religious hierarchies suggests its appropriateness in other life arenas. In other words, it is as if this arrangement is sacred and ordained by God. As Daly (1971) suggests, the situation provides images of the rightness of male rule. A second problem is what it communicates to women about themselves. A number of people suggest that the exclusion of women from religion's public spaces conditions women to view them-

---

BOX 7.3   *The Lay of the Holy Land in the United States*

The following is the total number of female bishops, priests, ministers, and rabbis in the United States as of 1996.

Denomination	Number
Baptist	2,313 ministers
Episcopal	6 bishops; 1,452 priests
Evangelical Lutheran	1,838 pastors
Reform Jewish	259 rabbis
Conservative Jewish	72 rabbis
Orthodox Jewish	0 rabbis
Latter-Day Saints (Mormon)	0 priests
Methodist	10 bishops; 4,995 ministers
Presbyterian	3,026 ministers
Roman Catholic	0 priests
Seventh-Day Adventist	0 priests
Unitarian Universalist Association	4,443 ministers
United Church of Christ (Congregationalist)	2,080 ministers

Source: Niebur, 1996.

selves as inferior to men and to accept subordination. For instance, the French feminist Simone de Beauvoir (in Daly, 1985) writes:

> God's representatives on earth: the pope, the bishop (whose ring one kisses), the priest who says Mass, he who preaches, he before whom one kneels in the secrecy of the confessional—all these are men. . . . The Catholic religion among others exerts a most confused influence upon the young girl.

Likewise, South African Anglican Bishop Desmond Tutu once said when speaking about resistance to the ordination of women into the priesthood, "A child of God subjected to that kind of treatment, actually gets to doubt that he is, or she is, a child of God" (in Hampson, 1987, p. 140).

Religion plays a paradoxical role in the lives of women. In some ways it has contributed to women's oppression. In other ways religion often renders women's suffering more bearable by suggesting that it is a form of worship that will be amply rewarded at some later date. Eck and Jain (1987) note yet another paradox. They suggest that religion is both a problem (or *the* problem) where its structures of dominance have oppressed women and a solution where its vision of liberation or equality has generated powerful movements of social change. They also note that the same religion may be both a problem and a solution. Mosse (1993) makes a similar point when she says that although religion has been used to oppress women, it has also brought women together to fight oppression. She provides the example of Rigoberta Menchu, an Indian Guatemalan peasant woman who is an important leader in her country, and quotes from her autobiography (*I, Rigoberta Menchu,* 1984):

> At the end of 1977, I decided to join a more formal group—a group of peasants in Heuheutenango . . . and yet, I still hadn't reached the rewarding stage of participating fully, as an Indian first, then as a woman, a peasant, a Christian, in the struggle of my people. That's when I started to get more involved. . . . I began traveling to different areas, discussing everything. . . . Why do they reject us? Why is the Indian not accepted? Why is it that the land used to belong to us? . . . Why don't outsiders accept Indian ways?. . . I started to work as an organiser. No one taught me to organise because, having been a catechist, I already knew. We began forming groups of women who wanted to join the struggle. . . . Our main weapon. . . is the Bible. We began to study the Bible as a text which represented each one of us. We tried to relate them to our Indian culture. We took the example of Moses for the men, and we have the example of Judith , who was a very famous woman in her times. She fought hard for her people. . . . We feel it is the duty of Christians to create the kingdom of God on earth. . . . This kingdom will exist only when we all have enough to eat, when our children, brothers, parents don't have to die from malnutrition.

As this chapter ends, women's diversity must once again be acknowledged. In this case, the last thirty years have brought forth a multiplicity of feminist theologies. Feminist theological voices have been heard in North America and Europe since the late 1960s, but Third World feminist theologies and feminist theologies of women of color are more recent and much less known (King, 1994). King (1994), in a book on feminist theology from the Third World, notes the ways in which First World feminist theology and **Third World feminist theology** are similar and different. As King views it, feminist theology is in general an advocacy theology concerned with the liberation of women from oppression, guided by the principle of seeking to achieve the full humanity of women.

In the Third World context, feminist theology is much more of a **liberation theology,** as it develops where the oppression of women and the denial of their full humanity is often much greater. The above paragraph from Rigoberta Menchu is an example of liberation theology. This is also true of theologies developed in the First World by women from traditionally oppressed groups. For instance, **Womanist theology** is a newly developing African American Christian feminist theology. Womanist theology brings Black women's social, reli-

BOX 7.4   *Firsts for Women in Religion in the United States*

1970	First female Lutheran minister—Elizabeth Platz
1972	First female Reform rabbi—Sally Preisand
1974	First Reconstructionist rabbi—Sandy Eisenberg
1976	Episcopal Church votes to allow the ordination of women as bishops and priests
1980	First female Methodist bishop—Majorie Swank Matthews
1984	First female African American Methodist bishop—Leotine Kelly
1985	First female Conservative rabbi—Amy Eilberg
1989	First female Episcopal bishop—Barbara Harris
1991	First female Lutheran bishop—April Ulring Larson
1993	First female Diocesan Episcopal bishop—Mary Adelia McLeod
1994	First female senior rabbi of a large Reform congregation—Laura Geller
1994	First Catholic altar girls
1996	First female evangelical minister in the Christian Reformed Church—Lesli van Milligen
1996	First chairwoman of the Methodist World Council—Frances Alguire

gious, and cultural experiences into the theological discourse (Williams, 1994). Womanist theology is a liberation theology in that it emphasizes justice for women and the oppressed and is envisioned as an instrument for theological and social change. Likewise, *Mujerista* **theology,** a Latin American feminist theology, has as its goal the liberation of Hispanic women and all people and the changing of church structures such that Hispanic women may participate fully in them (Isasi-Diaz, 1994). *Mujerista* theology also emphasizes the discovery and affirmation of God in Hispanic women's daily lives and communities.

Once again it is important to acknowledge women's activism, for it is through such activism that progress toward gender equality in religion is made. In virtually every religious tradition women have called their lower status into question. The last thirty years of the twentieth century evidenced remarkable change toward greater gender equality in many of the world's religions. (Box 7.4 gives some examples of important firsts for women in U.S. religions.)

Increases in women's status in secular society have, to some extent, preceded and stimulated women to question patriarchy within their religions and to work actively to promote change. There is great courage involved in this work. Calling for equality is especially difficult for religious women who have been socialized to think that virtuous religious women are quiet and long-suffering. Those who do this work face many obstacles. They must work to change old and entrenched organizational structures that typically exclude women. Their opponents point to tradition and to religious texts as evidence that things should not change. Calls for equality are also typically met with the response that change represents an assault on the traditional family, and therefore women's equality poses a threat to the religious group's survival. Women calling for change are likely to be ignored, and if they persist, threatened with abandonment or branded as traitors and betrayers to their religious community. For example, at the Wailing Wall in Israel, Orthodox Jewish men will not worship beside women, and, for the most part, women do not challenge this segregation. In 1994, the Israeli Supreme Court dismissed a petition requesting that women be allowed to pray out loud at the wall. The petition was viewed by religious authorities as an outrageous act of rebellion and a usurpation of the male claim to exclusive communion with God (Shalev, 1995). In 1997, a group of Conservative and Reform Jewish women and men carried a Torah scroll to the wall to worship together. They were pelted by bags of stones and excrement hurled by Orthodox Jews shouting "Nazis! Nazis!" ("World in Brief," 1997).

This chapter, like the ones that preceded it, illustrates the persistence and prevalence of patriarchy. It also reminds us of the courage displayed by those who work for change and who defy tradition. Once again there is evidence of positive results from women's activism. This theme is a major focus of the remaining chapters, which center on women's political activities.

Terms and Concepts

feminist theology

masculine God language

sexism in religious texts

hermeneutics

revolutionary feminist theology

feminist spirituality movement

goddess worship

womanspirit movement

womanspaces

Third World feminist theology

liberation theology

Womanist theology

Mujerista theology

Study Questions

1. In what way is religion a part of the social systems that keep women lower in power and status?

2. What is masculine God language? Why do many feminists argue that the male imagery used by so many of the world's religions is problematic?

3. What are the key issues identified by feminists who critique religious texts?

4. What are the four common themes found in religious texts that perpetuate females' lower status and power? How are these themes illustrated with examples from each of the world's major religions?

5. In what ways are the religious rituals and practices of the major religions sex segregated? What progress has been made toward greater gender equality?

6. What basic assumptions underlie reformist efforts in feminist theology? What types of efforts are made by reformist theologians? Why is it difficult to "winnow the wheat from the sexist chaff of religion"?

7. What basic assumptions underlie revolutionary feminist theology? How do some revolutionary efforts focus on the present and others on the past?

8. What is feminist spirituality? What is the role of the goddess in feminist spirituality?

9. What are womanspaces? In what way are they beneficial? In what way are they problematic?

10. What is the role of diversity in feminist theology? How are First and Third World feminist theologies similar and different?

Discussion Questions and Activities

1. Are traditional religions (Christianity, Islam, Hinduism, Judaism, and Buddhism) fundamentally sexist or have they merely been misinterpreted? Is it feasible that traditional religions can be reconceived or reinterpreted in a way that permits gender equality? Or, will it be necessary for women to develop their own religions in order to achieve equality?

2. Does the use of "He" to refer to God and the exclusion of women from most religious hierarchies condition women to view themselves as inferior to men?

3. Make a list of masculine adjectives that describe God and another list of feminine adjectives that describe God. What does this tell you about your conceptions of God? Is God male?

4. Interview a woman minister or rabbi, a practitioner of feminist spirituality (for instance, a witch), or a traditional religious woman, using questions developed from the chapter.

Violeta de Chamorro, president of Nicaragua (1990–1996). Women as national leaders are still uncommon. However, women are very political and have a long history of involvement in economic, environmental, revolutionary, and peace and justice movements.

Women in Politics

Political space belongs to all citizens, but men monopolize it.
United Nations Human Development Report, 1995

*I*n their book on women and politics worldwide, Chowdhury and her colleagues (1994) conclude that *in no country do women have political status, access, or influence equal to men's.* The sweep of women's political subordination encompasses the great variety of cultures, economic arrangements, and regimes in which they live (Chowdhury et al., 1994). This political subordination is a symptom of women's inequality as well as a challenge to gender equality movements.

When people think of politics, they often think of activities such as registering to vote, voting, running for and holding political office, and lobbying elected officials. The political sphere is also typically viewed as a masculine one and politicians as male. This is not surprising given that: the majority of formal political positions continue to be held by men (see Box 8.1); politics are a public activity, and the public sphere is associated with male activities; media coverage of politics tends to be almost exclusively focused on male political actors; and political science has centered on male political activity and leaders.

A feminist might note two things about these perceptions. First, it is indeed important to note the domination of formal politics by men and to increase women's representation. Because laws tend to be made by men, they are frequently *for* men and do little to address women's subordination. Furthermore, policies that explicitly address the needs of women and children are less likely because male lawmakers are often unaware of these needs. The domination of formal politics by men also perpetuates the notion that politics are the domain of men and therefore discourages women from participating. Some might also argue that the dearth of female representation deprives policymaking of a needed feminine, humanistic, earth-centered perspective and that women's qualities and ways of working will bring a needed cooperative, power-sharing element to politics.

Second, a feminist perspective on politics recognizes that by limiting our definition of politics to electoral activities and offices, women seem less political than they actually are. In fact, if the definition of political activity is broadened to include women's involvement in social movements and protests, women are a lot more political than they appear to be at first glance. As Lister (1997) notes, a distinction should be made between the level of women's

> "We can't be certain that women would make different decisions than men, but they might if there were enough of them to affect the decision process and its environment."
> *Jeanne Kirkpatrick, first female U.S. ambassador to the UN, 1981–1985*

BOX 8.1 *Political Power Worldwide*

In 1997, of the 191 governments worldwide,

- There were four female heads of government, five female heads of state, ten female foreign ministers, and ten female UN ambassadors.

- Of the 173 countries with legislatures, women were leaders of legislatures in only 7 percent of the countries.

- Women comprised 10 percent of the membership of the upper house of legislatures.

- Women comprised 12 percent of the membership of the lower house of legislatures.

- The Nordic countries had the highest percentages of women in national legislatures: Sweden (40%), Norway (39%), Finland (33%), Denmark (33%), the Netherlands (31%).

- Germany (26%), China (21%), Canada (18%), and Mexico (14%) all have more women serving in national legislatures than do the United States (11%), Britain (9%), and France (6%).

- Globally, Japan (5%) and Kuwait (0%) have among the lowest percentages of women in their national legislatures.

- Only nine of the 173 countries had no women representatives.

- In the period from 1988 to 1997, the number of women in parliaments worldwide declined 3 percent—from 15 percent to 12 percent.

Source: Inter-Parliamentary Union.

political *representation* and women's political *activity*. Women for instance, have a long history as key players in antiwar and peace movements, revolutionary movements, and economic movements (Peterson & Runyan, 1993). Unfortunately, women's political activity is rarely recognized or documented by political scientists because it is more apt to be in the context of social movements and protests ("power from below"), and politics tend to be narrowly defined in terms of participation in **formal politics** ("power from above") (West & Blumberg, 1990). Women, as I've remarked before and will demonstrate in this and our last two chapters, do act politically despite significant obstacles. That so many women overcome the barriers to their participation, at least to some extent, is a testimony to their commitment to the ideals of political citizenship (Lister, 1997). This commitment is especially evident in the sphere of **informal politics,** which include local community-based action and national and international social movements (Lister, 1997). This chapter begins with a consideration of women's participation in formal politics or "power from above." From there, it moves to a discussion of women's "power from below" in the form of women's participation in social movements and protests.

Women's Participation in Formal Politics: Voting

Female **voting,** or **women's suffrage,** was a major aim of the early feminist movement from the mid-1880s through the first half of the twentieth century.

BOX 8.2   *Women Gain the Right to Vote: A Sampling*

Years	Countries
1893–1919	Australia, Canada, Finland, Germany, Greenland, Iceland, New Zealand, Norway, Russia, Sweden, Turkey
1920–1944	Brazil, Burma, Ecuador, France, Ireland, Lithuania, Philippines, Spain, Thailand, United Kingdom, United States
1945–1959	Argentina, Bolivia, Chad, Chile, China, Columbia, Costa Rica, El Salvador, Ethiopia, Guatemala, Honduras, India, Japan, Mali, Mexico, Morocco, Nicaragua, Niger, Pakistan, Portugal, Senegal, Venezuela, Vietnam
1960–1979	Algeria, Angola, Iran, Kenya, Libya, Nigeria, Paraguay, Peru, Sudan, Zaire
Since 1980	Hong Kong, Iraq, Marshall Islands, South Africa, Western Samoa

Source: Seager, 1997.

Voting rights for women were hard-won, and women worldwide were arrested and harassed demonstrating for this right. In 1907, Finland became the first country to elect women to public office. Swiss women were not allowed to vote in national elections until 1972. See Box 8.2 for a sampling of countries and the year women's suffrage was attained. It should be noted however, that there were often restrictions on *which* women could vote. For example, Native American women were not allowed to vote until 1924, four years after other American women, and in Australia, White women won the vote in 1902 but Aboriginal women had to wait until 1967 (Seager, 1997). On March 8, 1999, International Women's Day, women in Qatar were permitted to run for political office and to vote for the first time. Qatar is a prosperous, small country of 150,000 citizens on the Persian Gulf. It has a monarchy and is primarily Islamic. In the majority of nations today women have the right to vote. Exceptions include Kuwait and Bahrain and of course those countries in which voting rights are nonexistent, such as Saudi Arabia. There is evidence from a handful of countries (France, Germany, Russia, and the United States) that women, more than men, favor liberal or left-wing parties (Seager, 1997).

Voting does not by itself guarantee equality of opportunity in politics (Abukhalil, 1994). In some countries, women's fathers, brothers, or husbands may interfere in their voting choices or discourage them from voting at all. Women's ability to exercise their voting rights freely is also impaired in

In August, 1997, **Masoumeh Ebtekar** became the first woman vice-president in Iranian history.

those countries where there are discrepancies in the adult literacy rates of women and men. Perhaps it is not surprising, then, that in many countries, women vote at a lower rate than men. Also, in some countries, voting is a token gesture intended to ratify choices made by tyrannical rulers. In certain countries, women's independent political organizations are not permitted. Lastly, women's voting is only one form of political involvement. Although many years have passed since women in most countries have obtained voting rights, women remain underrepresented in political power positions.

Women's Participation in Formal Politics: Parliaments, Congresses, and Cabinets

The Presence of Women in Political Office

Political systems, whatever the ideology and form, rest on the virtual exclusion or marginalization of women from formal politics (Chowdhury et al., 1994). As Rule (1994, p. 15) put it,

> Government of the people, by the people, and for the people—Abraham Lincoln's concept of democracy—is an ideal unachieved in the world. Democracy falls short when women of whatever color or ethnic group cannot vote or cast an effective vote, cannot expect success in electing representatives of their choice or in being elected to the legislative bodies, and have little hope for enactment of laws they believe are critically needed.

Governments are complex organizational structures consisting not only of heads of state but of other formal political actors such as members of **parliaments and congresses.** As is evident in Box 8.1, women only rarely serve as heads of government and are consistently underrepresented in parliaments and congresses. Appendix A also illustrates how, on average, approximately 5 to 10 percent of formal government positions are held by women worldwide.

Women are even more rare in government **cabinets.*** Women appear to fare better in obtaining elected political positions than they do in obtaining powerful appointments such as these. This is not to say that there has not been improvement. In 1986, Norway became the first country to have a cabinet with close to half of its members women (Bystydzienski, 1994). An analysis of cabinet appointments in western Europe shows that the number of women in parliamentary cabinets increased from 1968 to 1992 in all of the countries studied,

---

*Cabinets consist of advisors to the head of state who frequently lead specific government agencies and wield considerable policymaking power. In many countries, cabinet members are called ministers (as in Minister of Finance), but in some, such as the United States, they are called secretaries (as in Secretary of Labor).

except Portugal (Davis, 1997). There was however, wide variation across countries and within countries over time (the researcher suggests that this is because cabinet appointments change with administration changes, and some appoint more women than others). In the Nordic countries of Norway, Finland, and Sweden, the representation of women approached parity with men. In contrast, in continental Europe (Austria, Belgium, Germany, France, and the Netherlands), representation ranged between 10 and 20 percent. In the United Kingdom and Spain, the levels of representation were between 5 and 10 percent, and in southern Europe, they were at or below 5 percent. Women are typically appointed to cabinet positions in the areas of family, social affairs, health, and education and rarely to economic and defense positions.

> In 1997, **Madeleine Albright,** former U.S. ambassador to the United Nations, became the highest-ranking woman in the history of the U.S. government when she became U.S. secretary of state.

Explaining the Low Numbers of Women in Political Office

Why are so few women in parliaments, congresses, and cabinets? In earlier chapters, I suggested that women's domestic responsibilities and private/domestic sphere activities make it difficult for them to participate politically. For example, in Chapter 2 I suggested that the hand that rocks the cradle is too tired to rule the world. I also noted that when we consider women's paid and unpaid labor, women generally have less leisure time than do men. Moreover, it is not only women's longer workday that interferes, it is their lack of control over when they will be available and whether (how) family obligations will interfere with political pursuits (Peterson & Runyan, 1993). Combining family responsibilities and political office are largely a problem *for women only;* men are not forced to make these choices because their political activities are considered separate from their domestic relations (Peterson & Runyan, 1993).

> "But what is true I think, is that women who want and need a life outside as well as inside the home have a much, much harder time than men because they carry such a heavy double burden . . . and the life of a working mother who lives without the constant presence and support of the father of her children is three times harder than that of any man I have ever met."
> *Golda Meir, 1975*

It is also the case that cultural norms currently adversely affect the prospect for election to public office in every nation (Zimmerman, 1994). I have already suggested that politics is stereotyped as a male domain, and as part of gender conformity, men are more likely to pursue formal politics than are women. As Peterson and Runyan (1993) suggest, women are socialized into domestic roles that are antithetical to public political sphere activities, and the traits associated with political efficacy (ambition, aggression, competitiveness, authority) are seen as distinctly *un*feminine. The result is that women do not see themselves comfortably in conventionally defined politics, and men and women have trouble accepting them as political agents (Peterson & Runyan, 1993). The jobs that often lead to formal political office are also ones that are gender-typed as male (law, military, career civil service, big business), and this too reduces the pool of women "qualified" for political office (Peterson & Runyan, 1993).

The situation is similar for cabinet appointees, who are largely recruited from a political elite. In most cases, cabinet ministers are drawn from the ranks of parliamentarians, especially those that have served on important committees or who have otherwise distinguished themselves, for instance through finesse in parliamentary debate (Davis, 1997). In addition, appointments are often given as rewards for loyal party service.

The problem is also one of demand: The culture and processes of formal political institutions (especially political parties) are major barriers to women's equal participation in institutional politics (Chowdhury et al., 1994). Women, in general, have not been welcome in the fraternity of formal politics. What Chowdhury (1994) says in regard to politics in Bangladesh is true in general: Women's participation in electoral politics is illustrative of male control of party organizations; men have a greater ability to build viable constituency and party support in favor of nominations; women lack access to the kind of money and patronage needed to win elections; and the aggressive electioneering tactics often employed discourage women's entrance into the fray—especially the threat of character assassination and innuendo that is damaging to women's honor.

Studies reveal that when women are first elected to parliament, they are typically members of families long active in electoral politics (Zimmerman, 1994). Many women found in parliaments and congresses are "political surrogates" for martyred husbands or fathers. For instance, in 1998 in the United States, Mary Bono took her deceased husband's place in the U.S. House of Representatives and Lois Capps assumed her late husband's place in the U.S. Senate. Both women were largely politically inexperienced. A second common path to power is that of the "party insider" whose decades of hard work and dedication are finally rewarded with party advancement. Many women in formal politics have paid serious party dues to get into office. A third path to power is that of the "political outsider." Female outsider candidates are occasionally elected, helped out by voters' assumptions that they represent an honest alternative to corrupt, male politicians.

Increasing the Number of Women in Political Office

In 1949, **Rachel Kagan** became the first feminist to be elected to the Israeli Parliament (the Knesset).

As long as the sexual division of labor keeps women tied closely to the private domestic sphere, only a minority of women will be able to enter the formal political sphere (Lister, 1997). Because the absence of women in formal politics is partly due to their domestic and reproductive responsibilities, it follows that more equitable divisions of child care and household labor could make some difference in women's political activity. It has also been suggested that changing the parliamentary/congressional environment to be more family friendly (such as provision of child-care facilities and changes in working hours) would help. Too often women are disadvantaged by the fact that political systems are run on the assumption that those who participate have no family responsibilities (Norris & Lovenduski, 1995). However, this alone will not result in significant improvements in the absence of changes within the organizational cultures of parties and the electoral rules of the game (Chowdhury et al., 1994). Unfortunately, changing the political cultures that reject women's participation in the political process is a difficult task that may take many generations (Zimmerman, 1994). For instance, women's parliamentary representation is especially low in countries where dominant religions (such as Islam in Kuwait) and philosophies (such as Confucianism in Korea) confine women to subordinate roles (Rule, 1994).

Electoral system reform is one way to increase women's legislative representation. The electoral system (the procedures by which representatives are elected) explains almost 30 percent of the varying proportions of women in democracies' national legislatures (Rule, 1994). Rule (1994) demonstrates this in an analysis of twenty-seven long-established democracies. The system that yields the greatest number of female parliamentarians has these characteristics: Seats are allocated roughly in proportion to the votes each party receives, there are five or more representatives per district, three or more parties prepare lists of candidates for election from each district, and the voter may choose candidates from the lists. Under this system, parties see an advantage in having some female candidates to attract more female voters and gain more seats. This type of system, called the **party list/proportional representation system** (PL/PR), is used in all of the countries with the highest percentages of female legislators. However, a positive outcome for women still depends upon the parties including women on their candidate list (Lakeman, 1994). Party list quotas are one means of ensuring this and are discussed a bit later in the chapter.

In contrast, non party list/nonproportional representation systems, or **single-member district systems** (SMD), such as those in the United Kingdom, the United States, Canada, and France, require that winning candidates obtain an absolute majority vote or a plurality in any one constituency. In such cases, parties will usually choose and support only those candidates believed capable of winning the required number of votes. For the most part, it is believed that running a male candidate is the safer bet. In short, women generally do better in multimember elections and constituencies in which people can choose more than one candidate and where they can elect a female candidate in addition to a male one(s).

Making electoral systems more "women friendly" is clearly part of the solution to increasing women's presence in legislatures, and newly developing democracies can conceivably choose PL/PR systems with ten to fifteen representatives per district in order to do so. The new democracy of Namibia adopted a PL/PR system in 1989. A total of fourteen women appeared on candidate lists, and women were elected to 6.9 percent of assembly seats. Although this may not seem significant, this was only the second election in which Namibian women were eligible to vote and run for office.

Quotas are also a way to increase the number of female parliamentarians. One type of quota that would increase both the number of women and other traditionally underrepresented groups in electoral systems would be the allocation of parliamentary or congressional seats to different groups in accordance with their proportions in the population (Zimmerman, 1994). However, no country has elected this route although other, less profound types of quota systems have been used with some success. For instance, in the PL/PR countries of Finland, Sweden, Norway, Denmark, and Iceland (which have the highest number of female representatives in the world), women working inside and outside of political parties sought and won quotas setting a minimum percentage of women for their parties' lists of candidates (Rule, 1994).

Similarly, in the PL/PR country of Argentina, a law passed in 1991 stipulates that 30 percent of the upper-level positions on party lists must be occupied by female candidates. The bill was introduced by Senator Margarita Malharro and Representatives Norma Allegrone de Fonte and Florentina Gomez Miranda. On the day of the parliamentary debate, huge numbers of women from different social classes and different ideologies mobilized in the gallery, the Chambers, and in the streets and squares near the Congress (Bonder & Nari, 1995). The first election following implementation of the law made an immediate difference in the number of female federal district senators: Of the fifty-four senators elected, nineteen (35%) were female (Molinelli, 1994). The quota law also increased women's representation in the Chamber of Deputies from 5.5 percent in 1991 to 12.8 percent in 1993, and in 1994 resulted in the election of eighty women representatives (26.4%) to the constitutional assembly (Feijoo, 1998). The percentage of women in the House of Representatives rose from 5.4 percent in 1991 to 13.3 percent in 1993 (Bonder & Nari, 1995). Some feminists remain skeptical about the results, suggesting that the positions are being filled by the private recruitment of the supporters, friends, and relatives of male politicians (Bonder & Nari, 1995; Feijoo, 1998). There is also a concern that many of the women elected are not committed to gender issues (Bonder & Nari, 1995). As Bonder and Nari (1995) noted after anonymous interviews with Argentinean women legislators, the quota law in Argentina is not a point of arrival but rather one of departure, an effort that requires constant monitoring so that its original significance will not be lost.

PL/PR systems appear most advantageous for increasing the number of women legislators. However, there are some changes that can overcome the disadvantages of the SMD system for women. Australia provides a good example of the role that political parties in SMD systems can play in increasing the number of female representatives. Sawer (1994) describes how changes in Australian political parties increased the percentage of female parliamentarians from 2 percent in 1972 to 18 percent in 1997. It began with the Labor party's desire to gain power. Party leaders figured out that if they could get 8 percent of the women's vote, they could gain control of the government (voting is mandatory in Australia so women's votes can make a big difference). The problem was that women generally did not vote Labor, because of its image as the working man's party. In 1981, the party adopted an affirmative action policy aimed at increasing women's representation at all levels of the party to approximately 25 percent. In addition, they also promoted some women-centered policies such as a sex discrimination bill. Their strategy was successful, and by 1983, they were able to take control of the government. Since 1985, the other political parties (the Liberal, National, and Australian Democratic parties) have also been fielding more female candidates. The Australian Democrats have the largest number of female parliamentary representatives as well as females occupying top leadership positions within the party.

Reserving a certain number of parliamentary seats for women also has the effect of increasing women's parliamentary presence. However, although it increases women's numbers, it does not necessarily increase women's political power. In Bangladesh, for instance, 30 out of 330 seats were reserved for women, but the way it works is that women are indirectly elected—the party obtaining the largest number of parliamentary seats gets to nominate women for the seats. Women's participation in the parliament is almost entirely dependent upon the male elite in power, and this accentuates women's political dependence and subordination (Chowdhury, 1994). Chowdhury (1994) points out that "a policy of protection hardly ever guarantees equality unless it is intended as a temporary device and orchestrated with measures designed to eliminate the factors that warrant the protection" (p. 99).

In the SMD system of the United States, feminist groups have attempted to increase the number of female candidates by funding their campaigns. EMILY's List (the acronym stands for Early Money Is Like Yeast), in the United States, is one such example. In the United States, the average cost of a congressional campaign in a district without an incumbent is over half a million dollars (in California, Senators Dianne Feinstein and Barbara Boxer spent $8 and $10 million, respectively, in the 1992 election). Compared to most other electoral democracies, American election districts cover large populations and vast geographic distances. At an average size of 550,000 residents, many U.S. congressional districts are larger than the entire populations of many nations (Lauter, 1995). U.S. congressional candidates must therefore reach voters through the mass media, but this of course costs big money. When women are able to run for congressional office, they win at the same rate as men. Unfortunately, fewer women run for office because they lack access to the traditional business, professional, and political networks that allow male candidates to raise funds (Lauter, 1995). Begun in 1985 by feminist Ellen R. Malcolm, EMILY's List helps female candidates by introducing them to a network of donors who provide funds. In 1992, EMILY's List raised and spent $6.2 million for congressional Democratic candidates, and of the fifty-two female candidates they supported, twenty-five won (Lauter, 1995).

> "A woman's place is in the house, and in the Senate."
> *American/feminist proverb*

Women's activism plays an important role in increasing female parliamentary representation. For instance, in the newly developing democracy of South Korea, Nakyun Sin, President of the Korean League of Women Voters, and Hyun-ja Kim, a former National Assembly representative, have been advocating a proportional representation system with quotas for women; public opinion is supportive of changes (Darcy & Hyun, 1994). Norway provides one of the most dramatic and successful examples of women's activism to increase the number of female political representatives. Bystydzienski (1992b, 1995) describes how a coalition of women's groups mobilized women to run for office, worked through political parties, and taught voters how to use flexible voting rules (the system permits the writing in of names on ballots). The result was the quadrupling of female political representation locally and nationally in a period of two decades. According to Bystydzienski (1994), Norway exemplifies the fact that although a PL/PR system is helpful for women's representation, it is only in combination with a strong, organized women's movement that the number of women representatives can be significantly increased. Female-only political parties exist in Armenia, Chad, Colombia, Iceland, and Lithuania. So far, only the Icelandic Women's Alliance has had candidates elected into office.

Women's organizations also work to increase women's understanding of the political process, or their political literacy. In most countries, getting elected is a complex, expensive, and bureaucratic process. Without the backing of those that know and understand complex election rules, it is typically difficult to run for office. Unfortunately, the political insiders and parties familiar with the process are often hesitant to mentor women through it. In some places, women's organizations have stepped in to close this gap. For example, Korean women's organizations such as the Women's Research Association, the Korean Research Institute for Women and Politics, and the Center for Korean Women in Politics work to educate and train potential female candidates (Darcy & Hyun, 1994). Another example comes from Norway, where women activists in the 1970s engaged in a door-to-door campaign to teach women how to use the ballot by making them aware that by crossing out men's names on the voting lists, women could ensure the election of women (Bystydzienski, 1994). According to Bystydzienski, this technique proved so successful that male politicians subsequently limited voters' ability to alter ballots. Fortunately, Norwegian activists also convinced political parties to nominate women candidates and accept gender quotas, and female parliamentary representation has remained high.

In 1997, **Yeh Chin-Fong** became the first Taiwanese woman to serve in the important cabinet position of interior minister.

Increasing the number of women in cabinet positions is largely dependent upon increasing the pool of qualified applicants. This is somewhat dependent upon changes in a number of gendered systems. Gender-role segregation and sexism are large contributors to a situation in which there are fewer qualified females available to tap for cabinet positions. According to Davis (1997), if women are to be appointed to cabinet positions, we must first increase the number of women in parliaments and congresses. Because some cabinet appointments come from the military or industry, it also follows that changes need to be made there. Secondly, they must maneuver such that they are politically powerful and visible. Unfortunately, given their frequent minority status in politics and the **masculinist political culture,** it is often difficult for women to gain appointment to important political committees and to assume leadership positions within political parties and congresses.

Women Make a Difference

"And I know, in the depth of my being and in all my knowledge of history and humanity, I know women will struggle for a social order of peace, equality and joy."
Joan Kelly, 1982

Remember that feminists are very interested in increasing the number of women in formal government positions, in part because of the assumption that legislation more favorable to women, children, families, and the needy will result. In fact, researchers consistently find a positive relationship between the number of female legislators and the amount of legislation favorable to women, children, families, education, and medical and welfare needs (Davis, 1997; Rule, 1994; Thomas, 1994). For instance, women state legislators in the United States are more likely than male legislators to emphasize issues that affect women and children (Beckman & D'Amico,

1995). It is important to note, however, that when women are present in only small numbers, they have a negligible effect on policy outcomes (Davis, 1997; Saint-Germain, 1989; Thomas, 1994).

Women's Participation in Formal Governments: Female Heads of State

The mid- to late-twentieth century saw a number of female heads of state, and their presence in world politics interests us for several reasons. First there is the question of how women come to occupy such visible and customarily male leadership positions. This is an important question to feminists concerned with increasing women's power. It is also important to examine women as national leaders because their existence often masks the problem of sexism in world politics. In this section, you will see that not only does sexism persist in countries with female heads of state, but as it turns out, gender plays a large role in the election, appointment, and retention of female leaders. Another interesting question has to do with whether female world leaders lead differently than men. Feminists frequently assume that things would be better for women, and for the world, if there were more female leaders. But does the evidence support this assumption? This next section examines the evidence to see whether female leaders are less likely to lead their countries into war, whether they are more likely to pursue domestic policies friendly to women and children, and whether they typically pursue feminist agendas.

In 1872, **Victoria Clafin Woodhull** ran for U.S. president on her own Equal Rights Party ticket.

Paths to Power

Women world leaders (heads of state) are still relatively uncommon, and only a handful are in power at any given time. Indeed, in politics as well as in business, glass ceilings are still common—there are many barriers preventing women from moving into the highest power positions in organizations. One barrier is the gender stereotypes that suggest that women will be ineffective leaders. For instance, the dominant image of women in most cultures is that of the wife–mother who is competent in the private sphere of life, not the public one. Likewise, political parties are unlikely to run or appoint women if they believe that stereotypes of women would interfere with a female leader's effectiveness and public support. Educational and organizational barriers also operate to reduce the pool of women qualified to run for and hold office. For instance, in many countries, elected politicians are lawyers or former military officers, and women have been largely excluded from law schools and high-level military positions. In addition, women are often structurally disadvantaged in political organizations by assignments that do not give them the opportunity to garner the experiences necessary to move up the organizational ladder. They are also less likely to be groomed and mentored for political power positions by powerful people within political organizations. Given these barriers, how do women break through the glass ceiling

BOX 8.3 *Paths to Power: Political Surrogates*

Leader/Year Appointed or Elected	Country/Position	Surrogate For
Corazon Cojuangco Aquino, 1986	Philippines, president	Husband
Sirimavo Ratwatte Dias Bandaranaike, 1959	Sri Lanka, prime minister	Husband
Benazir Bhutto, 1988	Pakistan, prime minister	Father
Violeta Barrios Torres de Chamorro, 1990	Nicaragua, president	Husband
Indira Nehru Gandhi, 1966	India, prime minister	Father
Maria Estela "Isabelita" Cartas Martinez de Peron, 1974	Argentina, president	Husband
Aung Sun Su Ki	Myanmar (Burma), expected head of state should military rule be suspended	Father

Source: D'Amico, 1995.

that so clearly characterizes world politics? D'Amico (1995) identifies three common paths to power for female heads of state. The first is the "widow's walk to power," or as it is sometimes called, the "political surrogate."

Political Surrogate Path to Power

According to D'Amico (1995), most women who govern are the daughters of privilege and politics. They are disproportionately from the upper classes and in many cases follow the "widow's walk" to power. In other words, they are **political surrogates** (stand-ins) for husbands killed by natural or political causes and, as such, are expected to act as their husbands would. Likewise, a handful of female leaders come into power as stand-ins for their deceased political fathers when there are no male offspring to assume this role. However, in contrast to the widows, the daughters of political martyrs typically have extensive political party experience and merely present themselves as surrogates to get elected. Upon election, they often stray significantly from their father's leadership style and policies. In many ways, these daughters fit better in the path to power described in the next section, that of political insider. Box 8.3 lists some of the political surrogates of the past half-century.

In the case of most surrogates, the husband or father was assassinated and subsequently martyred by the citizenry as a persecuted leader of democratic change or national independence. When it appeared that the government was going in the direction of prestruggle politics and there were no electable alternative candidates, political strategists sought the next best thing to the successful but now deceased challenger—his male offspring. Lacking a son of the right age, his widow or daughter would have to do. During the campaign, references to the achievements and martyrdom of the husband/father were made repeatedly, and it was implied that the female candidate would serve as a stand-in for the cherished leader. With all but a few exceptions, these women were well educated and came from wealthy, political families.

The world's first woman prime minister, Sirimavo Bandaranaike of Sri Lanka (1960–1965, 1970–1977, 1994–present), took the widow's walk to power. She came from an aristocratic, well-off family. Her husband, Solomon Dias Bandaranaike, was a popular political leader largely because of his nationalism. Following centuries of colonial rule, he campaigned to make Buddhism the national religion and Sinhalese the national language (replacing English), and he was part of the movement to gain independence from Britain. He became prime minister in 1956, only to be assassinated in September 1959. New elections were set for March 1960, and Sirimavo Bandaranaike was asked to campaign on behalf of her husband's political party, the Sri Lankan Freedom Party (SLFP). In May 1960, she reluctantly accepted headship of the SLFP, and when they won the majority of seats in the House of Representatives, as head of the party, she became prime minister. Like many women who walk the surrogate path to power, prior to her husband's death, Sirimavo Bandaranaike was active in service organizations and did not aspire to political office. At the beginning she acted as a surrogate for her dead husband, carrying out his political plans. However, over time she became a politician in her own right. Now in her seventies, she currently serves as prime minister of Sri Lanka, and her daughter, Chandrika Kumaratunge, serves as president.

In countries where attitudes toward women are especially traditional, the surrogate path appears to be the most likely route to female national leadership. In such countries, women are expected to devotedly serve and assist men and to have few ideas of their own. Consequently, it seems safe to expect females to serve as political surrogates for departed husbands or fathers. Violeta de Chamorro, president of Nicaragua (1990–1996) is a good example of this. According to Saint-Germain (1993), Nicaraguan women are expected to derive their identities through their male relatives and are respected to the extent that they sacrifice and submit to the demands of men. There is a clear demarcation between public (political) and private (home) spheres, and women are expected to stay within the home sphere. Given this dual gender system, it is difficult for women to be political. To do so, they must typically present their political activity as an extension of their role in the home. Thus, during elections, and even once elected, their wife and mother roles are emphasized. For instance, during Chamorro's campaign she said she was not a feminist but rather a woman dedicated to her home, as "taught" by her husband, Pedro Chamorro. She stated she was not a politician but was running "for Pedro and for her country." At one point she said that she was "marked with the Chamorro branding iron." Violeta Chamorro's advisors modeled

"Many women do not want to be mirror images of men in similar positions, but at the same time they must show authority or they will simply be swept aside."
Margaret Anstee, 1993, first woman to head a UN peacekeeping mission

her image after the Virgin Mary, the ultimate long-suffering maternal mother in Nicaraguan culture. The idea of a national mother who could bring together war-torn Nicaraguans appealed to voters. This, in combination with U.S. promises to provide aid and stop encouraging the Contras should she be elected, resulted in her election to president in 1990.*

Benazir Bhutto, prime minister of Pakistan (1988–1990, 1993–1996), is another example of how in gender-traditional countries, women's political activism is tolerated when it appears as though they are acting on behalf of male relatives. Bhutto was the first woman to head a Muslim country and almost certainly would not have been elected in the conservative country of Pakistan were it not for the popularity of her martyred father, Zulfikar Ali Bhutto. Following her father's imprisonment and her brothers' political exile abroad, Bhutto took over the male role in her family. As Bhutto said in 1989,

> In a way I had transcended gender. There was not a person who did not know the circumstances that had forced me out of the pattern of landowning families where young women were guarded zealously and rarely, if ever, allowed to leave their homes without a male relative. (Bhutto, 1989, p. 155)

And, as she said about campaigning,

> A woman standing on a political podium was not as strange to the crowd as it felt to me. Other women on the subcontinent had picked up the political banners of their husbands, brothers, and fathers before me. The legacies of political families passing down through the women had become a South Asian tradition. (Bhutto, 1989, p. 125).

Bhutto was extremely close to her father and dutifully carried on his struggle against the authoritarian regime of General Mohammad Zia. Her father was eventually put to death by Zia, and Benazir was imprisoned. This treatment only cemented the Pakistanis' adoration of the Bhuttos. In time, international and domestic pressure led Zia to release Benazir, and, in 1988, Zia allowed elections. His timing, however, was suspect for he called the elections to coincide with the birth of Benazir's first baby—not that this stopped Benazir from campaigning. She used her father's image skillfully, referring repeatedly to him in speeches and being photographed with his image in the background (Anderson, 1993). Although Zia was killed in a plane crash right before the election, his successor allowed the elections to go on. Benazir's party, the Pakistan People's Party, won the

---

*The Contras were a Nicaraguan military group opposed to the democratic-socialist government of the Sandanista National Liberation Front, also called the FSLN. Throughout the 1980s, the Contras waged war in small-scale attacks throughout the country.

majority of seats in the National Assembly, and Benazir became prime minister. In 1990, President Izhaq Khan dismissed Bhutto on charges of nepotism and corruption. She ran for office and won again in 1993, but three years into her five-year term, she was dismissed by President Farooq Leghari, again under charges of corruption.

Political party officials frequently assume that once elected or appointed, the female head of state will act as a figurehead and will leave the governing to party officials. For instance, although Chamorro was often portrayed as strong-willed, most substantive action was taken by others within her administration (in particular, by her son-in-law Antonio Lacayo) without her involvement. Indeed, it appears that few party officials had any intention of actually having Chamorro lead. As one of her brothers-in-law said, "We are not looking for someone to run the country. We are looking for someone who represents the ideal [of democracy]." One of her political advisors said, "Violeta wasn't chosen for her abilities as a president. Violeta was chosen to win" (Saint-Germain, 1993, p. 84). Likewise, Benazir Bhutto was chosen to head the Pakistani political party because she was a Bhutto and had suffered political persecution by Zia. However, the party elders assumed that she would serve primarily as a symbol and had a difficult time accepting her leadership (Anderson, 1993).

Political Insider/Climber Path to Power

A second path to power for female leaders is that of **political insider** or **climber** (D'Amico, 1995). Such leaders work their way up through a party hierarchy over a number of years. D'Amico (1995) hypothesizes that this is an infrequent path to power for women because women are statistically underrepresented in the professions that serve as political stepping stones (that is, the law, military service, and business). Therefore, there are relatively few women in the typical apprentice pool for political leadership. Box 8.4 lists some examples of women leaders who took the insider path to power.

Indira Gandhi of India is one example of a leader who took the insider path. She became a member of the Congress Party in 1948, was elected to its Working Committee in 1955, to its presidency in 1959, to the upper house of Parliament in 1964, and served an appointed position as Minister of Information and Broadcasting before assuming the presidency of India in 1966 (Carras, 1995). Although she certainly presented herself as a political surrogate (especially early on), her party granted her power in part because she had earned her status within the party hierarchy. Similarly, Margaret Thatcher of Great Britain began working for the Conservative Party in the 1950s, was elected to the House of Commons in 1959, became Parliamentary Secretary to the Ministry of Pensions and National Security in 1961, became Secretary of State for Education in 1970, leader of the Conservative Party in 1975, and finally, prime minister in 1979.

Golda Meir, prime minister of Israel, was clearly a political insider. Her government service to Israel began in the state's formative years. As a teenager in

202   Chapter 8   Women in Politics

BOX 8.4   *Paths to Power: Insiders/Climbers*

Leader/Year Elected or Appointed	Country/Position
Agatha Barbara, 1982	Malta, president
Kim Campbell, 1993	Canada, prime minister
Eugenia Charles, 1980	Dominica, prime minister
Tansu Ciller, 1993	Turkey, prime minister
Edith Campion Cresson, 1991	France, prime minister
Indira Nehru Gandhi,* 1966	India, prime minister
Golda Mabovitz Meir, 1969	Israel, prime minister
Milka Planic, 1982	Yugoslavia, prime minister
Mary Bourke Robinson,* 1990	Ireland, president
Margaret Roberts Thatcher,* 1979	United Kingdom, prime minister
Jeanne Benoit Sauve, 1984	Canada, governor general

*Gandhi's path has elements of "surrogacy," and Robinson and Thatcher's paths have elements of "outsider."

Source: D'Amico, 1995.

the United States, she became a Zionist and organized and raised funds for an independent Jewish state in Palestine. In 1921, she moved to Palestine. For a time, she lived on a kibbutz, a communal experience dedicated to Zionism. In 1928 she took a position as secretary of the Women's Labor Council. Meir raised hundreds of millions of dollars for the fledging Israeli state. She spent a good part of the 1930s and 1940s traveling the world raising funds for the Jewish settlers in Palestine. She was active in the formation of the Mapai political party and served in many positions. She was responsible for settling the thousands of immigrants arriving from Europe in the late 1940s and orchestrated the building of thousands of homes. She served as the first Israeli ambassador to the Soviet Union, served as Israeli secretary of Labor, Israeli foreign minister, head of the Mapai Party, and finally in 1970 as prime minister of Israel.

Women who take the insider path to power appear to function more as honorary males than women who take other paths to power. They appear more likely to dismiss the relevance of gender to their leadership and to see themselves as one of the political boys. Indira Gandhi once said, "As Prime Minister, I am not a woman. I am a human being" (quoted in Everett, 1993).

Likewise Golda Meir (1975) said, "The fact is that I have lived and worked with men all my life, but being a woman has never hindered me in any way at all. It has never caused me unease or given me an inferiority complex or made me think that men are better off than women—or that it is a disaster to give birth to children. Not at all." Perhaps without these attitudes these women would not have been able to rise through the party ranks.

Despite having paid their political dues through party service, a confluence of factors must occur before insider women are considered seriously as possible heads of state. In particular, it appears that most are compromise candidates in the case of a divided political party (D'Amico, 1995). For example, it is generally agreed that Indira Gandhi may not have come to power at all were it not for the unexpected death of Prime Minister Lal Bahadur Shastri, a divided political party, and a desire to prevent a particular individual (Morarji Desia) from becoming prime minister (Carras, 1995; Everett, 1993). Likewise, Margaret Thatcher became head of the Conservative political party because the most likely challenger refused to run against the former leader, and there was a shortage of qualified competitors. It was, to use the words of Kenneth Harris (1995, p. 61), "almost a bombshell of surprise and certainly an extraordinary achievement" and was testament to the "strength of her character and the quality of her political instincts." Thatcher benefited from a remarkable sense of timing. As Genovese (1993) suggests, Thatcher's first election to prime minister had more to do with the failure of the Labour Party to solve severe domestic and trade union problems than it did with her policy proposals or charisma.

Likewise, Golda Meir may never have become prime minister of Israel were it not for a series of unusual events. She had retired from government service in 1968, but in 1970, Israel's Prime Minister Levi Eskol died suddenly from a heart attack. It was a bad time for Israel. Tensions and violence were mounting between Israel and Egypt, and the prospect of war loomed. Increased defense expenditures taxed the economy. There were profound disagreements within Eskol's coalition cabinet about how to respond to these problems. Clearly, selecting a leader from the cabinet would be divisive and disruptive. It seemed to make sense to appoint the steady Meir as an interim prime minister rather than engage in political infighting when Israel was on the verge of war. During her term as interim prime minister, she emerged as a highly visible, action-oriented leader. This, combined with her history as a Zionist pioneer, led to her popularity and her national election to prime minister in October 1970 at age 72.

Tansu Ciller, prime minister of Turkey from 1993 to 1995 and currently deputy prime minister, was the first female head of state in a Muslim country to get there without taking the surrogate path to power. A smartly dressed American-educated economist and member of the Istanbul elite, she became finance minister in 1991 and was partly successful in easing a high inflation rate. Her election to prime minister in 1993 with only four years of political experience was a surprise to many. Her win is attributed to shrewd campaigning as well as many Turks' desires to keep Turkey secular, democratic, and capitalistic. Turkey was also positioning itself for admittance into the European Customs Union, a move expected to help Turkey's economic situation considerably. Ciller, with

In 1982, **Rosario Ibarra Piedra** became the first woman to run for president in Mexico.

In 1993, **Agathe Uwilingiyimana** became the first female prime minister of Rwanda but was assassinated in 1994.

> **BOX 8.5** *Paths to Power: Outsiders/Activists*
>
> | Leader/Year of Election or Appointment | Country/Position |
> |---|---|
> | Gro Harlem Brundtland, 1981 | Norway, president |
> | Vigdis Finnbogadottir, 1980 | Iceland, president |
> | Maria Liberia-Peters, 1984 | Netherlands Antilles, prime minister |
> | Ertha Pascal-Trouillot, 1990 | Haiti, interim president |
> | Mary Bourke Robinson,* 1990 | Ireland, president |
>
> *She can be also considered an "insider" because of extensive political party experience.
>
> Source: D'Amico, 1995.

her designer suits, Western education, and free market politics, was anticipated to help their chances. Her femaleness was an asset as well, for it signaled to Europe that Muslim Turkey was not under control of religious fundamentalists.

Political Outsider Path to Power

"I accept that women are gentler at the moment, but if they had the same amount of power as men, they wouldn't be more virtuous."
Lynne Segal, 1987

A third path to power described by D'Amico (1995) is that of **political outsider.** These candidates are more likely to enter politics from grassroots citizen movements. They are often elected at a time when citizens perceive insider politicians as corrupt and are looking for honesty and change. Because of the unusualness (statistically speaking) of female politicians, they are easily perceived as outsiders and as a departure from politics as usual. It should be noted that some insider political women got elected in part because of public perceptions of their outsider status. For instance, Margaret Thatcher presented herself as an outsider although she had served for years in a variety of positions in the British Conservative Party and was apt to toe the party line. Box 8.5 lists some women leaders who have risen to power following the outsider path to power.

Outsider/activist women politicians seem to be one of the few cases in which stereotypical female gender stereotypes are beneficial. The common gender stereotype of women as other centered may be valuable when citizens are reacting against corruption. Likewise, as D'Amico (1995) suggests, women tend to be seen as caring, compassionate, and accessible. These qualities are advantageous when the issues facing a country involve health care and domestic economic and social issues.

In some cases, the election of a woman to a presidential position is not as daring as it first appears, for in many countries, presidents act in a more ceremonial than policymaking role. For instance, the presidency in Iceland, occupied by the female Vigdis Finnbogadottir from 1980 to 1996, is a nonpolitical office in which the president has little power over domestic issues. The office is somewhat similar to the royalties of Europe and is largely ceremonial. Likewise, the presidency of Ireland is also largely ceremonial. Indeed, the Irish Constitution prevents the president from participating in politics. However, as former president of Ireland Mary Robinson once said, "I feel I can change perceptions about equality. . . . This office allows me to be more symbolic, more reflective, to engage in lateral thinking, to do the unexpected" (Orth, 1992, p. 122). Many outsider/activist women leaders have used the symbolic power of their offices to promote social reform. They may not have much official power, but they may be empowering.

Liberal civil rights lawyer Mary Robinson's election as the first female president of Ireland in 1990 is a good example of the outsider/activist woman national leader. Robinson served a twenty-year term in the Irish Senate, where she championed causes considered radical in Ireland, such as, the legalization of contraception and divorce, the removal of discriminatory taxation against working married women, and the overhauling of the Irish jury system to allow women the right to serve on juries. She was not expected to win the presidential election, and Dublin odds makers listed her as a 1,000 to 1 underdog. Her opponent Brian Lenihan was one of the most popular politicians in the country, and her ardent feminism seemed a liability in a country fiercely devoted to traditional women's roles. She campaigned tirelessly and made some progress in the polls, although Lenihan maintained the lead for most of the campaign. However, the electoral tides changed in the final weeks of the campaign with a political scandal involving Lenihan. In the end, none of the three candidates won the majority of votes. Under Irish law, in such cases the second preference votes of the minor candidates are tallied with the first preference votes to determine the winner. This resulted in Robinson's winning the election with 52 percent of the vote.

Robinson was a popular president despite and because of her feminism and femininity. A female symbol of Ireland is in some ways a comfortable one, for the Irish used feminine names to refer to Ireland when the ruling British forbade them to mention Ireland. Mary Robinson's popularity may have been due in part to her transformation of the image of Mother Ireland as a land of the dispossessed and forlorn to one of strength and pride. Many commentators have noted that Robinson represented change in a country ready to change (Orth, 1992). Furthermore, as a skilled politician and lawyer, she was able to present feminist ideas in ways that are acceptable to the electorate and that mirror their own opinions and concerns. For instance, she was critical of a feminism that devalues homemaking and bringing up children, saying "If we do not sufficiently value these activities and the skills involved in them, how can we persuade society as a whole of their value and the importance of ensuring that these activities are more evenly shared between parents?" (Frank, 1991).

"There is no democracy in our beautifully democratic countries. Why? Women have not the same part in decision making as men have."
Vigdis Finnbogadottir, President of Iceland

Wilma Mankiller was the first woman elected chief of an American Indian tribe (the Cherokee Nation), in 1987.

BOX 8.6   *Queens as National Leaders*

Although somewhat rare, powerful female leaders may be found throughout history. Women like Cleopatra (Egypt), Catherine the Great (Russia), Yaa Asantewaa (Ghana), and Tz'u-Hsi (China) acquired their positions through hereditary monarchies in countries where women were deemed largely incapable of exercising political power. Historian Antonia Fraser writes of many of these queens in her book *The Warrior Queens* (1988).

In the twentieth century, most nations lack a monarchy, and for those that don't, queens serve a largely ceremonial role. There are three queens currently reigning. Queen Elizabeth II, queen of the United Kingdom of Great Britain and Northern Ireland since 1952, was never expected to become ruler. Her uncle Edward VIII was slated to become king but abdicated to her father. According to British law, the British crown

goes to firstborn royal males, but in 1998, Queen Elizabeth II and the British prime minister agreed to support a change that would grant the British crown to first-borns regardless of gender. This change must be ratified by lawmakers in England, Wales, Scotland, and Northern Ireland, a process that may take five years.

The Danish constitution was changed in 1953 to permit female succession to the throne (female succession to the throne is still not permitted in Norway although efforts are underway to change this). This made it possible for the daughter of King Frederick IX to become Margrethe II, Queen of Denmark, in 1972.

Queen Beatrix of the Netherlands is the third in a line of successive female rulers. In 1980 Beatrix succeeded her mother, Queen Juliana (1948–1980), who succeeded her mother, Queen Wilhelmina (1890–1948).

It now looks as though Mary Robinson will become an international leader. In a move applauded by human rights activists and feminists, the 53-year-old Robinson assumed the role of the United Nations Human Rights Commissioner in 1997 when she finished her term as Ireland's president. Her job will not be easy for, as noted repeatedly throughout the book, although on paper the UN promotes women's rights as human rights, in practice the organization often falls short. (Before leaving the discussion on paths to power, take a look at Box 8.6 on queens as national leaders.)

Leadership Style

Accepting the characterization of aggressiveness and authoritarianism as male traits, many feminists have assumed that women world leaders would govern in a more peaceful and democratic way than do male leaders. However, evidence indicates that this is not necessarily true. Indeed, there is great variability in leadership styles in women, just as there is in men. Simply put, it is difficult to generalize about women leaders. Their policy agendas and styles of leadership are diverse and often challenge gender-based notions of feminine values and behavior (D'Amico, 1995).

Contrary to our images of women as nurturers and peacemakers, women leaders do not appear less likely to use their militaries to resolve conflicts. Many of the women profiled in this chapter did not hesitate to use the military against domestic protesters and to go to war to defend territorial interests. Indeed, Fraser (1988) suggests that many women leaders "have found in the crucible of war—if successfully survived—the fiery process which has guaranteed them passage into the realms of honorary men" (p. 10).

The world's first female prime minister, Sirimavo Bandaranaike of Sri Lanka, increased defense spending, bought armaments from all over the world, and used them to control rebellion against her government. The military was used to squash ultra-leftists, who felt Bandaranaike was not moving quickly enough, and to combat the Tamils, a minority group who revolted when she decreed Buddhism the national religion and Sinhalese the national language. Indira Gandhi oversaw the most ambitious program of military buildup in India's history, presided over India's first underground nuclear explosion, built up the navy to become the principal naval power in the region, and went to war with Pakistan over East Pakistan's desire to become an independent state (Bangladesh). Margaret Thatcher sent British forces to the Falkland Islands in 1982 to reclaim them from the Argentinean government. She did not hesitate to use the police in strike situations and showed little sympathy for the citizens injured (Genovese, 1993). Eugenia Charles, prime minister of Dominica, appealed to U.S. president Ronald Reagan for assistance in invading Grenada in 1983 following a political coup. Charles believed that if the coup succeeded the whole Caribbean would be susceptible to Communist takeover. Golda Meir was quite willing to use force in conflicts with Israel's neighbors, seeing it as necessary to the establishment and preservation of a Jewish state in Palestine. As foreign minister she was ready to use force against Egypt in 1956, and she supported the Six-Day War of 1967 with Egypt. That she did not launch a preemptive strike against Egypt and Syria prior to the Yom Kippur War of 1973 (called the October War by Arabs) is attributed to faulty military intelligence and poor advice from the United States rather than to an aversion to military solutions (Thompson, 1993).

Under Tansu Ciller of Turkey, tensions between Greece and Turkey over the island of Cyprus escalated in 1996. A Greek protester had tried to tear down a Turkish flag on the island and was subsequently killed. Ciller reportedly warned that anyone who tried to tear down the Turkish flag would have their hands broken. Human rights violations have continued during Ciller's administration. Human rights activists have repeatedly called attention to the imprisonment and torture of political opponents and the evacuation and destruction of over 1,000 Kurdish villages. Ciller also introduced a law allowing the seizure and government sale of land that does not have a title issued since the last coup. Ciller has apparently personally benefited from such land seizures.

Of course, some women world leaders do fit the feminist image of peacemaker. These include such leaders as Corazon Aquino, Violeta Chamorro, and Mary Robinson. These leaders worked hard to resolve major domestic conflicts without the use of military force. Aquino, president of the Philippines from 1986 to 1992 and a political surrogate for her martyred husband, Benigno Aquino, emphasized economic development and the peaceful resolution of long-standing internal conflicts (Boudreau, 1995; Col, 1993). She granted amnesty to guerrillas, declared ceasefires with rebels, and released political prisoners (Col, 1993). Chamorro, much to the chagrin of the UNO party that ran her as a candidate, cooperated with the defeated yet powerful FSLN party.

This she did by appointing General Humberto Ortega, a director of the FSLN, to be her senior military officer. By cooperating with the FSLN and the Contras, she undoubtedly quelled some civil strife. In a country torn for many years by civil war, she consistently advocated consensus and reconciliation over confrontation and vengeance (Williams, 1995). Mary Robinson is another example. She has consistently worked for a peaceful solution to the conflict in Northern Ireland.

As the evidence currently stands, female leaders are also not more likely than male leaders to exhibit a democratic leadership style. Some are, but it appears that many, like Turkey's Tansu Ciller, are described as combative, insensitive, arrogant, and power mad. It is all too easy to find autocratic female leaders. These leaders have strong convictions regarding the directions that their countries should take, and they believe that only they are qualified to lead their countries there. Margaret Thatcher and Indira Gandhi are some of the best-known examples and shared the moniker "Iron Lady." Their external gentle appearance was at odds with their shrewd and ruthless leadership style. Indira Gandhi, for instance, tolerated little dissent from political advisors and cabinet members. When threatened with public opposition, she imposed martial law and used the military against Indian citizens to repress dissent. For this she was ultimately killed. Gandhi authorized a military operation (resulting in at least 576 deaths) against a Sikh temple from which alleged terrorist activities were conducted. Several months later, she was assassinated by two of her Sikh security guards.

As the privileged and doted-upon daughter of a national hero, Benazir Bhutto was reputedly an arrogant and imperious leader who surrounded herself with family members who had proven their loyalty (Anderson, 1993). Contrary to the notion of women leaders as democratic and ethical, she lost her office amid charges of autocratic rule and corruption. As Zahid Hussain, a respected Pakistani journalist, said, "Instead of strengthening democratic institutions, which have been weakened by long periods of autocratic rule, Ms. Bhutto has virtually set out to destroy them" (Dahlburg & Bearak, 1996). Bhutto routinely by-passed parliament and awarded high positions in her administration to corrupt politicians, including her husband. In addition, many believe she was behind the death of her brother and political rival, who was ambushed and killed by police. In a country where the average person earns $1.18 a day, she proposed $1.1 billion in new taxes while she was in the process of purchasing a $4 million mansion in Britain (Dahlburg & Bearak, 1996).

Margaret Thatcher was also known for an aggressive leadership style and chose cabinet members based on their loyalty to her. As Genovese (1993) says, Thatcher's style was highly personalized and imperious. She did not believe in listening to divergent viewpoints within her cabinet, nor did she believe in seeking consensus. As she herself once said, "I am not a consensus politician, I'm a conviction politician" (Jenkins, 1988, p. 3), and on taking office, "It must be a conviction government. As Prime Minister I could not waste time with any internal arguments" (Genovese, 1993, p. 197). She believed in getting her way and did it by arguing, bullying, intimidating, and threatening, and was unapologetic about it. Genovese (1993) quotes her as saying, "I am not ruthless, but some things have to be done, and I know that when they are done one will be accused of all sorts of things" (p. 199). Like Indira Gandhi, she chose her cabinet based on loyalty and obedience and regularly shuffled her ministers in order to maintain control.

Although less extreme than Gandhi or Thatcher, Golda Meir was also known for being tough, especially when it came to international relations. As an ardent international champion of Israeli interests, she became known for her confrontational style and her uncompromising opposition to concessions in the Arab-Israeli conflict. Like her prime minister predecessors, Meir employed a consultative decision-making style with her cabinet. Indeed, a cabinet subgroup of her allies and advisors would often meet in her kitchen the night before cabinet meetings. A number of biographical accounts describe Meir making and serving cookies and coffee as policy issues were discussed. On the face of it, the "Kitchen Cabinet," as it was dubbed, appears to be evidence of a democratic leadership style. However, she set the agenda, she invited the participants, and she announced the decisions to the full cabinet the next day (Thompson, 1993).

Corazon Aquino is one of the few female national leaders who was clearly consensus oriented and democratic in her leadership style. She came to power during a time when Filipinos were tired of the dictatorship of Ferdinand Marcos and longed for democracy. After nineteen years of rule by Marcos, wealth and power were concentrated in the hands of a powerful few, and the people were angry. Cory Aquino represented human rights, civil liberties, and democracy. As leader of the Philippines, she sought to develop a political culture ruled by law, tolerance, and participation. In her commitment to democratic participation, she made decisions only after elaborate and lengthy consultations with as many people and groups as possible (Col, 1993). Although criticized as incompetent and indecisive, she remained committed to a democratic style of leadership.

At this time it is difficult to say why women national leaders lead remarkably like men. Many feminists believe that there are no clear-cut leadership differences because female leaders are so aware of their precarious hold on power that they feel compelled to lead as men would. Carras (1995) points out that in time this may change as the number of women leaders increases and as they feel less bound by the male rules of the current power game. Perhaps then the prediction that women leaders are more cooperative and community oriented in their approaches will be borne out. On the other hand, the fact that the behavior of female world leaders is not strikingly different from male behavior could be because leadership, male or female, is more influenced by situational factors and personality than it is by gender. Similarly, the customary ways of gaining, wielding, and holding on to power may erroneously be believed to be male ways of power because most power is held by males. If this is the case, the absence of a gender difference in world leader behavior is likely to persist regardless of women's increased presence in world politics. It may be that, regardless of gender, getting and maintaining political power may require a certain ruthlessness and defensiveness.

Whatever the case, at present it is true that in most political systems, obtaining and holding on to power require playing by those "male" rules. Therefore, at least for now, women may have to follow these rules before they will be allowed to play the political game. Once they have earned status and respect for doing so, they will probably stand a greater chance of being able to deviate without a loss of power. As Boudreau (1995) notes, perhaps we should not ask whether women bring new perspectives to politics, but whether they can defend those perspectives—when they exist—against the established political order.

Advocacy of Women's Issues

Many feminists believe that adding women to existing power structures will put so-called women's issues on policymaking agendas (Peterson & Runyan, 1993), and I have noted that there is some evidence for this position. However, this gender difference is not so clear at the international head-of-state level, probably because most female heads of state are aware that being seen as a "women's leader" would quickly result in the loss of their already tenuous hold on power. Recall that most of these women gained power under very unusual circumstances. It is probably safe to say that some of these women rationalized their avoidance of women's issues by thinking that they would be of no use to women if they couldn't hold on to the power position to begin with. Also, women typically come into power during economic and political transitional periods. Therefore, it is not surprising that women's issues are frequently subordinated to other seemingly more pressing concerns, particularly economic ones affecting all citizens.

There appear to be some women's advocacy variations based upon the different paths to power we've discussed here. For example, political surrogates who took the widow's walk to power, such as Violeta de Chamorro, are often gender-role traditional, reluctantly leading only because a husband died. Such women do not come to their leadership roles with any feminist agenda but rather as dutiful widows upholding a dead husband's agenda. They are unlikely to give women positions in their governments and are unlikely to fund programs that specifically benefit women and children. Chamorro, for instance, appointed no female ministers until three years into her term. She also suspended governmental support for feminist organizations, reduced funding for programs designed to address women's and children's needs, and eliminated programs for the rehabilitation of prostitutes and street children.

The fact that political surrogates typically come to power in gender-role-traditional cultures is also relevant to their women's issues advocacy. In gender-traditional countries, calls for gender equality are unlikely to be met with encouragement. Thus, even those sympathetic to women's issues such as Benazir Bhutto must tread lightly or compromise what power they have. Although Bhutto made women's rights a major theme of her campaign and in writings favored a feminist interpretation of Islam, she was nonetheless criticized by feminists as being more concerned with political power than with women's rights (Anderson, 1993). Her arranged marriage as well as the fact that she never appeared without the traditional Islamic head covering for women (the dupatta), further dismayed Islamic feminists. However, Islamic fundamentalism was on the rise at the time, and many were antagonistic to the idea of a woman leader—especially a Western-educated one. Furthermore, Bhutto's party did not have a majority in the congress, and there were laws limiting the prime minister's power. Given these constraints, she may have had little choice other than to soft-pedal her women's rights agenda. Even so, there were some improvements for women under Bhutto. For instance, women could appear in public without the dupatta. More importantly perhaps, Bhutto prevented passage of an amendment that would have reexamined all laws in terms of their conformity to Islam. (Movements in this direction under Zia's Islamization programs resulted in the severe repression of women.)

Political insiders and "honorary men"—such as Indira Gandhi, Margaret Thatcher, Edith Cresson, and Golda Meir—are also disinclined to pursue a feminist agenda. Women like these who worked their way up through their political party's ranks were socialized by these experiences to act in accordance with their party's political strategies and ideologies. They were allowed to advance precisely because they minded their manners and proved to the party that they would advance a party line, not a feminist agenda. Margaret Thatcher once said, "The battle for women's rights has largely been won," and "The days when they were demanded and discussed in strident tones should be gone forever" (quoted in Harris, 1995). Her policies, which drastically decreased funding for education and social programs, disproportionately affected poor women and children, earning her the nickname "Maggie Thatcher the Milk Snatcher." As "honorary male" politicians, insiders seem no more likely than male politicians to encourage the appointment and election of females to political posts. For instance, Indira Gandhi appointed no women to her cabinet, and the number of women in the British cabinet decreased under Thatcher. As Enloe (1989) says, "When a woman is let in by the men who control the political elite it is usually precisely because that woman has learned the lessons of masculinized political behavior well enough to know not to threaten male political privilege" (pp. 6–7).

Outsiders seem the most likely to be openly feminist, to have explicitly feminist agendas, and to increase the number of women in government positions. Gro Harlem Brundtland, prime minister of Norway, appointed seven women of seventeen posts in her first cabinet and eight of eighteen in her second (D'Amico, 1995). She also extended maternity leave to twenty-four weeks, is an open proponent of changing Norway's Constitution to include female inheritance of the throne, and was instrumental in the Labor Party's requirement that at least 40 percent of the party's candidates in any given election be female. Mary Robinson, Ireland's former president, is a vocal supporter of rights for women, greater reproductive freedom for women, and reform in family laws that limit women. As a member of the Irish Parliament, she introduced legislation to legalize contraception in Ireland (1969) and divorce (1976)—daring moves in a country dominated by the Roman Catholic Church. On February 15, 1980, in the *London Times Literary Supplement,* she wrote, "Equality of employment cannot become a reality in a country which has not yet fully legalized the sale of contraceptives; where there is no divorces, no maternity legislation, and virtually no state creche [day care] or nursery facilities."

Role of Gender in the Perception of Female World Leaders

Rosaldo (1974) argues that cultures emphasize women's maternal role, and because of this, there is a near-universal opposition between domestic and public roles. Because of the confining of women to the domestic sphere, women view the exercise of power as illegitimate. Thus, she says, the ways that women gain prestige and a sense of value are shaped and limited by women's association with the domestic world. This is indeed true. Politics are generally a game played out in the public sphere by those with stereotypically masculine qualities such as aggressiveness. Also, as mentioned earlier, women's confinement to the domestic sphere generally means that there are fewer in the apprentice pools of leadership. In addition, the strong association of women with the domestic sphere affects the perception and evaluation of female leaders.

It is important to note, though, that women heads of state often manage to turn gender stereotypes to their advantage, especially when campaigning. For instance, many of the women discussed in this chapter came to power in war-torn or politically corrupt countries where the image of women as peaceful, selfless, and dedicated to others helped them gain power. The "iron-fisted, velvet-gloved" Margaret Thatcher and Indira Gandhi used their femininity to disguise their ruthless accrual of power. These nice middle-aged motherly-looking ladies were not expected to be so single-mindedly political, and this served them well, at least until everyone caught on. This could also be said of Tansu Ciller, reputedly the most beautiful female world leader. Her good looks, Western education, and Western clothing led to the assumption that she would behave democratically and that corruption and human rights violations would decrease in Turkey. As increasing evidence surfaces regarding her involvement with drug cartels, death squads, and tax evasion, she battles for political survival.

For the most part it appears that any political advantage there is to being female is not long-lasting. Eventually, it seems, gender stereotypes are used against women leaders. If they are aggressive and decisive, they are chided for being "men"; if they are democratic, they are criticized for being weak and for not being in control. Women must do what is not expected of them while doing enough of what is expected of them to gain acceptance (Morrison, White, & Van Velsor, 1987). For instance, it was because of this dilemma that Benazir Bhutto made the very political decision to marry a man chosen by her family. In Pakistan, it is highly unusual for a woman in her thirties to be unmarried. There was constant speculation about her private life, she required a chaperone, and was under surveillance by the opposition party, who hoped to catch her in a sexual liaison. Her male colleagues were uncomfortable interacting with an unmarried woman. In short, her unmarried status became a political liability. Her arranged marriage afforded her respectability and made her seem more normal. Female leaders must be careful not to trigger those gender stereotypes that suggest they cannot lead, yet they must also avoid stepping too far outside of their gender role lest they be rejected or ridiculed.

The dominant response to powerful women has tended to be first violence, then hostility, then indifference and dismissal (Lips, 1991). Powerful women are frequently attacked and vilified, threatened and demeaned. Edith Cresson, prime minister of France for a mere ten months in 1991 and 1992, could testify to this. Despite her credentials and experience, it was repeatedly implied in the French press that she must have been sleeping with President Mitterand to obtain the appointment. French feminists commented that women who succeed in politics are commonly believed to have done so through seduction and that a media hate campaign with sexist overtones was partly responsible for Cresson's problems (Opfell, 1993).

Another example is Benazir Bhutto. Her gender made her less threatening initially such that she was not forced into exile like her brothers and she was trusted to be a representative of her father. However, over time being a female leader in a conservative country reduced her power as it was not seen as legitimate. One popular joke following the birth of her second child in 1990 was that as prime minister all she had been able to deliver was a baby (Anderson, 1993).

Margaret Thatcher was demeaned with such nicknames as "Attila the Hen" and "Her Malignancy," and slogans such as "Ditch the Bitch" were used by those who sought her ouster (Genovese, 1993). Note that these attacks are gendered. Research indicates that when a woman is a numerical minority in a job category, we are more likely to judge and evaluate her according to gender stereotypes (Burn, 1996; Ragins & Sundstrom, 1989). As Vignis Finnbogadottir, president of Iceland, said, "Women must be very cautious when embarking on a leadership path . . . . If you make a mistake you will be attacked with the strongest weapon—mockery. . . . Unlike men, mistakes made by women inevitably reflect on their entire gender" (Jones, 1992).

Women in Informal Politics: Social and Protest Movements

Although very few women are official "state actors" and politics continues to be stereotyped as a male domain, women all over the world are political, are active, do challenge gender dichotomies, and do change world politics by their political agency (Peterson & Runyan, 1993). As I said early in the chapter, the invisibility of women's political activity is in part due to defining politics narrowly as participation in formal politics. Women's political activity is especially high when we take into account local, community-based actions in which women are a driving force (Lister, 1997).

West and Blumberg (1990) suggest that there are four general types of issues that draw women into **social protest:** (1) issues linked to the economic survival of themselves and their children; (2) issues related to nationalist and racial/ethnic struggles; (3) issues addressing broad humanistic/nurturing problems; and (4) issues identified as women's rights issues. They also note that these may overlap—for instance, a protest of economic conditions may lead to a larger, nationalist struggle as was the case when women's demands for food helped to spark both the French and Russian revolutions. Other examples may be found in the fact that peace and environmental causes are often part of the agendas of feminist movements, and women's movements, particularly in the Third World, may connect their struggles as women to their struggles against racism.

Much of women's informal political activity can be viewed as an extension of their traditional feminine roles. Women who might be otherwise uncomfortable in the political sphere can use **maternalism** as a way to rationalize the expansion of their nurturing roles into the public sphere (West & Blumberg, 1990). As Lister (1997) says, it is primarily (but not solely) as mothers that women transgress, and feel justified in transgressing, the public-private divide in their struggle to protect their families and communities. Women who do not generally see themselves as political may take political action when their families and communities are threatened. It is interesting to think of this in private sphere–public sphere terms. In short, when public policies and conditions make it difficult for women to meet their private sphere responsibilities, they may act publicly on behalf of private sphere concerns such as the food, shelter, and safety needs of their families. This has been called **accidental activism** (Hyatt, 1992), wherein women are often the active citizens of deprived communities. One cross-national study found that "concern with care, health, and education of children is a unifying thread" in women's local political action (Chanan, 1992, p. 86). Feminists have some concerns about the fact that women's participation in social protest politics are so often an extension of their private sphere maternal role. Their main concern is that it reinforces women's traditional roles. Indeed, some feminists fear that by operating out of maternal concerns, many such activists perpetuate their own and all women's enslavement under patriarchy (Strange, 1990).

Although social protest actions taken by women as extensions of their nurturing wife–mother roles are viewed as less of a gender violation than women's participation in the formal political sphere, they are still somewhat dangerous. Women's political activism is frequently punished. This is perhaps not surprising when you consider that to be political activists, women violate their gender role and challenge male-dominated institutions of power. Violence as a consequence of women's social protest is well documented, and this punishment is frequently gendered in the sense that it may involve verbal sexual slurs, rape, sexual torture, and violence against their children (Amnesty International, 1990). Women also face criticism from their husbands and families, who may see them as stepping out of their proper role at the expense of their husbands and children.

West and Blumberg (1990), as well as others, have noted the historic invisibility of women in protest movements. In other words, the historical record does not often reflect the important roles that women have played. It seems that women often initiate movements at the local level, but once they expand to higher levels, men assume formal leadership. Likewise, women often play important roles but do so quietly with men occupying the official leadership roles.

The first three types of social protest described by West and Blumberg (1990) are examined below. The fourth type, political action for women's rights, is the focus of the final two chapters of the book.

Women's Action Around Economic Issues

Women have led and taken part in food riots, welfare protests, labor struggles, tenants rights, and other similar actions (West & Blumberg, 1990). In our chapter on women and work, women's labor organizing around the world was noted. In the chapter on women and economic development, I discussed women-organized grassroots organizations dedicated to promoting women's economic development. Many of women's actions in this category fit with what I said above about political activity being an extension of women's maternal, private sphere role. Bolivia, where formal politics are strongly dominated by men, provides a good example. There, women are relegated to the domestic sphere and are for the most part kept out of formal politics; they do not view themselves as political agents. The exception is when women participate in public affairs as wives, mothers, and housewives in an effort to improve family living conditions. For instance, the Housewives Committees of the Federacion Sindical Trabajadores Mineros de Bolivia (FTMB) is a women's grassroots organization of the wives and mothers of employees of the state-run mining corporation (COMIBOL). COMIBOL paid extremely low wages such that mining families lived in extreme poverty. The FTMB groups played an important part in the formation and success of the labor movement against COMIBOL, as well as making their own demands regarding food, medicines, and utility services (Salinas, 1994).

Women's Action Around Nationalist and Racial/Ethnic Issues

Throughout history, women have initiated and joined protests and movements demanding liberation and equality (West & Blumberg, 1990). In the United States, Black women were important organizers of civil rights actions, and Rosa Parks, famous for refusing to give her bus seat up for a White man, was a long-term activist in the NAACP, an important civil rights organization (West & Blumberg, 1990). Millions of women have participated in countless uprisings, guerrilla movements, and revolutions—ranging from the French, American, Russian, and Chinese revolutions to the more recent revolutionary struggles throughout Latin America, the Caribbean, Africa, and the Middle East (Peterson & Runyan, 1993). For example, women were visible participants in the political opposition to military rule in Argentina, Brazil, Chile, and Peru (Jaquette & Wolchik, 1998). There are many examples in the next chapter, on women's movements, as many women's movements originate in nationalist liberation struggles.

Women's Action Around Humanistic/Nurturing Issues

Women have been leaders and mass participants in movements that address such issues as peace, environmentalism, public education, prison reform, mental health care, and hospices (West & Blumberg, 1990). Their actions in these arenas are frequently extensions of their nurturing wife–mother roles. A good example of this is the Argentinean group, Mothers of the Plaza de Mayo. A military junta took over the government in 1976 and began a terrorist regime in which an estimated 30,000 citizens (thought to be a political threat to the government) were kidnapped and killed (Feijoo, 1998). People were taken without warning, and families were unable to obtain any information about the whereabouts of their loved ones, who came to be known as the "disappeared" or *desaparecidos.* The mothers (and grandmothers) marched defiantly and silently with photographs of their disappeared loved ones; they talked and made tapestries to share the truth about their loved ones; they used drama, speech, and other art forms to publicize their political message (West & Blumberg, 1990).

Women have been the backbone of peace movements worldwide (West & Blumberg, 1990), and their protests against war are often maternally inspired (Strange, 1990). One example of women's organized resistance to war occurred in 1915, when 1,500 women from twelve countries met at the International Congress of Women in The Hague to discuss women's role in ending World War I. They linked women's suffrage with peace, arguing that if women were allowed greater political participation, war would be less likely. After the meeting, envoys from the conference visited leaders in fourteen countries and called for peace and mediation by neutral countries. There is evidence that these women had a positive effect on the peace process (Stienstra, 1994). More recent examples include women in Northern Ireland, like Mairead Corrigan and Betty Williams, who won the Nobel Peace Prize in 1977 for their efforts to stop the bloodshed between Protestants and Catholics, and the Sri Lankan Voice of Women for Peace, who called for the end of the civil war between the Sinhalese and Tamils (Peterson & Runyan, 1993).

Women's groups have also been an important part of the movement against nuclear weapons' deployment and proliferation. In the 1980s, women's activist antinuclear groups emerged in Australia, Canada, Holland, Italy, the United States, the United Kingdom, and West Germany (Peterson & Runyan, 1993). Their activism here also appears to be strongly connected to their maternal roles; you can't, they declare, hug children with nuclear arms (Strange, 1990).

Although the motivation of much of women's activism against war and the military has been their association with and responsibility for mothering, you should realize that many mothers support the war effort. Not all women are maternalistic pacifists opposed to war (Strange, 1990). Maternalism and patriotism are often linked, and women frequently see their role as calling for their support of military operations (Strange, 1990). Women, like men, are not innately peaceful and have always served militaries and supported wars (Peterson & Runyan, 1993). Also, women do take up arms and support national liberation struggles, evidence that women are not naturally peaceful (Peterson & Runyan, 1993).

In the chapter on women and development, the role of women in the environmental sustainability movement was illustrated using the Chipko movement and the Greenbelt movement. In the United States, women have taken leadership roles in the movement against hazardous wastes. For example, Lois Gibbs of the United States uncovered the contamination of her

The **Northern Ireland Peace Women** were awarded a Nobel Peace Prize in 1977.

Jody Williams of the United States won the Nobel Peace Prize in 1997 for leading the international movement to ban landmines. Left after wartime, landmines maim or kill approximately 26,000 people a year. Williams has built a coalition of 1,000 nongovernmental organizations leading to the signing of a ban by 122 nations.

home community (Love Canal in New York state), organized collective action to protect those living there, and now runs an organization that helps other women fight pollution in their communities.

Conclusion

In this chapter you saw that there is more to women's political involvement and power than their presence in formal government decision-making bodies. Ordinary women act politically when they organize and put pressure on established power systems from the bottom up, and the results of these efforts are significant. As D'Amico and Beckman (1995) note, a feminist perspective on women in world politics sees women as engaged in politics when they are working to prevent rape, to stop female circumcision and dowry deaths, and to influence how development aid is allocated.

The value of informal politics does not provide an alibi for the continued underrepresentation of women and minority groups in the formal structures of power (Lister, 1997). Indeed, when we think about the true purpose of representative democracy, we should become alarmed that although they make up approximately half of the population, women typically comprise only 5 to 10 percent of legislatures and only rarely occupy chief political posts. As Lister (1997) suggests, increasing women's political representation is particularly important because women have special interests, some in conflict with men's interests, which need to be articulated directly by women in political debate and decision making. Of course, not all women representatives advance women's causes, but in sufficient numbers (at least 30 percent), they do appear to make a difference.

To achieve equal political representation and participate on equal footing with men, women will have to transform political structures and the masculine values on which they rest (Bystydzienski, 1995). In this chapter you saw how in some countries this has been done through the adoption of PL/PR electoral systems and the use of quotas. Research also suggests that women are deterred from entering politics because of the masculinist, combative, alienating culture that often permeates it (Lister, 1997). Jeanne Kirkpatrick, former UN ambassador for the United States, suggests that although there are structural barriers to women's participation in formal politics, it is not just these barriers that keep women out of politics. Women, she suggests, choose not to go into higher politics because they find the political game unappealing:

> I tend to think that the patterns of interaction in high politics are particularly unattractive to women—as unattractive to women as they are inhospitable to them. I find myself thinking of the great number of women who withdrew from high politics and government by personal decision—not because they can't hack it, but because they don't choose to. High politics involves a weirdly unbalanced kind of life-style, which requires continuous involvement with power. It is not simply necessary that one work eighty or ninety hour weeks;

this is true of many vocations. It is that the whole enterprise resembles that described by the philosopher Thomas Hobbes: "the restless striving after power which [one suspects] ceases only in death." (in D'Amico & Beckman, 1995, p. 107)

The institutions of politics are also masculinist in that the behavioral traits deemed suitable for success are stereotypically masculine ones such as aggressiveness, ambition, rationality, competitiveness, and toughness; also, the meeting times and locations, as well as networking activities, are convenient for men's, not women's, schedules (Peterson & Runyan, 1993). Lister (1997) suggests that the best antidote to this masculinist political culture, is achieving a critical mass of female representatives who might be able to change the masculinist political culture.

Terms and Concepts

formal politics	masculinist political culture
informal politics	political surrogates
voting/women's suffrage	political insider/climber path to power
parliaments and congresses	political outsider path to power
cabinets	social protest
party list/proportional	maternalism
representation system	accidental activism
single-member district system	

Study Questions

1. Why do we perceive politics as a masculine domain? Why does this perception concern feminists?

2. When did most of women's struggles to gain the vote occur? Why doesn't voting alone guarantee gender equality in politics?

3. On average, what percentage of formal government positions are held by women?

4. How do women's private sphere responsibilities and their image as wives and mothers affect their presence in formal politics? How do they affect their informal political activities?

5. How do the masculinist culture of politics and the processes of formal political institutions pose barriers to women's equal participation in formal politics? How can the number of women in parliaments, congresses, and cabinets be increased?

6. What are the three paths to power for female heads of state? Describe.

7. What is the role of gender in the perception of female world leaders?

8. Do female heads of state lead differently than male ones? Explain.

9. What are the four general types of issues that draw women into social protest? Describe.

10. Are formal political actors responsive to women's issues? Under what conditions? (Consider parliaments and congresses as well as female heads of state, as there are differences.)

Discussion Questions and Activities

1. Do you agree that were it not for the fact that women leaders must act like men to get and stay in office that they would lead differently than men? Why or why not?

2. The use of quotas, in which political parties must give a certain percentage of their political seats to women, are one of the main means of getting women into political office worldwide. For instance, in the Nordic countries, where the highest percentages of women in political office are found, most political parties have voluntarily adopted quotas. Some have argued that such quotas are a necessary first step because without them women would not get a chance to show that they have what it takes to hold political office. Others argue that quotas don't help to generate a situation in which women are equal partners in politics because it is assumed that "quota women" are not as capable as those elected without the help of quotas. What is your position regarding the use of quotas to increase the number of women holding political office?

3. Do a biographical essay on one of the women leaders listed in the boxes on paths to power but not discussed in the chapter. Explain how the woman you profile rose to power and whether she was an advocate for women's issues.

4. Write a report on West Germany's Green party. The party, founded in 1983, is an interesting case study of a new political party that attempts to incorporate a feminist agenda. The party has faced a number of challenges in doing so. The story of co-founder Petra Kelly is interesting in itself.

Muslim women students in Jakarta, Indonesia, protest government policies that negatively impact women. In every society, in every generation, women protest gender injustice.

Gender Equality Movements

In Mexico, in the 1970s, small consciousness-raising groups met to establish a link between women's daily life and their oppression and to help every woman understand that what is personal is also political. Once women gained feminist consciousness, they would often join feminist organizations taking action toward change.

In 1978 in Spain, there was a national campaign in support of women on trial for having abortions. A thousand women publicly proclaimed in a written document that they too had had abortions and should be tried. In a second document, both men and women stated that they had participated in abortions and insisted that they too be judged.

In 1984, women in Iceland protested gender wage discrimination by jamming grocery stores and markets and insisting that they should only have to pay sixty-six cents on the dollar for purchases. Their reasoning was that if they were only paid sixty-six cents for every dollar men earned, they should only have to pay 66 percent of the price of consumer goods.

The Centre de Promotion des Femmes Ouvrières (CPFO) was founded in Port-au-Prince, Haiti, in 1985. CPFO's work focuses on the rights of women workers, women's literacy, women's reproductive health, and legal counseling and assistance. They serve a population of about 30,000 women workers.

In the United States in the 1990s, feminists established centers for research on women, staged protests and demonstrations, developed policy and legislation, lobbied Congress, and developed service programs to meet women's needs.

In 1990, forty-seven veiled Saudi Arabian women protested the law prohibiting women from driving by driving cars on the King Abdul Aziz Highway in Riyadh.

The National Women's Lobby Group (NWLG) was formed in Zambia in 1991. This NGO aims to promote the end of laws and customs that discriminate against women, to increase women's education and political participation, and to put women in political decision-making positions. The NWLG intensely campaigns in order to get women's issues on the government agenda, forms alliances with other NGOs, and does outreach to educate women as to the law and their rights. The NWLG is recognized as a leading advocate for Zambian women.

In Tehran, Iran, in 1994, psychology professor Homa Darabi Tehrani set herself on fire to protest the government's oppressive rules against women. She had been dismissed from her post at Tehran University for nonadherence to the Islamic dress code. Her death led to widespread protests.

Approximately thirty thousand people attended her funeral despite the government's threat to ban it.

In Mostar, Bosnia-Herzegovina, in 1997, a Serb woman and two Muslim women founded the Zena Zenama (Woman to Woman) Association. Working out of a crowded apartment, they engage in a number of activities such as helping elderly women try to recover their homes, assisting battered wives, running support groups for survivors of ethnic massacres and war rape, and providing voter education.

The Sri Lanka Federation of University Women (SLFUW) was formed almost fifty years ago by a handful of graduate women. Today the organization's focus is on helping women graduates and undergraduates and on training programs to enhance women's employment opportunities. The organization networks with a number of other organizations both nationally and internationally.

Founded in 1975, Rights of Women is a London-based organization that informs women of their rights and promotes the interests of women in relation to the law. They provide free legal advice to women and have been part of a number of successful policy initiatives, including those related to abortion rights, the criminalization of marital rape, and lesbians' legal rights.

*M*ao Tse-tung, Chinese Communist Party Chairman (1893–1976), once said that "women hold up half the sky," yet I think that you will agree from your reading thus far that women's importance is underestimated by the majority of social systems. This chapter focuses on contemporary women's efforts to challenge women's subordinate status. These efforts occur cross-nationally and assume a variety of forms. The chapter begins with a consideration of the forces that operate against women's activism and **empowerment** (by empowerment I mean women's learning to break away from the social systems that require their submission to gender inequality). Women's movements are an important means of women's empowerment, and the remainder of the chapter focuses on women's movements worldwide, emphasizing the many different forms women's movements may take and how history, politics, culture, and current realities shape them.

Forces Operating Against Women's Activism

People often seem puzzled that women put up with gendered abuses and lower power and status. I have heard many people make the simple proclamation that it could all be stopped if women would just stand up for themselves. Yes, it is true that, as Lerner (1986) once said, that the system of patriarchy can function only with the cooperation of women. However, as Lerner points out, this cooperation is secured by a variety of means: gender indoctrination, educational deprivation, denying women their history of struggle and achievement, dividing women from one another, restraints and outright coercion, discrimination in access to economic resources and political power, and awarding class privileges to conforming women. In other words, it is not such a simple matter after all.

It is important to understand the risks of women's rebellion against patriarchy. One risk is the possible loss of social belongingness and social approval. We want to be normal as defined by our culture, and we want to be accepted by others. These desires are powerful instigators of conformity and constitute what social psychologists call "normative pressure" (Deutsch & Gerard, 1955). Even those of us in societies that emphasize individualism must admit that there is nothing like the pain of being socially ostracized, that we are quite anxious to avoid this experience, and that we generally avoid it by conforming. Now consider that in most societies social rejection typically results when a woman does not conform to what her society deems as appropriate female behavior, and that in some cultures, this rejection can be quite severe. In some countries, nonconforming individuals may even be punished by the government. Iran's and Afghanistan's penalties for women who are not adequately "covered" in public are one example. Taslima Nasrin, Bangladeshi physician turned novelist, writes about women straining against patriarchy. Nasrin must hide from her government as there is a warrant for her arrest (for insulting Islam), and the leaders of fundamentalist religious groups have offered generous rewards for her capture or slaying (Filkins, 1998). In many countries, deviation makes one unmarriageable, and there may be few economic options for women outside of marriage. For instance, we have already mentioned that female genital mutilation increases a woman's marriageability in the cultures that practice it. Further consider that social rejection may be experienced especially severely in collectivistic cultures that emphasize the subordination of individual goals for the sake of the community. In such cultures, the shame one might bring upon one's family or village may seriously deter one from deviating from accepted norms.

Individuals generally have little doubt about the gender norms and roles of their culture. The distinct differences between women's and men's roles in most societies clearly communicate that what is expected of individuals is based in part on their sex. Starting in early childhood we become aware of our identity as a male or female and notice that different things are expected of each sex. We then model the behaviors of same-gendered others in a tendency psychologists call differential modeling (Burn, 1996). Add to this that children are reinforced for behaviors depending upon the behavior's gender appropriateness. This is called differential reinforcement and has been documented cross-culturally (Low, 1989; Rogoff, 1981; Whiting & Edwards, 1988). In particular, there is a greater emphasis on nurturance, obedience, and responsibility for girls, and achievement and self-reliance for boys, especially in societies in which women have little control over resources (Low, 1989). As a result of differential socialization by gender, gender-inappropriate behavior is not within the individual's behavioral

"It has been difficult for me as an indigenous woman to find the confidence to speak publicly, particularly since we were raised to believe that the only role for women is to maintain a household and to bear children. If you broke with this role, you were seen as abandoning tradition and you would lose the respect of the people."
Rigoberta Menchu, Guatemalan winner of the Nobel Peace Prize

"Women have been taught for centuries that they are the slaves of men. I started writing because I wanted to wake them up."
Taslima Nasrin

repertoire. For females socialized to be obedient and submissive, challenging gender customs is especially foreign. For instance, in many parts of Mexico, the ability to put up with things, aguantar, is a mark of feminine virtue (Darling, 1995).

Williams and Best (1990a) once said that beliefs concerning the psychological makeup of men and women are absorbed into myth and religion, into oral history and written literature. A culture's gender stereotypes typically function as gender norms—prescriptive social rules specifying appropriate behavior based on gender. They are also taught as part of childhood socialization. For instance, in the United States, there are sayings such as "Girls are made of sugar and spice and everything nice" and "Boys are made of frogs and snails and puppy dogs' tails." In short, societies have beliefs regarding how males and females are different and typically model and reinforce behaviors consistent with gender stereotypes. Wanting acceptance and approval from adults and peers, we conform to these gender roles and stereotypes and become more comfortable performing gender-appropriate behaviors (Burn, 1996). This makes it difficult to behave in a way counter to one's gender role.

Another reason why women often do not resist is that their low power leads them to believe that there is not much point in defiance. **Self-efficacy** is the name psychologists give to a person's belief that he or she will be effective should he or she act (Bandura, 1986). **Perceived self-efficacy** (PSE) is a major determinant of whether we try to perform a behavior and whether we are persistent in doing so. Female-repressive cultures communicate that females' efforts to deviate are unlikely to be effective. For instance, in female-repressive cultures, governments often control civil society and punish political activity that challenges the status quo. Deviation from gender norms is likely to meet with severe disapproval and is sometimes physically punished. Females learn early that efforts to rebel are unlikely to be successful. Nonconformity is not considered an option. It is also the case that in female-repressive societies, females are unlikely to have ever seen females like themselves successfully step outside of their gender place. Instead, they have seen such individuals ostracized and otherwise punished. As Lerner (1986) points out, when there is no precedent, one cannot imagine alternatives to existing conditions. We must also consider that in female-repressive societies, there is unlikely to be social support from others for deviation. This is because conformity is equated with survival. Given that there are few options for women outside of conformity to traditional roles and knowing that punishment is the likely result of deviation, the loved ones of potential "deviates" encourage conformity.

By communicating to women that they are empowered or disempowered as women, societal and family norms also affect women's perceived self-efficacy. The laws, religion, and cultural practices of a society communicate to its people the relative status and power of women and men. These societal values regarding male and female are enacted in the family in the form of resources and decision-making power. In this way, the norms of the society and of the family act together to determine a woman's power to make and carry out decisions. In other words, it is not surprising that women who have little power and status may be more passive and accepting of their lower status. Not only may they be unaccustomed to acting independently because it is discouraged and even punished, but because of their low power, attempts at independent action may not have much effect. Consequently, their inclination to act is reduced. When individuals do not perceive a contingency between their actions and outcomes, they do not act. Psychologists call this phenomenon **learned helplessness.**

Women from cultures in which females are low in status and power are especially prone to learned helplessness, for in their experience, they do not have the power to change things. Passivity may be especially marked for women who are exposed to numerous uncontrollable life stressors—in particular, high indoor and outdoor density, poverty, poor sanitation, or other factors beyond their control. Such uncontrollable events further contribute to the perception that action will make little difference. Religions and religious leaders who suggest that women's life situations are God's will exacerbate women's passivity.

The amazing thing, then, is not that women don't always protest gender injustice, but that *they often do.* Indeed, in every society, in every generation, there have been efforts by women to fight their lower status. For instance, Fatimah Umm Salamih, who lived in Persia (now Iran) in the nineteenth century, fought for the equality of women. Murdered in 1852, thrown in a well, and covered with rocks, her last words were recorded as "You can kill me as soon as you like, but you cannot stop the emancipation of women" (Tomasevski, 1993).

Early Assumptions About Women's Movements

Until recently, Western feminist academics dominated the study of women's movements. Typically, they focused on movements in the United States and Europe and rarely on movements in postcolonial countries (Basu, 1995). These analyses often overemphasized the role of middle-class women, the role of economic development, and particular types of activities. This probably occurred because to Western scholars, the most visible feminist movements were those in industrialized nations dominated by middle- and upper-class women engaged in campaigns to gain equal rights under the law (such as the right to vote). These features of Western women's movements were overgeneralized and led to a narrow definition of women's movements. This narrow definition excluded the many different ways in which women struggle against gender inequality, and, as noted by Basu (1995), defined out of existence those movements from which the middle class is absent or unimportant.

As Basu (1995) and others (Bystydzienski, 1992a) point out, there is a long history of struggle for women's equality in the Middle East, Latin

Salima Ghezali is a feminist activist and editor of Algeria's major newspaper, *La Nation,* now banned for criticizing the government and the Islamic extremists for their part in the violence that terrorizes Algeria. In hiding, she continues to write articles in an effort to draw international attention to human rights violations in Algeria. Ghezali also founded the Association for the Emancipation of Women and the feminist journal *Nyssa.*

"Never doubt that a small group of thoughtful, committed citizens can change the world—indeed, it's the only thing that ever has."
Margaret Mead

"While gender subordination has universal elements, feminism cannot be based on a rigid concept of universality that negates the wide variation in women's experience. . . . There is, and must be, a diversity of feminisms, responsive to the different needs and concerns of different women, and *defined by them for themselves.*" *Gita Sen and Caren Grown of DAWN*

America, Asia, and Africa; economic development is no guarantee of a strong women's movement; and women's movements comprise a range of struggles by women against gender inequality. Women's movements may be independently organized or affiliated with political parties, they may be of short or long duration, they may rest on a narrow social base or on multiclass coalitions, they may focus on one issue or multiple issues, and they may be local or national (Basu, 1995). To exclude any of these forms is to restrict our understanding of a rich and multifaceted phenomenon (Basu, 1995).

Women's Movements' Rejection of Feminist Label

Many women's movements do not adopt the feminist label. However, don't let the fact that many women's activists distance themselves from the feminist label lead you to assume that women's movements are not prevalent or strong. At first glance, support for feminism appears highest in countries with active socialist or communist parties and strong labor movements (Katzenstein, 1987), and it is often in these countries that an easily identifiable feminist movement may be found. This is probably because feminism seems less foreign to a political ideology that emphasizes the wrongs of exploitation of lower classes by higher classes and the challenging of this tradition. It is important to realize, though, that many women's organizations that do the work of the women's movement avoid the feminist label. There are a number of reasons for this.

One reason is that feminism has a negative connotation in many cultures. In countries with a history of colonization (many African countries) or other antagonistic relationships with Western countries (many Muslim countries), the effectiveness of openly feminist organizations may be compromised by the public perception that feminism is a Western, imported notion. In other countries, antifeminist groups have successfully given feminism a negative image such that many with feminist leanings do not call themselves "feminists." For example, in the United States, the National Organization for Women (NOW) is overtly feminist, but many other women's activists and organizations are covertly feminist because of the perception that support for women's policies and programs is reduced by association with the feminist label. Indeed, research in the United States finds that terminology affects support for feminism (Breinlinger & Kelly, 1994; Buschman & Lenart, 1996; Jacobson, 1981). For instance, one study (Buschman & Lenart, 1996) found that the term *feminist* evoked more negative responses than did the term *women's movement.* This was true even among those respondents who scored high on feminism (as measured by a strong collective orientation, a strong dissatisfaction with women's status, insistence that a woman's place is not in the home, and a belief that individual action is not sufficient for female empowerment). The stigma associated with the feminist label is at least partially the result of the American political right and the American media. Both often portray feminists as unrepresentative of American women, antimother, man-hating, and lesbian.

Third World women may avoid the feminist label because the term *feminism* is frequently associated with a narrow, Western view of women's issues and strategies. In a number of Latin American countries where socialist struggles have resulted in changes toward democracy, feminism is associated with the bourgeoisie and imperialism. In Chile, for instance, feminists are considered bourgeois and elitist and insufficiently committed to the interests of the working class (Frohmann & Valdes, 1995). In Bolivia, feminism is viewed as alien to the working class and as divisive to the labor movement (Salinas, 1994). Similarly, feminist activists in Nicaragua often avoid the feminist label because feminism is often portrayed in the media as antifamily and antimale, and the traditional Latin American political left believes feminism to be bourgeois and inappropriate for women in a poor country like Nicaragua (Chinchilla, 1994).

Many Third World women feel that their struggle as women is connected to the struggles of their communities against racism, economic exploitation, and imperialism and believe that **Western** or **First World feminism** does not address this. To cite an instance, Black South African feminism is based on Black women's experience of multiple oppressions and includes issues, such as access to clean water and housing, that have not traditionally been defined as feminist (Kemp, Madlala, Moodley, & Salo, 1995). In other words, First World feminism is viewed by many Third World women as too singularly focused on the struggle against gender discrimination when their oppression cannot be limited to gender alone (Johnson-Odim, 1991). As Mohanty (1991) says, "To define feminism purely in gendered terms assumes our consciousness (or identity) of being 'women' has nothing to do with race, class, nation, or sexuality, just gender. But no-one becomes a woman purely because she is female. Ideologies of womanhood have as much to do with class and race as they have to do with sex" (p. 12). Or, as Kemp and colleagues (1995) say in a chapter on Black South African feminism,

> The challenge especially for Black feminists, has been to shape South African feminism based on three central assumptions. First, our identities as women are shaped by race, class, and gender, and these identities have molded our particular experiences of gender oppression. Second, our struggles as feminists encompass the struggle for national liberation from a brutal white state. Furthermore, the liberation of Black people as a whole is a feminist issue. Third, we have to challenge and transform Black patriarchies even though Black men have been our allies in the fight for national liberation. (p. 133)

Third World women distance themselves from Western feminism for other reasons as well. They are often aware, for instance, that First World women participated in the oppression of Third World Women (Johnson-Odim, 1991; Kemp et al., 1995). As Chase, a Black Namibian activist says,

"The minute you hear about feminism one immediately puts it in the connotation of the European and North American women's struggles. These are women from societies which have long been independent—people who . . . support the governments that . . . support our oppression. I could never feel solidarity with that. . . . I think there will be a different feminism coming out of Africa" (in Kemp et al., 1995, p. 141). **Third World women's activists** are also cognizant of the fact that racism was present in the early Western women's movement and that, up until recently, First World feminists have dominated international women's conferences (Johnson-Odim, 1991).

For these reasons, Third World feminists seek their own feminisms. As I've already suggested, African feminisms are shaped by African women's resistance to Western hegemony and by African culture. This means that some of the concerns that have driven Western feminism, such as female control over reproduction and choice within human sexuality, are not characteristic of African feminisms. Indeed, African feminism is "distinctly heterosexual, pro-natal, and concerned with bread, butter, culture and power issues" (Mikell, 1997, p. 4). Third World feminisms are often rooted in a precolonial past in which women played strong roles and were high in status. For instance, the creation of the first woman, according to the indigenous people of the Philippines, was simultaneous with the creation of the first man. Filipina feminists refer to this to show that as a person born whole and separate from man, the Filipina owns her body and self and can chart her own history and destiny (Santiago, 1995).

Western feminism is also frequently dismissed as an instrument of colonialism in Muslim countries. **Islamic feminists** often argue that Western feminism, with its emphasis on equality in the labor force and White middle-class women, is irrelevant to the majority of the world's women, who seek an honored place as wives and as mothers (Afshar, 1996). Like African feminists, women working toward equality in Muslim countries frequently distinguish themselves from Western feminists to avoid charges that they have been influenced by "foreign" ideologies (Moghadam, 1991). These efforts are centered around recovering their own women's history (which includes Muslim women rulers and theologians) and showing that women's equality is consistent with Islam (Moghadam, 1991).

"In Islam and the Arab world, and in all our cultures, we must claim those things that are positive and discard without hesitation those things that are negative. In Egypt we have a long tradition of women in power. For thousands of years, for example, we have had the Goddess Isis, and her tradition. Thank God, thank Goddess, we still have her spirit with us."
Nawal el Saadawi

Different Strands of Women's Movements

A Broad Definition

It is important to realize that nationally and cross-nationally, women's movements may take many forms. The term **women's movement** describes a sum of campaigns around issues of importance to women—campaigns that feed into a network of women's groups and increase awareness of women's problems and rights (Kumar, 1995). The women's movement is not a distinct organizational entity worldwide, or even in most countries; within a single country, the movement has broad ideological variety and a range of organizational expressions (Katzenstein, 1987). Indeed, it is inaccurate to talk of *a* women's movement; it is far more accurate to speak of women's movement*s*. Consider this example from Alvarez (1994), who describes the Brazilian women's movement of the 1970s and 1980s:

> Women spearheaded protests against the regime's human rights violations; poor and working-class women crafted creative solutions to meet community needs in response to gross government neglect of basic urban and social services; women workers swelled the ranks of Brazil's new trade union movement; rural women struggled for their rights to land that were increasingly being usurped by export-agribusiness; Afro-Brazilian women joined the United Black Movement and helped forge other organized expressions of a growing antiracist, Black-consciousness movement; Brazilian lesbians joined gay males to launch a struggle against homophobia; young women and university students enlisted in militant student movements; some took up arms against the military regime, and still others worked in legally sanctioned parties of the opposition. By the 1980s, thousands of women involved in these and other struggles had come to identify themselves as feminists. (p. 13)

Bystydzienski (1992a) suggests that in countries with a women's movement, there are generally two branches: an established older branch made up of organizations that have become institutionalized and that are more or less accepted as the mouthpiece for women's rights; and a younger, noninstitutionalized branch made up of small, loose groups outside of the mainstream. The older branch, she maintains, tends to be more ideologically liberal or moderate and essentially struggles for changes in laws and policies within the existing society. This branch also tends toward a hierarchical structure with some role specialization and formal rules. In contrast, the younger branch is more ideologically radical and seeks transformation of existing societies according to feminist principles. It consists of small, local groups, often linked by informal networks, and avoids formal rules and hierarchies. The activities of the younger branch focus on building alternatives outside of the system, such as cooperatives run by women, economic enterprises, women's shelters, health clinics, and day-care centers.

Three Major Strands

Jahan (1995b) describes three major strands of women's movements in Bangladesh. These are found in many countries: women's rights activist groups that raise women's issues at the national policy level; women's research and advocacy organizations that raise public awareness; and nongovernmental organizations that work to raise women's awareness and mobilize women at the grassroots level (Jahan, 1995b). Furthermore, these different types of groups often build coalitions in order to create change.

Jahan (1995b) illustrates this in her discussion of campaigns to eliminate violence against women in Bangladesh (from the late 1970s to early 1980s). Researchers documented violence against women, grassroots groups started intervention programs, and women's organizations pressured the government to enact laws against that violence.

Ichikawa Fusae (1893–1981) led the women's suffrage movement in Japan, founded one of the first feminist organizations in 1919 (the New Woman's Association), and was elected to the House of Councillors in 1952, where she continued her work on women's issues and served until her death.

Large, National Organizations

One especially visible form of women's movement is the large, national organization focused on legislative change. From the early to mid-twentieth century, women's organizations on every continent won women the right to vote. Here are several recent examples of change sought by large, national women's organizations:

- In Bangladesh, the country's largest women's organization, Mahila Parishad, collected 17,000 signatures and lobbied parliament for an antidowry law, which was passed in 1980.
- The Concertación Nacional de Mujeres por la Democracia (National Coalition of Women for Democracy, or CNMD) is a coalition of women's organizations in Chile that successfully lobbied to include women's issues on the agenda of the new democratic government formed in 1990.
- Japanese feminists struggle for effective anti-sex discrimination legislation (Tanaka, 1995).

Grassroots Women's Groups

Several women's movement scholars maintain that the vitality of women's movements does not lie primarily in the activities of large national organizations but is frequently found in small, local-level activist groups (Basu, 1995; Katzenstein, 1987). In the chapter on women and development, you read about grassroots organizations (GROs), locally based groups that work to develop and improve communities. I noted that many of these work on women's issues. As mentioned earlier, women's movements include small local-level groups that do things like provide shelter to battered women or give credit to female microentrepreneurs. Local women's groups may also focus on consciousness raising. **Feminist consciousness** refers to an awareness of and discontent with women's lower status and power, as well as an identification of oneself as a member of the oppressed group "woman." Feminist consciousness is viewed as essential to women's empowerment. Grassroots support organizations (GRSOs) are another type of nongovernmental organization characteristic of women's movements worldwide. GRSOs are nationally or regionally based assistance organizations, usually staffed by professionals, that channel funds and information to grassroots organizations. For example, GABRIELA is a GRSO founded in 1984 in the Philippines. A broad-based coalition of Filipino feminist organizations, GABRIELA rallies women and organizes campaigns against violations of women's rights in the home and workplace, sexual harassment, and sex trafficking.

The Journey to Gender Equality Differs Cross-Culturally

Women's Movements in Response to Different Issues

There is great diversity in the origins and character of women's movements worldwide, and the journey to gender equality differs based on culture. As noted by Margolis (1993), we must guard against the ethnocentric assumption that all gender equality movements will happen in the same way. For instance, because cultures differ, the issue that stimulates the women's movement in one country may hurt it in another. Margolis (1993) gives the example of family planning. In the West, family planning and abortion have served as major mobilizing forces for the women's movement, but such programs often arouse suspicion and opposition from Third World women, who may see these as attempts to limit the populations of their ethnic groups. This approach also does not make sense to women in countries where women's status is enhanced by having lots of children or where women need lots of children to help with the labor. Similarly, Basu (1995) acknowledges that women's movements often address common feminist issues in very different ways. For instance, with regard to reproductive rights, Irish women struggle for freer access to contraception, Bangladeshi women fight antinatalist government policies, Chinese women emphasize the connection between the one-child policy and female infanticide, and Filipino women's groups organize for prostitutes' rights, access to a greater range of contraception, and education to prevent AIDS.

Molyneaux (1985) suggests that women's movements may arise out of either "practical gender interests" or "strategic gender interests." **Practical gender interests** are usually in response to an immediate perceived need and do not generally have as their goal women's emancipation or equality. In contrast, **strategic gender interests** arise out of an awareness of a generalized patriarchy and a desire to challenge and change it. Both types of movements are important and necessary for easing, and eventually eliminating, women's oppression. Peterson and Runyan (1993) propose that movements arising out of practical gender interests tend to be attempts at reforms of existing systems whereas movements arising out of strategic gender interests are oriented toward larger transformations.

Peterson and Runyan (1993) also suggest that most women's activism arises out of local and immediate conditions that are perceived as obstacles to the realization of practical interests, but that as activists become aware of the relationship between local struggles and the overall system of gender subordination, they often move toward system-transforming politics. In this way, they say, participation in local resistance actions can lead to participation in (or at least support for) larger and sometimes global social movements. This point is driven home in the next chapter, on global feminism. It appears, however, that strategically motivated movements may also become more practically oriented.

"Believe not those who say

The upward path is smooth,

Lest thou should stumble on the way

And faint before the truth."

Anne Brontë (1820–1849), British writer

This seems to happen as activists discover just how deeply embedded gender inequality is in established social systems. They then focus on bringing about progress in recalcitrant social systems through incremental change. For example, Tanaka (1995) writes that the Japanese feminist movement that emerged in the 1970s changed from one that sought to "transform the whole set of cultural values" to one in the 1990s focused on "concrete social changes" and "women's assimilation into the male-dominated system" (p. 351).

Effect of Local Political and Economic Conditions

Local political and economic conditions also affect women's movements, both positively and negatively, and as these conditions change, women's movements change also. On the positive side, women's movements frequently arise out of other political struggles. These include working-class struggles, movements opposing state repression, and civil rights struggles. For instance, Nigeria's first women's activist association, the National Women's Union, was begun in 1947 by Funmilayo Ransome-Kuti, leader of a large women's march to protest the colonial power's taxation policies and those prohibiting assembly (Abdullah, 1995). Basu (1995) suggests that what initially motivates many women to organize is not necessarily a belief in the distinctive nature of their problems but rather a sense of shared oppression with other groups that have been denied their rights. West and Blumberg (1990) suggest that women's consciousness is also raised when they begin to see the contradictions in ignoring their own oppression while fighting other injustices. They add that in the course of participating in these other struggles, women also gain valuable leadership training, skills, and confidence.

"Hum Bharat ki nari hain, phool nahin, chingari hain." ("We, the women of India, are not flowers, but fiery sparks.")
Indian feminist slogan

Women's Movements Arising from Class Struggles

India in the 1970s provides numerous examples of women's organizations arising out of political movements fighting class differences. These include the Self-Employed Women's Association (SEWA), founded in 1970 in Gujarat by trade unionist Ela Bhatt; the Progressive Organization of Women (POW) of Hyderabad and the Stree Mukti Sangathana (Women's Liberation Organization) of Bombay, both of which arose out of the Maoist communist movement; and Mahila Samta Sainik Dal (League of Women Soldiers for Equality) of Maharashtra, which was associated with the anticaste *dalit* movement (Kumar, 1995). (Those born into the *dalit* or untouchable social class have the lowest status in India's caste system.) In many Latin American countries, the origin of women's movements are easily traced to efforts by the working class to organize, unionize, and struggle for better wages and working conditions. In Chile, for instance, women workers began organizing around both class and gender issues in the early 1900s (Frohmann & Valdes, 1995).

Women's Movements in Tandem with Nationalist Struggles

Historically, women have played important roles in movements for national liberation, and women's activists frequently promote women's rights in tandem with other nationalist struggles for freedom. New republics based on a democratic socialism, secularism, and the equitable distribution of resources lend themselves to the inclusion of women's rights. These new governments often recognize the important role that women play in the national liberation movement and see gender discrimination as incompatible with their desire to move toward a modern, democratic society. Such new republics sometimes grant women equal rights, at least in the public sphere; this occurs generally after some strong reminders from women's activists.

Spain is one example. The modern Spanish women's movement coincided with the end of a long struggle for democratic rule in 1975. Most of the movement leaders at this time were members or ex-members of leftist political groups who had struggled against the authoritarian rule of General Franco. Following the death of the dictator in 1975, Spanish feminists had to persuade the newly developing government that women's liberation was part of the task of building democracy and socialism (Threlfall, 1996). According to Threlfall (1996), the emerging movement was protected and encouraged by that fact that 1975 was the United Nations' International Women's Year. Feminists essentially got in on the ground floor of the newly developing government. From there, they encouraged the eradication of discriminatory legislation and the passing of legislation favorable to women. In 1983, the government set up the Instituto de la Mujer (Institute of Women). It is currently one of the largest women's public administrations in Europe and carries out functions similar to those that an independent feminist group might undertake, if it had the resources (Threlfall, 1996).

South Africa is yet another example of how feminism may emerge in the space created by national liberation. South Africa was colonized by the British and the Dutch. By 1948, the Dutch-descended Afrikaners controlled the government and the country. The Afrikan government promoted restricting the rights and movements of all non-White citizens under a system called apartheid. All Black opposition parties were banned, and individuals who violated this ban were arrested. The majority of Blacks were forced to live in desolate "homelands" called *bantustans,* were not allowed to own property, and when in White areas, were required to carry passes proving they had permission to be there. It wasn't until 1992, following years of national and international protest, that apartheid was outlawed and a new constitution granted equal rights to all South Africans.

As was the case in Spain, from the beginning, women's organizations in South Africa played an important role in the struggle for national liberation. They organized protests and other grassroots challenges to the state. National Women's Day, a public holiday on August 9, commemorates one particularly famous example. On August 9, 1956, despite the discouragement of male

"If particular care and attention is not paid to the ladies, we are determined to foment a rebellion and will not hold ourselves bound by any laws in which we have no voice or representation."
Abigail Adams, wife of U.S. President John Adams, and perhaps America's first feminist

comrades, 20,000 South African women marched on the Union Building in Pretoria to protest the extension of "pass laws" to Black women and their children (Kemp et al., 1996).

As South African women's level of political awareness and experience grew, they demanded that women's issues be addressed in the national agenda. As Asha Moodley of the Black Women's Federation said,

> Having taken on co-responsibility for waging the political struggle, for sustaining and conserving it when it was really embattled, there was no way women would continue their silence . . . their suspension of the gender struggle. When they said then that the liberation of women was "inextricably linked" with the national liberation of the country, they did not mean that political liberation meant overall freedom for women. It was to imply a warning that at some time in the future, when deemed it fit to do so, there would be also a direct confronation with patriarchy. (in Kemp et al., 1995, p. 138)

This was no empty promise. Following the fall of apartheid, new women's organizations formed and old ones emerged from hiding. In 1992, the Women's National Coalition (WNC), representing eighty-one diverse women's organizations, was formed to ensure that women's rights were represented in the new constitution. Because the WNC represented a broad range of women's perspectives and was strongly activist, it was able to add women's issues to the national agenda of the postapartheid government. In 1996, the new South African Constitution, which provides equality between women and men as well as protection for lesbian and gay rights, was ratified.

The Philippines also fit this model of the newly liberated country sympathetic to women's issues. As was the case in Chile, Spain, and South Africa, from the beginning Filipino women played important roles in the labor and liberation movements. Santiago (1995) shows that feminist organizing and consciousness have a long history in the Philippines. Beginning in the early 1900s, *feminista* organizations campaigned to achieve political equality. Philippine suffragists campaigned in the Philippine Assembly, in the media, in schools, and at gatherings, and in 1937 they became the first women in Asia to win the right to vote. During the liberation movement of the 1970s and 1980s, *feministas* became an integral part of the struggle and insisted that a feminist perspective be part of the national agenda. In 1984, they founded a feminist political party and the feminist coalition GABRIELA mentioned earlier in the chapter. In 1985, when dictator Ferdinand Marcos declared victory in the national elections, feminist organizations were central in challenging the election results. This challenge toppled the Marcos dictatorship and affirmed Corazon Aquino as president. The Filipino women's movement today is strong and consists of a large variety of women's organizations working on a wide variety of issues, including reproductive rights, eliminating violence against women, employment, and the dismantling of U.S. military bases (Santiago, 1995).

The involvement of women in nationalist struggles stimulates women's activism in yet another way. When women work hard in the battle for liberation only to discover the patriarchy within the very liberation movement in which they are working, their feminist consciousness is often raised. For instance, Elaine Salo, of the South African United Women's Congress (UWC), recalls how the UWC was called upon to provide the tea and snacks at a national conference on the media instead of being a full participant (in Kemp et al., 1995). Likewise, many of the present leaders of the Bangladeshi women's movement became aware of gender discrimination as a result of the war for independence from Pakistan. Despite their role in the national independence movement, women were marginalized by the new government. They responded by organizing the first autonomous women's research organization in Bangladesh (Women for Women). Their reports on the status of women provided the basis for much of women's activism from the mid-1970s onward (Jahan, 1995).

Nationalist Struggles May Not Enhance Gender Equality

Although the fall of oppressive governments may lead to the adoption of reforms favorable to women and to climates supportive of feminist activism, this is not always the case. This is demonstrated by the countries of the former Soviet Union. Yes, it is true that the Soviet government did not permit an independent feminist movement, and the majority of women were required to participate in the paid labor force *and* assume the bulk of household labor. However, women did receive some economic protections and reproductive rights, and female political representation was guaranteed by "set asides" for women. For the most part, these rights for women have been abandoned in the former Soviet republics, and women's political representation has declined significantly. Although there is variation, generally speaking, women of the countries that made up the former Soviet Union have lost ground. Women now constitute a higher proportion of the poorest, most disadvantaged sector of society, prostitution is on the rise, day care is increasingly unavailable, and reproductive choice has been curtailed (Matynia, 1995; Waters & Posadskaya, 1995). The new "masculine democracies" that have arisen in countries of the former Soviet Union give little space to women's needs, interests, civil rights, and organization in the policy process (Molyneaux, 1996). For instance, in Russia, politicians from across the political spectrum have omitted women's equal rights from their list of legitimate and desirable goals (Waters & Posadskaya, 1995).

Initially it is puzzling that the fall of oppressive governments in Spain, the Philippines, and South Africa have led to positive development for feminism but not in the former Soviet republics. However, there are important differences. First, in the former countries, recall that there were politically active feminists who played key roles in the nationalist struggle and were able to link the liberation of women to the national liberation of the country. In other words, there was already a fairly strong feminist consciousness and familarity with political advocacy. This was not the case in the majority of the Eastern bloc countries, although the countries with the most active women's movements (such as Poland) do have a longer history of organized rebellion against the Soviet Union.

Second, unlike the Spanish democracy that arose during the International Decade for Women and that was responsive to feminist requests for inclusion, the new democracies of the 1980s and 1990s arose in a climate emphasizing free markets and minimal government protections (Molyneaux, 1996). These issues combined mean that there is no mechanism for protecting women's rights and that women do not yet have the feminist consciousness and activist skills to push for the inclusion of women's rights in the new national agendas.

Third, unlike Spain, the Philippines, and South Africa, the former Soviet republics had a bad taste in their mouth with regard to feminism. These new republics illustrate how a large, repressive state bureaucracy can taint impressions of feminism. Unfortunately, feminism is currently associated with a Soviet program of social entitlement that came with an extremely high social and political price tag. Consequently, the very fact that the Soviet regime espoused the idea of women's equality is now enough to bring it under suspicion (Molyneaux, 1996; Waters & Posadskaya, 1995). Similarly, in the former Soviet republics of Czechoslovakia, Slovakia, Poland, and Hungary, women have been slow to organize. Matynia (1995) suggests that this is because large, nationwide organizations are still associated with the image of the *sodruzka,* the communist token woman. Her interviews also suggest that many women favor a return to traditional roles because "Soviet-style" gender equality forced women into the workplace without providing any relief at home, and the pre-Soviet past is romanticized.

Successful nationalist struggles may also interfere with women's equality when they lead to states where conservative religious laws became state laws. This type of nationalism often seeks inspiration from an imaginary past and usually advocates redomesticating women and controlling their sexuality (Basu, 1995). The battle between those who desire a secular modernist state and those favoring a traditional religious state continues to be waged in countries such as Turkey and Bangladesh, and those who win will greatly affect women's lives. Those favoring a traditional religious state have already won in some countries such as Afghanistan, where a nationalist religious movement succeeded in ending ten years of Soviet occupation. Prior to that, chaos reigned for almost nine years as the freedom fighters turned against one another. It was the nationalist Taliban group who brought peace. However, the ruling Taliban government enforces an extreme version of Islam that prohibits women from working outside the home, prevents girls from going to school, and requires that women in public be completely covered by a garment called a *chador* (they see out of a screenlike covering in their burqa veil).

Iran is yet another case in which women's rights were significantly curtailed following a nationalist religious revolution. However, despite efforts by the state to restrict women's activities and rights, Iranian women have successfully fought to regain much of the ground they lost (Afshar, 1996). According to Afshar (1996), they have done this by anchoring their arguments in favor of women's rights in the teachings of Islam. As Afshar (1996)

Meena (1957–1987), of Kabul, Afghanistan, dangerously campaigned against the occupying Soviet forces, began a feminist women's magazine, founded the Afghan feminist organization RAWA, advocated against Islamic fundamentalist views of women, and established schools for Afghanistan refugee children in Pakistan and microenterprises for their parents. She was assassinated in 1987 by the Soviet secret service (KGB) and their fundamentalist accomplices.

says, "Given the Islamic nature of the national political discourse, which posits the government as the defender of the faith, women were able to take the Republic to task for failing to deliver on its Islamic duty" (p. 203). They did this by referring to parts of the Koran that favor respect for women and support for females' education and training. Islamic women also referred to educated and powerful female role models such as Muhammad's wives Khadija (politician and businesswoman) and A'isha (politician and religious expert). Consequently, Iranian women were able to successfully argue for the removal of many of the barriers placed upon their education, their practicing of medicine and law, and their owning and running of businesses. They have also successfully sought representation in parliament. Although they have not recaptured all of the progress made before the revolution, they have managed to regain some of their rights and continue to work toward women's rights as consistent with Islam.

"The women's movement in Iran is very misunderstood by the West. If you could break the image that we are all one black mass under the hijab, you would understand women in Iran. What we care about is not what we wear on our heads, but much more important issues, more profound issues of law that affect our lives."
Mehranguiz Kar

Gender Equality Often Subordinate to Other Issues

Gender equality may also be subordinated to other political issues. War, for example, typically causes struggles for women's rights to put on hold. To illustrate, from the early 1900s until 1937, there was a strong women's movement in Japan. Women such as Kishida Toshiko, Fukuda Hideko, Ishimoto Shizue, and Ichikawa Fusae spoke against the oppression of women, advocated women's rights, organized women's groups, and joined political parties (Ling & Matsumo, 1992). However, when Japan invaded China, the Japanese women's movement was prohibited, feminist leaders were forced to cooperate with the war effort, and those who persisted in feminist organizing were arrested and some killed (Fujieda, 1995; Ling & Matsumo, 1992). Likewise, Black South African women began protesting "pass laws" in 1912, but the campaign was suspended at the outbreak of World War I (Kemp et al., 1995). In the 1990s, war in Bosnia-Herzegovina also left little attention on women's rights (Wilkinson, 1998).

Economic crisis may also interfere with the struggle for women's rights (Margolis, 1993). Slovakia, once part of the Soviet Union, is a case in point. Matynia (1995) reports that in Slovakia, women feel that most of the problems they face are not specific or exclusive to women but are family problems caused by the economic transformation. Feminism may be seen as a luxury when the majority of the people are hungry. Similarly, Chowdhury (1994) states that women's issues are not perceived as major issues in Bangladesh, hidden as they are behind the country's poverty and underdevelopment.

Likewise, during times of political turmoil and repression, women's resistance of male oppression is often relegated to the margins, separated from other class and national struggles and subordinated to the wider and presumed higher cause of national liberation (Acosta-Belen & Bose, 1995). In cases in which the state is highly repressive, the vast majority of men also experience oppression, and it is therefore difficult for women to present a case that they are particularly oppressed (Bystydzienski, 1992b). For instance, under Soviet communism, Polish, Hungarian, Czech, and Slovak women *and* men felt equally repressed by the state, and the energies of every social movement were directed toward activities with the potential for large-scale change (Matynia, 1995).

In some cases, feminists believe that gender progress will not occur until authoritarian governments are overthrown, and so they work for other social changes under the assumption that women's liberation will follow. The Philippines from 1950s until the 1970s is one such case. Many feminists joined the nationalist movement against dictator Ferdinand Marcos, believing that national liberation would bring about women's equality (Santiago, 1995). The newly developing Indian women's movement of the 1970s was interrupted by the declaration of a state of emergency by Prime Minister Indira Gandhi in 1975. Most political organizations were driven underground, and those that remained focused on civil rights such as freedom of speech and association and the right to protest (Kumar, 1995). Kemp and colleagues (1995) describe a similar phenomenon in regard to Black South African feminism in the twentieth century. In the 1950s, women's activism was banned along with other opposition to the White, separatist government. In the 1970s, a resistance movement reemerged, but the immediacy of the state's attack on Black people and the constant bannings and detentions of Black activists meant that the debate over issues of gender and women's oppression had to wait until the battle for national liberation was won.

The State and Feminism

State Feminism

How feminist movements accomplish their goals depends greatly on political institutions and state structures (Katzenstein, 1987). This section examines the relationship between governments and women's movements. Many governments have responded to women's activism and international pressures (such as pressure from the United Nations) by adding offices, commissions, agencies, ministries, committees, and advisors to deal with women's issues. Here are some samples: Office of the Status of Women (Australia), Canadian Advisory Council on the Status of Women (Canada), Danish Equal Status Council (Denmark), Frauenbeauftragte (Women's Affairs Offices, Germany), Ministry of State for Women's Affairs (Ireland), Equal Status and Equal Opportunity National Commission (Italy), Women's Bureau (United States), National Women's Service (SERNAM in Chile), and the Better Life for Rural Women Programme (Nigeria). These have been called "women's policy machinery," and the female bureaucrats who work as part of these government structures have been called "femocrats" (Stetson & Mazur, 1995). **State feminism** refers to activities of government structures that are formally charged with furthering women's status and rights (Stetson & Mazur, 1995).

Debate About the Role of the State

There is quite a bit of debate about the role of the state in promoting a feminist agenda. Some feminists and feminist groups look upon state feminism favorably and cultivate relationships with the state under the assumption that the best way to create change is from within (Gelb, 1989; Steinberg, 1988). The focus of these individuals and groups is often on changing laws and integrating women into the public sphere (this approach is often associated with liberal feminism). Feminist critics of this approach, such as MacKinnon (1989), point out that no matter how many laws are passed or how many women hold public office, the state reflects, promotes, maintains, and responds to a hierarchy of male prerogative and female subordination (Stetson & Mazur, 1995). According to MacKinnon (1989), this is why women haven't made that much progress, despite legal changes.

Although critics agree that states should play a role in solving women's problems, they remain concerned that many governments undermine change by co-opting women's organizations and weakening them, such that they become part of the system rather than a challenge to it. For example, in Mexico during the 1930s, the United Front for Women's Rights was founded and had more than 50,000 women members from different social classes and ideological viewpoints. The movement was incorporated into the official party, Partido Revolucionario Mexicana (predecessor of today's ruling Partido Revolucionario Institutional). Its activities were then restricted, ostensibly to prevent "political instability" (Pablos, 1992).

Typically at least some feminist groups criticize government-run women's organizations for their failure to become the locus of women's empowerment. Skeptics, such as Basu (1995), also point to cases in which governments created women's organizations that they could control and required that women's interests be pursued through these organizations and not independently. The problem is that under these conditions, governments decide what women's problems are and how to solve them. The result is the appearance of progress despite the fact that key women's issues are ignored, and traditional gender relations and gender power differentials remain largely intact. A number of examples come from Latin America. For instance, in Chile, SERNAM, the main governmental organization devoted to women's issues, is perceived by many feminists to be too cautious and conservative, to be an instrument through which the women's movement has been co-opted, and to have failed to establish good links with grassroots women's organizations (Frohmann & Valdes, 1995). Similar criticisms are made by grassroots feminists in Brazil regarding state women's organizations (Alvarez, 1994).

It is important that state feminist inclusion of societal actors empower those interests without co-opting or dominating them (Mazur & Stetson, 1995). As Mazur and Stetson (1995) caution, "If interests become overly dependent on the state, not only is their autonomy threatened, but their own fortunes become intertwined with those of the policy offices, and these are often linked to the fate of a governing party coalition" (p. 276). The United States is a typical example. In general, feminist organizations have worked to cement alliances with the Democratic Party, and when this party is in power, more policies consistent with feminist interests are made. However, some ground is lost when the Republicans control the government. For instance, from the 1980s until the early 1990s, it was very difficult to get equal rights legislation passed under Republican presidents Reagan and Bush. By the early 1990s, some of the gains made in the 1970s were significantly weakened by these two administrations. For instance, the Reagan administration prohibited public health-care providers who receive federal funds from discussing abortion as an option (Brenner, 1996).

Nicaragua provides yet another example of how feminist alliances with governments are somewhat risky when those governments change and state feminist machineries may be dismantled. As was the case in many Latin American countries, a nationalist struggle for independence from a dictatorship stimulated the growth of the women's movement. Nicaraguan women played an important role in the overthrow of the Somoza dictatorship and in the process, honed their political skills and confidence and earned the right to inclusion in the new Sandinista government. AMNLAE (Asociación de Mujeres Louisa Amanda Espinosa) became the Sandinista-affiliated women's organization and by 1985 played an aggressive role in educating Nicaraguan society about women's issues. The Sandinista government also funded a number of significant feminist research projects and created a Women's Legal Office, located in the President's Office, in order to participate in strategic planning (Chinchilla, 1994). In 1990, however, the Sandinistas lost the election to the conservative UNO party, and, as you may recall, Violeta de Chamorro became president. Once in power, the fundamentally conservative and antifeminist character of the Chamorro government became evident when the government advocated traditional gender roles and the rhythm method as the only acceptable form of birth control, and when it cut services that benefited women (Chinchilla, 1994). These events stimulated intense discussion within the Central American women's movement about the meaning and importance of autonomy for feminist organizations (Chinchilla, 1994). Although the Nicaraguan movement remains divided on this issue, it is a large and diverse movement. AMNLAE remains active; there are research and service centers, neighborhood women's groups, feminist collectives such as the Women's Radio Collective of Matagalpa, gay and lesbian groups, a university women's studies program, women's newspapers and foundations, and NGOs with a gender focus (Chinchilla, 1994).

Because of the dangers inherent in the state co-opting women's movements, defining women's interests, and failing to bring about real change in the underlying social norms that support women's lower status and power, some feminists, such as Abdullah (1995), argue that there must be women's movements independent of the state in order to bring about real change.

This is certainly true to a point. However, Ferree (1987) in an analysis of the West German women's movement demonstrates the limits of strict autonomy. Although feminists there have played a leading role in the running of shelters for battered women, their fear of co-optation and desire for autonomy have made them reluctant to work for legislative and political changes. West German feminists now reluctantly acknowledge that their concerns with boundaries and independence have reduced their influence on the lives of most women. The movement is currently struggling to develop alliances with political groups without sacrificing their autonomy. Achieving this balance seems to be key to the success of women's movements.

> "A true feminist agenda challenges the state."
> *Hussaina Abdullah*

Examples of State Feminism

In truth, whether the state helps or hinders women's movements often depends upon which state you are talking about. States may or may not allow independent women's organizations to participate in policy formation and implementation. States may or may not successfully co-opt and dominate women's organizations such that their influence is weakened. States may or may not provide state funds to independent organizations that advance women's interests. States may or may not have their own state-run women's bureaus or commissions, and these may be powerful or weak, focused on gender equality or on maintaining traditional women's roles. States may or may not require that women's organizations be state-run organizations. State women's policy machinery may or may not contribute to feminist policymaking and provide women's advocates with access to the policy process. The cases of China, Kenya, and Norway illustrate the point that state feminism varies quite a bit.

China In some countries there is not much of an independent women's movement, and almost all advocacy for women is done by government commissions and government-sponsored women's organizations. For instance, in the Soviet Union, the official women's organization during the communist period was the Soviet Women's Committee, and independent women's organizations were not permitted. China is another example of a state feminism in which a doctrine consistent with women's rights is professed, little independent political activity is permitted, and it is essentially a requirement that women's organizations be state organizations.

The contemporary women's movement in China developed alongside the country's political movement in the early part of the twentieth century. The movement away from dynastic rule involved the rejection of traditional culture and the Confucian philosophy that had so strongly influenced gender relations. In the 1920s, the move toward socialism involved a new Marxist ideology that linked women's oppression to the rise of private ownership and a class society and viewed women's liberation as part of socialist revolution (Zhang & Xu, 1995). Within this context arose many women's activist groups who promoted the rejection of traditional practices such as foot-binding.

By 1949, the Chinese Communist Party (CCP) ruled the country. To maximize the people's commitment and involvement in the revolution, the CCP established organizations to connect society to the state. According to Zhang and Xu (1995), the All-China Women's Federation (ACWF) was set up to mobilize and represent the interests of Chinese women. Early campaigns focused on helping women to see that they had been oppressed and to convince them that support of the CCP would bring them equality. Campaigns against traditional practices such as forced marriage and bride-price* were initiated. In 1956, China declared the socialist process virtually complete, and the ACWF as a wing of the CCP had to go along with the idea that women's equality had been reached as well. Women's issues were essentially buried, and the ACWF was actually abolished in the years from 1966 to 1978. In 1978 the government reactivated the ACWF as evidence of forced marriage, female infanticide arising from population control policies, and prostitution became harder to ignore.

The ACWF remains the primary way in which women's interests are addressed in China, and over time it has become more militant and independent in advocating for women's interests (Zhang & Xu, 1995). The ACWF currently documents women's inequality and pushes for the protection of women's rights and interests. In the 1990s the ACWF achieved some notable success in getting legislation favoring women's rights passed, in mobilizing state resources to work for women's benefit, and in encouraging the study of women's issues. As of 1994, the ACWF had over 98,000 employees. Since the early 1980s other women's organizations have arisen as well. These are of two types: women's professional and occupational organizations and women's organizations led by women intellectuals to bring attention to women's issues. However, these organizations are required by law to have a formal link with a state agency to supervise their activities. In short, women's activism in China is very much controlled by the government, but some significant gains in women's status have been made since 1949. Furthermore, the growth of women's studies as an academic discipline and the increasing number of women's publications and literature are evidence of an emerging women's movement independent of the state (Zhang & Xu, 1995).

Kenya   Kenya appears to be an example of what Abdullah (1995) calls **state pseudofeminism,** a situation in which state-controlled women's organizations reinforce a conservative image of women as wives, mothers, and secondary income earners and prevent real changes in women's roles. She suggests that state pseudofeminism's effect on women is far from emancipatory because women are not empowered to resist patriarchy, their ability

---

*Bride-price is a custom in which the groom pays money or goods to the parents of the bride. The bride typically has little say in the negotiations. Financially desperate parents may essentially sell their daughters into bad marriages.

to earn independent income is not enhanced, and they are prevented from becoming a credible political force. On the face of it, however, the state has the appearance of attending to women's issues. According to Bystydzienski (1992a), when women have little access to government structures and the overall culture is unsupportive of women's equality, women develop other strategies for empowerment derived from women's culture. Kenya is a good example of how women organize themselves into groups that address their oppression and help them respond to it, even when societal conditions are not exactly conducive to women's activism.

Kenya remains a very patriarchal country where the constitution and courts continue to uphold traditional practices that discriminate against women. For instance, female genital mutilation is still practiced among the Kikuyu, Masai, Kisii, Meru, and Kalenjin peoples despite laws forbidding it (Morgan, 1996). Bride-price and polygymy continue as well, and there is no law against marital rape. Given the potential power of a unified women's movement to challenge male dominance, the state uses tactics to divide diverse groups of women such as those from different classes, religions, and tribes. The government is also a repressive one and stifles political dissent by permitting torture and ill treatment, including rape, by the police. This means that women's activists must proceed carefully lest they be intimidated, harassed, and imprisoned. Consequently, women in Kenya try to gain equal rights by helping one another become self-sufficient. This fits in with Kenyan women's traditions. Indeed, traditionally, much of Kenyan women's resistance was conducted through nonconfrontational artistic methods such as song, poetry, and dance.

There is no national organized feminist movement in Kenya, and the women's movement there is synonymous with the emergence of women's groups (Oduol & Kabira, 1995). Indeed, there are over 40 registered national women's organizations and over 6,000 local women's groups in Kenya (Arungu-Olende, 1996). One of the first national women's organizations is Maendeleo Ya Wanawake (MYWO), an organization that dates back to colonial rule and that was founded by White settlers' and administrators' wives. MYMO currently coordinates over 3,000 registered women's groups, but critics say its effectiveness has been reduced by its close association with the repressive ruling government.

Other formal organizations in Kenya have programs that reinforce women's traditional roles (for instance, through welfare activities such as child care, family nutrition, and hygiene) but also work for women's empowerment. The National Council of Women of Kenya (NCWK) is one example. Although the NCWK offers home economics programs, it also launched the National Committee on the Status of Women to educate women on democracy and their political rights. In addition, they also launched the Greenbelt movement to combat desertification in Kenya and were instrumental in the national women's conventions of 1992 and 1993, at which women from all over the country were brought together to strategize and demonstrate their solidarity in the struggle against gender-based oppression (Oduol & Kabira, 1995).

Much of Kenyan women's activism is conducted at a small grassroots level. These women's groups have a long history. Kenyan women's self-help groups have historically helped women cope in a male-dominated society that has denied them resources. For example, thousands of women's groups engage in business enterprises, community projects, and loan programs. The Kenyan Women Finance Trust, founded in 1983 by women professionals to provide loans for female-owned business ventures, is one such case (Morgan, 1996). Another example is the Kayole Women's Self-Help Group in Nairobi. Members of this group produce building materials, such as cinder blocks, for use in construction (Oduol & Kabira, 1995).

> "We do not want a piece of the pie; we want to change the basic recipe of the pie."
> *Birgit Brock-Utne*

Norway Stetson and Mazur (1995) suggest that state feminism does the most for women when the state is culturally defined as the site of social justice, has the structural capacity to institutionalize new demands for equality, and sustains widely supported feminist organizations that challenge sexual hierarchies through both radical politics from outside the government and reform politics in unions and parties. These very conditions exist in the state of Norway, considered to be one of the most progressive countries in the world with regard to women's issues.

Norway serves as an example of a positive state feminism with centralized offices that have successfully integrated gender equity principles into many policy areas and that have fostered the empowerment of women's groups (Stetson & Mazur, 1995). Although the Equal Status Council (ESC) remains the main agency focused on gender equality, the goal of equal status has been mainstreamed into most state agencies. The state actively promotes women's equality through publicly appointed committees, boards, and councils, quotas to increase the number of women in the civil service and in male-dominated occupations, child-care subsidies, and parental leave.

Bystydzienski (1992b; 1995) explains that part of the success of Norwegian state feminism is due to Norway's committment to the values of equality and justice, as well as to a belief in the role of the government in equalizing economic and social differences. However, its success is also clearly due to women's activism. Norwegian women have always been strong and political, and this is reflected in Norwegian literature dating back to the tenth century (As, 1996). Bystydzienski (1992b; 1995) emphasizes the role of Norway's active women's movement in creating a state responsive to women's needs. The modern movement has its roots in the 1800s, when the Norwegian Association for the Rights of Women worked to improve women's education and the legal rights of married women, the Association for Women's Suffrage worked toward women's suffrage, and women's labor unions were formed (Morgan, 1996). In the 1920s, women's organizations focused on contraception and abortion rights, the election of women to parliament, and legislation regarding the family (Morgan, 1996).

During the 1960s and 1970s, women representing traditional women's organizations and the so-called new feminists formed a successful coalition that raised public consciousness regarding women's disadvantaged status and called on the government to respond. In the 1970s, they united on the issue of abortion, and the Storting (the Norwegian Parliament) gave women the right to abortion within the first twelve weeks of pregnancy. One particular goal of the feminist coalition that significantly impacted state feminism was to increase the number of women in public office (as discussed in Chapter 8). The growing responsiveness of the Norwegian government to feminist activists clearly coincides with the increased number of women in public offices, for many of these women received their political training in the women's movement and were sympathetic to feminist demands. As more women entered government, the state became more responsive to women's demands from below, and women began to participate in forming state policy. Because of the influence of feminist organizations, the major political parties have all adopted sex quotas for political campaigns (at least 40 percent female and 40 percent male in any given election). The case should not be overstated, however. Men are still advantaged in Norway, and Norwegian feminists face a dilemma of how to remain committed to the promotion of women's interests while participating fully in male-created and dominated institutions (Bystydzienski, 1995).

Conclusion

It has already been said that women's struggles for equality are by no means new, but this fact, combined with women's continued lower status and power, suggests that these struggles have been less than effective. Indeed, the record of success is mixed. On the one hand, significant gains have been made. You can see this by the increase in national laws favorable to women (such as the dowry prohibition laws in India), the growth of international laws (the topic of our next chapter), increased women's services, and women's greater gender consciousness. Success is also evident in the sheer number of grassroots women's organizations worldwide. Although less visible than public protests and demonstrations, these organizations have significantly improved the quality of women's lives through the provision of information, services, and organization for change. Basu (1995) suggests that the success of women's movements must also be gauged in terms of women's increased cultural visibility. For instance, feminist expression is increasingly found in theater, dance, music, and literature. The growth of women's studies and centers for the study of women and gender are also seen by Basu as gains of the women's movement.

It is true, however, that women's movements have not achieved many of their legislative demands, such as the legalization of abortion in Brazil, the passage of the Equal Rights Amendment in the United States, and the reform of family law in Kenya, India, and Bangladesh (Basu, 1995). It is also true that in cases in which legislation has been passed, it is frequently unenforced. Indeed, what Jahan (1995) said in regard to the success of the women's movement in Bangladesh has broad applicability: While public pronouncements on the importance of including women are common, and women's participation at all levels has increased, no serious effort has been made to change the social structures and institutions perpetuating women's inequality. According to Jahan, the Bangladesh government seeks to "contain" the discourse on

"The women's movement, not only here in the U.S., but worldwide, is bigger and stronger than ever before and in places where it has never been. It has arms. It has legs. And most importantly, it has heads.
Bella Abzug, U.S. Congresswoman and co-founder of Women's Environment & Development Organization (WEDO)

women's rights in narrow channels that keep traditional notions of womanhood intact. Unfortunately, this is true of many governments.

Many explanations have been offered for the uneven success of women's movements. One thought is that many middle-class women's movements have failed because they did not mobilize poor women and assumed that class interests could be subordinated to gender interests (Basu, 1995). For example, in the case of women of color in the United States and Australia and in the Third World, the most pressing concerns may be freedom from starvation and ethnic discrimination, not gender inequality. Similarly, Australian Aboriginal women frequently feel that talking about women's rights is irrelevant when they are oppressed by racism and poverty and when the destruction of Aborginal society deprives men, more than women, of status and self-respect (Sawer, 1994). Likewise, women's national, cultural, or ethnic identities may be of equal or greater concern to women, and movements that fail to take this into account may not be supported by many women. LaFromboise, Heyle, and Ozer (1990) note that Native American women are at least as concerned with the preservation of their race and culture as they are with women's equality. They also suggest that Native American gender equality movements will differ from non-Native movements as Native women seek a feminism that works within the context of Native American families, their nations, and their cultures.

The success of women's movements is often challenged by countermovements against feminism. These arise as women's movements begin to influence women's attitudes. Such **backlashes against feminism** were well in evidence in the 1980s and 1990s in a number of countries. In 1980s India, for instance, Indian feminists were accused of being Westernists, colonialists, and cultural imperialists. Feminists working against dowries, sati (a widow's immolation on her husband's funeral pyre), and arranged marriage were attacked by irate families, the police, and the courts, which ruled against feminist positions and in favor of Muslim traditional law regarding women (Kumar, 1995). In 1980s India, Hindu nationalist women feared that feminist activism would erode traditional religious practices and agitated in *favor* of women's right to sati (Kumar, 1995).

In the United States, feminists are accused of being manlike and man-haters, and antifeminists actively work to limit women's reproductive rights. Women often fear that change threatens women's power in the private familial sphere and are unsupportive of feminist goals (Rowbotham, 1996). Antifeminist movements often draw attention to their female members and then charge that feminists do not represent the true interests of women and are forcing women into change that they do not want. As Basu (1995) points out, the opposition to women's equal rights is often better funded and better organized and often has the weight of the state, and tradition, behind it. Changing deeply entrenched gender ideology is a long-term process, particularly in the face of resistance and hostility from conservative and extremist groups using religion to legitimize a bid for social and political control (Jahan, 1995b).

Women's movements sometimes face significant challenges from within, as feminist groups differ about what they see as critical issues and about how to go about solving them. As an instance, consider the case of Brazil. There the women's movement was torn apart in the 1980s because of profound differences between feminist groups on which party to support during the election and controversy regarding whether the movement should remain autonomous from the state (Alvarez, 1994; Soares et al., 1995). Simply put, there are a variety of feminisms, often within one country, and these differences frequently threaten the solidarity that it takes to challenge entrenched systems. In Muslim countries, for instance, Islamic feminists differ in their support of veiling. Some women openly rebel against it whereas others maintain that it is a positive expression of religious devotion, that it protects women from sexual objectification and sexual harassment, and that it liberates them from the dictates of fashion. Likewise, some feminists in Muslim countries, try to promote a liberation theology as a way toward gender equality whereas others fight for secularism (a separation of religion and state) as a way to gain equality (Moghadam, 1991). In short, success often depends upon feminist groups finding issues on which they can agree and putting aside differences in order to build movements with sufficient size and strength.

This chapter focused in particular on challenges to the traditional gender roles of a community by women in that community (that is, national and local movements). In contrast, the next chapter focuses on international legal instruments as a means for change. These two approaches to gender equality are not mutually exclusive and, in fact, are mutually supportive. Positive changes in international law frequently result from the coordinated efforts of grassroots women's movements. Furthermore, without the influence of grassroots movements, international law may not have relevance in the day-to-day lives of women and may coerce cultural variety into a false unity (Toro, 1995).

International laws regarding the equality of women also serve grassroots movements by legitimizing their struggles and providing mechanisms for change where women's movements are suppressed. By building regional and international linkages, women's ability to develop effective political and legal strategies for their local struggles are enhanced (Human Rights Watch, 1995). International laws also strengthen feminism worldwide by placing pressure on governments to respond to women's movements (Basu, 1995). Ideally, international law would allow women whose domestic legal systems fail to protect them to submit complaints to the United Nations for investigation and enforcement (Human Rights Watch, 1995).

Terms and Concepts

empowerment	learned helplessness
differential modeling	Western or First World feminism
differential reinforcement	Third World women's activists
self-efficacy	Islamic feminists
perceived self-efficacy	women's movement

feminist consciousness   state feminism

practical gender interests   state pseudofeminism

strategic gender interests   backlashes against feminism

Study Questions

1. What are the risks associated with women's resistance against patriarchy? What are women up against when they question their subordination?

2. What early (and false) assumptions were made about women's movements by Western feminist scholars?

3. Why do some women's movements distance themselves from the feminist label? What are some differences between Western and other feminisms?

4. What does it mean to describe women's movements as having broad ideological variety and a range of organizational expressions? What are the three major strands of women's movements found in most countries?

5. How do cultures differ in terms of what stimulates the development of a women's movement?

6. How may local political and economic conditions affect the development of women's movements, both positively and negatively?

7. What are some specific examples of how women's movements may arise out of nationalist struggles for liberation? What factors seem to explain those cases in which struggles for national liberation do not foster women's equality?

8. What is state feminism? What are some of the concerns about state feminism? What are some examples of state feminism not doing much to help women's equality and some examples of it helping? What accounts for the difference?

9. What gains have been made by women's equality movements?

10. What are some of the explanations given for the uneven success of women's movements?

Discussion Questions and Activities

1. Choose a local women's issue that concerns you and sketch out a plan to do something about it. For example, is women's safety an issue on your campus?

2. Considering the broad definition of women's movements given at the beginning of the chapter, identify the various GROs and GRSOs in your community and what they do.

3. Why is it that governments enact legislation and sign conventions supportive of women's rights but frequently fail to enforce them? What can be done to change this?

4. What do you think of the feminist label? Would you identify yourself as feminist? Why or why not? Alternatively, ask a number of people these same three questions, along with others (such as age, gender, and religion) that you think may correlate with their answers.

Women at the UN's Fourth Women's World Conference in Beijing, China (1995).
The United Nations has promoted international feminism by holding four world
women's conferences on the status of women.

Women's Rights as Human Rights **10**

Challenging prevailing concepts of, and reinterpreting the movement for, human rights from a feminist perspective is not merely a matter of semantics. It is about the lives and deaths of individual women, everywhere, every day. . . . Yet even as the international human rights community has begun to recognize gender-based violations as pervasive and insidious forms of human rights abuse, we must work further to see that concerted actions against such practices are taken. . . . Only through community responsibility and state accountability, day by day, place by place, will we counter the massive violation of women's human rights in the world.

CHARLOTTE BUNCH (1995), Center for Women's Global Leadership

*T*he last chapter focused on women's movements in different countries. Here the focus is on the **international women's movement,** or, as it is sometimes called, **global feminism.** Global feminism is not new. Indeed, in 1887, American suffragists Elizabeth Cady Stanton and Lucretia Mott called a meeting of the International Council of Women to be held in Washington, DC, in 1888. Their call recognized the "universal sisterhood" of women and noted that "the position of women anywhere affects the position of women everywhere." They expressed the hope that the international council would "devise new and more effective methods for securing the equality and justice of women" and would help them realize their power in combining together to these ends (Fraser, 1987). This meeting resulted in the first formal international women's organization, the International Congress of Women (ICW) (Stienstra, 1994). Some of the first international women's organizations emphasized women's suffrage (right to vote). In 1904, the International Women's Suffrage Alliance (IWSA) was formed by U.S. feminists Elizabeth Cady Stanton, Susan B. Anthony, and Carrie Chapman Catt. The purpose of this organization was to secure women's right to the vote. Following the first World War, international women's groups worked to ensure that the newly forming League of Nations (later the United Nations) included women's representatives and issues affecting women and children. This influence continues today as organizations such as ISIS (Women's International Cross-Cultural Exchange), DAWN (Development Alternatives for Women for a New Era), and IWRAW (International Women's Rights Action Watch), among others, work to keep issues of concern to women visible at the international level.

Former U.S. congress-woman **Bella Abzug** (1920–1998) was a pioneer of the U.S. women's movement and of global women's organizing. Abzug also fought to make governments accountable for their promises to promote women's equality. Toward this end, Abzug issued annual report cards to 187 nations, grading them on their progress toward women's equality. Abzug was also the founder of WEDO (Women's Environment and Development Organization). A few days before she died, she said, "This is the time to declare, as we approach the great millennium, that women must be made free."

251

This chapter focuses on global feminism through an examination of the four UN international conferences on women and international human rights law. The United Nations is a key player in a human rights approach to women's equality. Therefore, the chapter begins with a brief description of the United Nations.

The United Nations

General Description

The **United Nations** is an international organization established in 1945 immediately following the end of World War II. Its purposes are the maintenance of international peace and security, the development of international law, and the correction of international economic, social, and humanitarian problems. The UN is a large, complex, and political organization with many specialized agencies, including the World Bank, the World Health Organization (WHO), and the United Nations Children's Fund (UNICEF). UN organiza tions publish many reports of social and economic statistics, fund development projects throughout the world, and lend technical and informational assistance to member governments. The UN also has many commissions including the Commission on Human Rights, which figures prominently in this chapter. The General Assembly, which meets at least once a year and includes representatives from all member states, appoints councils, creates commissions, and receives reports from UN organizations. The UN commissions, as well as the General Assembly, may draft conventions, resolutions, and treaties that, when ratified by member states, are legally binding as part of international law. They may also draft and vote on declarations that are not legally binding but serve as international guidelines and general commitments. Each member nation, regardless of size and power, has one vote. Declarations, programs for action, and other nonbinding documents are often drafted and voted on at UN conferences.

The UN's Contribution to Gender Equality

The UN's contribution to global feminism is debatable. On one hand, the UN can be taken to task for its reluctance to characterize abuses against women as human rights violations and for its difficulties in ratifying important women's rights documents. Feminists also lament the sexism within the UN and the time it took for the UN to even consider women's low status and power. For instance, Article 8 of the UN Charter makes it clear that women are not to be excluded in any way from participation in the UN organization. However, a glass ceiling is well in place at the UN. Only a minority of positions are held by women, and the majority of these are low-level secretarial and clerical jobs. Only five women head UN delegations,* and only 20 percent of the UN General Assembly delegates are women (Seager, 1997). As Charlesworth, Chinkin,

BOX 10.1   *United Nations Agencies: Women Senior Managers as a Percentage of All Senior Managers*

Food and Agriculture Organization (FAO)	2%
General Agreement on Tariffs and Trade (GATT)	0%
International Monetary Fund (IMF)	8%
UN Center for Human Settlements (UNCHS)	0%
UN Children's Fund (UNICEF)	22%
UN Development Programme (UNDP)	16%
UN Environment Programme (UNEP)	11%
UN Population Fund (UNFPA)	28%
World Health Organization (WHO)	10%

Source: Seager, 1997.

and Wright (1991) point out, it is significant that the major institutions of **international law** are peopled largely by men (see Box 10.1). Because men are not usually the victims of domestic violence, sex discrimination, sexual degradation, and violence, these important human rights matters are often ignored. It is ironic that women's rights are not typically considered given the fact that the UN makes such an effort to accommodate the interests of various ideological and regional groups (Charlesworth et al., 1991). In short, there is evidence that the UN has developed a system of human rights that has largely excluded the rights of women. To paraphrase Charlesworth, Chinkin, and Wright (1991), international law is a thoroughly gendered system because both the structure and the content of international lawmaking privilege men; if women's interests are acknowledged at all, they are marginalized.

Sexual harassment has also been a problem within the UN organization. Indeed, this problem was brought to light when the UN was sued for sexual harassment by a female clerical worker in the mid-1990s. The UN responded

"I don't know how we have survived so many years by thinking of women as a separate chapter. We are not a separate chapter, we are half the book." *Rosario Green, 1996, Assistant Secretary for UN Political Affairs (highest-ranking woman in the UN Secretariat)*

*Five women run UN agencies: Carol Bellamy at UNICEF; Catherine Bertini of the World Food Program; Noeleen Heyzer of the UN Development Fund; Sadako Ogata, the High Commissioner for Refugees; and Nafis Sadik of the Population Fund.

in 1996 by appointing Mexican diplomat Rosario Green as assistant secretary for political affairs and coordinator of all women's issues in the UN system. She has written a handbook to educate UN men regarding the appropriate treatment of female staff, and she has developed procedures for filing sexual harassment complaints.

On the other hand, what the UN has accomplished is remarkable given that it is a male-dominated organization and that many member nations are resistant to UN efforts to increase the worldwide status of women. Set up in 1946, the Commission on the Status of Women (CSW) is one of the first UN bodies to specifically address the concerns of women. CSW monitors the situation of women and promotes their rights. It is involved in setting universal standards regarding the status of women and assumes a leading role in bringing women's concerns to the attention of the UN specialized agencies. Indeed, throughout the book I have referred to many UN agencies such as UNIFEM and INSTRAW that are dedicated to women's issues. In the next two sections we examine more closely the UN's role in global feminism. We conclude the chapter with a discussion of whether global women's human rights are compatible with respect for cultural diversity.

The Four World Women's Conferences and the UN's Decade for Women

General Description and Importance

The United Nations designated 1975 as International Women's Year and 1975 to 1985 as the Decade for Women. During this time, the UN promoted international feminism by creating national and international forums for action, stimulating the gathering of data about women, and holding three **world women's conferences.** These international conferences on the status of women (1975—Mexico City; 1980—Copenhagen, Denmark; 1985—Nairobi, Kenya) catapulted the international connections among women to a qualitatively different level as women from very different backgrounds worked together on committees, caucuses, and networking (Chowdhury et al., 1994). A fourth women's conference was held in 1995 in Beijing, China.

Because UN world conferences are media events, these conferences and the declaration of United Nations Decade for Women (1975–1985) publicized the low status and power of women in the world. In some cases this publicity led to increased grassroots activism. The international women's conferences and UN Decade for Women also encouraged national commitments to increase the status of women through the development of women's bureaus and commissions and through legal and constitutional changes. Preparations for the first international women's conference held in 1975 in Mexico City revealed that the UN had very little information on the status of women worldwide. As a result, the UN pushed for the collection of statistical data and now publishes regular reports on the status of women.

Besides the official UN conference with delegations from UN member nations, discussion of women's issues occurred in nongovernmental forums. The nongovernmental organizations (NGOs) represented at these forums play an important role in keeping UN attention focused on women's issues. Furthermore, the conferences serve as powerful informational and organizational forums for feminists from all over the world. For instance, at the Fourth World Conference on Women in Beijing, China, over 20,000 people, mostly women, participated in the Non-Governmental Organizations Forum on Women despite its location in the hard-to-reach suburb of Huairou, 35 miles from the conference site. The conference itself hosted 5,000 delegates from 189 countries.

Complexities of Obtaining Member Nation Agreement

The UN women's conferences are interesting in part because they illustrate the complexities of international politics and cooperation. All four of the conferences became bogged down at some point by international politics that had little to do with the status of women. For instance, at both the 1975 conference in Mexico City and the 1980 conference in Copenhagen, the United States as well as other countries spent a good deal of time fighting the inclusion of a statement in documents that equated Israel's actions in the former Palestine with racism and apartheid.

Adding to the arduous task of obtaining agreement are language issues and the fact that the UN uses a consensus model of decision making. The final conference documents are usually somewhat unwieldy because the language must be translated into all of the languages of the UN system and because each government wants to make sure its viewpoint is included (Fraser, 1987). For instance, at the Fourth World Conference, voting on the final document (the legally nonbinding 149-page "Platform of Action") was delayed by wording difficulties. There were translation problems with the word *gender,* which does not exist in some languages, as well as terms such as *gender-neutral* and *feminization.* Some countries had problems with the phrase "universal human rights," arguing that human rights are relative to the culture. Ultimately this issue was resolved by dropping the word *universal.* Likewise, it took sixteen hours of debate before a subcommittee could accommodate the contrary views of countries who believe that sex education encourages risky youth sexual behavior and those who insist such education reduces youth risk.

Evolving Character of the Women's Conferences

Although the preamble of the United Nations' charter states that it supports "faith in fundamental human rights, in the dignity and worth of the human person, in the equal rights of men and women, in nations large and small," it is only over time and with pressure from international women's groups that the UN has moved from mere talk about women's issues to documents guaranteeing women's rights. The evolving character of the four women's conferences symbolizes the development of women's issues within the UN. For instance, at the 1980 Copenhagen convention, male dominance was evident. Indeed, it became a joke that women delegates occupying the lead delegate chair were always replaced by male delegates during important votes and debates. By the end of the Nairobi conference in 1985, however, women delegates dominated (Fraser, 1987). Similarly, male delegates took over the early women's conferences to complain about issues they had with other countries (Bernard, 1987). By the Fourth World Women's Conference, political issues unrelated to women's status finally took a backseat.

The role of the conferences in global feminism is also apparent from the growth of the **NGO forums.** For instance, approximately 6,000 people attended the NGO forum in 1975 at Mexico City, approximately 8,000 attended in 1980 at Copenhagen, and approximately 14,000 attended in 1985 at Nairobi (Fraser, 1987). In 1995 at Beijing, this number grew to 20,000. The growth of the NGO forums is a testament to global feminism because it is due in large part to international feminist organizing. Fraser (1987) suggests that this growth is more than merely numerical. By the time of the Nairobi conference, women had moved from the consciousness raising and outrage of the early conferences to collective activism. The growth of the forums also sends a message to the world that there is determination and solidarity among diverse women (Fraser, 1987). The hope is that the next stage in UN evolution will be the monitoring of countries for compliance with convention documents and greater nation accountability for violations of women's human rights.

Women's Rights as Human Rights

Throughout the book you have read about women's unequal status and power. It is a fact that most human groups are hierarchically structured and that power is an inherent part of human relations. However, as humans, we can prevent the abuse of power by a surrounding community that takes responsibility for regulating the process of power (Lips, 1991). This is what the **international human rights movement** is about.

"If we consider women's rights to be human rights, then we must work to make the reality of our lives match the ideals laid out by the rights standards that international law extends to all human beings."
Ilka Tanya Payan, 1995

The Human Rights Perspective on Women's Rights

The human rights perspective views the unequal status of women as a violation of **women's human rights.** This is key to the development of a global feminism. The idea is to wed women's rights to human rights, which are protected under international law and are monitored and enforced by the United Nations. This lends legitimacy to political demands because it is already accepted by most governments and brings with it established protocols for dealing with abuses (Friedman, 1995). Describing a particular discriminatory act as a human rights violation gives it an importance that it cannot obtain by simply calling it unfair; it also opens the way for the affected women to seek redress and helps to prevent further violations (Tomasevski, 1993).

Casting discrimination against women as a violation of their human rights has not been easy. Human rights law has traditionally focused on violations in the public spheres of life, in particular violations committed by government agents (such as the imprisonment or torture of political dissenters). As Bunch (1995) notes, this is not surprising given that the Western-educated propertied men who first advanced the cause of human rights most feared the violation of their civil and political rights in the public sphere. They did not fear violations in the private sphere because they were the masters of that territory. In contrast, the most common violations of women's rights often occur in the private sphere of the family and are condoned by religious and cultural practices. As a result, these violations have traditionally been viewed as outside the scope of human rights law (Mertus, 1995; Sullivan, 1995). As advocates for women's rights point out, though, the public/private distinction breaks down upon examination because "private" behaviors such as wife murder, battery, and rape result from a public toleration of the subordination of women (Charlesworth, 1995). Governments condone abuses when they inadequately prosecute wife abuse, rape, and sexual harassment. Therefore, they are accountable for these abuses (Friedman, 1995). Furthermore, using the public/private distinction to justify states' lack of involvement with women's human rights abuses is hypocritical considering that marriage and family law is monitored by the state (Kerr, 1993).

Global feminists work to ensure that human rights instruments and mechanisms provide avenues for challenging the systemic abuse of women. Ideally, governments would implement laws against gender-based violations and increase the sensitivity of agencies handling these issues (Bunch, 1995). Already, significant pressure is placed upon countries who violate human rights through torture, imprisonment, and the killing of those with opposing political views from those in power. However, rarely is it acknowledged that women, by virtue of being female, are routinely subjected to torture, starvation, terrorism, humiliation, mutilation, and even murder, simply because they are female (Peters & Wolper, 1995). Battery of women, for instance, is a form of torture that often includes imprisonment in the home, either physically or psychologically, through terrorization (Bunch, 1995). Women are held involuntarily in slavery for prostitution and pornography, and domestic servants are beaten and raped. These abuses can be viewed as violations of international laws forbidding slavery. There are also international laws barring the use of torture and terrorism. Sexual assault is a form of terrorism, and rape is a form of torture. Female infanticide and neglect are forms of female genocide. Amartya Sen, a male Indian economist at Harvard, has done statistical analyses of sex ratios and concludes that somewhere between 80 to 100 million women are missing in the world today (Bunch, 1995).

> "Women's rights are human rights."
> *Slogan of women's human rights movement*

Gender-based abuses such as these need to be seen as **human rights abuses** so that international pressure can be applied to countries that permit them. For instance, because of human rights abuses, the United States has occasionally refused to trade with a country or to loan money. But never has a country, including the United States, based its aid and trade decisions on the treatment of women (Bunch, 1995). Indeed, in 1991, the United States fought Iraq to defend Kuwait—a country where women are not allowed to vote or run for political office, where top female students are ineligible for government grants to study abroad, where male polygamy is encouraged but female polygamy outlawed, and where the abuse of domestic servants is permitted.

Governments frequently support human rights by providing political asylum to those who flee persecution in their own countries. Refugee status is often granted to those who claim persecution on the basis of race, religion, or politics, but refugee status is rarely granted on the basis of gender persecution. For instance, in 1990 an Iranian woman who sought refugee status in Canada because she faced prosecution for going without a veil in her own home was sent back to Iran by the Canadian government (Kerr, 1993). Similarly, it was only after numerous vocal appeals by human rights lawyers and activists that a 17-year-old woman from the West African nation Togo was permitted to stay in the United States. Fauziya Kasinga was ordered by her family to enter into a polygamous marriage to a 45-year-old man following her ritual genital mutilation (she was to become the fourth wife). She escaped to the United States, and upon her arrival at the airport, she requested asylum on the grounds that she faced genital mutilation should she return. She was sent to prison to await a hearing. The immigration judge said her story was not credible and that she did not have a well-founded case of persecution. Human rights lawyers rallied. Two years later (1996), the Board of Immigration Appeals heard her case and Fauziya was released from prison and granted asylum.

The Role of Women's Activism

The United Nations has a long history of involvement in human rights, but it is only recently that women's human rights have received specific attention. Much of that attention is the result of lobbying by women's rights advocates. For instance, in 1993, women's rights advocates from all over the world organized and cooperated to get the United Nations World Conference on Human Rights to include discussions of women's human rights. At least 300,000 people from 123 countries signed a petition demanding that the conference address women's human rights. Out of that conference came the **Vienna Declaration and Programme of Action,** which documents women's rights abuses in five areas: abuse within the family, war crimes against women, violations of women's bodily integrity, socioeconomic abuses, and political participation and persecution abuses. The document also includes recommendations for the reduction of such abuses although it does not adequately address the problem of compliance with these (Friedman, 1995).

Also in 1993, the General Assembly of the United Nations finalized the **Draft Declaration on the Elimination of Violence Against Women.** It defines violence as "any act of gender-based violence that results in, or is likely to result in, physical, sexual, or psychological harm or suffering to women,

BOX 10.2   *Article 2 of the United Nation's Declaration on the Elimination of Violence Against Women*

Definition of violence against women:

a. Physical, sexual and psychological violence occurring in the family including battering, sexual abuse of female children in the household, dowry-related violence, marital rape, female genital mutilation and other traditional practices harmful to women, non-spousal violence and violence related to exploitation.

b. Physical, sexual and psychological violence occurring within the general community, including rape, sexual abuse, sexual harassment and intimidation at work, in educational institutions and elsewhere, trafficking in women and forced prostitution.

c. Physical, sexual and psychological violence perpetrated or condoned by the state, wherever it occurs.

Source: From Stamatopoulou, 1995.

including threats of such acts, coercion or arbitrary deprivation of liberty, whether occurring in public or private life." This document is a notable addition to the legal definition of the human rights of women because it condemns specific forms of violence against women in and out of the home and holds states responsible for averting and punishing it (see Box 10.2). Unfortunately, however, the document is not a treaty and therefore is not legally binding.

The global movement for women's human rights has made impressive progress. Because of the efforts of women's activists, major human rights groups such as Amnesty International and Human Rights Watch now document violations of women's rights (before 1989, these organizations paid very little attention to women's human rights). Also, the United Nations has begun to pay even greater attention to women's human rights. Still, there are many significant challenges to be met.

Challenges to a Women's Human Rights Agenda

One such challenge is that *we must continue to work and organize for an inclusive women's human rights agenda so that the interests of diverse women worldwide are represented* (Thomas in Friedman, 1995; my emphasis). Some feminists doubt that it is possible to universalize feminism given the wide variety of women's experiences. Consequently, they question the usefulness of the international legal approach to women's rights. In response, feminists supportive of the international human rights approach point out that regardless of differences, women worldwide share the experience of patriarchy and the devaluing of women and all that encompasses (such as rape, economic oppression, and so forth). Nevertheless, it is agreed that the form of the oppression of women

BOX 10.3   *Conventions Adopted by the UN General Assembly Dealing with the Specific Rights of Women*

A convention is an international instrument subject to ratification that legally binds the ratifying governments to give full effect to all provisions contained in its text.

- *Convention on the Political Rights of Women* (1952). State parties to the convention undertake to grant women full political rights: the right to vote and to be eligible for election to all publicly elected bodies, and to be entitled to hold public office and to exercise all public functions on equal terms with men, without any discrimination.

- *Convention on the Nationality of Married Women* (1957). This convention provides for the general principle that men and women have equal rights to acquire, change, or retain their nationality.

- *Convention on Consent to Marriage, Minimum Age for Marriage and Registration of Marriages* (1962). The purpose of this convention is to ensure by national legislation equal rights for both spouses in connection with marriage. Marriages should be entered into with the free and full consent of both

spouses. A minimum age for marriage is to be established, and all marriages are to be registered.

- *Convention on the Elimination of All Forms of Discrimination Against Women* (1979). This convention is a broad affirmation of a commitment to ensure equal rights for women in all fields of life: political, economic, social, and cultural.

Other conventions and convenants adopted by the General Assembly containing provisions concerning the status of women include: Convention for the Suppression of the Traffic in Persons and of the Exploitation of the Prostitution of Others; Supplementary Convention on the Abolition of Slavery, the Slave Trade, and Institutions and Practices Similar to Slavery; International Covenant on Economic, Social, and Cultural Rights; International Covenant on Civil and Political Rights; Optional Protocol to the International Covenant on Civil and Political Rights.

———————

Source: United Nations, 1988.

March 8 is International Women's Day (IWD). Celebrated since 1901, it was originally intended to highlight the struggles of working-class women and to promote women's suffrage. The idea is that on this day, every year, women would speak together with one voice. In many countries, IWD is a day for rallies and marches to call attention to women's economic, political, and reproductive rights.

varies from culture to culture and within cultures. Great efforts are being made to develop an inclusive feminism that takes into account how differences of class, ethnicity, and nationality affect women's experience and how cultural and class differences affect how male domination may be contested.

A second challenge is that *we must move from visibility of abuse to actual accountability of abuse* (Thomas in Friedman, 1995; my emphasis). It is remarkable that virtually all of the abuses you've read about in this book can be seen as violations of human rights according to *existing* UN conventions and treaties. Yet there is no question that these abuses continue. At this point the UN has issued some strongly worded "women's declarations," which specifically address violations of women's human rights. However, unlike treaties, conventions are not legally binding (they are more like suggestions). (Box 10.3 lists some conventions adopted by the UN General Assembly dealing with the rights of women.) The choice to go the convention route was made in part because the legally binding treaties would have to be considerably weakened before many member states would agree to ratify them. The UN Committee for the Elimination of Discrimination Against Women (CEDAW) monitors compliance with these conventions. This monitoring is done largely by the examination of reports submitted by member states and by dialogues with government representatives. However, this committee has not yet declared a government in violation of women's human rights conventions despite evidence to the contrary. The current truth of the matter is that there is very little litigation nationally and internationally concerning the violation of women's human rights (Tomasevski, 1993). In summary, there is a lack of proper implementation machinery and lack of women's awareness of that machinery that would empower them (Coomaraswamy, 1994). Indeed, one of the demands of women's groups present at the Vienna conference on human rights was that the UN appoint a Special Rapporteur on Violence Against Women. The UN responded to this demand by appointing Radhika Coomaraswamy from Sri Lanka. Her job is to collect information, make recommendations, and draw attention to human rights violations against women.

There are several other obstacles to implementation. One is that in many countries there is ideological resistance to human rights for women. Although the UN documents relevant to women's rights clearly imply that gender equality is a desirable value, this universal value is not so universal after all. As a consequence, local customs and national and religious laws often contradict the treatment of women required by UN conventions and declarations. Furthermore, because of beliefs in state and cultural sovereignty, those local customs and national laws are usually given precedence.

Implementation of international laws and conventions is also hampered by the fact that in some cultures, talk about rights is not meaningful. Particularly in cultures with a history of colonialism, such as India, the human rights movement is disrespected, virtually ignored, and viewed as another tool of the West to eradicate indigenous cultures (Coomaraswamy, 1994). This may mean that unless movements *within* a society cause human rights values to take root, women's human rights will not be enforced (Coomaraswamy, 1994). If a country's own people demand change, these attempts to change things cannot be as easily resisted with accusations of cultural insensitivity. On the other hand, it is very helpful to local women's groups to be able to appeal to international treaties. For instance, Plata (1994) explains how the Colombian government began to take women's groups seriously once they emphasized that their requests were consistent with Brazil's signing of the Convention on the Elimination of Discrimination Against Women. As Coomaraswamy (1994) says, civil society is necessary for creating the conditions for law to be relevant, but without law, any human rights activist will only be tilting at windmills.

A third challenge to an international approach to women's human rights is that *women's issues must become part of the mainstream of the human rights agenda such that they will be considered at every level of human rights discussions rather than marginalized* (Thomas in Friedman, 1995, my emphasis). The long-term male domination of all-powerful political bodies nationally and internationally means that issues of concern to men are seen as general human concerns whereas women's concerns are relegated to a specialized and marginalized sphere (Charlesworth, 1995, my emphasis). One way to bring women's human rights into the mainstream is to show how UN conventions and treaties can be interpreted in ways

"My responsibility as UN High Commissioner is to adopt and to foster a rights-based approach across the whole spectrum of 'civil, cultural, economic, political, and social rights, to promote and protect the realization of the right to development and specifically to include women's rights as human rights.' "
Mary Robinson

Rhonda Copelon is a U.S. law professor and international human rights activist. She is at the forefront of the use of international law to prevent and prosecute crimes against women such as war rape.

"The fundamental challenge for the movement for women's human rights is that it not become a reformist project: Its recipe should not read "Add women and stir," but "Add women and alter."
Dorothy Q. Thomas, 1995, Human Rights Watch

that include women's human rights violations. For instance, Copelon (1994) shows how domestic violence meets many of the criteria for torture according to international law. Still, this approach will only work if applied with great vigilance. Otherwise, as was evident from the 1993 UN Human Rights Conference, women's human rights will not receive a seat at the human rights discussion table.

Stamatopoulou (1995) suggests that the creation of specialized bodies for addressing women's issues within the United Nations has contributed to their marginalization. Because there are specific UN groups designated to deal with women's issues, the more powerful, mainstream organs of the UN, such as the Commission on Human Rights, have paid little attention to women's human rights violations such as rape, forced marriage, transboundary trafficking of women, honor killings, and genital mutilation. These special women's agencies have resulted in the treatment of women's rights as "lesser rights" (Stamatopoulou, 1995) and have created a "women's ghetto" within the UN (Reanda, 1992). On the other hand, prior to separate institutional mechanisms for dealing with women's issues, women's human rights violations were still ignored. It is not that specialized agencies devoted to women's issues are necessarily bad. The problem is that they are chronically underfunded, given little authority, and often excluded from power bodies within the UN.

Cherishing Cultural Diversity While Advocating Gender Equality

At the heart of the women's rights as human rights endeavor is **universalism**—the idea that all humans share the same inalienable rights. That being said, we must carefully consider the cultural relativist criticism that international human rights are incompatible with respect for cultural diversity. This issue is particularly acute in international law, which is concerned with transnational standards (Charlesworth, 1994).

The Cultural Relativist Objection to Human Rights and CEDAW

Cultural relativists argue that there are no legitimate cross-cultural human rights standards—it is up to a given culture to determine what constitutes right and wrong. Indeed, **cultural relativism** continues to be one of the major sticking points for ratification of the far-reaching UN treaty **Convention on the Elimination of All Forms of Discrimination Against Women** (sometimes called the Women's Convention and sometimes called CEDAW, although the monitoring committee also goes by this acronym). The 1979 treaty defines discrimination against women as "any distinction, exclusion, or restriction made on the basis of sex which has the effect or purpose of impairing or nullifying the recognition, enjoyment or exercise by women, irrespective of their marital status, on a basis of equality of men and women, of human rights and fundamental freedoms in the political, economic, social, cultural, civil or any other field."

BOX 10.4   *Countries That Have Not Ratified the Women's Convention**

Afghanistan	Lesotho	Somalia
Algeria	Marshall Islands	Sudan
Bahrain	Mauritania	Swaziland
Botswana	Micronesia	Switzerland
Brunei Darassalam	Mozambique	Syria
Burma	Niger	United Arab Emirates
Cameroon	Oman	United States
Djibouti	Qatar	
Iran	São Tomé and Príncipe	
Korean DPR	Saudi Arabia	
Lebanon	Solomon Islands	

Source: United Nations, 1996.
*As of 2/12/96.

Nations that ratify the Women's Convention are to eliminate discrimination against women in employment, education, and politics. As of 1996, 152 countries have signed and ratified CEDAW, although 56 of these countries registered a total of 177 official "reservations" (United Nations, 1996). (Box 10.4 lists countries that have not ratified the Women's Convention. Box 10.5 lists the reservations to the Women's Convention.) This is the highest number of reservations recorded for any international convention, and most of these are based on religious or cultural grounds. For instance, Israel filed a reservation to Article 16, which states that parties undertake to eliminate discrimination against women in all matters relating to marriage and family relations (Shalev, 1995). As we discussed in earlier chapters, Israel's religious laws give men greater power in marriage and the family. Likewise, Bangladesh, Egypt, Libya, and Tunisia all invoked Islam as the reason for their reservations to the Women's Convention (Mayer, 1995a). Charlesworth and colleagues (1991) suggest that the CEDAW process shows that the international community is ready to acknowledge the considerable problem of women's inequality only if they are not required to alter the patriarchal practices that subordinate women. The fact that the international community tolerates these reservations, many of which are incompatible with

"... the full and complete development of a country, the welfare of the world and the cause of peace require the maximum participation of women on equal terms with men in all fields."
From the Convention on the Elimination of All Forms of Discrimination Against Women (CEDAW)

BOX 10.5   *Some Reservations to the Women's Convention*

Substantive Provisions of the Convention	Reservations
Definition of discrimination (Art. 1)	United Kingdom
Commitment to eradicate discrimination (Art. 2)	Bangladesh, Cook Islands, Egypt, Iraq, Libya, Malawi, Tunisia, United Kingdom
Measures to accelerate de facto equality (Art. 4)	Malawi
Measures to eliminate prejudices and stereotyping (Art. 5)	Cook Islands, France, India
Elimination of discrimination in political and public life (Art. 7)	Austria, Belgium, Germany, Luxembourg, Spain, Thailand
Equal citizenship rights (Art. 9)	Cyprus, Egypt, France, Iraq, Jamaica, Jordan, Korea, Thailand, Tunisia, Turkey, United Kingdom
Elimination of discrimination in education (Art. 10)	Thailand, United Kingdom
Elimination of discrimination in employment (Art. 11)	Malta, Mauritius, New Zealand, Thailand, United Kingdom
Equal labor rights (Art. 12)	Australia, Austria, Ireland, New Zealand, Thailand, United Kingdom
Equal access to financial credit (Art. 13)	Bangladesh, Ireland, Malta, United Kingdom
Full legal capacity (Art. 15)	Austria, Brazil, Ireland, Jordan, Libya, Malta, Thailand, Tunisia, Turkey, United Kingdom
Elimination of discrimination in marriage and the family (Art. 16)	Bangladesh, Brazil, Egypt, France, India, Iraq, Ireland, Israel, Jordan, Libya, Luxembourg, Malta, Mauritius, Korea, Thailand, Tunisia, Turkey, United Kingdom

Source: Tomasevski, 1993.

the purpose of the CEDAW, further underlines the inadequacy of current international law regarding women's human rights (Charlesworth et al., 1991). (Box 10.6 outlines the reasons that the United States has not ratified CEDAW.)

The problems with CEDAW represent a problem that plagues the whole women's rights and human rights endeavor. In short, that problem is one of balancing respect for cultural diversity with the need for change. As Katzenstein (1989) remarks, feminist values may conflict with traditional customs, and it is a legitimate question to ask which should be privileged when this occurs. Cultural relativists answer that traditional customs should have prior-

BOX 10.6 *The United States and CEDAW*

In our country—where we have worked so hard against domestic violence, where we have worked so hard to empower women—it is to say the least, an embarrassment that the U.S. has not ratified CEDAW.
U.S. President Bill Clinton, 1996

It [ratifying CEDAW] would be like an equal rights amendment enforced by the UN. I don't believe in giving power over U.S. laws to a UN body.
Phyllis Schlafly, U.S. conservative and antifeminist, 1996

The United States is one of a minority of UN members that has not yet ratified CEDAW. President Carter signed it in 1980, but it still has not been ratified by the U.S.

Senate. Neither the Reagan nor Bush administrations sought Senate ratification. Some effort has been made under Clinton, but the Republican-controlled Congress and Senator Jesse Helms (R-NC), powerful head of the Foreign Relations Committee, has effectively prevented it from coming up for vote. The objections of conservatives like Helms focus on a general reluctance to give the UN power over U.S. laws. They also see CEDAW as a form of the Equal Rights Amendment (ERA) to the U.S. Constitution [the ERA proclaims "equality of rights under the law shall not be denied or abridged by the US or by any state on account of sex." It still has not been ratified by the necessary thirty-eight states]. Conservatives often argue that the ERA is unnecessary and that ratifying it and CEDAW would be giving in to "special interests" (read: feminists).

ity. In regard to women's rights, they suggest that Western condemnations of gender discrimination in other regions is insensitive and ethnocentric and is a version of cultural imperialism (Mayer, 1995a). For instance, El-Bakri and Kameir (1983) object to holding the role of women in the Middle East and Third World countries to the standards of Western democracies. Cultural relativists also emphasize that the treatment of women is often prescribed by a culture's religious practices, and consequently calls for change are instances of religious intolerance. For example, in India, the treatment of women is based primarily on religious law and tradition, and demands for change are resisted on the ground that they interfere with freedom of religion (Jaising, 1995). Making charges of cultural imperialism to avoid human rights responsibility is especially effective in the present political climate, which is characterized by a desire to be sensitive to cultural diversity.

Countering Cultural Relativism

We certainly do not want to be so presumptuous as to impose our worldview on others. Just because a culture is different from our own does not mean that it is wrong. Furthermore, there is no question that historically, Western imperialists and colonialists destroyed native cultures and defended their actions on the basis of the superiority of Western cultural practices. On the other hand, as Nussbaum (1992) points out, we can go too far in the worship of cultural difference. She cites a number of examples of scholars who defend disturbing cultural practices out of reverence for the culture at hand.

As philosopher Rachels (1993) points out, it does not stand to reason that just because cultures differ, that right and wrong are matters of opinion. If we were to take cultural relativism too seriously, we would have to agree that all sorts of questionable behaviors were not immoral because those countries in which they occur do not define them as immoral. Wife beating is, for example, an accepted cultural practice in Kuwait. Female circumcision is another example. Because of discomfort with interfering with other cultures' traditional practices, this harmful ritual received little attention from human rights organizations until the 1980s. Furthermore, although the 1995 Beijing Women's Conference's Platform for Action condemns genital mutilation as a form of violence against women, there is still no international law banning it.

It is true that we shouldn't reject cultural practices just because they are not our own and that we should not presume to understand the experiences of those in another culture. And it is true that many cultural practices are nothing more than what Rachels (1993) calls "social conventions," which, objectively speaking, are neither right nor wrong and about which we should keep an open mind. But should we accept cultural practices that obviously result in serious harm to large segments of a society out of respect for the existing culture? If this had been the case in the United States, slavery would not have been abolished, women would not have been allowed to vote, and civil rights legislation would not have been passed. As Rachels says, moral progress cannot occur if we take cultural relativism too far.

Another problem with the cultural relativist's position is that it implies that there is a homogeneous culture upon which there is agreement. However, "culture is not a static, unchanging, identifiable body of information," but rather is a "series of constantly contested and negotiated cultural practices" (Rao, 1995). For instance, Mayer (1995b) points out that contrary to the view of a monolithic Islamic position on human rights, Muslims actually espouse a wide range of opinions regarding international human rights. These range from the assertion that international human rights are fully compatible with Islam to the claim that international human rights are products of alien, Western culture and represent values contrary to Islam. Libya, Tunisia, and Algeria are all examples of Islamic countries that have found it prudent to make concessions to citizen demands for the observance of international human rights (Mayer, 1995b). When pressured about international human rights, repressive governments often hide behind insincere claims of cultural imperialism as a way to remove the pressure. Their insincerity is evident when they show little respect for cultural diversity within their own nations and when internal demands for the recognition of international human rights show there is not cultural agreement. As Peters and Wolper (1995) say, when considering local, national, or international rulings, one must ask questions about context: What is the status of the speaker? In whose name is the argument from culture advanced? To what extent have the social groups primarily affected participated in the formation of the cultural practices being protected?

In contrast to cultural relativists, universalists argue that some values transcend culture—that is, some values are desirable regardless of culture. For instance, most people will readily agree that prohibitions on slavery are uni-

Maryam Rajavi is president-elect of the National Council of Resistance of Iran. Rajavi uses UN women's human rights documents to critique what she calls the "gender apartheid" of Iran. Now living in exile, Rajavi continues to give speeches refuting the fundamentalists' use of the Koran to support their oppression of women. Rajavi emphasizes that democracy and world peace depend on the advancement of women.

versally desirable. Rachels (1993) notes that another such value should be the impartial promotion of the interests of everyone alike, except when individuals deserve particular responses as a result of their own past behavior. Such a principle rules out racism and sexism. It is not defensible to treat individuals differently solely on the basis of their sex or race. Rachels argues that this should be a universal standard because it stands even after intense scrutiny. The bottom line is that gender equality and cultural diversity may sometimes clash and that respecting cultural diversity need not require unquestioned acceptance of all cultural practices. There are some universal values, such as gender and racial equality, that should lead us to be critical of certain cultural practices and to promote their change.

Both universalism and cultural relativism can be used in ways compatible or incompatible with human rights. Universalism was once used by imperialists to justify ignoring the rights of indigenous peoples to self-determination. Imperialists argued that their economic system or religion was deserving of universal value status and imposed it upon other cultures. Now universalism is being used by human rights advocates to promote freedom and self-determination. It is not used by women's human rights advocates as an excuse or tool for economic or territorial gain, or to imply Western cultural superiority. Rather, it rests on the premise that peoples in the West and the East share a common humanity and are equally deserving of rights and freedoms (Mayer, 1995b).

Likewise, cultural relativism can be used to promote tolerance of one culture by another but is currently used by many governments to justify their own oppressive practices and their intolerance of internal and external criticism. Indeed, Mayer (1995a) suggests that the acceptance of cultural relativism as justification for violating women's rights is, upon closer examination, no more than a universal claim for the subordinate status of women. Mayer goes on to quote Dorothy Thomas, director of the Women's Rights Project of Human Rights Watch. Following the 1993 UN Vienna Conference on Human Rights, Thomas said,

> Women from every single culture and every part of the world are standing up and saying we won't accept cultural justification for abuses against us anymore. We are human, we have a right to have our human rights protected, and the world community must respond to that call and throw out any attempts to justify abuse on the grounds of culture. (p. 185)

Conclusion

You have seen in this chapter both the hope and challenges associated with a human rights approach to women's equality. The success of the women's human rights movement requires embracing both universal human rights and cultural difference. It is important to emphasize the separate identities and histories of groups of women based on religion, ethnicity, nationality, sexual orientation, and economic position while at the same time avoiding a dangerous fatalism of unbridgeable differences among women (Chowdhury et al.,

1994). We must agree that regardless of culture it is unacceptable to deny women their equal rights, yet we must acknowledge the diversity of women's experiences to make our efforts relevant. We must respect those cultural features that do not lead to the oppression of women (and others) so as to preserve cultural diversity. We must understand the nuances of a culture because they will affect the ease with which human rights mechanisms are applied. And, last but not least, to paraphrase Charlesworth and colleagues (1991), we must remember that the formal acknowledgment of women's rights as human rights by governments does not in and of itself resolve problems of inequality. That will require economic and cultural change that is unlikely to occur without women's political activity. As Bunch and Fried (1996) point out, the UN documents that affirm women's equal rights (such as CEDAW and the Beijing Platform for Action) are only tools. The potential of these tools can only be realized through vigorous leadership, difficult political dialogue among different groups of women, and women's political activity at all levels—from the global to the local.

Terms and Concepts

international women's movement (or global feminism)

United Nations

international law

world women's conferences

NGO forums

international human rights movement

women's human rights

human rights abuses

Vienna Declaration and Programme of Action

Draft Declaration on the Elimination of Violence Against Women

universalism

cultural relativism

Convention on the Elimination of All Forms of Discrimination Against Women (CEDAW)

Study Questions

1. Is global feminism new? When were the first international women's movements founded, and what was their focus?

2. In what way is the UN's contribution to global feminism debatable?

3. How have the four women's conferences contributed to global feminism? How have the conferences evolved since the first one in Mexico City? What is the role of NGOs in the conferences?

4. How do human rights activists cast discrimination against women as a violation of women's human rights? Why has this been difficult to do given the traditional focus of human rights laws?

5. How can human rights instruments and mechanisms be used to challenge the abuse of women?

6. What three challenges face the women's human rights movement?

7. What is the nature of the cultural relativist criticism that international human rights are incompatible with a respect for cultural diversity?

8. What is CEDAW? How is cultural relativism one of the major sticking points regarding its ratification? How do the problems in ratifying CEDAW represent a problem that plagues the whole women's rights as human rights endeavor?

9. How do universalists respond to cultural relativists' criticisms of the human rights approach?

10. How may both universalism and cultural relativism be used in ways compatible or incompatible with women's human rights? How does the success of the women's movement require that we embrace both universal human rights and cultural difference?

Discussion Questions and Activities

1. What should be done when local customs and national and religious laws contradict the treatment of women required by UN conventions and declarations?

2. Are you optimistic or pessimistic about the UN's role in bringing about women's equality?

3. Charlesworth and colleagues (1991) suggest that it is significant that the major institutions of international law are peopled by men. Do you agree or disagree with their assertion that until there are more women in UN leadership roles, women's human rights will not receive the attention needed? Can and will men advocate for women's human rights?

4. Check on efforts to ratify CEDAW in the United States and take some action of your own.

Appendix A: Status of Women Worldwide

Country	Afghanistan	Albania	Algeria	Angola	Argentina
Location	South Central Asia	Eastern Europe on Adriatic coast	NW Africa on coast	SW coast of Africa	Most of the southern portion of South America
Average Age at Marriage	17.8; polygamy legal	20.4	23.7	17.9	22.9
Education	86% girls not in school; 36–45% of all college students	63% literacy; 46–55% of all college students	44% literacy; 36–45% of all college students	28% literacy; 16–25% of all college students	96% literacy; 46–55% of all college students
Life Expectancy	42.0	75.5	65.0	46.1	75.7
Maternal Deaths	1,700 per 100,000 births	65 per 100,000 births	160 per 100,000 births	1,500 per 100,000 births	100 per 100,000 births
Deaths from Abortion	1 in 9	1 in 549	1 in 174	1 in 10	1 in 370
Contraceptive Use	2%	10%	47%	2%	74%
Abortion Law	Only to save life of mother	On request	Only if rape/incest; health reasons	Only if rape/incest; health reasons	Only if rape/incest; health reasons
Avg. Number of Children	6.6	2.8	3.6	6.9	2.7
% of Workforce	9%	41%	8%	38%	29%
Prof./Tech. Positions	1%	No data	3%	6%	54%
Admin./Mgmt. Positions	14%	No data	3%	6%	6%
Government Positions	None	6% of legislature; 7% of cabinet	7% of legislature	15% of legislature; 7% of cabinet	22% of legislature
Violence Against Women	Domestic abuse reportedly common; systematic rape of women by soldiers; attacks on women for immodest dress	Domestic abuse reportedly common; no rape data	Rape and wife beating reportedly common; attacks on women for immodest dress	Domestic abuse reportedly common; systematic rape of women by soldiers	Domestic abuse reportedly common; political prisoners raped; rapist can escape penalty if he marries victim

Country	Armenia	Australia	Austria	Azerbaijan	Bangladesh
Location	SW Asia; between Turkey and Iran	Between Pacific and Indian Oceans	South Central Europe	NW of Iran on Caspian Sea	South Central Asia
Average Age at Marriage	21.7	24.5	23.5	21.7	18.0
Education	98% literacy	99% literacy; 46–55% of all college students	99% literacy; 36–45% of all college students	96% literacy	24% literacy; 16–25% of all college students
Life Expectancy	74.7	80.9	79.5	74.2	55.6
Maternal Deaths	50 per 100,000 births	9 per 100,000 births	10 per 100,000 births	22 per 100,000 births	850 per 100,000 births
Deaths from Abortion	1 in 800	1 in 5,848	1 in 6,250	1 in 1,894	1 in 29
Contraceptive Use	22%	76%	71%	17%	40%
Abortion Law	On request	Only if rape/ incest or health reasons	On request	On request	Only to save life of mother
Avg. Number of children	2.5	1.9	1.6	2.4	4.1
% of Workforce	48%	42%	40%	43%	41%
Prof./Tech. Positions	no data	74%	48%	No data	23%
Admin./Mgmt. Positions	no data	43%	22%	No data	5%
Government Positions	6% of legislature	18% of legislature; 13% of cabinet	23% of legislature; 30% of cabinet	2% of legislature; 15% of cabinet	11% of legislature; 10% of cabinet
Violence Against Women	Domestic violence reportedly common; no rape data	2,259 rapes reported in one year; 20% say they have been battered by husband	12,377 incidents reported in one year; 529 rapes	Domestic violence reportedly common; no rape data	472 rapes reported in one year; only one shelter; attacks for immodest dress; dowry deaths and acid throwing

Country	Belarus	Belgium	Benin	Bolivia	Bosnia-Herzegovina
Location	Bordered by Poland, Russia, Ukraine, and Lithuania	Northern Europe	Western Africa	Bordered by Brazil, Paraguay, Argentina, and Peru	Bordered by Serbia, Montenegro, and Croatia
Average Age at Marriage	21.8	22.4	18.3	22.1	22.2
Education	97% literacy; 46–55% of all college students	99% literacy; 36–45% of all college students	65% of girls not in school; 16% literacy; 15% in college	73% literacy	88% literacy
Life Expectancy	76.4	79.1	53.7	65.4	78.9
Maternal Deaths	37 per 100,000 births	10 per 100,000 births	990 per 100,000 births	650 per 100,000 births	No data
Deaths from Abortions	1 in 1,590	1 in 5,882	1 in 15	1 in 33	No data
Contraceptive Use	23%	79%	9%	30%	No data
Abortion Law	On request	Only if rape/ incest; health reasons	Only to save life	Only if rape/ incest; health reasons	On request
Avg. Number of Children	1.7	1.7	6.9	4.6	1.6
% of Workforce	47%	34%	47%	26%	38%
Prof./Tech. Positions	No data	47%	30%	42%	No data
Admin./Mgmt. Positions	No data	13%	6%	17%	No data
Government Positions	5% of legislature; 8% of cabinet	15% of legislature; 13% of cabinet	7% of legislature; 20% of cabinet	6% of legislature	5% of legislature
Violence Against Women	Domestic abuse reportedly common; 484 rapes reported in one year	41% report domestic abuse; no rape data	Domestic abuse reportedly common; no rape data; female genital mutilation	Domestic abuse reportedly common; no rape data	Domestic abuse reportedly common; systematic rape of women by soldiers

Country	Brazil	Bulgaria	Burkina Faso	Burundi	Cambodia
Location	Largest country in South America	Balkan country located along the Black Sea	Western Africa	East Central Africa	Bordered by Vietnam, Thailand, and Laos
Average Age at Marriage	22.6	21.1	17.4; 51% polygamy	21.9; 12% polygamy	21.3
Education	77% literacy; 46–55% of all college students	97% literacy; 55% of all college students	75% girls not in school; 8% literacy	53% of girls not in school; 20% literacy	22% literacy
Life Expectancy	67.3	74.8	48.9	49.2	49.9
Maternal Deaths	220 per 100,000 births	27 per 100,000 births	930 per 100,000 births	1,300 per 100,000 births	900 per 100,000 births
Deaths from Abortions	1 in 162	1 in 2,469	1 in 17	1 in 12	1 in 22
Contraceptive Use	78%	76%	8%	9%	44%
Abortion Law	Only if rape/ incest; health reasons	On request	Only if rape/ incest; health reasons	Only if rape/ incest; health reasons	Only to save life
Avg. Number of Children	2.8	1.5	6.3	6.5	5.1
% of Workforce	36%	47%	46%	47%	41%
Prof./Tech. Positions	57%	60%	26%	30%	No data
Admin./Mgmt. Positions	17%	30%	14%	14%	No data
Government Positions	7% of legislature; 5% of cabinet	14% of legislature; 6% of cabinet	6% of legislature; 13% of cabinet	11% of legislature; 9% of cabinet	6% of legislature
Violence Against Women	50% of women killed due to domestic violence; rapist can escape penalty if he marries victim	Domestic abuse reportedly common; 662 rapes reported in one year	Domestic abuse reportedly common; no rape data available; 70% female genital mutilation	Domestic abuse reportedly common; no rape data	Domestic abuse reportedly common; systematic rape of women by soldiers

Country	Cameroon	Canada	Central African Rep.	Chad	Chile
Location	At junction of Western and Central Africa	Northern 2/5 of North America	Center of Africa	North Central Africa	Western seaboard of South America
Average Age at Marriage	19.7; 39% polygamy	26.2; 38% divorce rate	18.9; polygamy is common	16.5	23.6
Education	48% literacy	99% literacy; 46–55% of all college students	54% of girls not in school; 46% literacy	73% of girls not in school; 31% literacy	94% literacy
Life Expectancy	54.0	81.0	44.1	47.1	76.5
Maternal Deaths	550 per 100,000 births	6 per 100,000 births	700 per 100,000 births	1,500 per 100,000 births	65 per 100,000 births
Deaths from Abortions	1 in 33	1 in 8,772	1 in 26	1 in 12	1 in 615
Contraceptive Use	16%	73%	16%	20%	43%
Abortion Law	Only if rape/incest; health reasons	On request	Only to save life of mother	Only to save life of mother	Abortions illegal in all instances
Avg. Number of Children	5.5	1.9	5.5	5.7	2.5
% of Workforce	33%	45%	45%	21%	32%
Prof./Tech. Positions	24%	60%	18.6%	No data	32%
Admin./Mgmt. Positions	1%	40%	9%	No data	20%
Government Positions	12% of legislature; 5% of cabinet	19% of legislature; 23% of cabinet	4% of legislature; 8% of cabinet	8% of legislature; 10% of cabinet	7% of legislature; 14% of cabinet
Violence Against Women	Domestic violence reportedly common; no rape statistics; 20% FGM	20,530 rapes in one year; 51% report having been a victim of some act of violence by males since the age of 16	Domestic violence reportedly common; no rape statistics; 50% female genital mutilation	Domestic violence reportedly common; no rape statistics; 60% female genital mutilation	60–80% report abuse; systematic rape by soldiers; rapist can escape penalty if he marries victim

Country	China	Colombia	Congo	Costa Rica	Croatia
Location	East Asia	NW region of South America	West Central Africa	Bounded by Nicaragua and Panama	Central Europe
Average Age at Marriage	22.4	22.6	21.9; polygamy is common	22.2	23.6
Education	68% literacy; 26–35% of all college students	90% literacy; 46–55% of all college students	59% literacy; 16–25% of all college students	94% literacy	95% literacy
Life Expectancy	69.2	74.9	55.3	77.0	77.3
Maternal Deaths	95 per 100,000 births	100 per 100,000 births	890 per 100,000 births	55 per 100,000 births	10–100 per 100,000 births
Deaths from Abortions	1 in 526	1 in 385	1 in 18	1 in 606	No data
Contraceptive Use	83%	66%	15%	75%	8%
Abortion Law	On request	Only to save life	Only if rape/ incest; health reasons	Only if rape/ incest; health reasons	On request
Avg. Number of Children	2.0	2.6	6.1	3.0	1.7
% of Workforce	43%	22%	39%	22%	44%
Prof./Tech. Positions	45%	42%	28.5%	30%	55%
Admin./Mgmt. Positions	11%	27%	5%	23%	24%
Government Positions	21% of legislature; 8% of cabinet	10% of legislature; 18% of cabinet	1% of legislature; 14% of cabinet	16% of legislature; 8% of cabinet	7% of legislature; 4% of cabinet
Violence Against Women	39,121 rapes reported in one year; 20% claim abuse	Domestic abuse reportedly common; no rape data	Domestic abuse common; no rape data; % female genital mutilation unknown	54% claim abuse; only two shelters; no rape data	Domestic abuse reportedly common; no rape data

Country	Cuba	Czech Republic	Denmark	Dominican Republic	Ecuador
Location	Island state of West Indies in Atlantic Ocean	Between Austria, Germany, and Poland	Western Europe	West Indies, 670 miles SW of Florida	On equator on Pacific coast of South America
Average Age at Marriage	19.9	21.7	25.6	20.5	21.1
Education	94% literacy; over 55% of all college students	99% literacy; over 55% of all college students	99% literacy; 46–55% of all college students	81% literacy	87% literacy 36–45% of all college students
Life Expectancy	76.3	76.3	78.1	68.1	67.6
Maternal Deaths	95 per 100,000 births	15 per 100,000 births	9 per 100,000 births	110 per 100,000 births	150 per 100,000 births
Deaths from Abortions	1 in 585	1 in 3,704	1 in 6,536	1 in 313	1 in 202
Contraceptive Use	70%	69%	78%	56%	53%
Abortion Law	On request	On request	On request	Illegal in all circumstances	Only if rape/incest; health reasons
Avg. Number of Children	1.8	1.8	1.7	2.9	3.3
% of Workforce	33%	45%	45%	16%	19%
Prof./Tech. Positions	48%	No data	63%	49%	38%
Admin./Mgmt. Positions	19%	No data	15%	21%	28%
Government Positions	23% of legislature; 12% of cabinet	10% of legislature	33% of legislature; 35% of cabinet	10% of legislature; 38% of cabinet	5% of legislature; 6% of cabinet
Violence Against Women	Domestic abuse reportedly common; no rape data	Domestic abuse reportedly common; no rape data	Domestic abuse reportedly common; 587 rapes reported in one year	1,500 rapes reported in one year, but estimated that 7,000 occurred	366 rapes reported in one year; only one shelter

Country	Egypt	El Salvador	Eritrea	Estonia	Ethiopia
Location	NE corner of Africa	Central America	Northern Ethiopia	Eastern Europe	Eastern Africa
Average Age at Marriage	22.4	19.4	17.1	21.7; 74% divorce rate	17.1
Education	41% literacy; 36–45% of all college students	68% literacy; 46–55% of all college students	76% of girls not in school; 10% literacy	99% literacy; 46–55% of all college students	84% of girls not in school; 26% literacy; 16–25% of all college students
Life Expectancy	62.8	66.5	51.8	74.9	45.6
Maternal Deaths	170 per 100,000 births	300 per 100,000 births	1,400 per 100,000 births	41 per 100,000 births	1,400 per 100,000 births
Deaths from Abortions	1 in 159	1 in 88	1 in 13	1 in 1,525	1 in 11
Contraceptive Use	47%	53%	3%	No data	4%
Abortion Law	Illegal in all instances	Only if rape/incest; health reasons	Only if rape/incest; health reasons	On request	Only if rape/incest; health reasons
Avg. Number of Children	3.7	3.8	5.6	1.6	6.8
% of Workforce	23%	25%	37%	46%	37%
Prof./Tech. Positions	28%	43%	No data	No data	23%
Admin./Mgmt. Positions	10%	18%	12%	No data	11%
Government Positions	2% of legislature; 9% of cabinet	11% of legislature; 8% of cabinet	21% of legislature; 4% of cabinet	11% of legislature	10% of legislature; 13% of cabinet
Violence Against Women	50% female genital mutilation; rapist can escape penalty if he marries the victim	Domestic abuse reportedly common; systematic rape of women and children by soldiers	90% female genital mutilation; no rape data; domestic abuse reportedly common	Domestic abuse reportedly common; no rape data	90% female genital mutilation; domestic abuse reportedly common; no rape data

Country	Finland	France	Georgia	Germany	Ghana
Location	Bordered by Sweden, Norway, and Russia	Bordered by Spain, Italy, and Germany	SE shores of the Black Sea	North Central Europe	Coastal Western Africa
Average Age at Marriage	26.1	27.3	21.7	26.1	21.1; 33% polygamy
Education	99% literacy; 46–55% of all college students	99% literacy; 46–55% of all college students	98% literacy	99% literacy; 36–45% of all college students	49% literacy; 16–25% of all college students
Life Expectancy	79.6	82.0	75.7	79.1	55.8
Maternal Deaths	11 per 100,000 births	15 per 100,000 births	33 per 100,000 births	22 per 100,000 births	740 per 100,000 births
Deaths from Abortions	1 in 4,785	1 in 3,922	1 in 1,443	1 in 3,497	1 in 24
Contraceptive Use	80%	81%	17%	75%	13%
Abortion Law	Only if rape/incest; health reasons	Only if rape/incest; health reasons	On request	Only if rape/incest; health reasons	Only if rape/incest; health reasons
Avg. Number of Children	1.9	1.7	2.1	1.3	5.7
% of Workforce	47%	42%	45%	40%	35%
Prof./Tech. Positions	61%	41%	No data	No data	9%
Admin./Mgmt. Positions	25%	9%	No data	No data	10%
Government Positions	34% of legislature; 39% of cabinet	5% of legislature; 13% of cabinet	7% of legislature; 6% of cabinet	26% of legislature; 12% of cabinet	8% of legislature; 12% of cabinet
Violence Against Women	11,000 abuses; 292 rapes reported in one year	13,000 abuses; 2,937 rapes reported in one year	Domestic abuse reportedly common; no rape data	Estimated 4 million women a year are abused; 5,527 rapes reported in one year; 325 shelters	Female genital mutilation; domestic abuse reportedly common; no rape data

Country	Greece	Guatemala	Guinea	Haiti	Honduras
Location	Bordered by Albania, Bulgaria	Central America	Western Africa	West Indies	Central America
Average Age at Marriage	22.5	20.5	16.0	23.8	20.0
Education	89% literacy; 46–55% of all college students	47% literacy	19% literacy; 15% or less of all college students	74% of girls not in school; 40% literacy	70% literacy; 36–45% of all college students
Life Expectancy	80.1	64.4	43.0	56.4	66.1
Maternal Deaths	10 per 100,000 births	200 per 100,000 births	1,600 per 100,000 births	1,000 per 100,000 births	220 per 100,000 births
Deaths from Abortions	1 in 7,143	1 in 98	1 in 9	1 in 21	1 in 99
Contraceptive Use	No data	23%	1 to 5%	10%	47%
Abortion Law	On request	Only to save life	Only if rape/ incest; health reasons	Only if rape/ incest; health reasons	Only to save life
Avg. Number of Children	1.4	5.1	6.8	4.7	4.6
% of Workforce	27%	17%	39%	41%	20%
Prof./Tech. Positions	43%	45%	No data	39%	50%
Admin./Mgmt. Positions	9%	32%	No data	32%	27%
Government Positions	6% of legislature; 7% of cabinet	14% of legislature; 13% of cabinet	None in legislature; 15% of cabinet	3% of legislature; 15% of cabinet	11% of legislature; 7% of cabinet
Violence Against Women	600 rapes reported in one year; domestic abuse reportedly common	49% claim abuse; rapist can escape penalty if he marries the victim	Female genital mutilation; 30% claim abuse; no rape data	Domestic abuse reportedly common; no rape data	Domestic abuse reportedly common; 62 rapes reported in one year

Country	Hungary	India	Indonesia	Iran	Iraq
Location	Central Europe	Southern Asia	SE Asia	SW Asia	SW Asia
Average Age at Marriage	21.0	19.5	21.1	19.7	22.3
Education	99% literacy; 46–55% of all college students	39% literacy; 26–35% of all college students	79% literacy	55% literacy; 26–35% of all college students	41% literacy; 26–35% of all college students
Life Expectancy	73.8	59.1	64.0	65.5	64.8
Maternal Deaths	30 per 100,000 births	570 per 100,000 births	650 per 100,000 births	120 per 100,000 births	310 per 100,000 births
Deaths from Abortions	1 in 1,961	1 in 49	1 in 55	1 in 174	1 in 59
Contraceptive Use	73%	45%	50%	65%	14%
Abortion Law	Only if rape/ incest; health reasons	Only if rape/ incest; health reasons	Only to save life	Only to save life	Only if rape/ incest; health reasons; must have husband's consent
Avg. Number of Children	1.7	3.6	2.8	4.8	5.5
% of Workforce	46%	25%	39%	19%	22%
Prof./Tech. Positions	49%	21%	40%	32%	44%
Admin./Mgmt. Positions	58%	2%	6%	4%	13%
Government Positions	11% of legislature; 7% of cabinet	9% of legislature; 4% of cabinet	11% of legislature; 5% of cabinet	4% of legislature	11% of legislature
Violence Against Women	Domestic abuse reportedly common; 1,128 rapes reported in one year	82,818 domestic abuses, 9,783 rapes, 7,000 dowry deaths in one year; systematic rape of women by soldiers and while in police custody	Domestic abuse reportedly common; 1,341 rapes reported in one year	Domestic abuse reportedly common; no rape data; mandatory dress code; attacks for immodest dress	Domestic abuse reportedly common; 264 rapes reported in one year; systematic rape of women by soldiers

Country	Ireland	Israel	Italy	Ivory Coast	Jamaica
Location	Island west of Great Britain	Mid-East	South Central Europe	South shore of West Africa	West Indies
Average Age at Marriage	23.4	23.9	23.2	18.9	29.7
Education	99% literacy	89% literacy	99% literacy; 46–55% of all college students	26% literacy	88% literacy; over 55% of all college students
Life Expectancy	77.9	78.5	80.5	54.2	74.8
Maternal Deaths	10 per 100,000 births	7 per 100,000 births	12 per 100,000 births	810 per 100,000 births	120 per 100,000 births
Deaths from Abortions	1 in 4,762	1 in 5,102	1 in 6,410	1 in 17	1 in 379
Contraceptive Use	60%	65%	78%	3%	67%
Abortion Law	Only to save life	Only if rape/incest; health reasons	Only if rape/incest; health reasons	Only to save life	Only if rape/incest; health reasons; husband's consent needed
Avg. Number of Children	2.1	2.8	1.3	7.1	2.2
% of Workforce	30%	42%	32%	34%	46%
Prof./Tech Positions	47%	54%	46%	15%	60%
Admin./Mgmt. Positions	15%	19%	4%	No data	No data
Government Positions	13% of legislature; 13% of cabinet	9% of legislature; 6% of cabinet	9% of legislature; 15% of cabinet	8% of legislature; 10% of cabinet	12% of legislature; 13% of cabinet
Violence Against Women	Domestic abuse reportedly common; 5,000 rapes reported in one year; ten shelters	Estimated 200,000 women abused by husbands in 1995; 2,000 sexual assaults and 1,500 rapes reported each year; seven shelters	Domestic abuse reportedly common; 672 rapes reported in one year	Wife abuse uncommon, not socially accepted; harsh penalties; no rape data	Domestic abuse reportedly common. 1,520 reported rapes in one year

Country	Japan	Jordan	Kazakhstan	Kenya	Korea, North
Location	East coast of Asia	SW Asia	Republic of Russia	Along Indian Ocean in Africa	East Asia
Average Age at Marriage	26.9	24.7	21.7	21.1	No data
Education	99% literacy; 26–35% of all college students	73% literacy; 36–45% of all college students	96% literacy; 46–55% of all college students	65% literacy; 26–35% of all college students	99% literacy; 26–35% of all college students
Life Expectancy	83.0	67.8	73.1	60.5	73.0
Maternal Deaths	18 per 100,000 births	150 per 100,000 births	80 per 100,000 births	650 per 100,000 births	70 per 100,000 births
Deaths from Abortions	1 in 3,704	1 in 123	1 in 521	1 in 26	1 in 621
Contraceptive Use	64%	35%	30%	33%	67%
Abortion Law	Only if rape/ incest; health reasons	Only if rape/ incest; health reasons	On request	Only if rape/ incest; health reasons; need husband's consent	On request
Avg. Number of Children	1.5	5.4	2.4	6.0	2.3
% of Workforce	40%	34%	43%	39%	46%
Prof./Tech. Positions	42%	5%	66%	No data	25%
Admin./Mgmt. Positions	8%	6%	48%	No data	4%
Government Positions	8% of legislature	3% of legislature; 7% of cabinet	11% of legislature; 3% of cabinet	4% of legislature; 5% of cabinet	20% of legislature; 4% of cabinet
Violence Against Women	1,600 reported rapes per year; 59% claim abuse	Domestic abuse reportedly common; 34 reported rapes in one year	Domestic abuse reportedly common; no rape data	Female genital mutilation; 42% claim abuse; 454 reported rapes in one year	Domestic abuse reportedly common; no rape data

Country	Korea, South	Kuwait	Kyrgyzstan	Laos	Latvia
Location	East Asia	NW corner of Persian Gulf	Asia	SE Asia	NW Russia
Average Age at Marriage	24.7	22.4	21.7	No data	22.4
Education	96% literacy; 26–35% of all college students	73% literacy; over 55% of all college students	96% literacy	41% literacy; 36–45% of all college students	99% literacy
Life Expectancy	74.0	75.4	72.4	50.0	75.2
Maternal Deaths	130 in 100,000 births	29 in 100,000 births	110 in 100,000 births	650 in 100,000 births	40 in 100,000 births
Deaths from Abortions	1 in 427	1 in 1,149	1 in 260	1 in 24	1 in 1,563
Contraceptive Use	79%	35%	31%	18%	19%
Abortion Law	Only if rape/incest; health reasons	Only if rape/incest; health reasons	On request	Only to save life	On request
Avg. Number of Children	1.8	3.0	3.5	6.4	1.6
% of Workforce	40%	16%	44%	44%	47%
Prof./Tech. Positions	42%	37%	No data	No data	No data
Admin./Mgmt. Positions	4%	4%	No data	No data	No data
Government Positions	3% of legislature; 5% of cabinet	None; only country where women cannot vote	6% of legislature; 12% of cabinet	9% of legislature	15% of legislature
Violence Against Women	3,909 reported rapes per year; 38% claim abuse	Domestic abuse reportedly common; systematic rape of women by soldiers	Domestic abuse reportedly common; no rape data	Wife abuse uncommon; not socially acceptable; harsh penalties; no rape data	Domestic abuse reportedly common; no rape data

Country	Lebanon	Liberia	Libya	Lithuania	Macedonia
Location	SW Asia	Western Africa	North Africa	Russian Republic	SW Europe
Average Age at Marriage	23.2	19.7	18.7	21.7	22.2
Education	89% literacy	18% literacy; 16–25% of all college students	57% literacy; 46–55% of all college students	98% literacy; 46–55% of all college students	88% literacy
Life Expectancy	67.0	54.0	62.5	76.2	75.9
Maternal Deaths	300 in 100,000 births	560 in 100,000 births	220 in 100,000 births	36 in 100,000 births	No data
Deaths from Abortions	1 in 115	1 in 27	1 in 73	1 in 1,543	No data
Contraceptive Use	55%	6%	14%	12%	No data
Abortion Law	Only to save life	Only if rape/ incest; health reasons	Only to save life	On request	On request
Avg. Number of Children	2.9	6.6	6.2	1.8	2.0
% of Workforce	27%	29%	10%	45%	41%
Prof./Tech. Positions	38%	25%	No data	No data	No data
Admin./Mgmt. Positions	2%	11%	No data	No data	No data
Government Positions	2% of legislature	6% of legislature; 17% of cabinet	6% of cabinet	7% of legislature	3% of legislature; 10% of cabinet
Violence Against Women	Domestic abuse reportedly common; no rape data	Female genital mutilation domestic abuse reportedly common; 27 rapes reported in one year	Domestic abuse reportedly common; no rape data	33% claim abuse; no rape data	No data

Country	Madagascar	Malawi	Malaysia	Mali	Mauritania
Location	SE coast of Africa	SE Africa	SE Asia	Western Africa	NW Africa
Average Age at Marriage	20.3	17.8	23.5	16.4; 45% polygamy	23.1; 18% polygamy
Education	75% literacy; 36–45% of all college students	39% literacy; 16–25% of all college students	75% literacy; 46–55% of all college students	86% of girls are not in school; 20% literacy	25% literacy; 16–25% of all college students
Life Expectancy	55.0	47.7	71.6	45.6	47.6
Maternal Deaths	490 per 100,000 births	560 per 100,000 births	80 per 100,000 births	1,200 per 100,000 births	930 per 100,000 births
Deaths from Abortions	1 in 35	1 in 26	1 in 368	1 in 12	1 in 21
Contraceptive Use	17%	13%	48%	5%	3%
Abortion Law	Only to save life	Only if rape/incest; health reasons; need husband's consent	Only if rape/incest; health reasons	Only to save life	Only to save life
Avg. Number of Children	5.9	6.9	3.4	6.9	5.2
% of Workforce	39%	40%	35%	16%	23%
Prof./Tech. Positions	No data	28%	46%	17%	21%
Admin./Mgmt. Positions	No data	8%	1%	20%	7%
Government Positions	6% of legislature; 5% of cabinet	6% of legislature; 4% of cabinet	11% of legislature; 8% of cabinet	3% of legislature; 25% of cabinet	None in legislature; 4% of cabinet
Violence Against Women	Wife abuse uncommon; not socially accepted; harsh penalties; no rape data	Domestic abuse reportedly common; systematic rape of women by soldiers	39% claim abuse; 912 reported rapes in one year; two shelters	Domestic abuse reportedly common; female genital mutilation; 136 reported rapes in one year	Domestic abuse reportedly common; no rape data

Country	Mexico	Moldova	Morocco	Mozambique	Myanmar (Burma)
Location	Northern Latin America	Extreme SW of European portion of Russia	NW corner of Africa	SE coast of Africa	SE Asia
Average Age at Marriage	20.6	21.7	22.3; 5% polygamy	22.2	22.4
Education	86% literacy; 46–55% of all college students	94% literacy	22% literacy; 36–45% of all college students	65% of girls not in school; 20% literacy; 26–35% of all college students	76% literacy
Life Expectancy	75.2	72.3	62.5	48.1	62.2
Maternal Deaths	110 per 100,000 births	60 per 100,000 births	610 per 100,000 births	1,500 per 100,000 births	580 per 100,000 births
Deaths from Abortions	1 in 303	1 in 794	1 in 48	1 in 11	1 in 43
Contraceptive Use	53%	15–22%	42%	4%	13%
Abortion Law	Only if rape/ incest; health reasons	On request	Only if rape/ incest; health reasons; husband's consent needed	On request	Only to save life
Avg. Number of Children	3.0	2.1	3.4	6.3	4.0
% of Workforce	30%	48%	21%	47%	36%
Prof./Tech. Positions	34%	No data	24%	21%	42%
Admin./Mgmt. Positions	20%	No data	25%	12%	12%
Government Positions	14% of legislature; 12% of cabinet	5% of legislature	1% of legislature	25% of legislature; 5% of cabinet	No women in government
Violence Against Women	Domestic abuse reportedly common; systematic rape and abuse of women in police custody	No data	Domestic abuse common; no penalty if rapist marries victim	Domestic abuse common; systematic rape of women by soldiers	Wife abuse uncommon; socially unacceptable; harsh penalties; no rape data

Country	Nepal	Netherlands	New Zealand	Nicaragua	Niger
Location	SE Asia	NW Europe	Island in South Pacific; SE of Australia	Central America	Western Africa
Average Age at Marriage	17.9	23.2	26.7	20.2	16.3; 36% polygamy
Education	13% literacy; 16–25% of all college students	99% literacy; 36–45% of all college students	99% literacy; 46–55% of all college students	66% literacy; 46–55% of all college students	86% of girls not in school; 7% literacy; 15% or less in college
Life Expectancy	50.3	80.4	78.0	64.6	46.1
Maternal Deaths	1,500 per 100,000 births	12 per 100,000 births	25 per 100,000 births	160 per 100,000 births	1,200 per 100,000 births
Deaths from Abortions	1 in 13	1 in 5,208	1 in 1,905	1 in 130	1 in 11
Contraceptive Use	23%	76%	70%	49%	4%
Abortion Law	Only if rape/incest; health reasons	On request	Only if rape/incest; health reasons	Only to save life	Only to save life
Avg. Number of Children	5.2	1.6	2.1	4.8	7.3
% of Workforce	33%	38%	36%	26%	46%
Prof./Tech. Positions	36%	43%	48%	43%	No data
Admin./Mgmt. Positions	23%	14%	32%	12%	No data
Government Positions	3% of legislature	30% of legislature; 31% of cabinet	29% of legislature; 4% of cabinet	16% of legislature; 6% of cabinet	4% of legislature; 13% of cabinet
Violence Against Women	Domestic abuse reportedly common; 71 reported rapes in one year	1,200 reported rapes in one year; 21% claim abuse	8,472 domestic violence reports in one year; 1,205 rapes	1,045 domestic violence reports in one year; 696 rapes	Domestic abuse reportedly common; no rape data; female genital mutilation

Country	Nigeria	Norway	Pakistan	Panama	Paraguay
Location	Southern coast of Western Africa	Western part of Scandinavian peninsula	NW portion of Asia's Indian subcontinent	Southern extension of Central America	South Central South America
Average Age at Marriage	18.7; 41% polygamy	24.0	21.7; 5% polygamy	21.9	21.8
Education	51% of girls not in school; 42% literacy; 26–35% of all college students	99% literacy; 46–55% of all college students	22% literacy; 15% or less in college	89% literacy	90% literacy; 36–45% of all college students
Life Expectancy	56.6	80.3	58.1	74.1	69.1
Maternal Deaths	1,000 per 100,000 births	6 per 100,000 births	340 per 100,000 births	55 per 100,000 births	160 per 100,000 births
Deaths from Abortions	1 in 16	1 in 8,333	1 in 50	1 in 649	1 in 152
Contraceptive Use	6%	76%	12%	58%	48%
Abortion Law	Only to save life	On request	Only if rape/incest; health reasons	Only if rape/incest; health reasons	Only to save life
Avg. Number of Children	6.2	2.0	5.9	2.8	4.1
% of Workforce	34%	41%	13%	28%	21%
Prof./Tech. Positions	26%	56%	18%	51%	51%
Admin./Mgmt. Positions	6%	25%	3%	1%	16%
Government Positions	9% of cabinet	39% of legislature; 39% of cabinet	2% of legislature; 7% of cabinet	7% of legislature; 27% of cabinet	4% of legislature; 9% of cabinet
Violence Against Women	Men are allowed to "correct" wives as long as it doesn't leave a scar or require a hospital stay longer than three weeks; female genital mutilation; no rape data	255 reported rapes in one year; 25% claim abuse	80% abused by husband; 4,000 rapes in one year; attacks for immodest dress	Domestic abuse reportedly common; no rape data	Domestic abuse reportedly common; no rape data

Country	Peru	Philippines	Poland	Portugal	Puerto Rico
Location	South America	Island off the coast of Asia	Europe	Atlantic coast of the Iberian Peninsula	Island of West Indies
Average Age at Marriage	22.7	23.8	23.0	22.1	22.3
Education	81% literacy	93% literacy; over 55% of all college students	99% literacy; 46–55% of all college students	81% literacy; over 55% of all college students	88% literacy
Life Expectancy	67.9	70.2	75.8	78.2	77.9
Maternal Deaths	280 per 100,000 births	280 per 100,000 births	19 per 100,000 births	15 per 100,000 births	No data
Deaths from Abortions	1 in 108	1 in 94	1 in 2,770	1 in 4,167	No data
Contraceptive Use	59%	40%	75%	66%	70%
Abortion Law	Only if rape/ incest; health reasons	Illegal under any circumstances	Only if rape/ incest; health reasons	Only if rape/ incest; health reasons	On request
Avg. Number of Children	3.3	3.8	1.9	1.6	2.2
% of Workforce	24%	31%	46%	37%	29%
Prof./Tech. Positions	41%	37%	60%	54%	53%
Admin./Mgmt. Positions	22%	33%	15%	17%	29%
Government Positions	9% of legislature; 14% of cabinet	13% of legislature; 14% of cabinet	13% of legislature; 6% of cabinet	9% of legislature; 13% of cabinet	No women in legislature or cabinet
Violence Against Women	3,912 domestic violence reports in one year; 2,421 rapes	Estimated 60% of wives are abused; a rape occurs every five hours, but this is only 5% of actual number	Domestic abuse reportedly common; 1,894 rapes reported in one year	Domestic abuse reportedly common; 200 rapes reported in one year	Domestic abuse reportedly common; no rape data

Country	Romania	Russia	Rwanda	Saudi Arabia	Senegal
Location	SE Europe	Border meets Baltic Sea and Artic/Pacific Oceans	South of the equator in Central Africa	Occupies 4/5 of Arabian Peninsula	Westernmost area of Western Africa
Average Age at Marriage	21.1	21.7; 68% divorce rate	21.2; 14% polygamy	21.7	23.7
Education	95% literacy; 46–55% of all college students	99% literacy; 46–55% of all college students	44% literacy	46% literacy; 36–45% of all college students	70% of girls not in school; 19% literacy; 16–25% of all college students
Life Expectancy	73.3	71.0	50.2	65.2	48.3
Maternal Deaths	130 per 100,000 births	75 per 100,000 births	1,300 per 100,000 births	130 per 100,000 births	1,200 per 100,000 births
Deaths from Abortions	1 in 51	1 in 889	1 in 12	1 in 124	1 in 14
Contraceptive Use	57%	21–32%	21%	14%	7%
Abortion Law	On request	On request	Only if rape/incest; health reasons	Only if rape/incest; health reasons, then need husband's consent	Only to save life
Avg. Number of Children	1.5	1.5	6.3	6.2	5.8
% of Workforce	47%	48%	47%	8%	39%
Prof./Tech. Positions	53%	No data	32%	9%	17%
Admin./Mgmt. Positions	26%	No data	8%	None	4%
Government Positions	5% of legislature	7% of legislature; 3% of cabinet	17% of legislature; 5% of cabinet	No women in government	12% of legislature; 9% of cabinet
Violence Against Women	Domestic abuse reportedly common; no rape data	14,000 rapes reported in one year; estimate is 700,000; in 1993, 14,000 women killed by partners	Domestic abuse reportedly common; no rape data	Domestic abuse common; no rape data; attacks reported for immodest dress	Domestic abuse common; female genital mutilation; 136 rapes reported in one year

Country	Sierra Leone	Singapore	Slovakia	Slovenia	Somalia
Location	Western Africa	Southern tip of Malay Peninsula	Western Europe	NW Bosnia	NE Africa
Average Age at Marriage	18.0	27.0	22.2	24.1	20.1
Education	16% literacy; 16–25% of all college students	84% literacy	99% literacy; 46–55% of all college students	88% literacy	94% of girls not in school; 14% literacy; 16–25% of all college students
Life Expectancy	42.6	76.4	77.2	78.4	46.6
Maternal Deaths	1,800 per 100,000 births	10 per 100,000 births	No data	13 per 100,000 births	1,600 per 100,000 births
Deaths from Abortions	1 in 9	1 in 5,882	No data	1 in 5,128	1 in 9
Contraceptive Use	4%	74%	74%	No data	1%
Abortion Law	Only if rape/incest; health reasons	On request	On request	On request	Only to save life
Avg. Number of Children	6.3	1.7	1.9	1.5	6.8
% of Workforce	32%	31%	46%	50%	38%
Prof./Tech. Positions	32%	40%	58%	55%	No data
Admin./Mgmt. Positions	8%	16%	23%	22%	No data
Government Positions	8% of legislature; 5% of cabinet	5% of legislature	15% of legislature; 13% of cabinet	14% of legislature; 13% of cabinet	No women in government
Violence Against Women	Domestic abuse reportedly common; no rape data; female genital mutilation	Wife abuse uncommon; not socially acceptable; harsh penalties; 111 rapes in one year	Domestic abuse reportedly common; no rape data	Domestic abuse reportedly common; no rape data	Domestic abuse reportedly common; no rape data; female genital mutilation

Country	South Africa	Spain	Sri Lanka	Sudan	Sweden
Location	Southernmost country in Africa	SW corner of Europe	Island off the SE coast of India	NE Africa	Scandinavian peninsula of Europe
Average Age at Marriage	25.7	23.1	24.4	24.1; 20% polygamy	30.4; 44% divorce rate
Education	70% literacy; 46–55% of all college students	98% literacy; 46–55% of all college students	86% literacy	31% literacy; 46–55% of all college students	99% literacy; 46–55% of all college students
Life Expectancy	67.9	80.5	72.5	51.0	80.8
Maternal Deaths	230 per 100,000 births	7 per 100,000 births	140 per 100,000 births	660 per 100,000 births	7 per 100,000 births
Deaths from Abortions	1 in 109	1 in 11,904	1 in 298	1 in 27	1 in 6,803
Contraceptive Use	50%	59%	62%	9%	78%
Abortion Law	On request	Only if rape/incest; health reasons	Only to save life	Only if rape/incest; health reasons	On request
Avg. Number of Children	4.0	1.2	2.4	5.6	2.1
% of Workforce	36%	25%	27%	23%	48%
Prof./Tech. Positions	51%	47%	48%	26%	56%
Admin./Mgmt. Positions	19%	9%	17%	2%	39%
Government Positions	25% of legislature; 11% of cabinet	18% of legislature; 25% of cabinet	5% of legislature; 21% of cabinet	4% of legislature; 4% of cabinet	41% of legislature; 52% of cabinet
Violence Against Women	A rape every 83 seconds; 26,000 rapes reported, but estimate is 386,000 in one year; 43% claim abuse	Domestic abuse reportedly common; 1,466 rapes reported in one year	Domestic abuse reportedly common; 274 rapes reported in one year	Systematic rape of women by soldiers; women not allowed to testify in own rape trials; female genital mutilation	Nearly 18,600 incidents of abuse reported in 1994; 1,800 rapes

Country	Switzerland	Syria	Taiwan	Tajikistan	Tanzania
Location	Central Europe	SW fringe of Asia	Off SE coast of China	South Central Asia	East Africa
Average Age at Marriage	25.0	21.5	25.8	21.7	20.6
Education	99% literacy	52% literacy; 36–45% of all college students	79% literacy	97% literacy	52% literacy
Life Expectancy	81.7	66.9	78.6	71.7	50.0
Maternal Deaths	6 per 100,000 births	180 per 100,000 births	No data	130 per 100,000 births	770 per 100,000 births
Deaths from Abortions	1 in 10,417	1 in 99	No data	1 in 164	1 in 23
Contraceptive Use	71%	20%	75%	21%	10%
Abortion Law	Only if rape/incest; health reasons	Only to save life, then need husband's consent	Only if rape/incest; health reasons	On request	Only to save life
Avg. Number of Children	1.6	5.6	1.7	4.7	5.7
% of Workforce	36%	18%	33%	43%	47%
Prof./Tech. Positions	40%	37%	No data	No data	No data
Admin./Mgmt. Positions	28%	3%	No data	No data	No data
Government Positions	17% of legislature; 14% of cabinet	10% of legislature; 6% of cabinet	11% of legislature; 3% of cabinet	3% of legislature; 13% of cabinet	17% of legislature; 13% of cabinet
Violence Against Women	Domestic abuse reportedly common; 398 rapes reported in one year	Domestic abuse reportedly common; no rape data	7,000 estimated rapes per year; 35% claim abuse	Domestic abuse reportedly common; no rape data	Domestic abuse reportedly common; 60% claim abuse

Country	Thailand	Togo	Trinidad and Tobago	Tunisia	Turkey
Location	SE Asia	Western Africa	West Indies, off coast of Venezuela	North Africa	95% in Asia, 5% in Europe
Average Age at Marriage	22.7	20.3; 52% polygamy	22.3	25.0	21.5
Education	91% literacy; 46–55% of all college students	33% literacy; 15% or less of all college students	96% literacy; 46–55% of all college students	50% literacy; 36–45% of all college students	69% literacy; 36–45% of all college students
Life Expectancy	71.9	54.8	73.5	70.2	73.4
Maternal Deaths	200 per 100,000 births	640 per 100,000 births	90 per 100,000 births	170 per 100,000 births	180 per 100,000 births
Deaths from Abortions	1 in 238	1 in 25	1 in 483	1 in 196	1 in 174
Contraceptive Use	66%	12%	53%	50%	63%
Abortion Law	Only if rape/incest; health reasons	Only if rape/incest; health reasons, then need husband's consent	Only if rape/incest; health reasons	On request	On request, but need husband's consent
Avg. Number of Children	2.1	6.3	2.3	3.0	3.2
% of Workforce	44%	36%	30%	25%	34%
Prof./Tech. Positions	52%	21%	55%	30%	30%
Admin./Mgmt. Positions	22%	8%	22%	9%	10%
Government Positions	6% of legislature; 5% of cabinet	1% of legislature; 5% of cabinet	18% of legislature; 14% of cabinet	7% of legislature; 4% of cabinet	2% of legislature; 5% of cabinet
Violence Against Women	Domestic abuse reportedly common; 3,356 rapes reported in one year	Domestic abuse reportedly common; no rape data; female genital mutilation	Domestic abuse reportedly common; 148 reported rapes in one year; five shelters	Domestic abuse reportedly common; no rape data; only one shelter	Domestic abuse reportedly common; systematic rape of women by soldiers

Country	Turkmenistan	Uganda	Ukraine	United Arab Emirates	United Kingdom
Location	North of Iran and Afghanistan on the Caspian Sea	Eastern Africa	Between Russia and Poland on the Black Sea	East coast of Arabian peninsula	NW coast of Europe
Average Age at Marriage	21.7	19.0	21.7; 57% divorce rate	23.1	23.1; 42% divorce rate
Education	97% literacy	46% literacy; 26–35% of all college students	97% literacy; 46–55% of all college students	77% literacy; over 55% of all college students	99% literacy; 36–45% of all college students
Life Expectancy	68.4	52.7	74.8	72.9	79.0
Maternal Deaths	55 per 100,000 births	1,200 per 100,000 births	50 per 100,000 births	26 per 100,000 births	9 per 100,000 births
Deaths from Abortions	1 in 478	1 in 12	1 in 1,250	1 in 938	1 in 6,173
Contraceptive Use	20%	5%	23%	41%	81%
Abortion Law	On request	Only if rape/incest; health reasons	On request	Only to save life, then need husband's consent	Only if rape/incest; health reasons
Avg. Number of Children	3.8	7.0	1.6	4.1	1.8
% of Workforce	44%	40%	46%	9%	44%
Prof./Tech. Positions	No data	No data	No data	25%	45%
Admin./Mgmt. Positions	No data	No data	No data	2%	33%
Government Positions	5% of legislature	17% of legislature; 13% of cabinet	4% of legislature; 4% of cabinet	No women in government	10% of legislature; 8% of cabinet
Violence Against Women	Domestic abuse reportedly common; systematic rape of women by soldiers	Domestic abuse reportedly common; no rape data; female genital mutilation	Domestic abuse reportedly common; 2,315 rapes reported in one year	Domestic abuse reportedly common; no rape data; female genital mutilation	50,000 abuses and 4,000 rapes reported in each year

Country	United States	Uruguay	Uzbekistan	Venezuela	Vietnam
Location	North America	South America	Bordered by Afghanistan, Turkmenistan, and Kazakinstan on the Aral Sea	Northern extremity of South America	Eastern coast of SE Asia
Average Age at Marriage	25.8	22.9	21.7	21.2	23.2
Education	99% literacy; 46–55% of all college students	97% literacy	96% literacy	90% literacy	89% literacy
Life Expectancy	79.7	75.3	72.1	75.2	67.6
Maternal Deaths	12 per 100,000 births	85 per 100,000 births	55 per 100,000 births	120 per 100,000 births	160 per 100,000 births
Deaths from Abortions	1 in 3,968	1 in 512	1 in 491	1 in 269	1 in 169
Contraceptive Use	74%	72%	28%	49%	53%
Abortion Law	On request	Only if rape/incest; health reasons	On request	Only to save life	On request
Avg. Number of Children	2.1	2.3	3.7	3.1	3.7
% of Workforce	46%	32%	45%	28%	47%
Prof./Tech. Positions	51%	41%	No data	33%	No data
Admin./Mgmt. Positions	43%	28%	No data	23%	No data
Government Positions	11% of legislature; 29% of cabinet	6% of legislature; 8% of cabinet	5% of legislature; 5% of cabinet	6% of legislature; 7% of cabinet	19% of legislature; 6% of cabinet
Violence Against Women	A rape every three minutes; ten women killed each day; 90,430 reported rapes in one year; but estimate is that 310,000 occur	Domestic abuse reportedly common; 855 rapes reported in one year	Domestic abuse reportedly common; no rape data	Domestic abuse reportedly common; 3,985 rapes reported in one year	Of 22,000 divorces in 1991, 70% were due to violence; no rape data

Country	Yemen	Zaire	Zambia	Zimbabwe
Location	SW corner of Arabian peninsula	West Central Africa	Southern Africa	Southern Africa
Average Age at Marriage	15.0	20.0	20.0; 18% polygamy	20.7; 17% polygamy practiced; widows become property of brothers-in-law
Education	64% of girls not in school; 20% literacy; 16–25% of all college students	53% of girls not in school; 64% literacy	67% literacy; 16–25% of all college students	78% literacy; 26–35% of all college students
Life Expectancy	52.4	53.7	54.5	60.1
Maternal Deaths	1,400 per 100,000 births	870 per 100,000 births	940 per 100,000 births	570 per 100,000 births
Deaths from Abortions	1 in 10	1 in 18	1 in 19	1 in 37
Contraceptive Use	7%	9%	15%	43%
Abortion Law	Only to save life	Only if rape/incest; health reasons	Only if rape/incest; health reasons	Only if rape/incest; health reasons
Avg. Number of Children	7.4	6.5	5.7	4.8
% of Workforce	14%	35%	30%	34%
Prof./Tech. Positions	12%	17%	32%	40%
Admin./Mgmt. Positions	2%	9%	6%	15%
Government Positions	1% of legislature	6% of legislature; 4% of cabinet	7% of legislature; 9% of cabinet	11% of legislature; 12% of cabinet
Violence Against Women	Domestic abuse reportedly common; no rape data; female genital mutilation	Domestic abuse reportedly common; no rape data	Domestic abuse reportedly common; no rape data	Domestic abuse reportedly common; 964 rapes reported in one year

Appendix B: Annotated Web Bibliography

The Internet is a powerful networking and informational tool for women worldwide, and its role in global feminism continues to grow. Below you will find some sites to get you started. Keep in mind, however, that the web is constantly evolving, and patience and persistence are required. This list is far from exhaustive, and despite my best efforts to choose sites I deemed dependable, some of them may not work by the time you try them. If an address doesn't work, remember you can type the name of the organization or topic into a web search engine.

Search Engines Focused on Women

Femina: http://femina.cybergrrl.com/
Pridelinks: www.pridelinks.com/
Womensguide: www.netguide.com/women
WWWomen: www.wwwomen.com/

General Sites Providing Links and Statistics on the Status of Women

AVIVA *is an international website for women that provides listings of events, organizations, and resources from around the world. Click on a map to explore the expansive resources of dozens of countries for a global guide to women's movements:* www.aviva.org/index.html

Feminist.com *is a comprehensive site with links to a variety of women's issues and services:* www.feminist.com/

Feminist Internet Gateway, *good links to many feminist sites:* www.feminist.org/gateway/master2.html

Feminist Majority Foundation, *excellent links to international and national sites on women's issues:* www.feminist.org

The Global Fund for Women *is an international organization focused on a variety of women's rights and issues. The organization provides funding and support for women's groups and links women's groups worldwide:* www.igc.org/gfw

National Organization for Women *(NOW), the U.S. organization's global issues' site with international news and links:* www.now.org/issues/global

Women in Development Network (WIDNET), *women's organizations, resources on women's issues, and statistics on women worldwide:* www.focusintl.com/widnet.htm

Women's International Net (WIN), *a magazine about women, by women, and for women, all over the world:* www.geocities.com/Wellesley/3321/

WomensNet *supports women's organizations locally, nationally, and worldwide by providing and adapting telecommunications technology to enhance their work. Contains late-breaking news from around the world and good links:* www.igc.org/igc/womensnet/

WomenWatch *is a joint initiative of three UN entities: DAW, INSTRAW, and UNIFEM. The site serves as a gateway to UN information and data on women worldwide:* www.un.org/womenwatch

Feminist Organizations (NGOs)

Feminist Theory Website *provides information about different national and ethnic feminisms. You may click on continents, and from there, countries:* www.utc.edu/~kswitala/Feminism/Ethnic.html

Network of East-West women *has links to women's organizations in eastern Europe:* www.neww.org

Other links to women's organizations: *See the general sites at the beginning of the Web bibliography; most have links to local, national, and international women's organizations.*

South Asian Women's Network (SAWNET) *focuses on women's issues and organizations in South Asia and promotes networking:* www.umiacs.umd. edu:80/users/sawweb/sawnet/SAW.orgn.html

Female Genital Mutilation

The FGM Education and Networking Project *contains good links to informational and action-oriented sites:* www.hollyfeld.org/fgm/

Online United Nations document "Women, Culture, and Traditional Practices": gopher.undp. org:70/00/unifem/poli-eco/poli/whr/cedaw/cedawkit/wctp

Lesbianism

The International Association of Lesbian/Gay Pride Coordinators (IAL/GPC) *exists to promote lesbian, gay, bisexual, and transgender pride on an international level, to increase networking and communication among Pride groups, to encourage diverse communities to hold Pride events, and to act as a source of education:* www.interpride.org

The International Gay and Lesbian Human Rights Commission (IGLHRC) *monitors, documents, and mobilizes action against the human rights violations of lesbians, gays, bisexuals, and people with HIV and AIDS. Click on a map for regional and country information and IGLHRC actions and resources:* www.iglhrc.org/

The International Lesbian and Gay Association (ILGA), *a worldwide federation of national and local groups, is dedicated to achieving equal rights for lesbians, gay men, bisexuals, and transgendered individuals. The site includes a comprehensive review of the developments affecting the lesbian and gay movement in each of the main international human rights bodies and in-depth reports from regions and countries:* www.ilga.org/

The Lesbian History Project, *a product of* Lesbian.org, *promoting lesbian visibility on the Internet:* www.geocities.com/WestHollywood/9993/

Religion

A bibliography on women and religion *compiled by Susan Walter Lau, Ph.D. (religious studies):* www.nd.edu/~archives/lau_bib.html
Catholic Perspectives on Women and Society *is a heavily linked site from the Catholic Perspectives Project of the Newman Center at Caltech:* www.cco.caltech.edu/~newman/women.html
Christians for Biblical Equality *is an organization devoted to demonstrating that biblical scriptures are consistent with gender equality:* www.cbeinternational.org/
A goddess bibliography *prepared by Pat Monaghan, author of* Goddesses and Heroines: www.iit.edu/ ~phillips/personal/basic/goddess.html
Links to sites on women and Islam: www.jannah.org/sisters/
The Mary Page, *maintained by the Marian Library/International Marian Research Institute at the University of Dayton in Ohio (USA), reflects the institute's research and study on the role of Mary in Christian life:* www.udayton.edu/mary/
Matrix *is an ongoing collaborative effort by an international group of scholars of medieval history, religion, history of art, archeology, religion, and other disciplines, as well as librarians and experts in computer technology to collect all existing data about Christian women in Europe between 500 and 1500 C.E.:* http://matrix.divinity.yale.edu/MatrixWebData/about.html
Sadyekbita: The International Association of Buddhist Women: www2.hawaii.edu/~tsomo/
Women Active in Buddhism *is a comprehensive Web collection of links and resources on contemporary Buddhist women:* http://members.tripod.com/~Llamo/
Women in Judaism: A Multidisciplinary Journal: www.utoronto.ca/wjudaism/

Reproductive Rights

The Alan Guttmacher Institute (AGI) *seeks to protect and expand the reproductive choices of women and men in freedom and dignity. Its aim is to enable individuals everywhere to have access to the information and services they need to exercise their rights and responsibilities concerning sexual activity, reproduction, and family information:* www.agi-usa.org
The Center for Reproductive Law and Public Policy (CRLP) *is a nonprofit legal and policy advocacy organization dedicated to promoting women's reproductive rights. The site features a map of the world. Click on regions, and then countries, for specific country-by-country information:* www.crlp.org/searchworld.html
The International Planned Parenthood Federation (IPPF) *links national autonomous family planning associations (FPAs) in over 150 countries worldwide. It is the largest voluntary family planning organization in the world:* www.ippf.org/

Online document on women's reproductive and sexual rights, *posted by the United Nations Development Fund for Women (UNIFEM):* gopher://gopher.undp.org:70/00/unifem/poli-eco/poli/whr/cedaw/cedawkit/rrsr

PATH, the Program for Appropriate Technology in Health, *is an international, nonprofit organization whose mission is to improve health, especially the health of women and children:* www.path.org/

United Nations Population Fund (UNFPA) *assists developing countries to improve reproductive health and family planning services on the basis of individual choice and to form population policies in support of efforts toward sustainable development:* www.unfpa.org/

UN's Agenda for Action for Women and AIDS: www.unaids.org/unaids/document/women/agenda.html

The World Health Organization's Department of Reproductive Health and Research *aims to strengthen the capacity of countries to promote and protect sexual and reproductive health:* www.who.int/rht/

Sexploitation

Coalition Against Trafficking of Women: www.uri.edu/artsci/wms/hughes/catw/catw.htm

Global Alliance Against Traffic in Women *supports grassroots women's groups, provides relevant articles and information:* www.inet.co.th/org/gaatw/

Mail order bride sites *(advertising mail-order brides):*
    www.mailorderbrides.com/
    www.aarens.com/dating/mailord.html
    www.tigerlilies.com/

The Prostitutes Education Network, *links to sites concerning prostitution internationally:* www.bayswan.org/penet.html

Violence Against Women

UNIFEM's Global Campaign to Eliminate Violence Against Women: www.unifem.undp.org/campaign/violence

UN policy paper on various forms of violence against women: www.un.org/rights/dpi1772e.htm

UN's Declaration on the Elimination of Violence Against Women: www1.umn.edu/humanrts/instree/e4devw.htm

Women and Development

The FAO is the Food and Agriculture Organization of the United Nations. *This page, from the women and population sustainable development section, provides information on NGOs, research institutes, and information centers; links to special features on population, poverty and the environment, and gender and food security; and twenty-three articles on key issues in women and development, as well as other resources:* www.fao.org/WAICENT/FAOINFO/SUST/WPdirect/WPhomepg.htm

INSTRAW is the UN's International Research and Training Institute for the Advancement of Women. *INSTRAW performs research, training, and information activities worldwide to promote women as key agents for sustainable development:* www.un.org/instraw/

The International Center for Research on Women in Development (ICRW) *generates empirical information and technical assistance:* www.icrw.org/

Linkages is a product of the International Institute for Sustainable Development (IISD), *an organization dedicated to environmentally sustainable development:* www.iisd.ca/index.html

UNIFEM is the United Nations Development Fund for Women. *UNIFEM is an advocate for women in the developing world. It provides direct financial and technical support to development projects for women in developing countries:* www.unifem.undp.org

The Women's Environment and Development Organization (WEDO) *is a global organization actively working to increase women's visibility and leadership at all political levels:* www.wedo.org

The World Bank's gender equality site *includes research and statistics on gender and development, policy documents, bank lending operations, country gender profiles, and efforts to promote gender equality:* www.worldbank.org/gender/

Women in Politics

The Center for the American Woman and Politics (CAWP) *is a university-based research, education, and public service center with a mission of promoting women in politics:* www.rci.rutgers.edu/ ~cawp/index.html

The Center for Women's Global Leadership *seeks to develop an understanding of the ways in which gender affects the exercise of power and works to enhance women's leadership:* www.feminist.com/cfwgl.htm

Emily's List *identifies viable pro-choice Democratic women candidates for key federal and statewide offices (United States):* www.emilyslist.org/home.htm

The International Institute for Democracy and Electoral Assistance (IDEA) *promotes women's presence in formal politics:* www.idea.int/women/

The Inter-Parliamentary Union (IPU) *is the world organization of parliaments of sovereign states. Established in 1889, the IPU works for the establishment of representative democracy. These pages contain the most recent information on the number of women in parliaments and a worldwide chronology of women's achievement of the right to vote and hold political office:* www.ipu.org/wmn-e/classif.htm *and* www.ipu.org/wmn-e/world.htm

Women's Speeches from Around the World *includes speeches from many of the world's notable women:* http://gos.sbc.edu/index.html

Women's Rights as Human Rights

Amnesty International *is an international human rights organization. This site provides articles and reports about women's human rights violations:* www.amnesty.se/women/week.htm

The Beijing Platform for Action from the Fourth World Women's Conference *is available at:* www.un.org/womenwatch/daw/beijing/platform

The Global Fund for Women, *an international organization with a human rights focus, funds activism for women's issues worldwide:* www.igc.apc.org/gfw/

Human Rights Watch *is an international human rights organization. This site includes reports on women's human rights:* www.hrw.org

Leading to Beijing: Voices of Global Women *radio interviews with Devaki Jain, Nawal el Saadawi, Peggy Antrobus, Gertrude Mongella, Arvonne Fraser, Mitsuko Horiuchi, Vignis Finnabogadottir, Charlotte Bunch:* www.cee.umn.edu:80/radiok/beijing/index.html

MADRE *is an international women's rights organization based in New York City:* www.madre.org

Sisterhood Is Global Institute *is an international nongovernment, nonprofit organization dedicated to the support and promotion of women's rights at the local, national, regional, and global levels:* www.sigi.org/

UN Convention on the Elimination of All Forms of Discrimination Against Women (CEDAW): gopher://gopher.undp.org/1/ecosocdocs/cedaw/

UN Division for the Advancement of Women (DAW): www.un.org/DPCSD/daw

Women's Human Rights, *law, documents, internet links from the University of Toronto:* www.law-lib. utoronto.ca/diana/

Work

The International Labour Organization (ILO) *was created by the United Nations in 1919 and has a long history of focusing on gender equality in the world of work. At this site you can find briefing notes on gender issues, news and events related to the promotion of women's work equality, examples of ongoing ILO programs, ILO conventions, as well as links to related sites:* www.ilo.mirror.who.or.jp/public/english/140femme/index.htm

The Women's Bureau of the U.S. Department of Labor *alerts women about their rights in the workplace, proposes policies and legislation that benefit working women, researches and analyzes information about women and work, and reports its findings to the president, Congress, and the public. The site includes statistics and data, programs and services, and links to related sites:* www.dol.gov/dol/wb/publicinfo

References

Abdel Halim, A. M. (1995). Challenges to the application of international women's human rights in the Sudan. In R. J. Cook (Ed.), *Human rights of women: National and international perspectives* (pp. 397–422). Philadelphia: University of Pennsylvania Press.

Abdullah, H. (1995). Wifeism and activism: The Nigerian women's movements. In A. Basu (Ed.), *The challenge of local feminisms: Women's movements in global perspective* (pp. 209–225). Boulder, CO: Westview Press.

AbuKhalil, A. (1994). Women and electoral politics in Arab states. In W. Rule & J. F. Zimmerman (Eds.), *Electoral systems in comparative perspective: Their impact on women and minorities* (pp. 127–138). Westport, CT: Greenwood Press.

Acevedo, L. (1995). Feminist inroads in the study of women's work and development. In C. E. Bose & E. Acosta-Belen (Eds.), *Women in the Latin American development process* (pp. 65–98). Philadelphia: Temple University Press.

Acosta-Belen, E., & Bose, C. E. (1995). Colonialism, structural subordination, and empowerment: Women in the development process in Latin America and the Caribbean. In C. E. Bose & E. Acosta-Belen (Eds.), *Women in the Latin American development process* (pp. 15–36). Philadelphia: Temple University Press.

Afshar, H. (1991). *Women, development, and survival in the Third World.* New York: Longman.

Afshar, H. (1996). Islam and feminism: An analysis of political strategies. In M. Yamani (Ed.), *Feminism and Islam: Legal and literary perspectives* (pp. 197–216). New York: New York University Press.

Allen, P. G. (1992). *The sacred hoop: Recovering the feminine in American Indian traditions.* Boston: Beacon Press.

Almeida Acosta, E., & Sanchez de Almeida, M. E. (1983). Psychological factors affecting change in women's role and status: A cross-cultural study. *International Journal of Psychology, 18,* 3–35.

Alvarez, S. E. (1994). The (trans)formation of feminism(s) and gender politics in Brazil. In J. S. Jaquette (Ed.), *The women's movement in Latin America: Participation and democracy* (2nd ed.). Boulder, CO: Westview Press.

American Medical Association. (1995). Council report: Female genital mutilation. *Journal of the American Medicine, 274,* 1714–1716.

Amin, R., & Li, Y. (1997). NGO-promoted women's credit program, immunization coverage, and child mortality in rural Bangladesh. *Women & Health, 25,* 71–87.

Amnesty International (1990). *Women in the front line: Human rights violations against women.* New York: Author.

Amnesty International. (1997a). *Breaking the silence: Human rights violations based on sexual orientation.* London: Author.

Amnesty International (1997b). *Pakistan: Women's human rights remain a dead letter.* www.amnesty.org/ailib/aipub/1997/ASA/33300797.htm

Amoah, E. (1987). Women, witches, and social change in Ghana. In D. L. Eck & D. Jain (Eds.), *Speaking of faith: Global perspectives on women, religion, and social change* (pp. 84–94). Philadelphia: New Society Publishers.

Anand, A. (1993). Introduction. In *The power to change: Women in the Third World redefine their environment* (pp. 1–21). London: Zed.

Anderson, J. (1994, Winter). Separatism, feminism, and the betrayal of reform. *Signs,* 437–448.

Anderson, N. F. (1993). Benazir Bhutto and dynastic politics: Her father's daughter, her people's sister. In M. A. Genovese (Ed.), *Women as national leaders* (pp. 41–69). Newbury Park, CA: Sage.

Anderson, T. (1992, July 10). Summit weighs women's role in changing world. *Los Angeles Times,* p. A6.

Anson, O., Levenson, A., & Bonneh, D. Y. (1990). Gender and health on the kibbutz. *Sex Roles, 22,* 213–236.

Antrobus, P. (1991, November). Paper presented to the World Women's Congress for a Healthy Planet, Miami, FL.

Arthur, R. H. (1987). The wisdom goddess and the masculinization of western religion. In U. King (Ed.), *Women in the world's religions, past and present* (pp. 24–37). New York: Paragon House.

Arungu-Olende, R. A. (1996). Kenya: Not just the literacy but wisdom. In R. Morgan (Ed.), *Sisterhood is global* (pp. 394–398). New York: Feminist Press.

As, B. (1996). Norway: More power to women. In R. Morgan (Ed.), *Sisterhood is global* (pp. 509–514). New York: Feminist Press.

Asian Women Workers Newsletter. (1992). Sexual harassment at work. *Women's International Network News, 18,* 46.

Bachofen, J. J. (1967). *Myth, religion, and mother right.* Princeton, NJ: Princeton University Press.

Bacon, D. (1997, March 5). Workers in maquiladoras from Tijuana to Juarez are fighting back against NAFTA-driven exploitation. *San Francisco Bay Guardian.*

Bamberger, J. (1974). The myth of matriarchy: Why men rule in primitive society. In M. Z. Rosaldo & L. Lamphere (Eds.), *Women, culture, and society* (pp. 263–281). Stanford, CA: Stanford University Press.

Bancroft, A. (1987). Women in Buddhism. In U. King (Ed.), *Women in the world's religions, past and present* (pp. 81–106). New York: Paragon House.

Bandura, A. (1986). *Social foundations of thought and action.* Englewood Cliffs, NJ: Prentice-Hall.

Barnes, N. S. (1987). Buddhism. In A. Sharma (Ed.), *Women in world religions* (pp. 59–104). Albany: State University of New York Press.

Barnes, N. S. (1994). Women in Buddhism. In A. Sharma (Ed.), *Today's woman in world religions* (pp. 137–170). Albany: State University of New York Press.

Baron, J. N., Davis-Blake, A., & Bielby, W. T. (1986). The structure of opportunity: How promotion ladders vary within and among organizations. *Administrative Science Quarterly, 31,* 248–273.

Barry, K. (1995). *The prostitution of sexuality.* New York: New York University Press.

Barstow, A. L. (1994). *Witchcraze: A new history of the European witch hunts.* New York: HarperCollins.

Baruch, G. K., & Barnett, R. C. (1986). Role quality, multiple role involvement, and psychological well-being in midlife women. *Journal of Personality and Social Psychology, 51,* 578–585.

Baruch, G. K., & Barnett, R. C. (1987). Role quality and psychological well-being. In F. J. Crosby (Ed.), *Spouse, parent, and worker: On gender and multiple gender roles* (pp. 63–73). New Haven, CT: Yale University Press.

Basu, A. (Ed.). (1995). *The challenge of local feminisms: Women's movements in global perspective.* Boulder, CO: Westview Press.

Beckman, P. R., & D'Amico, F. (1995). Conclusion: An end and a beginning. In F. D'Amico & P. R. Beckman (Eds.), *Women in world politics: An introduction* (pp. 199–213). Westport, CT: Bergin & Garvey.

Bem, S. L. (1993). *The lenses of gender: Transforming the debate on sexual inequality.* New Haven, CT: Yale University Press.

Beneria, L., & Roldan, M. (1987). *The crossroads of class and gender: Industrial homework, subcontracting, and household dynamics in Mexico City.* Chicago: University of Chicago Press.

Berger, M. (1995). Key issues on women's access to and use of credit in the micro-and-small-scale enterprise sector. In L. Divard & J. Havet (Eds.), *Women in micro-and-small-scale enterprise development* (pp. 189–216). Boulder, CO: Westview Press.

Bergmann, B. R. (1989). Does the market for women's labor need fixing? *Journal of Economic Perspectives, 3,* 43–60.

Bernard, J. (1972). *The future of marriage.* New York: World.

Bernard, J. (1987). *The female world from a global perspective.* Bloomington: Indiana University Press.

Bhatnagar, D. (1988). Professional women in organizations: New paradigms for research and action. *Sex Roles, 18,* 343–355.

Bhatt, E. (1995). Women and development alternatives: Micro-and-small-scale enterprises in India. In L. Divard & J. Havet (Eds.), *Women in micro-and-small-scale enterprise development* (pp. 85–100). Boulder, CO: Westview Press.

Bhutto, B. (1989). *Daughter of destiny: An autobiography.* New York: Simon & Schuster.

Biehl, J. (1991). *Rethinking ecofeminist politics.* Boston: South End Press.

Bjorkqvist, K., Osterman, K., & Lagerspetz, K. M. J. (1994). Sex differences in covert aggression among adults. *Aggressive Behavior, 20,* 27–33.

Blackwood, E. (1984). Sexuality and gender in certain Native American tribes: The case of cross-gender females. *Signs, 10,* 27–42.

Blackwood, E. (1986). Breaking the mirror: The construction of lesbianism and the anthropological discourse on homosexuality. In E. Blackwood (Ed.), *The many faces of homosexuality: Anthropological approaches to homosexual behavior* (pp. 1–19). New York: Harrington Park.

Blair, S. L., & Lichter, D. T. (1991). Measuring the division of household labor: Gender segregation of housework among American couples. *Journal of Family Issues, 12,* 91–113.

Blau, F. D., & Ferber, M. A. (1987). Occupations and earnings of women works. In K. S. Koziara, M. H. Moskow, & L. D. Tanner (Eds.), *Working women: Past, present, future* (pp. 37–68). Washington, DC: BNA Books.

Blau, F. D., & Kahn, L. M. (1996). Wage structure and gender earnings differentials: An international comparison. *Economica, 63,* 529–562.

Bloom-Feshbach, J. (1981). Historical perspectives on the father's role. In M. E. Lamb (Ed.), *The role of the father in child development* (pp. 71–112). New York: Wiley.

Blumberg, R. L. (1991). Income under female versus male control: Hypotheses from a theory of gender stratification and data from the Third World. In R. L. Blumberg (Ed.), *Gender, family, and economy: The triple overlap* (pp. 97–127). Newbury Park, CA: Sage.

Blumberg, R. L. (1995). Gender, microenterprise, performance, and power: Case studies from the Dominican Republic, Ecuador, Guatemala, and Swaziland. In C. E. Bose & E. Acosta-Belen (Eds.), *Women in the Latin American development process* (pp. 194–226). Philadelphia: Temple University Press.

Blumstein, P., & Schwartz, P. (1991). In R. L. Blumberg (Ed.), *Gender, family, and economy: The triple overlap* (pp. 261–288). Newbury Park, CA: Sage.

Bonder, G., & Nari, M. (1995). The 30 percent quota law: A turning point for women's political participation in Argentina. In A. Brill (Ed.), *A rising public voice: Women in politics worldwide* (pp. 183–194). New York: Feminist Press.

Boserup, E. (1970). *Women's role in economic development.* New York: St. Martin's Press.

Boston Women's Health Collective. (1992). *The new our bodies, ourselves.* New York: Simon & Schuster.

Boudreau, V. G. (1995). Corazon Aquino: Gender, class, and the people power president. In F. D'Amico & P. R. Beckman (Eds.), *Women in world politics: An introduction* (pp. 71–83). Westport, CT: Bergin & Garvey.

Brandell, S. G. (1998, May/June). FGM roundup. *Ms., 8,* 26.

Brandiotti, R., Charkiewicz, E., Hausler, S., & Wieringa, S. (1994). *Women, the environment, and sustainable development.* Santo Domingo, Dominican Republic: INSTRAW.

Braun, S. (1998, June 12). Mitsubishi to pay $34 million in sex harassment case. *Los Angeles Times,* pp. A1, A18, A19.

Braverman, L. (1991). The dilemma of housework: A feminist response to Gottman, Napier, and Pittman. *Journal of Marital and Family Therapy, 17,* 25–28.

Breinlinger, S., & Kelly, C. (1994). Women's responses to status inequality: A test of social identity theory. *Psychology of Women Quarterly, 18,* 1–16.

Brenner, J. (1996). The best of times, the worst of times: Feminism in the United States. In M. Threlfall (Ed.), *Mapping the women's movement: Feminist politics and social transformation in the North* (pp. 17–73). London: Verso & New Left Review.

Brenner, O. C., Tomkiewicz, J., & Schein, V. E. (1989). The relationship between sex role stereotypes and requisite management characteristics revisited. *Academy of Management Journal, 32,* 662–669.

Brownmiller, S. (1986). *Against our will.* New York: Simon & Schuster.

Bruce, J. (1995). The economics of motherhood. In N. Heyer (Ed.), *A commitment to the world's children: Perspectives on development for Beijing and beyond.* New York: UNIFEM.

Bryceson, D. F. (1995). Wishful thinking: Theory and practice of western donor efforts to raise women's status in rural Africa. In D. F. Bryceson (Ed.), *Women wielding the hoe: Lessons for feminist theory and development practice* (pp. 201–222). Oxford: Berg Publishers.

Bullock, S. (1994). *Women and work.* London: Zed.

Bumiller, E. (1990). *May you be the mother of a hundred sons: A journey among the women of India.* New York: Random House.

Bunch, C. (1995). Transforming human rights from a feminist perspective. In J. Peters & A. Wolper (Eds.), *Women's rights, human rights: International feminist perspectives* (pp. 11–17). New York: Routledge.

Bunch, C., & Fried, S. (1996, Autumn). Beijing '95: Moving women's human rights from margin to center. *Signs,* 200–204.

Burke, R., & McKeen, C. (1988). Work and family: What we know and what we need to know. *Canadian Journal of Administrative Sciences, 5,* 30–40.

Burn, S. M. (1996). *The social psychology of gender.* New York: McGraw-Hill.

Buschman, J. K., & Lenart, S. (1996). "I am not a feminist, but . . .": College women, feminism, and negative experiences. *Political Psychology, 17,* 59–75.

Buss, D. M., & Barnes, M. (1986). Preferences in human mate selection. *Journal of Personality and Social Psychology, 50,* 559–570.

Buvinic, M. (1995). Women's income generation activities in Latin America and the Caribbean: A commentary. In A. Leonard (Ed.), *Seeds 2* (pp. 219–222). New York: Feminist Press.

Buvinic, M., Gwin, C., & Bates, L. M. (1996). *Investing in women: Progress and prospects for the World Bank.* Washington, DC: Johns Hopkins University Press.

Bystydzienski, J. M. (1992a). Introduction. In J. Bystydzienski (Ed.), *Women transforming politics: Worldwide strategies for empowerment* (pp. 1–10). Bloomington: Indiana University Press.

Bystydzienski, J. M. (1992b). Influence of women's culture on public policies in Norway. In J. Bystydzienski (Ed.), *Women transforming politics: Worldwide strategies for empowerment* (pp. 11–23). Bloomington: Indiana University Press.

Bystydzienski, J. M. (1994). Norway: Achieving world-record women's representation in government. In W. Rule & J. F. Zimmerman (Eds.), *Electoral systems in comparative perspective: Their impact on women and minorities* (pp. 55–64). Westport, CT: Greenwood Press.

Bystydzienski, J. M. (1995). *Women in electoral politics: Lessons from Norway.* Westport, CT: Praeger.

Cannon, C. M. (1997, October). The Adams chronicle. *Working Woman,* 24–27, 88, 91.

Cantor, A. (1995). *Jewish women, Jewish men: The legacy of patriarchy in Jewish life.* New York: Harper & Row.

Carillo, R. (1992). *Battered dreams: Violence against women as an obstacle to development.* New York: UNIFEM.

Carmody, D. L. (1974). *Women and world religions.* Nashville: Parthenon Press.

Carmody, D. L. (1979). *Women and world religions.* Nashville: Abingdon.

Carmody, D. L. (1989). *Women and world religions.* Englewood Cliffs, NJ: Prentice-Hall.

Carmody, D. L. (1994). Today's Jewish women. In A. Sharma (Ed.), *Today's woman in world religions* (pp. 245–266). Albany: State University of New York Press.

Carras, M. C. (1995). Indira Gandhi: Gender and foreign policy. In F. D'Amico & P. R. Beckman (Eds.), *Women in world politics: An introduction* (pp. 45–58). Westport, CT: Bergin & Garvey.

Cartright, D. W., & Zander, A. (1968). *Group dynamics: Research and theory* (3rd ed.). New York: Harper & Row.

Cath. (1995). Country report on lesbians in India. In R. Rosenbloom (Ed.), *Unspoken rules: Sexual orientation and women's human rights* (pp. 77–88). San Francisco: International Gay and Lesbian Human Rights Commission.

Cavin, S. (1985). *Lesbian origins.* San Francisco: Ism Press.

Chafetz, J. S. (1990). *Gender equity: An integrated theory of stability and change.* Newbury Park, CA: Sage.

Chafetz, J. S. (1991). The gender division of labor and the reproduction of female disadvantage: Toward an integrated theory. In R. L. Blumberg (Ed.), *Gender, family, and economy: The triple overlap* (74–96). Newbury Park, CA: Sage.

Chanan, G. (1992). *Out of the shadows: Local community action and the European community.* Dublin: European Foundation for the Improvement of Living and Working Conditions.

Charles, M., & Hopflinger, F. (1992). Gender, culture, and the division of household labor: A replication of US studies for the case of Switzerland. *Journal of Comparative Family Studies, 23,* 375–387.

Charlesworth, H. (1994). What are "women's international human rights"? In R. Cook (Ed.), *Human rights of women* (pp. 58–84). Philadelphia: University of Pennsylvania Press.

Charlesworth, H. (1995). Human rights as men's rights. In J. Peters & A. Wolper (Eds.), *Women's rights, human rights: International feminist perspectives* (pp. 103–113). New York: Routledge.

Charlesworth, H., Chinkin, C., & Wright, S. (1991). Feminist approaches to international law. *The American Journal of International Law, 85,* 613–645.

Chen, M. A. (1995). Introduction. In A. Leonard (Ed.), *Seeds 2* (pp. 1–16). New York: Feminist Press.

Chesler, P. (1996, Winter). What is justice for a rape victim? *On the Issues,* 12–16, 56–57.

Chinchilla, N. S. (1994). Feminism, revolution, and democratic transitions in Nicaragua. In J. S. Jaquette (Ed.), *The women's movement in Latin America: Participation and democracy* (2nd ed., pp. 177–198). Boulder, CO: Westview Press.

Chinery-Hesse, M. (1995). Speech as Deputy Director-General, International Labour Office at the Fourth World Conference on Women. *gopher.un.org/00/conf/fwcw/conf/una/950906203352.txt*

Chinkin, C. M. (1993). Peace and force in international law. In D. G. Dallmeyer (Ed.), *Reconceiving reality: Women and international law.* New York: Asil.

Chodorow, N. (1978). *The reproduction of mothering: Psychoanalysis and the sociology of gender.* Berkeley: University of California Press.

Chow, E. N., & Chen, K. (1994). The impact of the one-child policy on women and the patriarchical family in the People's Republic of China. In E. N. Chow & C. W. Berheide (Eds.), *Women, the family, and policy* (pp. 71–98). Albany: State University of New York Press.

Chowdhury, N. (1994). Bangladesh: Gender issues and politics in a patriarchy. In B. J. Nelson & N. Chowdhury (Eds.), *Women and politics worldwide* (pp. 92–113). New Haven, CT: Yale University Press.

Chowdhury, N., Nelson, B. J., Carver, K. A., Johnson, N. J., & O'Loughlin, P. L. (1994). Redefining politics: Patterns of women's political engagement from a global perspective. In B. J. Nelson & N. Chowdhury (Eds.), *Women and politics worldwide* (pp. 3–24). New Haven, CT: Yale University Press.

Christ, C. P., & Plaskow, J. (1979). Introduction: Womanspirit rising. In C. P. Christ & J. Plaskow (Eds.), *Womanspirit rising: A feminist reader in religion* (pp. 1–18). San Francisco: Harper & Row.

Cisernos, S. (1996). Guadalupe the sex goddess. *Ms., 7,* 43–46.

Clark, B. (1995). Country report on lesbians in Zimbabwe. In R. Rosenbloom (Ed.), *Unspoken rules: Sexual orientation and women's human rights* (pp. 237–242). San Francisco: International Gay and Lesbian Human Rights Commission.

Cleveland, J. N., & McNamara, K. (1996). Understanding sexual harassment: Contributions from research on domestic violence and organizational change. In M. S. Stockdale (Ed.), *Sexual harassment in the workplace: Perspectives, frontiers, and response strategies* (pp. 217–240). Thousand Oaks, CA: Sage.

Col, J. (1993). Managing softly in turbulent times: Corazon C. Aquino, President of the Philippines. In M. Genovese (Ed.), *Women as national leaders* (pp. 13–40). Newbury Park, CA: Sage.

Collins, P. H. (1990). *Black feminist thought: Knowledge, consciousness, and the politics of empowerment.* Boston: Irwin Hyman.

Cook, R. J. (1995). International human rights and women's reproductive health. In J. Peters & A. Wolper (Eds.), *Women's rights, human rights: International feminist perspectives* (pp. 256–278). New York: Routledge.

Coomaraswamy, R. (1994). To bellow like a cow: Women, ethnicity, and the discourse of rights. In R. Cook (Ed.), *Human rights of women* (pp. 39–57). Philadelphia: University of Pennsylvania Press.

Cooper, G. (1997, July/August). Lesbian mothers. *Networker,* 15.

Copelon, R. (1994). Intimate terror: Understanding domestic violence as torture. In R. Cook (Ed.), *Human rights of women* (pp. 116–152). Philadelphia: University of Pennsylvania Press.

Copelon, R. (1995). War crimes: Reconceptualizing rape in time of war. In J. Peters & A. Wolper (Eds.), *Women's rights, human rights: International feminist perspectives* (pp. 197–204). New York: Routledge.

Corea, G. (1991). Depo-Provera and the politics of knowledge. In H. P. Hynes (Ed.), *Reconstructing Babylon* (pp. 161–184). Bloomington: Indiana University Press.

Coronel, S., & Rosca, N. (1993). For the boys: Filipinas expose years of sexual slavery by the U.S. and Japan. *Ms., 5,* 10–15.

Crampton, S. M., Hodge, J. W., & Mishra, J. M. (1997). The Equal Pay Act: The first 30 years. *Public Personnel Management, 26,* 335–344.

Cray, C. (1997, October). Conducive to sexual harassment: The EEOC's case against Mitsubishi. *Multinational Monitor,* 24–26.

Crosby, F. J. (1991). *Juggling: The unexpected advantages of balancing career and home for women and their families.* New York: Free Press.

Curtius, M. (1995, March 12). Paying a high price for honor. *Los Angeles Times,* pp. A1, A6.

Dahlburg, J. T., & Bearak, B. (1996, November 6). Pakistani president sacks Bhutto and government. *Los Angeles Times,* pp. A1, A26.

D'Alusio, F., & Menzel, P. (1996). *Women in the material world.* New York: Random House.

Daly, M. (1971, March 12). After the death of God the Father. *Commonweal,* 7–11.

Daly, M. (1973). *Beyond God the Father.* Boston: Beacon Press.

Daly, M. (1974). Theology after the demise of God the Father: A call for the castration of sexist religion. In A. L. Hageman (Ed.), *Sexist religion and women in the church: No more silence* (pp. 125–142). New York: Association Press.

Daly, M. (1985). *The church and the second sex* (2nd ed.). Boston: Beacon Press.

D'Amico, F. (1995). Women as national leaders. In F. D'Amico & P. R. Beckman (Eds.), *Women in world politics: An introduction* (pp. 15–30). Westport, CT: Bergin & Garvey.

D'Amico, F., & Beckman, P. R. (1995). *Women in world politics: An introduction.* Westport, CT: Bergin & Garvey.

Daniszewski, J. (1997, May 3). Egyptian women scarred by hate. *Los Angeles Times,* pp. A1, A8, A9.

Dankelman, I., & Davidson, J. (1988). *Women and environment in the Third World: Alliance for the future.* London: Earthscan.

Dankelman, I., & Davidson, J. (1991). Land: Women at the centre of the food crisis. In S. Sontheimer (Ed.), *Women and the environment: A reader on crisis and development in the Third World.* New York: Monthly Review Press.

Darcy, R., & Hyun, C. M. (1994). Women in the South Korean electoral system. In W. Rule & J. F. Zimmerman (Eds.), *Electoral systems in comparative perspective: Their impact on women and minorities* (pp. 171–182). Westport, CT: Greenwood Press.

Darling, J. (1995, March 31). The women who run Juchitán. *Los Angeles Times,* pp. A1, A11, A13.

D'Augelli, A. R. (1992). Lesbian and gay male undergraduates' experiences of harassment and fear on campus. *Journal of Interpersonal Violence, 7,* 383–395.

Davidson, A. R., & Thomson, E. (1980). Cross-cultural studies of attitudes and beliefs. In H. C. Triandis & W. W. Lambert (Eds.), *Handbook of cross-cultural psychology* (Vol. 5, pp. 25–72). Boston: Allyn & Bacon.

Davis, E. G. (1971). *The first sex.* New York: Putnam.

Davis, R. H. (1997). *Women and power in parliamentary democracies: Cabinet appointments in Western Europe, 1968–1992.* Lincoln: University of Nebraska Press.

de Beauvoir, S. (1953). *The second sex.* New York: Alfred Knopf.

Degler, C. N. (1990). Darwinians confront gender; or, there is more to it than history. In D. L. Rhode (Ed.), *Theoretical perspectives on sexual difference* (pp. 33–46). New Haven, CT: Yale University Press.

Deutsch, M., & Gerard, H. B. (1955). A study of normative and informational social influence on social judgment. *Journal of Abnormal and Social Psychology, 51,* 629–636.

Dignard, L., & Havet, J. (1995). Introduction. In L. Divard & J. Havet (Eds.), *Women in micro-and-small-scale enterprise development* (pp. 1–24). Boulder, CO: Westview Press.

Diner, H. (1975). *Mothers and Amazons.* New York: Julian Press.

Dinnerstein, D. (1976). *The rocking of the cradle and the ruling of the world.* London: Souvenir.

Dion, K. L., & Schuller, R. A. (1990). Ms. and the manager: A tale of two stereotypes. *Sex Roles, 22,* 569–577.

Dixon-Mueller, R. (1993). *Population policy & women's rights: Transforming reproductive choice.* Westport, CT: Praeger.

Dorf, J., & Perez, G. C. (1995). Discrimination and tolerance of difference: International lesbian human rights. In J. Peters & A. Wolper (Eds.), *Women's rights, human rights: International feminist perspectives* (pp. 324–334). New York: Routledge.

Doyle, P. M. (1974). Women and religion: Psychological and cultural implications. In R. R. Reuther (Ed.), *Religion and sexism: Images of woman in the Jewish and Christian traditions* (pp. 15–40). New York: Simon & Schuster.

Drury, C. (1994). *Christianity.* In J. Holm (Ed.), *Women in religion* (pp. 30–58). New York: St. Martin's Press.

Dubisch, J. (1993). "Foreign chickens" and other outsiders: Gender and community in Greece. *American Ethnologist, 20,* 272–287.

Duda, A., & Wuch, M. (1995). Country report on lesbians in Germany. In R. Rosenbloom (Ed.), *Unspoken rules: Sexual orientation and women's human rights* (pp. 59–66). San Francisco: International Gay and Lesbian Human Rights Commission.

Duley, M. I., & Diduk, S. (1986). Women, colonialism, and development. In M. I. Duley & M. I. Edwards (Eds.), *The cross-cultural study of women: A comprehensive guide* (pp. 48–77). New York: Feminist Press.

Duley, M. I., & Edwards, M. I. (1986). *The cross-cultural study of women: A comprehensive guide.* New York: Feminist Press.

Duley, M. I., Sinclair, K., & Edwards, M. I. (1986). Biology vs. culture. In M. I. Duley & M. I. Edwards (Eds.), *The cross-cultural study of women: A comprehensive guide* (pp. 3–25). New York: Feminist Press.

Eck, D. L., & Jain, D. (1987). Introduction. *Speaking of faith: Global perspectives on women, religion, and social change* (pp. 17–21). Philadelphia: New Society Publishers.

Ehrenberg, M. (1989). *Women in prehistory.* Norman: University of Oklahoma Press.

Ehrenreich, B., Dowie, M., & Minkin, S. (1979, November). The charge: Gynocide, the accused: The United States government. *Mother Jones, 32.*

Eisler, R. (1987). *The chalice and the blade.* San Francisco: Harper & Row.

El-Bakri, Z. B., & Kameir, E. M. (1983). Aspects of women's political participation in Sudan. *International Social Science Journal, 35,* 605–623.

El Dareer, A. (1982). *Woman, why do you weep?: Circumcision and its consequences.* London: Zed.

Elliot, L. (1996). Women, gender, feminism, and the environment. In J. Turpin & L. A. Lorentzen (Eds.), *The gendered new world order* (pp. 13–34). New York: Routledge.

el Saadawi, N. (1987). Toward women's power, nationally and internationally. In D. L. Eck & D. Jain (Eds.), *Speaking of faith: Global perspectives on women, religion, and social change* (pp. 17–21). Philadelphia: New Society Publishers.

Engle, P. L. (1993). Influences of mothers' and fathers' income on children's nutritional status in Guatemala. *Social Science & Medicine, 37,* 1303–1312.

Engle, P. L., & Breaux, C. (1994). *Is there a father instinct? Fathers' responsibility for children.* Report for the Population Council (New York) and the International Center for Research on Women (Washington, DC).

Enloe, C. (1989). *Bananas, beaches, and bases: Making feminist sense of international relations.* Berkeley: University of California Press.

Enloe, C. (1995a). The globetrotting sneaker. *Ms., 6,* 10–15.

Enloe, C. (1996). Spoils of war. *Ms., 6,* 15.

Everett, J. (1993). Indira Gandhi and the exercise of power. In M. A. Genovese (Ed.), *Women as national leaders* (pp. 103–134). Newbury Park, CA: Sage.

Faderman, L. (1981). *Surpassing the love of men: Romantic friendship and love between women from the Renaissance to the present.* New York: William Morrow.

Falbo, T., & Peplau, L. A. (1980). Power strategies in intimate relationships. *Journal of Personality and Social Psychology, 38,* 618–628.

Farley, M. (1998, December 26). In Lugo Lake, marriage is a ticklish affair. *Los Angeles Times,* pp. A1, A5, A6.

Fausto-Sterling, A. (1985). *The myths of gender.* New York: Basic Books.

Feijoo, M. D. C. (1998). Democratic participation and women in Argentina. In J. S. Jaquette & S. L. Wolchik (Eds.), *Women and democracy: Latin America and Central and Eastern Europe* (pp. 29–46). Baltimore: Johns Hopkins University Press.

Ferguson, A. (1981). Patriarchy, sexual identity, and the sexual revolution. *Signs, 7,* 157–172.

Ferguson, A. (1990). Is there a lesbian culture? In J. Allen (Ed.), *Lesbian philosophies and cultures* (pp. 63–88). Albany: State University of New York Press.

Ferree, M. M. (1987). Equality and autonomy: Feminist politics in the U.S. and West Germany. In M. F. Katzenstein & C. M. Mueller (Eds.), *The women's movements of the U.S. and Western Europe* (pp. 172–195). Philadelphia: Temple University Press.

Filer, R. (1985). Male-female wage differences: The importance of compensating differentials. *Industrial and Labor Relations Review, 38,* 426–437.

Filer, R. (1989). Occupational segregation, compensating differentials, and comparable worth. In R. Michael, H. Hartmann, & B. O'Farrell (Eds.), *Pay equity: Empirical inquiries* (pp. 153–170). Washington, DC: National Academy.

Filkins, D. (1998, November 13). Writer risks threats, arrest on her return to Bangladesh. *Los Angeles Times*, p. A5.

Fiorenza, E. S. (1979). Women in the early Christian movement. In C. P. Christ & J. Plaskow (Eds.), *Womanspirit rising: A feminist reader in religion* (pp. 84–92). New York: Harper & Row.

Fisher, J. (1996). Sustainable development and women: The role of NGOs. In J. Turpin & L. A. Lorentzen (Eds.), *The gendered new world order: Militarism, development, and the environment* (pp. 95–112). New York: Routledge.

Fitzgerald, L. F. (1993). Sexual harassment: Violence against women in the workplace. *American Psychologist, 48,* 1070–1076.

Foek, A. (1997). Sweat-shop Barbie: Exploitation of Third World labor. *The Humanist, 57,* 9–13.

Food and Agriculture Organization. (a). *Q & A with Marie Randriamamonjy. www.fao.org/news/1997/970304-e.htm*

Food and Agriculture Organization. (b). *Research and extension: A gender perspective. www.fao.org/ focus/e/Women/Extens-e.htm*

Food and Agriculture Organization. (c). *Women and land tenure. www.fao.org/focus/e/Women/tenure-e.htm*

Food and Agriculture Organization. (d). *Women hold the key to food security. www.fao.org/focus/e/Women/Wo-Hm-e.htm*

Food and Agriculture Organization. (e). *Women: Users, preservers and managers of agro-biodiversity. www.fao.org/focus/e/Women/Biodiv-e.htm*

Food and Agriculture Organization. (f). *Women and water resources. www.fao.org/focus/e/Women/Water-e.htm*

Forbes, G. H. (1987). *Women in modern India.* New York: Cambridge University Press.

Forrester, A. (1995). From stabilization to growth with equity: A case for financing women in development programs. In F. C. Steady & R. Toure (Eds.), *Women and the United Nations* (pp. 81–88). Rochester, VT: Schenkman Books.

Forsyth, D. (1999). *Group dynamics.* Pacific Grove, CA: ITP.

Frank, T. (1991, October 20). Irish leader decries narrow definition of women's success. *Providence, Rhode Island, Bulletin,* p. E3.

Frankson, J. R. (1998, May/June). Getting our day in court. *Ms., 7,* 19.

Fraser, A. (1988). *The warrior queens: The legends and life of the women who have led their nations in war.* New York: Random House.

Fraser, A. S. (1987). *The U.N. Decade for Women: Documents and dialogue.* Boulder, CO: Westview Press.

Freedman, S. M., & Phillips, J. S. (1988). The changing nature of research on women at work. *Journal of Management, 14,* 231–251.

Freeman, M. A. (1995). The human rights of women in the family: Issues and recommendations for implementation of the women's convention. In J. Peters & A. Wolper (Eds.), *Women's rights, human rights: International feminist perspectives* (pp. 149–164). New York: Routledge.

French, M. (1992). *The war against women.* New York: Simon & Schuster.

Friedman, E. (1995). Women's human rights: The emergence of a movement. In J. Peters & A. Wolper (Eds.), *Women's rights, human rights: International feminist perspectives* (pp. 18–35). New York: Routledge.

Friedman, R. C., & Downey, J. (1995). Internalized homophobia and the negative therapeutic reaction. *Journal of the American Academy of Psychoanalysis, 23,* 99–113.

Frohmann, A., & Valdes, T. (1995). Democracy in the country and in the home: The women's movement in Chile. In A. Basu (Ed.), *The challenge of local feminisms: Women's movements in global perspective* (pp. 276–301). Boulder, CO: Westview Press.

Frymer-Kensky, T. (1994). The Bible and women's studies. In L. Davidman & S. Tenenbaum (Eds.), *Feminist perspectives on Jewish studies* (pp. 16–39). New Haven, CT: Yale University Press.

Fujieda, M. (1995). Japan's first phase of feminism. In K. Fujimura-Fanselow & A. Kameda (Eds.), *Japanese women: New feminist perspectives on the past, present, and future* (pp. 323–342). New York: Feminist Press.

Gardini, W. (1987). The feminine aspect of God in Christianity. In U. King (Ed.), *Women in the world's religions, past and present* (pp. 56–67). New York: Paragon House.

Garnier, J. (1995). Country report on lesbians in Poland. In R. Rosenbloom (Ed.), *Unspoken rules: Sexual orientation and women's human rights* (pp. 155–160). San Francisco: International Gay and Lesbian Human Rights Commission.

Gay, J. (1986). "Mummies and babies" and friends of lovers in Lesotho. In E. Blackwood (Ed.), *The many faces of homosexuality: Anthropological approaches to homosexual behavior* (pp. 97–116). New York: Harrington Park.

Gebara, I., & Bingemer, M. C. (1994). Mary—Mother of God, mother of the poor. In U. King (Ed.), *Feminist theology from the Third World* (pp. 275–282). New York: Orbis.

Geis, F. L. (1993). Self-fulfilling prophecies: A social psychological view of gender. In A. E. Beall & R. J. Sternberg (Eds.), *The psychology of gender* (pp. 9–54). New York: Guilford Press.

Gelb, J. (1989). *Feminism and politics*. Berkeley: University of California Press.

Genovese, M. A. (1993). Margaret Thatcher and the politics of conviction leadership. In M. A. Genovese (Ed.), *Women as national leaders* (pp. 211–218). Newbury Park, CA: Sage.

Ghorayshi, P. (1996). Women, paid work, and the family in the Islamic Republic of Iran. *Journal of Comparative Family Studies, 27,* 453–466.

Gimbutas, M. (1991). *The civilization of the goddess: The world of Old Europe.* San Francisco: Harper & Row.

Ginsberg, F. D., & Rapp, R. (1995). Introduction: Conceiving the new world order. In F. D. Ginsberg & R. Rapp (Eds.), *Conceiving the new world order: The global politics of reproduction* (pp. 1–18). Berkeley: University of California Press.

Glass, J., & Camarigg, V. (1992). Gender, parenthood, and job-family compatibility. *American Journal of Sociology, 98,* 131–151.

Glenn, E. N. (1992). From servitude to service work: Historical continuities in the racial division of paid reproductive labor. *Signs,* 1–43.

Glick, P. (1991). Trait-based and sex-based discrimination in occupational prestige, occupational salary, and hiring. *Sex Roles, 25,* 351–378.

Glick, P., Zion, C., & Nelson, C. (1988). What mediates sex discrimination in hiring decisions? *Journal of Personality and Social Psychology, 55,* 178–186.

Golden, K. (1998, July/August). Rana Husseini: A voice for justice. *Ms., 9,* 36–39.

Gonzalez, M. B. (1995). Country report on lesbians in Nicaragua. In R. Rosenbloom (Ed.), *Unspoken rules: Sexual orientation and women's human rights* (pp. 133–138). San Francisco: International Gay and Lesbian Human Rights Commission.

Goodwin, J. (1994). *Price of honor: Muslim women lift the veil of violence on the Islamic world.* Boston: Little Brown.

Goodwin, J. (1997, January/February). Prisoners of biology. *Utne Reader,* 66–71.

Gross, R. M. (1979). Female God language in a Jewish context. In C. P. Christ & J. Plaskow (Eds.), *Womanspirit rising: A feminist reader in religion* (pp. 167–173). San Francisco: Harper & Row.

Gross, R. M. (1993). *Buddhism after patriarchy: A feminist history, analysis, and reconstruction of Buddhism.* Albany: State University of New York Press.

Gross, R. M. (1996). *Feminism and religion: An introduction.* Boston: Beacon Press.

Gruber, J. E., Smith, M., & Kauppinen-Toropainen, K. (1996). Sexual harassment types and severity: Linking research and policy. In M. S. Stockdale (Ed.), *Sexual harassment in the workplace: Perspectives, frontiers, and response strategies* (pp. 151–173). Thousand Oaks, CA: Sage.

Gunderson, M. (1995). Comparable worth and gender discrimination: An international perspective. *WIN News, 21.*

Gupta, L. (1991). Kali the savior. In P. Cooey, W. Eakin, & J. McDaniel (Eds.), *After patriarchy: Feminist transformations of the world religions.* Maryknoll, NY: Orbis.

Gutek, B. A., Cohen, A. G., & Konrad, A. M. (1990). Predicting social-sexual behavior at work: A contact hypothesis. *Academy of Management Journal, 33,* 560–577.

Gutek, B. A., & Koss, M. P. (1993). Changed women and changed organizations: Consequences of and coping with sexual harassment. *Journal of Vocational Behavior, 42,* 28–48.

Haavio-Mannila, E. (1993). Family, work, and gender equality: A policy comparison of Scandinavia, the United States, and the former Soviet Union. *SIECUS Report, 21,* 1–5.

Hada, A. (1995). Domestic violence. In K. Fujimura-Fanselow & A. Kameda (Eds.), *Japanese women: New feminist perspectives on the past, present and future* (pp. 265–268). New York: Feminist Press.

Hadley, J. (1996). *Abortion: Between freedom and necessity.* Philadelphia: Temple University Press.

Hampson, D. (1987). Women, ordination and the Christian Church. In D. L. Eck & D. Jain (Eds.), *Speaking of faith: Global perspectives on women, religion, and social change* (pp. 138–147). Philadelphia: New Society Publishers.

Hardy, E. (1996). Long-acting contraception in Brazil and the Dominican Republic. In E. H. Moskowitz & B. Jennings (Eds.), *Coerced contraception? Moral and policy challenges of long-acting birth control* (pp. 206–216). Washington, DC: Georgetown University Press.

Harris, K. (1995). Prime Minister Margaret Thatcher: The influence of her gender on her foreign policy. In F. D'Amico & P. R. Beckman (Eds.), *Women in politics: An introduction* (pp. 60–69). Westport, CT: Bergin & Garvey.

Hartmann, B. (1987). *Reproductive rights and reproductive wrongs.* New York: Harper & Row.

Hartmann, B. (1995). *Reproductive rights and wrongs: The global politics of population control.* Boston: South End Press.

Hartmann, H. (1984). The unhappy marriage of Marxism and feminism: Towards a more progressive union. In A. Jaggar & P. Rothenberg (Eds.), *Feminist frameworks: Alternative theoretical accounts of the relations between women and men* (pp. 172–189). New York: McGraw-Hill.

Hassan, R. (1991). Muslim women and post-patriarchal Islam. In P. Cooey, W. Eakin, & J. McDaniel (Eds.), *After patriarchy: Feminist transformations of the world religions.* Maryknoll, NY: Orbis.

Heilbroner, R. (1963). *The great ascent.* New York: Harper & Row.

Heilman, M. E., Block, C. J., Martell, R. F., & Simon, M. C. (1989). Has anything changed? Current conceptions of men, women, and managers. *Journal of Applied Psychology, 74,* 935–942.

Heilman, M. E., & Martell, R. F. (1986). Exposure to successful women: Antidote to sex discrimination in applicant screening decisions? *Organizational Behavior and Human Decision Processes, 37,* 376–390.

Heise, L. L. (1995). Freedom close to home: The impact of violence against women on reproductive rights. In J. Peters & A. Wolper (Eds.), *Women's rights, human rights: International feminist perspectives* (pp. 238–255). New York: Routledge.

Helie-Lucas, M. A. (1993). Women living under Muslim laws. In J. Kerr (Ed.), *Ours by right: Women's rights as human rights* (pp. 52–64). Ottawa, Canada: North South Institute.

Herbert, B. (1995, October 9). Not a living wage. *New York Times,* p. A17.

Herbert, B. (1996, June 26). From sweatshops to aerobics. *New York Times,* p. A15.

Herbert, B. (1997, March 31). Nike's boot camps. *New York Times,* p. A15.

Hesson-McInnis, M., & Fitzgerald, L. F. (1995). *Modeling sexual harassment.* Unpublished manuscript.

Hewlett, B. S. (1992). Husband-wife reciprocity and the father-infant relationship among Aka pygmies. In B. S. Hewlett (Ed.), *Father-child relations: Cultural and biosocial contexts* (pp. 153–176). New York: Aldine de Gruyter.

Holm, J. (1994). Introduction. In *Women in religion.* New York: St. Martin's Press.

Hong, L. K. (1987). Potential effects of the one-child policy on gender equality in the People's Republic of China. *Gender & Society, 1,* 317–326.

Hong, Z. (1995). The testimony of women writers: The situation of women in China today. In J. Peters & A. Wolper (Eds.), *Women's rights, human rights: International feminist perspectives* (pp. 96–102). New York: Routledge.

Horney, K. (1967). *Feminine psychology.* New York: Norton.

Howard, J. A., Blumstein, P., & Schwartz, P. (1986). Sex, power, and influence tactics in intimate relationships. *Journal of Personality and Social Psychology, 51,* 102–109.

Howard, R. E. (1995). Women's rights and the right to development. In J. Peters & A. Wolper (Eds.), *Women's rights, human rights: International feminist perspectives* (pp. 301–316). New York: Routledge.

Hubbard, D., & Solomon, C. (1995). The many faces of feminism in Namibia. In A. Basu (Ed.), *The challenge of local feminisms: Women's movements in global perspective* (pp. 163–186). Boulder, CO: Westview Press.

Hulin, C. L., Fitzgerald, L. F., & Drasgow, F. (1996). Organizational influences on sexual harassment. In M. S. Stockdale (Ed.), *Sexual harassment in the workplace: Perspectives, frontiers, and response strategies* (pp. 127–150). Thousand Oaks, CA: Sage.

Human Rights Watch. (1995). *The Human Rights Watch global report on women's human rights.* New York: Human Rights Watch.

Human Rights Watch. (1998). *The women's rights project. www.hrw.org/hrw/worldreport/Back-04.htm*

Hyatt, S. (1992). *Putting bread on the table: The women's work of community activism.* University of Bradford, Work & Gender Research Unit.

Ilgen, D. R., & Youtz, M. A. (1986). Factors affecting the evaluation and development of minorities in organizations. *Personnel and Human Resources Management, 4,* 307–337.

Ilyas, Q. S. M. (1990). Determinants of perceived role conflict among women in Bangladesh. *Sex Roles, 22,* 237–248.

International Labour Organization. (1995). Press releases. *www.essential.org/ilo/press_releases/ilo1.html*

International Labour Organization. (1996a). Women swell ranks of working poor, says ILO. *www.ilo.org/public/english/235press/pr/96-25.htm*

International Labour Organization. (1996b). Gender issues in micro-enterprise development. *www.ilo.org/public/english/140femme/guides/enterpri.htm*

International Labour Organization. (1997). Gender issues in workers' activities. *www.ilo.org/public/english/140femme/guides/workers.htm*

International Labour Organization. (1998). Will the glass ceiling ever be broken? Women in management: It's still lonely at the top. *www.ilo.org/public/english/235press/magazine/23/glass.htm*

International Research and Training Institute for the Advancement of Women (INSTRAW). (1991). Women, water, and sanitation. In S. Sontheimer (Ed.), *Women and the environment: A reader on crisis and development in the Third World* (pp. 119–132). New York: Monthly Review Press.

International Research and Training Institute for the Advancement of Women (INSTRAW). (1995). Measuring women's unpaid work. *Women's International Network News, 21,* 7–8.

Inter-Parliamentary Union. (1999). *www.ipu.org/wmn-e/world.htm*

Isasi-Diaz, A. M. (1994). The task of Hispanic women's liberation theology—*Mujeristas:* Who we are and what we are about. In U. King (Ed.), *Feminist theology from the Third World* (pp. 88–104). Maryknoll, NY: Orbis.

Ishii-Kuntz, M. (1993). Japanese fathers: Work demands and family roles. In J. C. Hood (Ed.), *Men, work, and family* (pp. 45–67). Newbury Park, CA: Sage.

Ishino, S. & Wakabayashi, N. (1995). Country report on lesbians in Japan. In R. Rosenbloom (Ed.),

Unspoken rules: Sexual orientation and women's human rights (pp. 101–108). San Francisco: International Gay and Lesbian Human Rights Commission.

Jacobs, J. A., & Steinberg, R. (1990). Compensating differentials and the male-female wage gap: Evidence from the New York State Comparable Worth Study. *Social Forces, 69,* 439–468.

Jacobson, J. L. (1992). Women's reproductive health: The silent emergency. *New Frontiers in Education, 22,* 1–54.

Jacobson, M. B. (1981). You say potato and I say potahto: Attitudes toward feminism as a function of its subject-selected label. *Sex Roles, 7,* 349–354.

Jahan, R. (1995a). The elusive agenda: Mainstreaming women in development. In A. Leonard (Ed.), *Seeds 2* (pp. 214–218). New York: Feminist Press.

Jahan, R. (1995b). Men in seclusion, women in public: Rokeya's dream and women's struggles in Bangladesh. In A. Basu (Ed.), *The challenge of local feminisms: Women's movements in global perspective* (pp. 87–109). Boulder, CO: Westview Press.

Jain, S. (1991). Standing up for trees: Women's role in the Chipko movement. In S. Sontheimer (Ed.), *Women and the environment: A reader on crisis and development in the Third World* (pp. 163–178). New York: Monthly Review Press.

Jaising, I. (1995). Violence against women: The Indian perspective. In J. Peters & A. Wolper (Eds.), *Women's rights, human rights: International feminist perspectives* (pp. 51–56). New York: Routledge.

Jankowiak, W. (1992). Father-child relations in urban China. In B. S. Hewlett (Ed.), *Father-child relations: Cultural and biosocial contexts* (pp. 345–363). New York: Aldine de Gruyter.

Jaquette, J. S., & Wolchik, S. L. (1998). Women and democratization in Latin America and Central and Eastern Europe: A comparative introduction. In J. S. Jaquette & S. L. Wolchik (Eds.), *Women and democracy: Latin America and Central and Eastern Europe* (pp. 1–28). Baltimore: Johns Hopkins Press.

Jeffrey, D. (1996). Sweatshop update. *Ms., 6,* 38.

Jenkins, P. (1988). *Mrs. Thatcher's revolution.* Cambridge, MA: Harvard University Press.

Jenson, J. (1995). Extending the boundaries of citizenship: Women's movements of Western

Europe. In A. Basu (Ed.), *The challenge of local feminisms, Women's movements in global perspective* (pp. 405–434). Boulder, CO: Westview Press.

Johnson, P. (1976). Women and power: Toward a theory of effectiveness. *Journal of Social Issues, 32,* 99–110.

Johnson-Odim, C. (1991). Common themes, different contexts: Third World women and feminism. In C. T. Mohanty, A. Russo, & L. Torres (Eds.), *Third world women and the politics of feminism* (pp. 314–327). Bloomington: Indiana University Press.

Jones, T. (1992, July 10). Summit weighs women's role in changing world. *Los Angeles Times,* p. A6.

Kabilsingh, C. (1987). The future of the Bhikkhuni Samgha in Thailand. In D. L. Eck & D. Jain (Eds.), *Speaking of faith: Global perspectives on women, religion, and social change* (pp. 148–158). Philadelphia: New Society Publishers.

Kalin, R., & Tilby, R. (1978). Development and validation of a sex-role ideology scale. *Psychological Report, 42,* 731–738.

Kanno, N. (1991). The failure of Western family planning. In H. P. Hynes (Ed.), *Reconstructing Babylon: Essays on women and technology* (pp. 19–40). Bloomington: Indiana University Press.

Kanno, N. (1996). Lesotho and Nepal: The failure of Western "family planning." In H. P. Hynes (Ed.), *Reconstructing Babylon: Essays on women and technology* (pp. 19–40). Washington, DC: Georgetown University Press.

Kanter, R. M. (1976). The impact of hierarchical structures on the work behavior of women and men. *Social Problems, 23,* 415–430.

Katumba, R., & Akute, W. (1993). Greening takes root. In *The Power to Change* (pp. 55–58). London: Zed.

Katzenstein, M. F. (1987). Comparing the feminist movements of the United States and Western Europe: An overview. In M. F. Katzenstein & C. M. Mueller (Eds.), *The women's movements of the United States and Central Europe: Consciousness, political opportunity, and public policy* (pp. 3–22). Philadelphia: Temple University Press.

Katzenstein, M. F. (1989). Organizing against violence: Strategies of the Indian women's movement. *Pacific Affairs, 62,* 53–71.

Kaur-Singh, K. (1994). Sikhism. In J. Holm (Ed.), *Women in religion* (pp. 141–157). New York: St. Martin's Press.

Kawashima, Y. (1995). Female workers: An overview of past and current trends. In K. Fujimura-Fanselow & A. Kameda (Eds.), *Japanese women: New feminist perspectives on the past, present and future* (pp. 271–294). New York: Feminist Press.

Kehoe, A. B. (1983). The shackles of tradition. In P. Albers & B. Medicine (Eds.), *The hidden half: Studies of plains Indian women.* Washington, DC: University Press of America.

Kemp, A., Madlala, N., Moodley, A., & Salo, E. (1995). The dawn of a new day: Redefining South African feminism. In A. Basu (Ed.), *The challenge of local feminisms: Women's movements in global perspective* (pp. 131–162). Boulder, CO: Westview Press.

Kendall. (1998). "When a woman loves a woman" in Lesotho: Love, sex, and the (Western) construction of homophobia. In S. O. Murray & W. Roscoe (Eds.), *Boy-wives and female husbands: Studies of African homosexualities* (pp. 223–242). New York: St. Martin's Press.

Kenrick, D. T., Sadalla, E. K., Groth, G., & Trost, M. R. (1990). Evolution, traits, and the stages of human courtship: Qualifying the parental investment model. *Journal of Personality, 58,* 97–116.

Kerig, P. K., Alyoshina, Y. Y., & Volovich, A. S. (1993). Gender-role socialization in contemporary Russia. *Psychology of Women Quarterly, 17,* 389–408.

Kernaghan, C. (1997, April 30). A living wage to end sweatshops. *San Francisco Examiner,* p. A19.

Kerr, J. (1993). *Ours by right: Women's rights as human rights.* London: Zed.

Kilic, D., & Uncu, G. (1995). Turkey. In R. Rosenbloom (Ed.), *Unspoken rules: Sexual orientation and women's human rights* (pp. 209–214). San Francisco: International Gay and Lesbian Human Rights Commission.

King, U. (1987). Goddesses, witches, androgyny and beyond? Feminism and the transformation of religious consciousness. In U. King (Ed.), *Women in the world's religions, past and present* (pp. 201–218). New York: Paragon House.

King, U. (1994). Introduction. In U. King (Ed.), *Feminist theology from the Third World* (pp. 1–22). Maryknoll, NY: Orbis.

King, W. C., Jr., Miles, E. W., & Kniska, J. (1991). Boys will be boys (and girls will be girls): The attribution of gender role stereotypes in a gaming situation. *Sex Roles, 25,* 607–623.

Knapp, D. E., & Kustis, G. A. (1996). The real "Disclosure": Sexual harassment and the bottom line. In M. S. Stockdale (Ed.), *Sexual harassment in the workplace: Perspectives, frontiers, and response strategies* (pp. 199–216). Thousand Oaks, CA: Sage.

Koen, K., & Terry, P. (1995). South Africa. In R. Rosenbloom (Ed.), *Unspoken rules: Sexual orientation and women's human rights* (pp. 187–198). San Francisco: International Gay and Lesbian Human Rights Commission.

Kotter, L. (1995). Country report on lesbians in Estonia. In R. Rosenbloom (Ed.), *Unspoken rules: Sexual orientation and women's human rights* (pp. 53–58). San Francisco: International Gay and Lesbian Human Rights Commission.

Kumar, R. (1995). From Chipko to Sati: The contemporary Indian women's movement. In A. Basu (Ed.), *The challenge of local feminisms: Women's movements in global perspective* (pp. 58–86). Boulder, CO: Westview Press.

Kusha, H. R. (1995). Minority status of women in Islam: A debate between traditional and modern Islam. *Journal of the Institute of Muslim Minority Affairs, 11,* 58–72.

Kuzmanovic, J. (1995). Legacies of invisibility: Past silence, present violence against women in the former Yugoslavia. In J. Peters & A. Wolper (Eds.), *Women's rights, human rights: International feminist perspectives* (pp. 57–61). New York: Routledge.

LaBotz, D. (1993, May). Manufacturing poverty: The maquiladorization of Mexico. *Multinational Monitor,* 18–23.

LaFromboise, T. D., Heyle, A. M., & Ozer, E. J. (1990). Changing and diverse roles of women in American Indian cultures. *Sex Roles, 22,* 455–486.

Lakeman, E. (1994). Comparing political opportunities in Great Britain and Ireland. In W. Rule & J. F. Zimmerman (Eds.), *Electoral systems in comparative perspective: Their impact on women and minorities* (pp. 45–54). Westport, CT: Greenwood Press.

Lamas, M., Martinez, A., Tarres, M. L., Tunon, E. (1995). Building bridges: The growth of popular feminism in Mexico. In A. Basu (Ed.). *The challenge of local feminisms: Women's movements in global perspective* (pp. 324–347). Boulder, CO: Westview Press.

Lamb, M. E. (1981). Fathers and child development: An integrative overview. In M. E. Lamb (Ed.), *The role of the father in child development* (pp. 1–70). New York: Wiley.

Lang, P. (1998, May/June). Update: Still a woman's burden? *Ms., 7,* 21.

Larwood, L., Szwajkowski, E., & Rose, S. (1988). Sex and race discrimination resulting from manager-client relationships: Applying the rational bias theory of managerial discrimination. *Sex Roles, 18,* 9–29.

Lauter, D. (1995). EMILY's List: Overcoming barriers to political participation. In A. Brill (Ed.), *A rising public voice: Women in politics worldwide* (pp. 217–228). New York: Feminist Press.

Lazarowitz, E. (1997, February 22). Panel prepares to ok use of pill after thirty-year ban. *Los Angeles Times.*

Lazarowitz, E. (1997, January 8). A woman's place now is in the sumo ring. *Los Angeles Times,* pp. A1, A10.

Leacock, E. B. (1981). Women in an egalitarian society: The Montagnais-Naskapi of Canada. In *Myths of male dominance* (pp. 33–81). New York: Monthly Review Press.

Lebra, T. S. (1984). *Japanese women: Constraint and fulfillment.* Honolulu: University of Hawaii.

Lerner, G. (1986). *The creation of patriarchy* (Vol. 1). New York: Oxford.

Leslie, L. A., Anderson, E. A., & Branson, M. P. (1991). Responsibility for children: The role of gender and employment. *Journal of Family Issues, 12,* 197–210.

Lim, L. Y. C. (1990). Women's work in export factories: The politics of a cause. In I. Tinker (Ed.), *Persistent inequalities* (pp. 101–149). Oxford: Oxford University Press.

Lindau, R. (1993, June). A sexualized image of lesbians in Sweden. *Off Our Backs,* 10, 20.

Ling, Y., & Matsumo, A. (1992). Women's struggle for empowerment in Japan. In J. Bystydzienski (Ed.), *Women transforming politics: Worldwide strategies for empowerment* (pp. 51–66). Bloomington: Indiana University Press.

Lips, H. M. (1991). *Women, men, and power.* Mountain View, CA: Mayfield.

Lister, R. (1997). *Citizenship: Feminist perspectives.* New York: New York University Press.

Livingston, J. A. (1982). Responses to sexual harassment on the job: Legal, organizational, and individual actions. *Journal of Social Issues, 38,* 5–22.

Lorentzen, L. A., & Turpin, J. (1996). Introduction: The gendered new world order. In J. Turpin & L. A. Lorentzen (Eds.), *The gendered new world order* (pp. 11–12). New York: Routledge.

Low, B. S. (1989). Cross-cultural patterns in the training of children: An evolutionary perspective. *Journal of Comparative Psychology, 103,* 311–319.

MacKinnon, C. A. (1989). *Toward a feminist theory of the state.* Cambridge, MA: Harvard University Press.

Macklin, R. (1996). Cultural difference and long-acting contraception. In E. H. Moskowitz & B. Jennings (Eds.), *Coerced contraception? Moral and policy challenges of long-acting birth control* (pp. 173–190). Washington, DC: Georgetown University Press.

Mak, A., Hui, K., Poone, J., & King, M. A. (1995). Country report on lesbians in Argentina. In R. Rosenbloom (Ed.), *Unspoken rules: Sexual orientation and women's human rights* (pp. 67–76). San Francisco: International Gay and Lesbian Human Rights Commission.

Margolis, D. R. (1993). Women's movements around the world: Cross-cultural comparisons. *Gender and Society, 7,* 379–399.

Marin, M. S. (1995). Country report on lesbians in Argentina. In R. Rosenbloom (Ed.), *Unspoken rules: Sexual orientation and women's human rights* (pp. 145–154). San Francisco: International Gay and Lesbian Human Rights Commission.

Martinez, A. (1995). Country report on lesbians in Uruguay. In R. Rosenbloom (Ed.), *Unspoken rules: Sexual orientation and women's human rights* (pp. 229–236). San Francisco: International Gay and Lesbian Human Rights Commission.

Martinho, M. (1995). Country report on lesbians in Brazil. In R. Rosenbloom (Ed.), *Unspoken rules: Sexual orientation and women's human rights* (pp. 15–24). San Francisco: International Gay and Lesbian Human Rights Commission.

Martinho, M. J., & Gardner, J. (1983). A methodological review of sex-related access discrimination problems. *Sex Roles, 9,* 825–839.

Massengill, D., & DiMarco, N. (1979). Sex-role stereotypes and requisite management characteristics: A current replication. *Sex Roles, 5,* 561–569.

Matynia, E. (1995). Finding a voice: Women in postcommunist Central Europe. In A. Basu (Ed.), *The challenge of local feminisms: Women's movements in global perspective* (pp. 374–404). Boulder, CO: Westview Press.

Mayer, A. M. (1995a). Cultural particularism as a bar to women's rights: Reflections on the Middle Eastern experience. In J. Peters & A. Wolper (Eds.), *Women's rights, human rights: International feminist perspectives* (pp. 176–188). New York: Routledge.

Mayer, A. M. (1995b). *Islam and human rights: Tradition and politics* (2nd ed.). Boulder, CO: Westview Press.

Mbon, F. M. (1987). Women in African traditional religions. In U. King (Ed.), *Women in the world's religions, past and present* (pp. 7–23). New York: Paragon House.

Mead, M. (1935). *Sex and temperament in three primitive societies.* London: Morrow.

Meir, G. (1975). *My life.* New York: Putnam.

Menon, S. A., & Kanekar, S. (1992). Attitudes toward sexual harassment of women in India. *Journal of Applied Social Psychology, 22,* 1940–1952.

Merchant, C. (1992). *Radical ecology: The search for a livable world.* New York: Routledge.

Mermel, A., & Simons, J. (1991). *Women and world development: An education and action guide.* Washington, DC: OEF International.

Mernissi, F. (1987). *The veil and the male elite: A feminist interpretation of women's rights in Islam.* Reading, MA: Addison-Wesley.

Mertus, J. (1995). State discriminatory family law and customary abuses. In J. Peters & A. Wolper (Eds.), *Women's rights, human rights: International feminist perspectives* (pp. 135–148). New York: Routledge.

Mikell, G. (1997). Introduction. In G. Mikell (Ed.), *African feminism: The politics of survival in sub-Saharan Africa* (pp. 1–52). Philadelphia: University of Pennsylvania Press.

Minter, S. (1995). Country report on lesbians in the United States. In R. Rosenbloom (Ed.), *Unspoken rules: Sexual orientation and women's human rights* (pp. 215–228). San Francisco: International Gay and Lesbian Human Rights Commission.

Mirhosseini, A. (1995). After the revolution: Violations of women's human rights in Iran. In J. Peters & A. Wolper (Eds.), *Women's rights, human*

rights: International feminist perspectives
(pp. 72–77). New York: Routledge.

Moghadam, V. M. (1991). Islamist movements and
women's responses in the Middle East. *Gender &
History, 3,* 268–284.

Mohanty, C. (1991). *Third World women and feminism.*
Bloomington: Indiana University Press.

Molinelli, N. G. (1994). Argentina: The (no) ceteris
paribus case. In W. Rule & J. F. Zimmerman
(Eds.), *Electoral systems in comparative perspective:
Their impact on women and minorities* (pp. 197–
202). Westport, CT: Greenwood Press.

Molyneaux, M. (1985). Mobilization with
emancipation? Women's interests, the state, and
revolution in Nicaragua. *Feminist Studies, 11,*
227–255.

Molyneaux, M. (1996). Women's rights and
international context in the post-communist
states. In M. Threlfall (Ed.), *Mapping the women's
movement: Feminist politics and social transformation
in the North* (pp. 217–232). London: Verso & New
Left Review.

Morgan, R. (1984). *Sisterhood is global* (1st ed.). New
York: Feminist Press.

Morgan, R. (Ed.). (1996). *Sisterhood is global.* New
York: Feminist Press.

Morrison, A. M., & Von Glinow, M. A. (1990).
Women and minorities in management.
American Psychologist, 45, 200–208.

Morrison, A. M., White, R. P., & Van Velsor, E. (1987).
*Breaking the glass ceiling: Can women reach the top of
America's largest corporations?* New York: Addison
Wesley.

Moser, C. (1989). Gender planning in the Third
World: Meeting practical and strategical gender
needs. *World Development, 17,*
1799–1825.

Moser, C. (1995). From Nairobi to Beijing: The
transition from women in development to
gender and development. In A. Leonard (Ed.),
Seeds 2 (pp. 209–213). New York: Feminist Press.

Mosse, J. C. (1993). *Half the world, half a chance: An
introduction to gender and development.* Oxford:
Oxfam.

Munroe, R. L., & Munroe, R. H. (1975). *Cross-cultural
human development.* Monterey, CA: Brooks Cole.

Munroe, R. L., & Munroe, R. H. (1992). Fathers in
children's environments: A four culture study. In
B. S. Hewlett (Ed.), *Father-child relations: Cultural
and biosocial contexts* (pp. 213–230). New York:
Aldine de Gruyter.

Murray, B. (1998). Psychology's voice in sexual
harassment law. *American Psychological Association
Monitor, 29,* 50–51.

Murrell, A. J. (1996). Sexual harassment and women
of color: Issues, challenges, and future
directions. In M. S. Stockdale (Ed.), *Sexual
harassment in the workplace: Perspectives, frontiers,
and response strategies* (pp. 51–66). Thousand
Oaks, CA: Sage.

Myers, D. G. (1998). *Social psychology* (3rd ed.). New
York: McGraw-Hill.

Narayan, U. (1993). Paying the price of change:
Women, modernization, and arranged marriages
in India. In M. Turshen & B. Holcomb (Eds.),
*Women's lives and public policy: The international
experience* (pp. 159–170). Westport, CT:
Greenwood Press.

Nauman, A. K., & Hutchison, M. (1997). The
integration of women into the Mexican labor
force since NAFTA. *American Behavioral Scientist,
40,* 950–956.

Neft, N., & Levine, A. D. (1998). *Where women stand:
An international report on the status of women in
140 countries 1997–1998.* New York: Random
House.

Nelson, D. L., Quick, J. C., Hitt, M. A., & Moesel, D.
(1990). Politics, lack of career progress, and
work/home conflict: Stress and strain for
working women. *Sex Roles, 23,* 169–184.

Niarchos, C. N. (1995). Women, war, and rape:
Challenges facing the international tribunal for
the former Yugoslavia. *Human Rights Quarterly,
17,* 649–690.

Niebur, G. (1996, Nov./Dec.). The lay of the holy
land. *Working woman.*

Nikolic-Ristanovic, V. (1996). War and violence
against women. In J. Turpin & L. A. Lorentzen
(Eds.), *The gendered new world order: Militarism,
development and the environment* (pp. 195–210).
New York: Routledge.

Nkomo, S. M., & Cox, T., Jr. (1989). Gender
differences in the upward mobility of black
managers: Double whammy or double
advantage? *Sex Roles, 21,*
825–839.

Noe, R. A. (1988). Women and mentoring: A review
and research agenda. *Academy of Management
Review, 13,* 65–78.

Norris, P., & Lovenduski, J. (1995). *Political recruitment,
gender, race, and class in the British Parliament.*
Cambridge: Cambridge University Press.

Nsamenang, B. A. (1992). Perceptions of parenting among the Nso of Cameroon. In B. S. Hewlett (Ed.), *Father-child relations: Cultural and biosocial contexts* (pp. 321–344). New York: Aldine de Gruyter.

Nur, R. (1995). Country report on lesbians in Malaysia. In R. Rosenbloom (Ed.), *Unspoken rules: Sexual orientation and women's human rights* (pp. 111–116). San Francisco: International Gay and Lesbian Human Rights Commission.

Nussbaum, M. (1992). Human functioning and social justice: In defense of Aristotelian essentialism. *Political Theory, 20,* 202–246.

Oduol, W., & Kabira, W. M. (1995). In A. Basu (Ed.), *The challenge of local feminisms: Women's movements in global perspective* (pp. 187–208). Boulder, CO: Westview Press.

Olsen, C. (Ed.). (1983). *The book of the goddess: Past and present.* New York: Crossroad.

Olson, J. E., & Frieze, I. H. (1987). Income determinants for women in business. In A. H. Stromberg, L. Larwood, & B. A. Gutek (Eds.), *Women and work: An annual review* (Vol. 2, pp. 173–206). Newbury Park, CA: Sage.

Opfell, O. S. (1993). *Women prime ministers and presidents.* Jefferson, NC: McFarland.

Orth, M. (1992, July). Proud Mary. *Vanity Fair,* 121–132.

Pablos, E. T. (1992). Women's struggles for empowerment in Mexico: Accomplishments, problems, and challenges. In J. Bystydzienski (Ed.), *Women transforming politics: Worldwide strategies for empowerment* (pp. 95–107). Bloomington: Indiana University Press.

Pagelow, M. D. (1992). Adult victims of domestic violence. *Journal of Interpersonal Violence, 7,* 87–120.

Pagels, E. H. (1976). What became of God the Mother? Conflicting images of God in early Christianity. In C. P. Christ & J. Plaskow (Eds.), *Womanspirit rising: A feminist reader in religion* (pp. 105–119). San Francisco: Harper & Row.

Palmer, A. (1995). Country report on lesbians in Britain. In R. Rosenbloom (Ed.), *Unspoken rules: Sexual orientation and women's human rights* (pp. 25–34). San Francisco: International Gay and Lesbian Human Rights Commission.

Papanek, H. (1990). To each less than she needs, from each more than she can do: Allocations, entitlements, and value. In I. Tinker (Ed.), *Persistent inequalities* (pp. 162–184). Oxford: Oxford University Press

Parvey, C. F. (1974). The theology and leadership of women in the New Testament. In R. R. Reuther (Ed.), *Religion and sexism: Images of woman in the Jewish and Christian traditions* (pp. 17–149). New York: Simon & Schuster.

Patterson, C. J., & Redding R. E. (1996). Lesbian and gay families with children: Implications of social science research for policy. *Journal of Social Issues, 52,* 29–50.

Paul, D. Y. (1979). *Women in Buddhism: Images of the feminine in Mahayana tradition.* Berkeley: Asian Humanities Press.

Pearce, T. O. (1996). Ethical issues in the importation of long-acting contraceptives to Nigeria. In E. H. Moskowitz & B. Jennings (Eds.), *Coerced contraception? Moral and policy challenges of long-acting birth control* (pp. 192–205). Washington, DC: Georgetown University Press.

Penelope, J. (1990). Introduction. RU12? In J. Penelope & S. Valentine (Eds.), *Finding the lesbians: Personal accounts from around the world.* Freedom, CA: Crossing Press.

Perez, G. C., & Jimenez, P. (1995). Country report on lesbians in Mexico. In R. Rosenbloom (Ed.), *Unspoken rules: Sexual orientation and women's human rights* (pp. 117–126). San Francisco: International Gay and Lesbian Human Rights Commission.

Petchesky, R. P. (1984), *Abortion and women's choice.* New York: Longman.

Peters, J., & Wolper, A. (1995). Introduction. In J. Peters & A. Wolper (Eds.), *Women's rights, human rights: International feminist perspectives* (pp. 1–8). New York: Routledge.

Peterson, V. S., & Runyan, A. S. (1993). *Global gender issues.* Boulder, CO: Westview Press.

Pharr, S. (1988). Homophobia: A weapon of sexism. In S. Ruth (Ed.), *Issues in feminism* (3rd ed., pp. 253–263). Mountain View, CA: Mayfield.

Plaskow, J. (1991). *Standing again at Sinai.* San Francisco: HarperCollins.

Plata, M. I. (1994). Reproductive rights as human rights: The Colombian case. In R. J. Cook (Ed.), *Human rights of women: National and international perspectives* (pp. 515–531). Philadelphia: University of Pennsylvania Press.

Pleck, J. H. (1985). *Working wives/Working husbands.* Beverly Hills: Sage.

Powell, G. N., & Butterfield, D. A. (1984). If "good managers" are masculine, what are "bad managers"? *Sex Roles, 10,* 477–484.

Powell, G. N., & Mainiero, L. A. (1992). Cross-currents in the river of time: Conceptualizing the complexities of women's careers. *Journal of Management, 18,* 215–237.

Prusak, B. P. (1974). Woman: Seductive siren and source of sin? In R. R. Reuther (Ed.), *Religion and sexism: Images of woman in the Jewish and Christian traditions* (pp. 89–116). New York: Simon & Schuster.

Pryor, J. B., Giedd, J. L., & Williams, K. B. (1995). A social psychological model for predicting sexual harassment. *Journal of Social Issues, 51,* 69–84.

Pyne, H. H. (1995). AIDS and gender violence: The enslavement of Burmese women in the Thai sex industry. In J. Peters & A. Wolper (Eds.), *Women's rights, human rights: International feminist perspectives* (pp. 215–223). New York: Routledge.

Rachels, J. (1993). *The elements of moral philosophy* (2nd ed.). New York: McGraw-Hill.

Ragins, B. R., & Sundstrom, E. (1989). Gender and power in organizations: A longitudinal perspective. *Psychological Bulletin, 105,* 51–88.

Rajesh, N. (1997, July/August). Working to death in Thailand. *Multinational Monitor,* 7–8.

Ramalingaswami, V., Jonsson, U., & Rohde, R. (1996). Commentary: The Asian Enigma. In *The Progress of Nations 1996,* UNICEF.

Rao, A. (1995). The politics of gender and culture in international human rights discourse. In J. Peters & A. Wolper (Eds.), *Women's rights, human rights: International feminist perspectives* (pp. 167–175). New York: Routledge.

Ray, R. (1999). *Fields of protest: Women's movements in India.* Minneapolis: University of Minnesota Press.

Reanda, L. (1992). The commission on the status of women. In P. Alston (Ed.), *The United Nations and human rights: A critical appraisal.* Oxford: Oxford University Press.

Renzetti, C. M., & Curran, D. J. (1995). *Women, men, and society* (3rd ed.). Boston: Allyn & Bacon.

Reske, H. J. (1995, July). Lesbianism at center of custody dispute. *American Bar Association Journal, 28.*

Reuther, R. (1985). *Womanguides: Readings toward a feminist theology,* Boston: Beacon Press.

Reuther, R. R. (1974). *Religion and sexism: Images of woman in the Jewish and Christian traditions.* New York: Simon & Schuster.

Rich, A. (1976). *Of woman born: Motherhood as experience and institution.* New York: Norton.

Rich, A. (1980). Compulsory heterosexuality and lesbian existence. *Signs, 5,* 631–660.

Robinson, S. P. (1985). Hindu paradigms of women: Images and values. In Y. Y. Haddad & E. B. Findly (Eds.), *Women, religion, and social change* (pp. 181–215). Albany: State University of New York Press.

Rodin, J., & Ickovics, J. R. (1990). Women's health: Review and research agenda as we approach the 21st century. *American Psychologist, 45,* 1018–1034.

Rogers, B. (1980). *The domestication of women: Discrimination in developing societies.* New York: St. Martin's Press.

Rogers, S. C. (1985). Gender in Southwestern France: The myth of male dominance revisited. *Anthropology, 9,* 65–86.

Rogers, S. G. (1982). Efforts towards women's development in Tanzania: Gender rhetoric vs. gender realities. *Women in Politics, 2,* 23–41.

Rogoff, B. (1981). The relation of age and sex to experiences during childhood in a highland community. *Anthropology UCLA, 11,* 25–41.

Rondon, E. (1995). Country report on lesbians in Colombia. In R. Rosenbloom (Ed.), *Unspoken rules: Sexual orientation and women's human rights,* pp. 49–52. San Francisco: International Gay and Lesbian Human Rights Commission.

Roopnarine, J. L., & Ahmeduzzaman, M. (1993). Puerto Rican fathers' involvement with their preschool-aged children. *Hispanic Journal of Behavioral Sciences, 15,* 96–107.

Rosaldo, M. Z. (1974). Women, culture, and society: A theoretical overview. In M. Z. Rosaldo & L. Lamphere (Eds.), *Women, culture, and society,* (pp. 17–42). Stanford, CA: Stanford University Press.

Rosaldo, M. Z., & Lamphere, L. (1974). *Women, culture, and society.* Stanford, CA: Stanford University Press.

Rosenbloom, R. (1995). Introduction. In R. Rosenbloom (Ed.), *Unspoken rules: Sexual orientation and women's human rights* (pp. ix–xxvii). San Francisco: International Gay and Lesbian Human Rights Commission.

Rosenthal, R., & Rubin, D. B. (1982). Further meta-analytic procedures for assessing cognitive gender differences. *Journal of Educational Psychology, 74,* 706–712.

Rourke, M. (1997, October 22). It must be what birth is like. *Los Angeles Times,* pp. E1, E6.

Rowbotham, S. (1996). Introduction: Mapping the women's movement. In M. Threlfall (Ed.), *Mapping the women's movement: Feminist politics and social transformation in the North* (pp. 1–16). London: Verso & New Left Review.

Ruan, F. F., & Bullough, V. (1992). Lesbianism in China. *Archives of Sexual Behavior, 21,* 217–228.

Rule, W. (1994). Parliaments of, by, and for the people: Except for women? In W. Rule & J. F. Zimmerman (Eds.), *Electoral systems in comparative perspective: Their impact on women and minorities* (pp. 15–30). Westport, CT: Greenwood Press.

Russell, G., & Radin, N. (1983). Increased paternal participation: The father's perspective. In M. E. Lamb & A. Sagi (Eds.), *Fatherhood and family policy* (pp. 139–166). Hillsdale, NJ: Erlbaum.

Ruth, S. (1995). *Issues in feminism* (3rd ed.). Mountain View, CA: Mayfield.

Sachs, C. E. (1997). Introduction: Connecting women and the environment. In C. E. Sachs (Ed.), *Women working in the environment* (pp. 1–10). Washington, DC: Taylor & Francis.

Sacks, K. (1982). The case against universal subordination. In *Sisters and wives: The past and future of sexual equality.* Urbana: University of Illinois Press.

Saint-Germain, M. (1993). Women in power in Nicaragua: Myth & reality. In M. A. Genovese (Ed.), *Women as national leaders* (pp. 70–102). Newbury Park, CA: Sage.

Saint-Germain, M. A. (1989). Does their difference make a difference? The impact of women on public policy in the Arizona legislature. *Social Science Quarterly, 70,* 956–967.

Salinas, G. A. (1994). Women and politics: Gender relations in Bolivian political organizations and labor unions. In B. J. Nelson & N. Chowdhury (Eds.), *Women and politics worldwide* (pp. 114–126). New Haven, CT: Yale University Press.

Sanday, P. R. (1974). Female status in the public domain. In M. Z. Rosaldo & L. Lamphere (Eds.), *Women, culture, and society* (pp. 189–206). Stanford, CA: Stanford University Press.

Sanday, P. R. (1981). *Female power and male dominance: On the origins of sexual inequality.* Cambridge: Cambridge University Press.

Santiago, L. Q. (1995). Rebirthing *Babaye:* The women's movement in the Philippines. In A. Basu (Ed.), *The challenge of local feminisms: Women's movements in global perspective* (pp. 110–130). Boulder, CO: Westview Press.

Sarda, A. (1995). Country report on lesbians in Argentina. In R. Rosenbloom (Ed.), *Unspoken rules: Sexual orientation and women's human rights* (pp. 1–8). San Francisco: International Gay and Lesbian Human Rights Commission.

Sawer, M. (1994). Locked out or locked in? Women and politics in Australia. In B. J. Nelson & N. Chowdhury (Eds.), *Women and politics worldwide* (pp. 73–91). New Haven, CT: Yale University Press.

Schein, V. E. (1973). The relationship between sex role stereotypes and requisite management characteristics. *Journal of Applied Psychology, 57,* 95–100.

Schein, V. E. (1975). The relationship between sex role stereotypes and requisite management characteristics among female managers. *Journal of Applied Psychology, 60,* 340–344.

Schein, V. E., & Mueller, R. (1992). Sex role stereotyping and requisite management characteristics: A cross-cultural look. *Journal of Organizational Behavior, 13,* 439–447.

Schein, V. E., Mueller, R., & Jacobson, C. (1989). The relationship between sex role stereotypes and requisite management characteristics among college students. *Sex Roles, 20,* 103–111.

Schneider, K. T., Swann, S., & Fitzgerald, L. F. (1997). Job-related and psychological effects of sexual harassment in the workplace: Empirical evidence from two organizations. *Journal of Applied Psychology, 82,* 401–415.

Schoepf, B. G. (1997). AIDS, gender, and sexuality during Africa's economic crisis. In G. Mikell (Ed.), *African feminism: The politics of survival in sub-Saharan Africa* (pp. 310–332). Philadelphia: University of Pennsylvania Press.

Schulman, G. B. (1974). View from the back of the synagogue. In A. L. Hageman (Ed.), *Sexist religion and women in the church* (pp. 143–166). New York: Association Press.

Seager, J. (1993). *Earth follies.* New York: Routledge.

Seager, J. (1997). *The state of women in the world atlas.* London: Penguin.

Sen, G., & Grown, C. (1987). *Development crises and alternative visions.* New York: Monthly Review Press.

Sered, S. S. (1994). *Priestess, mother, sacred sister.* Oxford: Oxford University Press.

Shalev, C. (1995). Women in Israel: Fighting tradition. In J. Peters & A. Wolper (Eds.), *Women's rights, human rights: International feminist perspectives* (pp. 89–95). New York: Routledge.

Sherif, C. W. (1982). Needed concepts in the study of gender identity. *Psychology of Women Quarterly, 6,* 375–395.

Sherif, M., & Sherif, C. (1964). *Reference groups.* New York: Harper & Row.

Shiva, V. (1988). Interview. In I. Dankelman & J. Davidson, *Women and environment in the Third World: Alliance for the future* (pp. 117–119). London: Earthscan.

Shiva, V. (1989). *Staying alive: Women, ecology and development.* London: Zed.

Shiva, V. (1994). *Closer to home: Women reconnect ecology, health and development worldwide.* Philadelphia: New Society Publishers.

Shiva, V. (1996). Let us survive: Women, ecology, and development. In R. R. Reuther (Ed.), *Women healing earth: Third World women on ecology, feminism, and religion* (pp. 65–73). New York: Orbis.

Simmons, A. M. (1998, December 29). Abortion deaths in Nigeria attributed to archaic methods. *Los Angeles Times,* p. A4.

Simons, M. (1996, June 28). U.N. court for the first time, defines rape as war crime. *New York Times,* pp. A1, A10.

Singapore Asian Christian Women's Conference. (1994). Summary statement on feminist Mariology. In U. King (Ed.), *Feminist theology from the Third World* (pp. 275–282). Maryknoll, NY: Orbis.

Slocum, S. (1975). Woman the gatherer: Male bias in anthropology. In R. R. Reiter (Ed.), *Toward an anthropology of women* (pp. 36–50). New York: Monthly Review Press.

Smith, J. I. (1987). Islam. In A. Sharma (Ed.), *Women in world religions* (pp. 235–250). Albany: State University of New York Press.

Snow, R. C. (1994). Each to her own: Investigating women's response to contraception. In G. Sen & R. C. Snow (Eds.), *Power and decision: The social control of reproduction* (pp. 233–254). Cambridge, MA: Harvard University Press.

Soares, V., Alcantara Costa, A. A., Buarque, C. M., Dora, D. D., & Sant'Anna, W. (1995). Brazilian feminism and women's movements: A two-way street. In A. Basu (Ed.), *The challenge of local feminisms: Women's movements in global perspective* (pp. 302–323). Boulder, CO: Westview Press.

Sontheimer, S. (1991). *Women and the environment: A reader on crisis and development in the Third World.* New York: Monthly Review Press.

Stacey, J. (1983). *Patriarchy and social revolution in China.* Berkeley: University of California Press.

Stamatopoulou, E. (1995). Women's rights and the United Nations. In J. Peters & A. Wolper (Eds.), *Women's rights, human rights: International feminist perspectives* (pp. 36–50). New York: Routledge.

Starhawk. (1979). Witchcraft and women's culture. In C. P. Christ & J. Plaskow (Eds.), *Womanspirit rising: A feminist reader in religion* (pp. 259–268). New York: Harper & Row.

Stark, C. (1996, October 22). One woman's life in a sweatshop. *Bangor Daily News.*

Stark, R. (1995). Reconstructing the rise of Christianity: The role of women. *Sociology of Religion, 56,* 229–244.

Staudt, K. (1995). Planting *Seeds 2* in the classroom. In A. Leonard (Ed.), *Seeds 2* (pp. 229–236). New York: Feminist Press.

Steady, F. C. (1995). Women and the environment in developing countries: The challenge of implementing Agenda 21. In F. C. Steady & R. Toure (Eds.), *Women and the United Nations* (pp. 89–108). Rochester, VT: Schenkman Books.

Steinberg, R. (1988). Women, the state, and equal employment. In J. Jenson, E. Hagen, & C. Ruddy (Eds.), *Feminization of the labor force: Paradoxes and promises* (pp. 189–213). New York: Oxford University Press.

Stetson, D. M., & Mazur, A. G. (1995). Introduction. In D. M. Stetson & A. G. Mazur (Eds.), *Comparative state feminism* (pp. 1–21). Newbury Park, CA: Sage.

Stevens, G. E. (1984). Women in business: The view of future male and female managers. *Journal of Business Education, 59,* 314–317.

Stevens, P. E., & Hall, J. M. (1991). A critical historical analysis of the medical construction of lesbianism. *International Journal of Health Services, 21,* 291–307.

Stienstra, D. (1994). *Women's movements and international organizations.* New York: St. Martin's Press.

Stockard, J., & Johnson, M. (1979). The social origins of male dominance. *Sex Roles, 5,* 199–218.

Strange, C. (1990). Mothers on the march: Maternalism in women's protest for peace in North America and Western Europe, 1900–1985. In G. West & R. L. Blumberg (Eds.), *Women and social protest* (pp. 209–224). Oxford: Oxford University Press.

Stroh, L. K., Brett, J. M., & Reilly, A. (1992). All the right stuff: A comparison of female and male managers' career progression. *Journal of Applied Psychology, 77,* 251–260.

Sturgeon, N. (1997). *Ecofeminist natures: Race, gender, feminist theory, and political action.* New York: Routledge.

Sugirtharajah, S. (1994). Hinduism. In J. Holm (Ed.), *Women in religion* (pp. 59–83). New York: St. Martin's Press.

Sugisaki, K. (1986). From the moon to the sun: Women's liberation in Japan. In L. B. Iglitzin & R. Ross (Eds.), *Women in the world: 1975–1985, the women's decade.* Santa Barbara, CA: ABC-Clio.

Sullivan, D. (1995). The public/private distinction in international human rights law. In J. Peters & A. Wolper (Eds.), *Women's rights, human rights: International feminist perspectives* (pp. 126–134). New York: Routledge.

Tanaka, K. (1995). Work, education, and the family. In K. Fujimura-Fanselow & A. Kameda (Eds.), *Japanese women: New feminist perspectives on the past, present and future* (pp. 295–308). New York: Feminist Press.

Tarawan, K. (1995). Country report on lesbians in Thailand. In R. Rosenbloom (Ed.), *Unspoken rules: Sexual orientation and women's human rights* (pp. 203–208). San Francisco: International Gay and Lesbian Human Rights Commission.

Tavris, C., & Wade, C. (1984). *The longest war: Sex differences in perspective.* New York: Harcourt Brace Jovanovich.

Taylor, V., & Rupp, L. J. (1993, Autumn). Women's culture and lesbian feminist activism: A reconsideration of cultural feminism. *Signs,* 32–61.

Thomas, K. (1998, March/April). FGM watch. *Ms., 8,* 28.

Thomas, S. (1994). *How women legislate.* New York: Oxford University Press.

Thompson, S. (1993). Golda Meir: A very public life. In M. A. Genovese (Ed.), *Women as national leaders* (pp. 135–160). Newbury Park, CA: Sage.

Threlfall, M. (1996). Feminist politics and social change in Spain. In M. Threlfall (Ed.), *Mapping the women's movement: Feminist politics and social transformation in the North* (pp. 1–16). London: Verso & New Left Review.

Thurman, J. E., & Trah, G. (1990). Part-time work in international perspective. *International Labour Review, 129,* 23–40.

Tinker, I. (1990). A context for the field and for the book. In I. Tinker (Ed.), *Persistent inequalities: Women and world development* (pp. 3–13). Oxford: Oxford University Press.

Tinker, I. (1994). Women and community forestry in Nepal: Expectations and realities. *Society and Natural Resources, 7,* 367–381.

Tinker, I. (1995). The human economy of microentrepreneurs. In L. Divard & J. Havet (Eds.), *Women in micro-and-small-scale enterprise development* (pp. 25–40). Boulder, CO: Westview Press.

Todosijevic, J. (1995). Country report on lesbians in Serbia. In R. Rosenbloom (Ed.), *Unspoken rules: Sexual orientation and women's human rights* (pp. 177–186). San Francisco: International Gay and Lesbian Human Rights Commission.

Tomasevski, K. (1993). *Women and human rights.* London: Zed.

Toro, M. S. (1995). Popularizing women's human rights at the local level: A grassroots methodology for setting the international agenda. In J. Peters & A. Wolper (Eds.), *Women's rights, human rights: International feminist perspectives* (pp. 189–196). New York: Routledge.

Triandis, H. C. (1994). *Culture and social behavior.* New York: McGraw-Hill.

Trible, P. (1973). Eve and Adam: Genesis 2–3 reread. In C. P. Christ & J. Plaskow (Eds.), *Womanspirit rising: A feminist reader in religion* (pp. 74–83). New York: Harper & Row.

Trujillo, C. (1991). Chicana lesbians: Fear and loathing in the Chicano community. In A. Kesselman, L. D. McNair, & N. Schniedewind (Eds.), *Women images and realities: A multicultural anthology* (pp. 255–260). Mountain View, CA: Mayfield.

Tulananda, O., Young, D. M., & Roopnarine, J. L. (1994). Thai and American fathers' involvement with preschool-aged children. *Early Child Development and Care, 97,* 123–133.

Uchino, K. (1987). The status elevation process of Soto sect nuns in modern Japan. In D. L. Eck & D. Jain (Eds.), *Speaking of faith: Global perspectives*

on women, religion, and social change
(pp. 159–174). Philadelphia: New Society
Publishers.

UNIFEM. (1998). *gopher://gopher.undp.org:70/
00/unifem/polieco/poli/whr/cedaw/
cadaswkit/wctp*

United Nations. (1985). *The state of the world's women.*
Oxford: New Internationalist Publications.

United Nations. (1988). *Compendium of international
conventions concerning the status of women.*
New York: Author.

United Nations. (1989). *Violence against women in the
family.* New York: Author.

United Nations. (1991a). *Report of the working group on
contemporary forms of slavery on its sixteenth session,*
UN Doc. E/CN.4/Sub.2/1991/41 of August,
1991, paras. 1 and 3.

United Nations. (1991b). *The world's women: Trends
and statistics, 1970–1990.* New York: Author.

United Nations. (1993). *Abortion politics: A global
review, Volume II.* New York: Author.

United Nations. (1994, August). Equal pay, urban
women problems discussed by commission. *UN
Chronicle,* 60–61.

United Nations. (1996). *The United Nations and the
advancement of women: 1945–1996.* New York:
Author.

United Nations. (1997a). *Human Development Report
1997.* New York: Author.

United Nations. (1997b). *Work.*
www.un.org/Depts/unsd/gender/sum5.htm

United Nations. (1998). *Too young to die: Genes or
gender?* New York: Author.

U.S. Department of Commerce. (1997). *Statistical
abstracts of the United States.* Washington, DC:
Author.

Vahme-Sabz. (1995). Country report on lesbians in
Iran. In R. Rosenbloom (Ed.), *Unspoken rules:
Sexual orientation and women's human rights*
(pp. 89–94). San Francisco, CA: International
Gay and Lesbian Human Rights Commission.

Van Vianen, A. E. M., & Willemsen, T. M. (1992). The
employment interview: The role of sex
stereotypes in the evaluation of male and female
job applicants in the Netherlands. *Journal of
Applied Social Psychology, 22,* 471–491.

Via, E. J. (1987). Women in the gospel of Luke. In U.
King (Ed.), *Women in the world's religions, past and
present* (pp. 38–55). New York: Paragon House.

Vogel, L. (1983). *Marxism and the oppression of women:
Toward a unitary theory.* New Brunswick, NJ:
Rutgers University Press.

Waldfogel, J. (1997). The effect of children on
women's wages. *American Sociological Review, 62,*
209–217.

Wallace, C. P. (1992, September 22). Doing business:
new shots fired in Indonesia wage war. *Los
Angeles Times,* p. 2.

Ward, K. B., & Pyle, J. L. (1995). Gender,
industrialization, transnational corporations, and
development: An overview of trends and patterns.
In C. E. Bose & E. Acosta-Belen (Eds.), *Women in
the Latin American development process* (pp. 37–64).
Philadelphia: Temple University Press.

Waring, M. (1988). *If women counted: A new feminist
economics.* New York: Harper & Row.

Watanabe, T. (1999, April 10). Sikhs celebrate major
anniversary. *Los Angeles Times,* p. B2.

Waters, E., & Posadskaya, A. (1995). Democracy
without women is no democracy: Women's
struggles in postcommunist Russia. In A. Basu
(Ed.), *The challenge of local feminisms: Women's
movements in global perspective* (pp. 351–373).
Boulder, CO: Westview Press.

Weissinger, C. (1993). Introduction: Going beyond
and retaining charisma: Women's leadership in
marginal religions. In *Women's leadership in
marginal religions: Explorations outside the
mainstream* (pp. 1–22). Chicago: University of
Illinois Press.

West, G., & Blumberg, R. L. (1990). Reconstructing
social protest from a feminist perspective. In G.
West & R. L. Blumberg (Eds.), *Women and social
protest* (pp. 3–36). New York: Oxford University
Press.

Whitam, F. L., & Mathy, R. M. (1991). Childhood
cross-gender behavior of homosexual females in
Brazil, Peru, the Philippines, and the United
States. *Archives of Sexual Behavior, 20,* 151–170.

Whiting, B. B., & Edwards, C. P. (1988). *Children of
different worlds: The formation of social behavior.*
Cambridge, MA: Harvard University Press.

Wilkinson, T. (1998, October 7). She seeks women's
rights—quietly. *Los Angeles Times,* pp. A1, A6.

Williams, D. S. (1994). Womanist theology: Black
women's voices. In U. King (Ed.), *Feminist
theology from the Third World* (pp. 77–87).
Maryknoll, NY: Orbis.

Williams, H. (1995). Violeta Barrios de Chamorro. In F. D'Amico & P. R. Beckman (Eds.), *Women in world politics: An introduction* (pp. 31–44). Westport, CT: Bergin & Garvey.

Williams, J. E., & Best, D. L. (1990a). *Measuring sex stereotypes: A thirty nation study* (Rev. ed). Beverly Hills, CA: Sage.

Williams, J. E., & Best, D. L. (1990b). *Sex and psyche: Gender and self viewed cross-culturally.* Beverly Hills: Sage.

Willis, J. D. (1985). Nuns and benefactresses: The role of women in the development of Buddhism. In Y. Y. Haddad & E. B. Findly (Eds.), *Women, religion, and social change* (pp. 58–86). New York: State University of New York Press.

Wilshire, R. (1995). Gender in development: A critical issue for sustainable development. In F. C. Steady & R. Toure (Eds.), *Women and the United Nations* (pp. 127–132). Rochester, VT: Schenkman Books.

Wilson, E. O. (1978). *On human nature.* Cambridge, MA: Harvard University Press.

WIN. (1992). Sexual harassment at work. *Women's International Network News, 18,* 46–47.

WIN. (1993). Hong Kong: Sex discrimination in the work force. *Women's International Network News, 19,* 60.

Wolfe, L. R., & Tucker, J. (1995). Feminism lives: Building a multicultural women's movement in the United States. In A. Basu (Ed.), *The challenge of local feminisms: Women's movements in global perspective* (pp. 435–462). Boulder, CO: Westview Press.

World Commission on Environment and Development. (1987). *Our common future.* Oxford: Oxford University Press.

World in brief: Orthodox Jews pelt worshippers at Wall. (1997, June 12). *Los Angeles Times,* p. A12.

World Resources Institute. (1994–95). *World resources: A guide to the global environment.* Oxford: Oxford University Press.

Wright, R. (1995a, August 25). Economic progress comes slow for women worldwide, UN study finds. *Detroit News. http://detnews.com/menu/stories/1469.htm*

Wright, R. (1995b, August 27). *Los Angeles Times. http://detnews.com/menu/stories/1469.htm*

Yoko, H. (1995). The path to gender equality in Japan. *Japan-Asia Quarterly Review, 25,* 18–19.

Yoshizumi, K. (1995). Marriage and the family: Past and present. In K. Fujimura-Fanselow & A. Kameda (Eds.), *Japanese women: New feminist perspectives on the past, present, and future* (pp. 183–198). New York: Feminist Press.

Young, K. K. (1987). Hinduism. In A. Sharma (Ed.), *Women in world religions* (pp. 59–104). Albany: State University of New York Press.

Young, K. K. (1994). Women in Hinduism. In A. Sharma (Ed.), *Today's woman in world religions* (pp. 137–170). Albany: State University of New York Press.

Youseff, N. H. (1995). Women's access to productive resources: The need for legal instruments to protect women's development rights. In J. Peters & A. Wolper (Eds.), *Women's rights, human rights: International feminist perspectives* (pp. 279–288). New York: Routledge.

Zhang, N., & Xu, W. (1995). Discovering the positive within the negative: The women's movement in a changing China. In A. Basu (Ed.), *The challenge of local feminisms: Women's movements in global perspective* (pp. 25–57). Boulder, CO: Westview Press.

Zimmerman, J. F. (1994). Equity in representation for women and minorities. In W. Rule & J. F. Zimmerman (Eds.), *Electoral systems in comparative perspective: Their impact on women and minorities* (pp. 3–14). Westport, CT: Greenwood Press.

Zita, J. N. (1981). Historical amnesia and the lesbian continuum. *Signs, 7,* 172–187.

Index

Key terms and the pages on which they are defined are boldfaced.